Real Tourism

Over the past decade tourism studies has broken out of its traditional institutional affiliation with business and management programs to take its legitimate place as an interdisciplinary social science field of cutting-edge scholarship. The field has emerged as central to ongoing debates in social theory concerning such diverse topics as postcolonialism, mobility, and postmodernism, to name just a few. While there has been a diverse body of empirical research on this transformation, the theoretical discussions in tourism studies remain largely attached to theories of modernity and Anglocentric assumptions about tourism. There is a need for the field to come to terms theoretically with the contemporary and future realities of tourism as a truly global phenomenon.

Real Tourism is a significant volume, which sets this new theoretical agenda, engaging directly with what tourism does in practice and in place, and demonstrates the need for a theoretical intervention that moves tourism scholarship beyond the province of anglophone thinking. The volume achieves this by explicitly bridging "Western" and "non-Western" scholarship on tourism; reframing theoretical discussions around "real practices" instead of abstract typologies; and radically delinking tourism theory from the grand narratives of modernity and assumptions about authenticity, identity, tradition, and development. The book brings together leading academics in the field, and provides provocative multidisciplinary and multicontextual reflection on the future of tourism.

This original, timely, and compelling volume puts forward new postmodernist ideas and arguments about tourism today and in the future. It is essential reading for students, researchers, and academics interested in tourism.

Claudio Minca is Head and Professor of the Cultural Geography Department at Wageningen University, the Netherlands, and Research Professor of Geography at Royal Holloway, the University of London, UK.

Tim Oakes is Professor of Geography at the University of Colorado, Boulder, USA, and Visiting Professor at Guizhou Nationalities University, China.

Contemporary Geographies of Leisure, Tourism and Mobility

Series Editor: C. Michael Hall

Professor at the Department of Management, College of Business & Economics, University of Canterbury, Private Bag 4800, Christchurch, New Zealand

The aim of this series is to explore and communicate the intersections and relationships between leisure, tourism and human mobility within the social sciences.

It will incorporate both traditional and new perspectives on leisure and tourism from contemporary geography, e.g. notions of identity, representation and culture, while also providing for perspectives from cognate areas such as anthropology, cultural studies, gastronomy and food studies, marketing, policy studies and political economy, regional and urban planning, and sociology, within the development of an integrated field of leisure and tourism studies.

Also, increasingly, tourism and leisure are regarded as steps in a continuum of human mobility. Inclusion of mobility in the series offers the prospect to examine the relationship between tourism and migration, the sojourner, educational travel, and second home and retirement travel phenomena.

The series comprises two strands:

Contemporary Geographies of Leisure, Tourism and Mobility aims to address the needs of students and academics, and the titles will be published in hardback and paperback. Titles include:

1. **The Moralisation of Tourism**
   Sun, sand . . . and saving the world?
   Jim Butcher

2. **The Ethics of Tourism Development**
   Mick Smith and Rosaleen Duffy

3. **Tourism in the Caribbean**
   Trends, development, prospects
   Edited by David Timothy Duval

4. **Qualitative Research in Tourism**
   Ontologies, epistemologies and methodologies
   Edited by Jenny Phillimore and Lisa Goodson

5. **The Media and the Tourist Imagination**
   Converging cultures
   Edited by David Crouch, Rhona Jackson and Felix Thompson

6. **Tourism and Global Environmental Change**
   Ecological, social, economic and political interrelationships
   Edited by Stefan Gössling and C. Michael Hall

7. **Cultural Heritage of Tourism in the Developing World**
   Edited by Dallen J. Timothy and Gyan Nyaupane

8. **Understanding and Managing Tourism Impacts**
   An integrated approach
   Michael Hall and Alan Lew

9. **An Introduction to Visual Research Methods in Tourism**
   Edited by Tijana Rakic and Donna Chambers

10. **Tourism and Climate Change**
    Impacts, adaptation and mitigation
    C. Michael Hall, Stefan Gössling and Daniel Scott

Routledge Studies in Contemporary Geographies of Leisure, Tourism and Mobility is a forum for innovative new research intended for research students and academics, and the titles will be available in hardback only. Titles include:

Real Tourism

Practice, care, and politics in contemporary travel culture

Edited by
Claudio Minca and
Tim Oakes

Routledge
Taylor & Francis Group

LONDON AND NEW YORK

First published 2012
by Routledge
2 Park Square, Milton Park, Abingdon, Oxon OX14 4RN

Simultaneously published in the USA and Canada
by Routledge
711 Third Avenue, New York, NY 10017

Routledge is an imprint of the Taylor & Francis Group, an informa business

British Library Cataloguing in Publication Data
A catalogue record for this book is available from the British Library

Library of Congress Cataloging in Publication Data
Minca, Claudio.
  Real tourism/Claudio Minca and Tim Oakes.
      p. cm.
    Includes bibliographical references and index.
  1. Tourism–Research. 2. Tourism–Social aspects.
  3. Postcolonialism. 4. Postmodernism. I. Oakes, Tim.   II. Title.
  G155.A1M523 2011
  306.4'819—dc23
  2011019818

ISBN: 978-0-415-58224-7 (hbk)
ISBN: 978-0-203-18096-9 (ebk)

Typeset in Times New Roman
by Florence Production, Stoodleigh, Devon

MIX
Paper from
responsible sources
FSC
www.fsc.org   FSC® C013604

Printed and bound in Great Britain by
CPI Antony Rowe, Chippenham, Wiltshire

Contents

Figures

Contributors

Tim Edensor teaches cultural geography at Manchester Metropolitan University. He is the author of *Tourists at the Taj* (1998), *National Identity, Popular Culture and Everyday Life* (2002), and *Industrial Ruins: Space, Aesthetics and Materiality* (2005), as well as the editor of *Geographies of Rhythm* (2010), and co-editor of *Spaces of Vernacular Creativity* (2009) and *Urban Theory Beyond the West: A World of Cities* (2011). He is the editor of the international journal *Tourist Studies* and has written extensively on national identity, tourism, industrial ruins, walking, driving, football cultures and urban materiality, and is currently investigating landscapes of illumination.

Steven Flusty is Associate Professor of Geography at York University. His primary obsession is the everyday practices of global formation, a topic he has interrogated most ruthlessly in *De-Coca-Colonization: Making the Globe from the Inside Out* (2004). His work has also appeared in assorted electronic media, and a selection of academic, professional, and popular journals of varying degrees of repute.

Jamie Gillen is an Assistant Professor of Geography at the National University of Singapore. His research interests are focused on entrepreneurialism and the urban cultural economy in Vietnam and Southeast Asia. His work is published in *Political Geography*, *Geografiska Annaler B*, *Urban Geography*, and other journals.

Eeva Jokinen is Professor of Social Policy at the University of Eastern Finland. Currently, she is Director of the research project "Fourth shift: on the borders of home, labour and affects" (Academy of Finland 2008–2011), which explores the blurring borders of work and home in a post-Fordist society. She has published and edited several books on motherhood, embodiment and everyday practices. Her publications in the area include "The makings of motherhood in diary narratives" (in *Qualitative Inquiry*, 2004). She has written several articles on tourism theories together with Soile Veijola, including "The disoriented tourist" (1998) and "Mountains and landscapes: towards embodied visualities" (2003). They have also co-authored two books: *Oman elämänsä turistit* [*Tourists of Their Own Lives*] (1990) and *Voiko naista rakastaa? Avion ja eron karuselli* [*Can Woman be Loved? The Grim Cell of Marriage and Divorce*] (2001).

Claudio Minca is Head and Professor of the Cultural Geography Department at Wageningen University, and Research Professor of Geography at Royal Holloway, the University of London. He is also Visiting Professor at the College of Tourism, Rikkyo University, Tokyo. His current research centers on three major themes: tourism and travel theories of modernity; the spatialization of (bio)politics; and the relationship between modern knowledge, space, and landscape in postcolonial geography. His most recent books are *Social Capital and Urban Networks of Trust* (with J. Hakli, 2009) and *Travels in Paradox: Remapping Tourism* (with T. Oakes, 2006).

Kazuo Murakami is Professor of Tourism and Head of the Graduate School in the College of Tourism at Rikkyo University, Japan, where he is also the Director of RARC (Rikkyo Amusement Research Centre). The main focus of his work is on rural tourism and the study of travelogues. Recent publications include *Innovation for Tourist Destination Management* (2008) and *Introduction to Amusement Studies* (Gendai, 2008).

Tim Oakes is Professor of Geography at the University of Colorado, Boulder, USA, and Visiting Professor at Guizhou Nationalities University, China. His research focuses on China's regional cultural development, culture industries, tourism, heritage, and place-based identities. In addition to numerous journal articles and book chapters, he is the author of *Tourism and Modernity in China* (1998), and co-editor of *Translocal China* (2006), *Travels in Paradox* (2006), *Reinventing Tunpu: Cultural Tourism and Social Change in Guizhou* (in Chinese, 2007), *The Cultural Geography Reader* (2008), and *Faiths on Display: Tourism and Religion in China* (2010).

Meghann Ormond is Lecturer at the Cultural Geography Department, Wageningen University, the Netherlands. Her research focuses on questions of transnational mobility, health and care. Focusing on responses to international medical travel within Southeast Asia, her work examines postcolonial development strategies and their negotiation of the benefits and challenges generated by extending care to non-national mobile subjects. She is co-author of the book *Family Reunification and Immigration in Portugal* (in Portuguese, 2005) and author of the forthcoming book *Neoliberal Governance and International Medical Travel in Malaysia*.

Saithong Phommavong is a political scientist working on issues of economic development. He began his career working as lecturer at the Department of Political Science and the Research and Post-Graduate Division, Faculty of Social Sciences, National University of Laos. He is currently completing his PhD at the Department of Social and Economic Geography, Umea

University, Sweden. His research interest is focused on tourism development and poverty reduction in Lao PDR and more specifically on policy analysis, on practice of tourism policy, on gender aspect and, more generally, on the economic impacts of tourism.

Harng Luh Sin is a PhD Candidate at the Department of Geography, Royal Holloway, University of London, and a Teaching Assistant at the National University of Singapore. Her current research focuses on the ethical and responsible possibilities as enacted in tourism, situated within the larger context of social initiatives like sustainable development, ethical consumerism, and 'first world responsibilities' to the 'third world'. Her work is published in *Annals of Tourism Research, Geoforum*, and other journals.

Soile Veijola is Professor of Cultural Studies of Tourism at the University of Lapland, Finland, and works at the Lapland Institute for Tourism Research and Education (LUC Tourism) launched by the Lapland Universities Consortium. She is also Adjunct Professor (Dozent) in Sports Tourism at the University of Jyväskylä. Her earlier publications related to tourism include *The Body in Tourism* (1994) and *Towards a Hostessing Society* (2008), both co-authored with Eeva Jokinen, and *Sleep in Tourism* (2011), co-authored with Anu Valtonen. She has guest-edited a special issue of *Tourist Studies* on the topic of Tourism as Work, including her own article "Gender as work in the tourism industry" (2009). Her current research is focused on designing culturally and ecologically sustainable tourist communities for the future.

Eriko Yasue received her PhD at the Department of Geography at Royal Holloway, University of London. Her doctoral research concerns the practice and reproduction of landscapes in Japanese tourism. In particular, her work focuses on issues of nostalgia and the production of the past through visual representations, and tourist practices and performances.

Acknowledgments

This book is the result of a project that began in 2007 and involved the contribution of many people over the years. The project itself would not have been possible without the assistance and inspiration of Kazuo Murakami and the Recreation Amusement Research Center (RARC) at Rikkyo University, Japan, which also hosted the final workshop in Tokyo. Among those at RARC, we are especially indebted to Kenichi Ohashi, Yuji Nakamish, Eiji Keyamura, and, in particular, Ms Yuko Murata for all her logistical and organizational support. Our workshops were enhanced greatly by the additional contributions of Mike Crang, Tim Winter, Bounpong Keorodom, Dexanourath Senedouangdeth, Phouth Simmalavong, and Takashi Yamazaki. In addition, we would like to thank the National University of Laos and the University of London, Royal Holloway for hosting workshops in Vientiane and London. The volume is also the result of the support and encouragement of Emma Travis and Faye Leerink at Routledge. Crucial support was provided by the Cultural Geography Chair Group at Wageningen University, the Netherlands. Finally, very special thanks go to Maartje Roelofsen, our "Wageningen copy-editor," for doing an excellent job in putting the whole manuscript together while copy-editing it to perfection, but also for her overall dedication to this project.

1   Real tourism

Claudio Minca and Tim Oakes

Why "real" tourism? Some readers may assume that our title signals some sort of claim to the truth about tourism, but our intention is quite different. Rather than establishing a definitive argument for what tourism actually *is*, as a particular category of social phenomena, our aim in this volume is to unbound tourism from the confines of a scholarly discourse that works to separate and distinguish tourism from the rest of the social world. Adrian Franklin (2003) has argued that we should not be treating tourism as a marginal space and activity located somewhere outside of presumably more central social phenomena such as work, production, and the everyday worlds of home and habit, but rather as a fundamental *social force* that assembles a broad array of social, political, economic, cultural, and material processes. Here we take this approach one step further by insisting on tourism as a comprehensive analytic capable of reassembling our understandings of contemporary life. Not only do we view tourism as a social force, then, but we also view tourism as an analytic through which new insights into "the social," "the cultural," and "the political," and thus our theorizations about those domains, are gained. This is important, we believe, not for what it reveals about tourism, but for what it reveals about the social world and how it is changing. Tourism is "real," then, as a constitutive force in the social world. It is also "real" in the sense of actual practices that defy simple categorizations or disembodied abstractions (on this see, for example, Bærenholdt *et al.* 2004; Crang, M. 1999, 2004, 2006; Crouch 2004, 2005; Edensor 2001, 2006a, 2007; Minca and Oakes 2006; Minca 2007; Obrador 2007). Our approach to tourism thus emphasizes placed practice and, as a result, a theoretical pluralism that resists closure around orderly ideas such as authenticity or modernity.

The field of tourism studies appears to be at a critical turning point. As evidenced by published monographs, edited volumes, new academic journals, dissertations and theses, as well as curriculum developments in geography, anthropology, sociology, cultural studies, and other related fields, tourism studies over the past decade has broken out of its traditional institutional affiliation with business and management programs to take its legitimate place as a transdisciplinary field of cutting- edge scholarship (see, among others, Meethan 2001; Urry 2002; Gibson, C. 2008). Tourism has thus emerged as central to ongoing debates in social theory concerning such diverse topics as postcolonialism, mobility, and postmodernism, to name just a few. Yet while this has enabled an increasingly coherent body of theoretical work interpreting tourism in relation to broader questions of social theory, the "empirical ground" upon which tourism studies is purportedly based has been undergoing profound transformation. A diverse body of empirical research on tourism has been describing this transformation in rich and compelling ways, and yet much of the theoretical discussion in tourism studies seems to proceed as if the world of travel were the same today as it was a few decades ago.

This volume is the result of a project entitled "Re-tracing modern tourism" (again, a deliberately ambitious title), which was conceived initially by Minca in partnership with Kazuo Murakami and the Recreation Amusement Research Center (RARC) at Rikkyo University in Tokyo. The project began with the premise that tourism scholarship needs to come to terms theoretically with the contemporary and future realities of tourism as a truly global phenomenon. Through a series of workshops held in London, Vientiane, and Tokyo, the project sought to bridge "Western" and "non-Western" scholarship on tourism, reframe theoretical discussions around "real practices" (instead of abstract typologies) in tourism, and radically delink tourism theory from the grand narratives of modernity and their assumptions about authenticity, identity, tradition, progress, and development.

Yet the outcome – in the form of the papers collected for this volume – suggested something more fundamental going on than simply bringing to bear different intellectual contexts on the study of tourism. We found inescapable the fact that, in each case, tourism was presenting ways to think through basic questions and issues in social theory in productive new directions. This told us as much about social theory as it did about tourism, if not more. If we are to take seriously, then, the claim that tourism is a social process, then *Real Tourism* makes a case for the ways tourism builds social theory not by applying that theory to "tourism cases" but by building theory through an engagement with tourism as a highly contextual, or "placed," process. We have found ourselves, in other words, relearning social theory from tourism. This is quite different, it turns out, from simply legitimizing tourism as a serious field of scholarship and by articulating it in the vernaculars of social theory. Because our initial bridging efforts resulted in an engagement with scholars who work in Asia and who are themselves of Asian origin, the volume takes Asian contexts as its predominant empirical focus. Our point is not to suggest anything particular about "Asia" as an alternative, non-Western standpoint from which to critique the Eurocentric scholarly edifice of social theory (though we have no real objection to such a standpoint). But we do recognize that a study focusing on tourism as a social process ignores the Asian contexts of those social processes at its peril. Asia increasingly dominates the world's tourist destinations, and is increasingly the predominant region of origin for tourists themselves. We have found in Asia a rich grounding for our relearning of social theory as tourist practice.

When examining the actual practices related to some of the most innovative and creative forms of tourism, we have also found that the "colonial travel tradition" lives on, but that it often blends "modernities" that are born out of very specific Asian contexts. This blending has had an enormous (and rather original) impact on the new directions that tourism has been taking in the last decade or so, and might be taking in the near future, in Asia and elsewhere. With this in mind, instead of asking "What can we learn from Asia?", we decided to focus on practices, experiences and interpretations of these practices and experiences that suggest the difficulty of approaching tourism as a phenomenon uniquely rooted in European modern culture. We find it impossible to isolate a typology of "Asian tourism" as a sort of regional expression of a global phenomenon. Instead, many of the most "conventional" tourist practices, linked as they are to the long European travel tradition, are intertwined with a set of entirely new practices that, in many ways, overcome the very idea of tourism as we knew it; that is, as a mere expression of Western modernity "gone global."

Approaching tourism this way, we find it impossible to speak of *the tourist* as a self-standing subject characterized by a set of distinct behaviors, languages, representation, identities, even geographies. *Real Tourism* continues the ongoing efforts (see Franklin and Crang 2001), then, to put to rest the lingering structuralism that continues its remarkable staying power in tourism theory. The analysis of a series of tourist practices *in situ* developed by the volume's contributors shows, rather, the emergence of an enormous, only partially explored space of banal and mundane practices that make up the contemporary tourist experience "as it is." As many chapters in this volume will demonstrate, this realization entails a radical rethinking of tourism as a specific/unique experience of subject formation, and suggests that tourism should be studied as one form (out of many others) of contemporary mobility, notwithstanding its capacity of colonizing and exploiting places, cultural productions, consumption patterns and ways of understanding "the social," "the cultural," and "the political" at a global scale. In particular, we focus on the different forms of experimentation that tourists develop "on the ground."

This approach also means that tourism can no longer be explained simply as the local manifestation of a general project and process of modernity. Quite the contrary: the relationship between representations, practices and the "material" dimension of the contemporary tourist experience dismantle the very possibility of grand narrative of the modern. While this in itself is not a novel claim, tourism studies have yet to fully engage broader debates on practice and the material in the social sciences and the humanities. Emphasizing the "real practice" of tourism allows for a more imaginative use of theoretical and methodological tools to interpret the ever-changing nature of contemporary travel (see Franklin 2004). In concrete terms, this means that each chapter of *Real Tourism* is characterized, on the one hand, by a shared set of postcolonial "arrangements" and theoretical perspectives on the question of practice, and on the other by an experimental challenge to these very theorizations accompanied by an effort to imagine new possible trajectories inspired by "real tourism" practices. Rather than "applying" social theory to the "empirical case" of tourism, then, *Real Tourism* suggests that new imaginations and experimentations, together with their related practices, will require equally new theories, languages and methods.

While each of the volume's chapters can be read as a stand-alone case study reflecting upon the theoretical implications of place-based tourism practices, we have attempted to arrange them in a progression that brings out particularly salient themes emerging in the volume. Perhaps the most consistent theme throughout the volume revolves around the question of care, and how tourism practices refocus our attention on care as fundamental to social relations in ways often missed in more conventional social theorizations. We therefore begin with a group of chapters addressing the question of care and the biopolitical in relation to tourism. Biopolitical arrangements are indeed pervasive in many aspects of the tourist experience. At the same time, the question of care is central to the operations of the biopolitical dispositive, as well to issues of gender and hostessing in late modern Western societies. By opening the volume with two chapters intervening in these issues, we highlight the increasing importance given by academia to the politicization of the body and to the ways in which the *bios* has become the object of growing attention on the part of late capitalist organizations and their regimes of governance.

In addition to this, the first set of chapters intentionally addresses "mainstream" academic debates and preoccupations, and tries to show that not only should tourism studies incorporate the findings of those very debates, but that indeed tourism and the experience of tourism have something important to say about those debates. This is true for the two opening chapters, written by Claudio Minca and by Soile Veijola and Eeva Jokinen – where questions of care (and life) are analyzed in depth, although from two rather different perspectives – but also for Tim Edensor's chapter that follows, which focuses on the questions of rhythm and their implications for the tourist and tourism studies.

Claudio Minca's chapter directly addresses the question of the biopolitical. By engaging with philosopher Giorgio Agamben's speculations on the post-historical condition and his biopolitical interpretation of the separation between "the human" and "the animal," Minca's chapter claims that the *anthropotouristic machine* (after Agamben's description of the anthropogenic machine) is at work on many occasions in which the body of the tourist and of the "locals" are "put on display" and presented as if they were an abstract body, eternally smiling and healthy. The complicated implications of the biopolitical in tourism are then articulated via three distinct but closely correlated "moves." In the first case, Minca reflects on the obsession in the tourism industry with the quest for "community," where a sort of utopian communitarian experience is offered, adopting a post-romantic nostalgic rhetoric (Esposito 2009). The second "move" concerns questions of postcoloniality and culture in relation to the exposure of "humans" on tourist stages. Biopolitics here operate on these tourist bodies with endless caesurae that investigate and "inspect" – in the contact zones between the body of the tourist and the body of the touristified local – the existential thresholds of the post-historical condition. Finally, the chapter focuses on the question of care – of the individual and collective body – using the example of Nazi tourism in order to show the deep biopolitical nature of many tourist experiences contended between issues of happiness, health, and well-being, but also control.

Care and life are treated in a different but somewhat complementary way by Veijola and Jokinen's chapter. Here, care is put in direct relation to gender. For Veijola and Jokinen, "tourism can never be fully grasped without a broad and subtle conception of gender, nor without acknowledging the role that gender plays in organizing life and symbolic orders in today's societies." Gender is to be defined as a "contingent habit." In late modern societies, gender divisions are becoming increasingly porous or blurred (along with other divisions: public/private, inside/outside, work/leisure). This is true in tourism as well, where the indistinction between labor and free time (especially for emotional labor) is becoming increasingly important. Tourism is presented here as a practice of giving and receiving care. For this reason, it is important to reflect on the highly gendered provision of care in contemporary societies, which are gradually moving toward an increased valorization of "hostessing." Hostessing is not only becoming more pervasive, but is also producing more and more unequal gender relationships. The labor of hostessing requires a flexibility and a precariousness that can only be provided by deeply unequal social relations, of which gender is perhaps the most basic, but which also involves relations of ethnicity or nationality, mobility, and of course class.

Tim Edensor's intervention deals with the question of rhythm in tourism. This is a rather different issue, but his chapter speaks in an important way to the previous two chapters. Edensor emphasizes the inadequacy of a broad, general theory of tourism applied across the globe without acknowledging cultural contexts in which tourist practice emerges. He engages directly with mainstream conceptualizations of rhythm and how to incorporate them in the methodologies of tourism studies. At the same time, like many other chapters in the volume, there is something revealing about the tourist rhythm here that can help to understand the question of rhythm in more general terms. For Edensor, rhythmanalysis provides an extremely useful framing device, a conceptual approach with which to appreciate the plurality of the contemporary travel experience, often based on a intriguing but complicated negotiation between the rhythm of tourism and the rhythm of the places visited. The importance of the plural examples from Asia that populate his chapter is at the basis of Edensor's attempt to suggest a much-needed pluralization in tourism theory, since

> tourists cannot be insulated from ordinary everyday activities but must accommodate themselves to, and improvise around, these regular rhythmic practices that occur in work places, schools, cafes, extemporized leisure

sites, transport termini, bathing points, offices, administrative centers, houses and flats, and places of worship (p. 58).

Tourism constitutes a particular rhythmic way of being-in-the-world – unreflexive and habitual, reproducing another kind of everyday home away from home. Tourists of all stripes do this. This means tourism cannot be counted on to provide the basis of some kind of project; it cannot be relied on as some sort of "improving" activity. The rhythm of tourism is thus not only worthwhile as a deeper investigation, but becomes in this way the site for a new direction in thinking, philosophically and methodologically, through the everyday of space and time.

This concern with the everyday, and with exploring the everyday in terms of tourist practice (rather than the more conventional viewing of tourism as an exceptional activity separate from our mundane and ordinary lives), also calls into question some assumptions about the relationship between tourism and modernity. Tourism theory has long reflected a great variety of efforts to account intellectually for (and otherwise come to terms with) modernity as a certain kind of experience, and as a particular epistemological approach to the world. Structuralist approaches emphasizing tourism as uniquely revelatory of the hidden grand designs of modernity were prominent early in the development of the tourism studies field (e.g. MacCannell 1999 [1976]; Britton 1982; Wang, N. 2000; Urry 2002). In these studies, tourism tended to occupy a particular conceptual space where certain modern behaviors and beliefs – a yearning for authenticity somewhere else, a need for ludic escape from the ordinary and humdrum of daily life, an outlet for existential anxiety over the precariousness of the modern condition, and so on – found their expression. These were in turn challenged by more poststructural orientations toward tourism that questioned claims to any grand design, and the tidy categories around which that design was thought to be built (Edensor 2001; Franklin 2003; Gibson, C. 2008; Larsen 2008). Such challenges have been particularly significant in calls for gendered and embodied accounts of tourism (Veijola and Jokinen 1994; Kaplan 1996; Johnston 2001).

The chapters by Steven Flusty and Tim Oakes both examine and extend this analytical engagement with the modern condition as understood in the highly contextualized and embodied practices of tourism. More precisely, they explore how practices of travel vary according to time and space, and how this variance reveals as problematic some of our assumptions about the relationships between the "global spread" of modernity and a particular kind of modern traveling subjectivity thought to be inherent in tourism.

Flusty begins his chapter with what has, in some ways, been a classic trope of modernity: a deeply anxious subjectivity discontented by the ephemerality of modern life, conveyed by the question, "What am I missing?" To be modern was to both exhilarate and despair in the impermanence of know-ledge and the sense that "something else" was always just beyond the horizon. But Flusty approaches the question through the practical narrative of a souvenir-collecting and sightseeing traveler rather, than the analyzing abstractions of a theorist. That he travels with an imaginary pachyderm companion – the reflexive and unsettling voice of modernity interrogating all knowledge with critical scrutiny – only adds to our sense that we are indeed missing something. There are, it turns out, many levels in which to understand "what is missing" – both when we travel and when we try and understand the tourism experience. For colonial Europeans, what was missing was the exotic non-modern, and they traveled to find it, making themselves modern and constructing "the modern" as they went. Their leisure was always an extension of the colonial project, and their travel constructed new colonial entanglements that, in many ways, remain hidden in the mundane practices of tourism to this day. Yet at the same time – and this is where Flusty's emphasis lies – there was a counter-movement. For elites from the colonies and colonies-to-be, travel was also necessary for the acquisition of modernity and for bringing the modern home. These "grand ambassadors" of the colonial realm traveled to erase their difference from the modern, not to reinforce it. Their traveling practices *also* served to make themselves modern *and* to construct "the modern" as they went, but in vastly different terms in relation to colonial power, capital, and the politics of racial and other discriminations. Rather than viewing tourism, then, as a reflection or outcome of the modern experience, as has so often been done in tourism studies, Flusty's chapter turns the relationship on its head: modernity itself is a tourist production. This implicates tourism in modernity's legacy of colonialism and conquest in disturbingly new ways. Tourism and travel, Flusty reminds us, have always been intimately and inextricably connected to conquest. And this fact becomes the "elephant in the room" – his pachyderm companion – a presence so obvious that it could only hide in plain sight, in the mundane practices of everyday tourism.

While tourism, for Flusty, thus helps us appreciate that intimate relationship between modernity's power of conquest and the mundane objects of tourism, Tim Oakes's chapter reminds us that modernity's power is always spinning out of control, producing unintended outcomes and new forms of disorder, even as it professes to bring order into a world of chaos. Perhaps "what is missing" when we travel is that orderly world always promised by modernity, yet always somehow just out of reach, beyond the horizon. Tourism, then, becomes a way of understanding both the modernist will to order *and* the continuous disordering that modern projects churn out, paradoxically, in their attempts to produce order. Oakes argues that the actual care-giving and care-receiving practices of the tourism experience provide the key to understanding modernity as an always incomplete project of ordering, rather than a process by which societies are in fact brought to order. The host–guest relationship underlying much of the tourism experience, when framed as a project of ordering, reveals unintended consequences in actual practice. The implication of this argument for tourism studies, then, is to dispense with any notion that tourism itself can be viewed as a set of distinct categories of behaviors and motivations. While state ordering projects, such as those implemented in the name of China's modernization, may conceive of tourists and tourism as stable subjects and categories, "real tourism" suggests the much more fluid processes of ordering and disordering that capture that actual experience of modernity in China.

Concern for actual practices of tourism also shapes Eriko Yasue and Kazuo Murakami's study of landscape photography in Japan. While their study offers a rich ethnographic portrait of tourist–photographers, it aims more importantly to demonstrate the ways that such a portrait can complicate and deepen our understanding of landscape formation as a multivocal performance. Here, tourism offers a means by which a central concept in geography – landscape – might be rethought as something constituted through our practical engagement with the world around us. Rather than interpreting landscape through the analytical lens of representation, then, Yasue and Murakami explore its embodied and performative dimensions. In addition to arguing that tourist practices offer something important to say about how we understand analytical concepts, then, their chapter *also* makes clear that paying attention to such practices requires an accounting of the rich social, cultural, and political contexts conditioning those practices. Their study thus points out how tourism might also be a productive lens through which to problematize "Western" conceptual framings by subjecting them to critical, contextualized analysis of social practices in different parts of the world.

The four chapters that round out the volume return us to some more explicit explorations of care – and the precarious qualities of host–guest relationships – as a central feature of social relations revealed with particular clarity when seen in the light of the tourism experience. These chapters also raise a set of questions – of ethics, social responsibility, and the moral imperatives brought about by inequality and injustice – that shape, energize, and politicize the practices of tourism. These chapters take us further into the realm of place-based tourism practice by exploring specific contexts in which questions of care emerge in their own localized ways. These questions are raised in the contexts of Malaysian medical tourism, the "social responsibilities" of Thai tour operators, the difficulties of mobilizing tourism for poverty relief in Laos, and the ways tourism mediates post-war trauma across host–guest relations in Vietnam. In these cases, we find that tourism practices suggest novel approaches to issues of ethics and responsibility, such as the need to rethink medical travelers as "exiles" seeking care when they cannot find it at home, the need to question assumptions about ethical versus non-ethical consumption practices, the need to recognize the ways "socially responsible tourism" often goes awry when mixed with other poverty-relief projects, and the need to understand tourism-mediated reconciliation and post-war healing as inherently limited by the complex practices of host–guest relations.

Meghann Ormond's chapter rethinks "hospitality" from the perspective of the medical tourist and exile. This allows her to develop a concept of "productive hospitality," up-ending the assumption that medical tourists are simply wealthy Western travelers flitting to the Third World for plastic surgery. Medical travel, she argues, is no longer exceptional but everyday. Paying attention to medical travel reveals the shifting centers of medical expertise around the world and emphasizes the ways consumer-market liberalization has altered state biopolitical approaches to outsiders. In this way, we begin to appreciate the complex negotiations between hosting and guesting as well. At the heart of these negotiations lie significant moral and ethical questions: Ormond argues that "If recognizing courted patient–consumers as being in 'medical exile' implies recognizing their dignity and the gravity of their unmet needs 'at home,' then [medical tourism/exile] destinations are entering into an ethical playing field in which they are challenged by the political consequences" of such market-based recognition. Her focus on Malaysia also reminds us of emerging, but still generally ignored, flows of medical travel *within* the so-called developing world, complicating more typical assumptions about care and hostessing within an industry dominated by developed-to-developing world flows. These assumptions, she argues, have led to "an impoverished awareness of [medical tourism/exile] destinations' multifaceted 'care' relationships with an array of foreign patient–consumers and their implications".

The moral and ethical questions underlying tourist practices also concern Harng Luh Sin's chapter on corporate social responsibility and tourism. Beginning from the perspective that all consumption decisions and consumer choices are moral choices of one kind or another, Sin argues that there is no ethical or unethical consumption (or, by extension, tourism). Rather, there are tourism choices, each of which reflects particular moral and ethical decisions. The ethics of Sin's tourists are not absolute, or abstract, but are negotiated at the place of consumption. Since, in the tourism experience, this is also the place of production, tourism offers a uniquely rich site within which to interrogate the relationship between the social responsibilities of producers (in this case, hosts) and those of consumers (their guests). Sin's chapter raises questions about the ethical and moral choices we make every day, and not just in terms of the kinds of products that we buy. Tourism's "post-ethics" has that everyday and contingent quality to it. And with Sin's chapter we also encounter the importance of modesty in tourism theory, the plurality of local contexts in which tourism occurs, and thus in the ways tourism might be theorized.

Sin's chapter raises important questions that are also tackled in the chapter by Saithong Phommavong: the practicalities and complexities of tourism as poverty relief. Phommavong argues that the success of tourism as a project of poverty alleviation is entirely dependent on the placed contexts within which it is practiced, and that the well-intentioned efforts of broader-scale actors such as the state and international donors and NGOs must account for these actual practices. This is important obviously for practical reasons of improving local livelihoods, but it is also important as a lesson in same kind of "post-ethics" articulated in Sin's chapter, for the success of tourism-as-poverty-relief lies

in dispensing with a one-size-fits-all approach and recognizing local pluralism
inherent in tourism development. Tourism, Phommavong argues, is not a
particular kind of development model, but is rather a social process through
which development gets practiced. It can be viewed as an assemblage of
contingent and contextual processes, rather than a particular kind of industry.
Viewing tourism as a social process requires us to derive solutions directly
from local social contexts, approaching tourism as poverty reduction in
pluralistic ways that derive from actual social practices rather than a given
theoretical apparatus.

We conclude the volume with Jamie Gillen's chapter on how the traumatic
memory of war is mediated through tourism. As with many of the volume's
other contributors, Gillen explores questions of care across the host–guest
relationship and the ways care disrupts our assumptions about the polarized
dichotomies of that relationship. This allows Gillen to use tourism to explore
broader questions about the geopolitics and diplomacy of post-war relations
in novel ways. Tourism, in other words, links areas of inquiry that typically
remain separated. By examining, ethnographically, the more mundane,
informal, and interpersonal practices between tourists and guides during the
tourism experience in Vietnam, Gillen argues that post-war tourism indeed
opens up spaces of reconciliation and healing, but that these spaces are con-
strained by broader state projects that maintain post-war trauma for a variety
of political, economic, and cultural reasons. While the Vietnamese state
promotes tourism as part of this broader project, actual tourist practices always
disrupt and disorder – but never break away from – the social constraints within
which they occur. For this reason, Gillen's chapter demonstrates, again, how
tourism offers ways of understanding "the social" across a diverse array of
scales and through a great variety of contextualized practices.

Real Tourism is a deliberately provocative title for a book. We accept that
tourism is "real" in many different ways. What is normally defined as the
"tourist experience" has become a fundamental part of how people learn about
and travel through the world. As tourism increasingly shapes the formation
of our subjectivities, the world increasingly presents itself to us as a visitable
place (Dicks 2003). Likewise, the presumed boundaries between daily life
and the tourist experience can no longer be sustained. However, real tourism also assumes a critical stance toward a well-established tradition in
tourism studies that considers "the tourist" as a special subject and, at the
same time, as a distinct object of analysis. By claiming provocatively that everything is indeed "real" in tourism, and that tourism is by now fully embedded
in the drama of the everyday of millions of people, we have attempted to breach
that tradition and to show not only how some of the central preoccupations
in philosophy and the social sciences are relevant for the understanding
of contemporary tourism practice, but also that the study of tourism can be of
help in reflecting on broader issues of care and politics of life in productive
new ways. These are issues that have long been (and remain today) at the core
of the epistemology and the experience of modernity. Tourism, then, is not a

category of behavior, or a certain kind of space, but a remarkably versatile analytic.

In some ways, to be even more provocative, the implications of our approach point to a radical undermining of the remit for tourism studies as a distinct and coherent field. While our objective with this volume is not aimed at any kind of institutional dismantling of tourism studies, we accept that the de-ghettoization of tourism might productively lead to the integration of a tourist analytic across the social sciences and humanities. It might, in other words, lead to a "tourist turn" of sorts.

2   No country for old men

Claudio Minca

Introduction

This chapter is about tourism and biopolitics. Or, better, about the biopolitical in tourism. The title's reference to Cormac McCarthy's book (and the Coen brothers' film that it inspired) is intentionally provocative; the country with no old men here is the country of "post-historical tourism," the domain of a specific biopolitical understanding of the business of free time and leisure, associated with a specifically biopolitical understanding of the human body – the unreachable and abstract body that populates tourist literature, and often also inhabits the spaces of tourism.

Two preliminary observations are in order. Leisure and tourism have often been taken very seriously by totalitarian biopolitical regimes, as the most recent literature on the Third Reich clearly shows (see, among others, Baranowski 2004; Semmens 2005). This fact alone would justify an investigation of the biopolitical in tourism. However, the relationship between tourism and biopolitics cannot be simply relegated to the experience of totalitarianism. Tourism is, in fact, deeply involved in the politicization of the human body, of many actual bodies. One of the purposes of this chapter is thus that of highlighting the importance and the pervasiveness of the biopolitical in modern Western cultures of travel.

The literature on this aspect of tourism is surprisingly scarce and sporadic (see, among others, Diken and Laustsen 2004; Ek and Hultman 2008; Minca 2009; Veijola 2009a). Despite the increasing "management of bodies" operated by the police and other authorities on tourists, often in collaboration with the tourism industry, a full debate on this issue is still to come. In particular, relatively little attention has been paid in the field of tourism studies to the ways in which new forms of individual and collective pleasure and control walk side by side and are part of a broader biopolitical apparatus.

The "biopolitical" has, instead, occupied in the past few decades the core of an increasingly influential and sophisticated academic literature, especially in philosophy and in political theory. Italian philosopher Roberto Esposito has perhaps developed the most articulate analysis of the genealogy and the workings of biopolitics in his trilogy *Communitas*, *Immunitas* and *Bíos*, to which this chapter will make extensive reference (Esposito 1998, 2002, 2004). Esposito is convinced that the task of analyzing biopolitics in all its forms and expressions is an urgent and dramatic one for anyone concerned with the definition and the implications of "the political" in contemporary Western societies. The question of life, of "a good life," of individual and collective well-being, has been and indeed remains central to the production of political and cultural subjectivities in Western societies. Tourism, especially in its preoccupation with the care for and happiness of individuals (but also for the body politics), will thus be considered here as an integral part of the machinery of biopower, as illustrated on many occasions by Michel Foucault (2003, 2004b; see also Chomsky and Foucault 1994).

This chapter moves from this basic claim in order to pursue several objectives. First, to show how important aspects of tourism host at their core a biopolitical element, which is becoming increasingly pervasive. The traditional focus on well-being and the quest for happiness and personal regeneration is indeed taking on new forms today that mobilize a very specific, biopolitical presentation and re-presentation of bodies, of the human body. This is not particularly new, and in many ways relates to past strategies of the colonization, desubjectivation and objectification of others' bodies, especially in what used to be the real and imagined relationship between modern Europe and the many "others" produced by its imperialist discourses and practices, including modern travel. However, what is perhaps relatively new is the emerging philosophical debate on how questions of life and care relate to biopolitics and to the redefinition of what Giorgio Agamben (2004: 79) has described as the modern *anthropogenesis*, the process of definition of the separation between the human and the non-human/animal in Man (sic) throughout modernity.

Second, this chapter attempts to link this specific discussion to the social and political "meaning of tourism," especially in relation to questions of community, immunity, and the post-historical condition as presented, again, by Agamben (1993). What Kojève, in his influential lectures at the Ecole des Hautes Etudes (cited in Agamben 2004: 6), has described as the Man (sic) at the end of History (Kojève 1980 [1947]) is a man mainly defined by non-essential forms of social reproduction, an individual who has entered a new condition in which he tends to seek compensation for the lack of the "historical," also as a reaction to the pervasiveness of nihilism in modern life. Activities traditionally associated with tourism, leisure, and travel (such as art, play, eroticism, hedonism, boredom, etc.) are central to this very condition, a condition driven at the same time by a biopolitical imperative that deserves close inspection.

To be sure, it is not the intention of this chapter to claim that all tourism and all tourists are simply caught in a sort of biopolitical "anthropogenic machinery." However, it does claim that the tourist condition and some of its key manifestations are often pervaded by a biopolitical logic. This logic certainly pays tribute to the colonial tradition of displaying bodies and their parts, but also to a more recent tendency toward a celebrative, almost obsessive emphasis placed on the individual body and its well-being. A crowd of abstract and normalized bodies has, indeed, come to populate the rhetoric employed by the travel industry. This emphasis on real and imagined bodies – of the tourists, but *also* of the people subjected to the tourist gaze – seems to be supported by two parallel and sometimes intersecting tropes: that of health, youth, happiness, regeneration, and self-enhancement on the one hand, and that of control, and spatial and emotional "containment" on the other.

This chapter explores some of the key articulations of this growing biopolitical dimension of tourism and contemporary travel. It does so in one "overture" and three following parallel "moves." In the theoretical "overture," it reflects on the nature of what is provocatively referred to here as the "anthropotouristic machine;" that is, the biopolitical arrangements at the basis of a modern culture of travel faced with questions of value and meaning. This travel culture is invested with all the problems inherent to the nihilistic approach to life, which transverse many venues of modern life, while being driven, at the same time, by the imperative of health and well-being. Such an imperative seems to be centered more on a set of formal gestures than on genuine content. The biopolitical in tourism, it is argued, is about the definition of "the human" in late modernity, but it is also about "care," for the individual and the collective – a preoccupation often presented as self-evident in content and meaning, yet one that has become a crucial political task for the state and a leitmotif for the tourism industry (see Chapter 3).

These hypotheses are investigated via three distinct articulations. The first deals with the "question of the origins" and the neo-communitarian rhetoric that feeds into so much of the popular tourist literature. Following Esposito's understanding of *Communitas* (1998, 2009), it shows how the myth of the community is indeed a constitutive element of the anthropotouristic machine. The second articulation focuses on the ways in which a specific culture of display, of people and of things, pervades the tourist experience and our own understanding of travel and difference. The contemporary interest on the part of tourists for visits to remote and "traditional" people and regions is discussed as part of a reassuring practice of the reaffirmation of "what-it-is-to-be-human," and of the confirmation of the existence of threshold figures (normally the natives and, in particular, their local representatives) that hypothetically stand between the human and the non-human. Contemporary travels allow for an apparently unmediated contact with these abstract figures and for a negotiation of that complicated threshold. The third articulation discusses the question of care in relation to Nazi leisure and tourism, but also in relation to the immunitary paradigm exposed by Esposito's reading of biopolitics. The present-day celebration of a perfect and perfectible individual body, the zombie-like beautified body that is at the core of so much of the rhetoric of contemporary mass tourism, will be presented as a key site for the enactment of the biopolitical.

The chapter concludes by suggesting that the dreams of perfection and body regeneration and enhancement that occupy so much space in contemporary tourism and in the promotional material produced by the industry must be investigated in a biopolitical perspective in order to grasp their deep immunitary nature and to explore what can possibly be learned from tourism about what Kojève presented as the post-historical (post-human?) condition.

The anthropotouristic machine

In *The Open*, Giorgio Agamben (2004) reflects on the indirect dialogue between Georges Bataille and Alexander Kojève about the "end of History" and its implications for "what-it-means-to-be-human." In the "post-historical" condition – for Agamben – the very definition of what it is to be human is put into question, "as a result of the completion of the long-lasting process according to which the animal of the species, *Homo sapiens*, had become finally human." Let us recall Kojève here:

> the disappearance of Man at the end of History is a not a cosmic catastrophe: the natural World remains what it has been from all eternity, and it is not a biological catastrophe either: Man remains alive as animal in harmony with nature or given Being. What disappears is Man properly so called [. . .], in point of fact, the end of time or history [. . .] means quite simply the cessation of Action in the strong sense of the term. Practically, this means: the disappearance of *Philosophy*; for since Man no longer changes himself essentially, there is no longer any reason to change the (true) principles which are at the basis of his knowledge of the world and of himself. But all the rest can be preserved indefinitely; art, love, play, etc.; in short, everything that makes Man *happy*.
>
> (Kojève 1980 [1947]: 434–35; cited in Agamben 2004: 6)

According to Agamben, Bataille disagreed precisely on the nature of this "rest," that is, on the nature of what outlives/survives after the "death" of a Man returned to his animal condition at the end of history. What Bataille could not accept was that art, love, play, but also laughter, ecstasy, luxury, etc., instead of being considered as superhuman characteristics, were qualified by Kojève, in their post-historical dimension, as an expression of the "return" of the (happy) animal-in-us, as non-human: "if history is nothing but the patient dialectical work of negation [of Action], and man both the subject and the stakes of this negating action, then the completion of history necessarily entails the end of Man . . ." (Agamben 2004: 7). The end of History implies, then, an epilogue, when human lack of Action is simply maintained as "a rest" in the form of eroticism, of laughter, of "joy in the face of death" (Agamben 2004: 7).

It is necessary to follow another passage of Agamben's argument. In 1968, in fact, Kojève returns to this question to argue that "the post-historical animals of the species *Homo sapiens* (which will live amidst abundance and complete security) will be content as a result of their artistic, erotic, and playful behavior, inasmuch as, by definition, they will be contented with it" (Kojève 1979 [1946]: 436; cited in Agamben 2004: 9). (Incidentally, isn't this nothing other than the ultimate dream of perfection promoted by the tourism industry, a timeless dream, that is? I shall return to this point later.) Importantly, Agamben identifies a key threshold here between the human and the non-human in the post-historical condition. In theoretical terms, if we adopt Kojève's post-historical figure of the human, then Man is not

> a biologically defined species, nor is he a substance given once and for all; he is rather a field of dialectical tensions always already cut by internal caesurae that every time separate – at least virtually – "anthropophorous" animality and the humanity which takes bodily form from in it. Man exists historically only in this tension; he can be human only to the degree that he transcends and transforms the anthropophorous animal which supports him, and only because, through the action of negation, he is capable of mastering and, eventually, destroying his own animality.
>
> (Agamben 2004: 9)

But what happens to Man's animality in the post-historical condition? With modernity, this "animality" – Man's natural life, his *bios* – is treated as if it was separated from his relational and political life in order to become the *object of care*, in particular on the part of the state – a state left (especially after the end of World War I) with no clear and credible historical task. This is a common argument in the mainstream literature on biopolitics, as we all know. Foucault has indeed famously defined this form of institutionalized care as "biopower." In this understanding of the "animal-in-us," modern Man ends up being conceived as a sort of mobile threshold, a frontier in/on which the modern political economy of animality is constantly negotiated. As part of this negotiation, argues Agamben, a critical passage is represented precisely by the strategic isolation of "vegetative" and "relational" life, a distinction that has become paramount in modern medicine. This caesura in the life of human beings operates as if life were something that could not really be defined, and for this reason must be constantly articulated and divided (Agamben 2004: 13). The post-historical Man then looks like a figure finally separated from his original animality and allowed (condemned?) to be defined by a "political economy of pleasure," so to speak, an economy centered around eroticism, play, conspicuous consumption, boredom, contemplation, personal enhancement, well-being, care of the body, etc.

This "fully human" post-historical Man is then the result of the completion of that process of biopolitical "cuts" that operated across the whole of modernity in order to produce a clear separation, in the individual and in the body of the population, between two forms of life: the biological and the relational – that is, the political. The literature on this passage is vast and articulated, and I do not have the space here for a proper engagement with it (see, among many others, Agamben 1998; Cavalletti 2005; Esposito 2008). But one hint could help link this argument to the question of the biopolitical in tourism. Isn't this perfected being disturbingly similar to the hypothetical tourist as conceived and represented by the industry? That is, a sort of mindless mobile subject who wanders the globe seeking distilled forms of well-being or personal enhancement; who walks our cities for the mere "pleasure" of doing it and out of "curiosity;" who pursues accidental and temporary identities in the dedicated spaces of leisure where (s)he is invited to forget about life back at home and abandon himself/herself to the flow of the vacation; who is entranced by dreams of eternal youth; who must be (or at least look) healthy and joyful; and who is offered an ephemeral citizenship in a world marked by repetition and a permanent festival (see Bataille 1985, 2001; also, Diken and Laustsen 2004).

However, the links between the post-historical condition described above and the "tourist condition" do not stop here. Let us follow Agamben's thought for a couple more passages. He significantly recalls Linnaeus's decision to include/inscribe humans in his classification of beings developed in the *Sistema Naturae*, a decision opening up the field to scientific and philosophical speculations that will mark the centuries to come, during which the definition of that threshold between the human and the animal will become a (often implicit) crucial task for the social sciences, and in particular for the work of the anthropologist (Agamben 2004: 23; but also Ewen and Ewen 2006).

Modern debates on what makes "the human" distinct have often translated into a set of practices aimed at investigating "the animal in the human" and, especially, in keeping these two clearly separate. This is what Agamben (2004) calls the "anthropogenic" or anthropological machine:

> the anthropogenic [. . .] machine is an optical one [. . .] constructed of a series of mirrors in which man, looking at himself, sees his own image always already deformed in the features of an ape. *Homo* is a constitutively "anthropomorphous" animal (that is, "resembling man", according to the term that Linnaeus constantly uses [. . .]), who must recognize himself in a non-man in order to be human.
>
> (Agamben 2004: 26–27)

> The anthropological machine of humanism is an ironic apparatus that verifies the absence of a nature proper to *Homo*, holding him suspended between a celestial and a terrestrial nature, between animal and nature.
>
> (Agamben 2004: 29)

This machine relies on the belief in the existence of a set of intermediate figures bridging the human and the animal, "from man to ape" as some literature from the past would have had it (Ewen and Ewen 2006). According to Agamben, what makes man "human" is his awareness of being human, his capacity for locating the human in himself (2004: 26). This process of recognition and awareness requires a constant identification and definition of these threshold figures, but also of their links with the animal/human dialectic. The "monkey-man" famously presented by Ernst Haeckel in his seminal *Die Welträtsel* (1899), also cited by Agamben, is indeed a key bridging figure of this kind, a "missing link" of sorts. The monkey-man, noticeably, is a being that does not speak, or does not speak *yet*:

> what distinguishes man from animal is language, but this is not a natural given already inherent in the psychophysical structure of man; it is, rather, a historical production which, as such, can be properly assigned neither to man nor to animal. If this element is taken away, the difference between man and animal vanishes, unless we imagine a nonspeaking man – *Homo alalus*, precisely – who would function as a bridge that passes from the animal to the human.
>
> (Agamben 2004: 36)

As tourists or tourism scholars, we are indeed often faced with the enigmatic look of a native "representative" on the cover of a brochure inviting us to visit this or that country, to meet this or that culture, to penetrate these or those people's living space. This somewhat hieratic being, often smiling and very "native" in his/her pose, is indeed mute; (s)he is a non-speaking being, similar, perhaps too similar, to the *Homo alalus*, the bridging figure described by Agamben.

Why are we attracted to the "encounter" with the thousands of hypothetical monkey-men that populate the colorful pages produced by the industry? What are we expecting to obtain out of the mirroring experience of the confrontation with these (often funny) radical others, with the primitive, the folkloric wax manikin, with those zombies who perform and who appear to be there merely as a sign (of their "culture")? Is it just post-historical curiosity, a speculative need for cheap and spectacular difference at a glance? This is certainly a possibility, but perhaps there is more, and this more has perhaps to do with the biopolitical nature of the anthropological machine.

The silent monkey-men of the tourist political economy are, in fact, presented as hospitable inhabitants of a colorful world marked by reassuring images of a culture-in-place, of a single patchwork-world in which things and people have their place, are clearly distinct and available for inspection. The "inspection" is what the brochures seem to promise and is one of the engines of the anthropotouristic machine. This machine operates biopolitically in several different ways. First, it allows for the post-historical tourist to test the threshold between the human and the animal through the visual inspection of the monkey-men encountered, who seem to be trained to provide precisely that reassuring performance of otherness and not-too-radical difference. It is in the inspection of these silenced others that the existence of the threshold-monkey-man can be reaffirmed and consolidated. I shall return to this point later. Second, paradoxically, the globalized tourists who visit many places and cultures, in collecting their various "experiences" seem to be constantly preyed upon by a strange post-historical boredom, by the anxiety of a world populated by things that "have nothing to offer" (Agamben 2004: 64). Boredom here must be intended as a metaphysical *dispositif*, as the condition that distinguishes humanity from animality – animals do not get bored, for Kojève (and Agamben) – but also as a pervasive post-historical tourist condition.

The "bored" tourist is a human suspended in a strange threshold where he seems to look for meaning and purpose in the real and imagined worlds produced by the anthropotouristic machine. But a problem with this is that the machine gravitates around an empty center and is driven by an insurmountable aporia. On one hand, its task seems to be that of providing precisely a sort of geography of meaning and purpose. By visiting, seeing and touching different humans (or, better, their representatives and representations), the tourists should find comfort in these realms of total humanity in an age of nihilism and shifting cultural borders. The monkey-men populating these bizarre geographies of touch-and-go experiences should indeed provide the missing link, the compensation for the disappearance of a historical sense in the late modern subject. They seem to be ready to incorporate all kinds of "heritage" and "culture" in order to fill out the spaces of those empty cartographies of meaning. At the same time – and here is the aporia – tourists are invited to get themselves involved in this machinery by entering spaces with no sense of place and time, by dealing with hosts with no age and subjectivity, by attending performances of sticky cultural essentialism. *This is no country for old men.* Both the tourists and the subhuman objects of their gaze, in their encounters, are putatively placed in a sort of ideal stable cultural relationship. In the specialist literature, the images inviting to penetrate these placid waters of culture indeed refer to hypothetical happy and healthy tourists entering a *contact zone* (Pratt 1992) together with an equally placid, happy and docile "local" subject. Their bodies, in the political economy of the machine, are a referent and an abstraction at the same time, a biopolitical horizon where both (the tourist and the "local") are subject(ed) to a timeless and spaceless narrative of spiritual enhancement and relational endeavor. In the attempt to operate the biopolitical caesurae that aim at keeping the animal and the human separate "in us," the anthropogenic tourist machine ends up producing two abstract kinds of bodies identically suspended in a threshold where no meaning and no life can be clearly defined, only performed through repetition and boredom (for both).

These considerations, to which I will return in the next sections, bring us to a second crucial biopolitical element in contemporary tourism; that is, the preoccupation with care and well-being, often associated with a nostalgic sense of (the lack of) community. According to Agamben's reading of contemporary biopolitics, traditional Western expressions of meaning and purpose, such as poetry, religion and philosophy, have been progressively transformed into performances and private experiences, and have lost every historical dimension:

> faced with this eclipse, the only task that still seems to retain some seriousness is the assumption of the burden – and of the "total manage-ment" – of biological life, that is, of the very animality of man. Genome, global economy, and humanitarian ideology are the three united faces of this process in which post-historical humanity seems to take on its own physiology at its last, apolitical mandate.
>
> (Agamben 2004: 77)

This may explain the growing nostalgia for community, a disturbingly empty concept when employed in tourism, a concept around which the whole anthropological machine seems to spin today at an increasing speed. According to Esposito, in the contemporary condition the paradox is that

> the individual desires what he fears (precisely losing the limits that make him be), set in motion by an irresistible nostalgia for his previous and subsequent state of not-being-individual. Out of this arises the perennial contradiction between desire and life. [. . .] life is nothing other than desire (for community), but the desire (for community) is necessarily configured as the negation of life.
>
> (Esposito 2009: 121)

The desire for community can be seen also as the need for experience, for historical experience in a post-historical condition, that is. But as Bataille has shown, in the contemporary search for the experience of community what we experience is only the experience of the lack of that experience. Bataille, however, according to Esposito, at the same time identifies in the community a limit in which experience is indeed possible, but it is only a flash, a moment; one cannot remain in it except for "instants" – of laughter, of sex, of blood – in which "our existence reaches both its apex and abyss, fleeing outside of itself" (Esposito 2009: 122).

> Stripping naked is the decisive action. Nakedness offers a contrast to self-possession, to discontinuous existence, in other words. It is a state of communication revealing a quest for a possible continuance of being beyond the confines of the self. Bodies open out to a state of continuity through secret channels that give us a feeling of obscenity. Obscenity is our name for the uneasiness which upsets the physical state associated with self-possession, with the possession of a recognized and stable individuality.
>
> (Bataille 2001: 17–18; cited in Diken and Laustsen 2004)

This is a potentially intriguing interpretation of the post-historical tourist condition as well, and it would explain to some extent the endless desire for the event, for a moment of emotional intensity, for a glance of a life worth living on the part of the post-historical traveler. For Littlewood, tourism sets up, against the religion of the spirit, an "anti-religion of the senses" characterized by the supremacy of the senses and the primacy of enjoyment: a "coded promise of sexual adventure" (Littlewood 2001: 193, 210; cited in Diken and Laustsen 2004). Order is then constantly faced with the impulse of desire and the vertigo of risk. In tourism, this translates into the messiness of the tourist experience and practice in place, as described by Tim Oakes (Chapter 6 in this volume) and Tim Edensor (Chapter 4 in this volume), an interplay between orderings and disorderings that the academic literature has been only recently analyzing in depth.

A close inspection of this aporia at the core of the anthropogenic machine is possibly a useful way to think through the relationship between tourism and the biopolitical. The biopolitical here is that *dispositif* at the basis of the anthropotourist machine that, while rotating around the void of meaning and content that characterizes the post-historical condition, activates a political economy of care *and* control – of the individual *and* of the collective – of compensation *and* exoneration, all generated by the aporiae at the core of that same void around which the machine continues to rotate.

The biopolitical in tourism is also a *dispositif* at the center of contemporary attempts at redefining the threshold between the animal and the human, and it does so by operating endless caesurae on real and imagined bodies, post-historical bodies at work and on display, mobilized bodies constantly on the move but often presented as if they were frozen in space and time. The rest of the chapter is thus dedicated to a preliminary exploration of this *dispositif*, in order to investigate its broader implications for the constitution of "the political," well beyond tourism and its tropes – an investigation about the politicized bodies on the move that populate the spaces of contemporary travel.

The missing community

Contemporary tourism seems to be obsessed with the question of community. The word "community" is just about everywhere in the promotional material produced by tourist organizations. Tourists are invited to visit local communities in remote villages in every corner of the planet in order to appreciate their hospitality and traditions – marginal populations, in the tourism popular literature, are always hospitable and traditional. One example among others is the "Philippines community-based marine conservation" where dedicated volunteers (they are not called "tourists" any more) are offered the opportunity to work as part of a coral reef research team that supports and assists local non-profit organizations, the local communities around Sogod Bay, and the provincial government of Southern Leyte. As the website promises, there is the very engaging and thoroughly rewarding community aspect that will see you undertake community education and capacity building programs in order to: increase local awareness of marine environmental issues; highlight the importance and economic benefits of MPAs and initiate the planning of a coastal zone management scheme for Southern Leyte with full stakeholder involvement.[1]

In other cases, tourists are offered the chance to help the local community directly: for example, La Ruta Moskitia, a Rio Plátano Biosphere Reserve in Honduras and a UNESCO World Heritage Site,

has created an example of how sustainable tourism development can provide training and education, support infrastructure development, and
foster cultural preservation and environmental awareness. Founded in
2003 [. . .] this area's first indigenously operated NGO is run by a board
of directors comprised entirely of community members. The project
consists of community-run ecolodges and tours, with a focus on long-term
commitment to an authentic travel experience grounded in quality service.
(Tourism for Tomorrow 2009)

But the tourists themselves are also a community of sorts. Communities of travelers exchange material, experiences, hints, etc. via several media, but they also share a specialist literature – think, for example, of the symbolic (and somewhat political) meaning of traveling with a Lonely Planet guide, instead of a Michelin Guide. What is perhaps even more important for our argument, however, is the new communitarian and somewhat utopian culture that is inherent to many tourist experiences.

The book and film *The Beach* (1996/2000) wonderfully illustrates the tensions and the paradoxes at the heart of newly founded communities of tourists/travelers/drifters, especially when ideas of purity and separation are taken too seriously – which is often the case with radical forms of communitarianism. Tourist villages are also organized around the bizarre but powerful concept of a temporary exclusive community. Walls separate the guests of "total resorts" for a week or so from the rest of the world, while questions of fun, well-being and mindless relaxation are the mantras of what is in fact a rather regimented kind of space. The academic literature on this is vast and very helpful in understanding this increasing tendency (see, among many others, Diken and Laustsen 2004; Edensor 2001, 2006a, b).

Despite the rhetoric of togetherness and freedom that promotes them, what these temporary communities of strangers actually have in common is the fact that their accidental members share practically nothing, but they share this nothingness in the same place and in a similar way. The whole spatial rhetoric of any enclavic tourist space tends to confirm this strange negotiation between alienation and commonality. Why do people decide to spend their time and money with total strangers in such a bizarre reconstruction of what a human community should be (at least in its most conventional understanding), since it is at this understanding the total resorts seem to hint in all their promotional material?[2] Driven as they are by a subtle post-romantic vibe and by a less subtle therapeutic intent, enclavic "tourist communities" claim indeed to provide a specific culture of being together and a set of typically post-historical values; that is, a "well-organized" collectively experienced nothingness based on the myth of the foundations and on the nostalgic drive that are found in each and every experimental form of radical communitarianism today.

This shared "nothingness" challenges in an interesting way the very idea of community. For this reason, in this first articulation of my exploration of the biopolitical in tourism, I would like to suggest that academic discussions on the meaning of community today (see Nancy 1991; Agamben 1993; De Petra 2010; Meazza 2010; but also current reinterpretations of Blanchot's work) can learn something also from the excesses and the paradoxes of the tourist community.

Some background theory is thus in order here. Roberto Esposito, in his seminal *Communitas*, explains why it is so important and urgent to interrogate the question of community today:

> Nothing seems more appropriate today than thinking community; nothing more necessary, demanded and heralded by a situation that joins in a unique epochal knot the failure of all communisms with the misery of new individualisms. Nevertheless, nothing is further from view; nothing so remote, repressed, and put off until later, to a distant and indecipherable horizon.
>
> (Esposito 2009: 1)

In particular, for the Italian philosopher, it is its reduction to "object" on the part of many political–philosophical discourses

> that forces community into a conceptual language that radically alters it [. . .]: that of the individual and totality; of identity and the particular; of the origin and the end or, more simply of the subject with its most unassailable metaphysical connotations of unity, absoluteness and interiority.
>
> (Esposito 2009: 1)

An urgent question for this chapter is, then, what is the foundational myth of the tourist community? The imagined (coming?) tourist community indeed often implicitly makes reference to the dream of a self-sufficient isolated human consortium, a utopian space where the individual subject can merge into, and become part of, a larger collective Self. But this myth is also based on the belief in the possibility of realizing a sort of transparent community, a biopolitical experiment based on the dominion of absolute immanence. In other words, a post-historical community.

The tourist community is thus a sort of political horizon; literally, a happy community of tomorrow (a leitmotif in the Disney-*lands*), in the sense that it can never be realized, but only deferred, endlessly deferred (see also Chapter 5 in this volume). This community of nothingness is important biopolitically for two main reasons: first, because, once again, it has at its core an aporia that is based on its claim to offer the purity of a transparent *community in the making*, and, at the same time, the experience of a temporary transient space of separation and desire, escapism and freedom from responsibility: fully immanent and somewhat transcendental at the same time, a sort of low-cost ticket to paradise. Second, because it seems to provide the ideal ground for biopolitical "regeneration" based on care *and* control. I will return to this second point in the final section.

Now, since it is apparent in its inception that this kind of community could be home only to the gods, the question remains: why are people, who should be well aware of its aporiae, be so keen to submit themselves to its "deep" experience? Again, Esposito's critique of *communitas* provides some useful hints here. According to him, community is too often presented simply as a sort of wider (than the individual one) subjectivity, a conception based on the assumption that it is a property belonging to subjects that join together, or some sort of substance produced by their union (Esposito 2009: 2). From this perspective,

> the organicistic sociology of *Gemeinschaft*, of American neo-communitarianism, and of the various "ethics of communication" lie beyond the same line [. . .] for these philosophies, in fact, it is a full, or a whole, or even a good, a value, an essence, which can be lost and then re-found as "something that once belonged to us" and that therefore can once again belong to us; an origin to be mourned or a destiny foreshadowed based on the perfect symmetry that links *arche* and *telos*.
>
> (Esposito 2009: 2)

What they have in common – this is the conventional claim – is that which unites the ethnic, territorial, and spiritual property of every one of its members (Esposito 2009: 2). Be that as it may, the romantic rhetoric of community, together with some traces of past *Gemeinschaft* culture, are significantly present in the ways in which community is promoted and organized by the tourism industry today. The realization of the essentialized and sublimated "communitas," we all know, is the ultimate (and phantasmagoric) goal of totalitarianism (Esposito 2009: 143). But Esposito famously claims that "communitas" is instead the totality of persons united not by a property, but by an obligation, by a *munus*, a due gift; it is not an addition but rather a subtraction of what is "proper" in each of us, a subtraction operated by the space of the "common." In other words, "being of a community" is the condition by which we lose something that belongs to us in order to be with others – with whom we share precisely this loss of the "proper" (Esposito 2009: 4–6).

The tourist community is also, in many ways, the product of a subtraction, but of a different kind, and of the related need for compensation. Influenced, as it seems to be, by the legacy of those very communitarian philosophies/ideologies, it responds to a widespread popular rhetoric of loss, of betrayal (of the original community), of protection from the devastating power of the nihilism that pervades modern societies (see Esposito 2009: 134). The perceived lack and loss of an original community is precisely the referent of so much tourism promotional material that promises an impossible but desirable return/compensation[3] (see Chapter 9 in this volume). The result is a sort of imagined phantasmagoric geography of peculiar communities, often presented as a response to the insufficiency of the individualistic model. For example, the community of the total resorts inhabited by these temporary citizens becomes a sort of island of ephemeral togetherness, in contrast to the messiness of the real world, out there:

> the rules are suspended rather than destroyed. The transgressions of the holidaymaker do not, in this sense, perform a "back-to-nature movement" [. . .] the identity of the tourist is stripped of its public connotations and his desire is moved by the promise of an eroticized, corporeal, "animal" world experienced as freedom from the "city": the dark, routinized, disciplinary "iron cage" of the citizen [. . .] transgression does not suppress but suspends the rule.
>
> (Bataille, 2001: 36, cited in Diken and Laustsen 2004)

This community becomes, then, hypothetically at least, a place of content and meaning, a substance, a value of sorts, a putative compensation for the nothingness of the post-historical.

The paradox here is that the enclavic tourist community is constitutively founded precisely on the nothingness shared by its "inhabitants." The tourist experience is the result of the workings of a nihilistic community, a community that is purely formal and substantially empty, which claims affection for its nothingness, and which will suddenly evaporate when the tourist returns home. The gist of tourist communitarianism is then about filling up a void determined by the nothingness of the whole tourism business. What the brochures of hedonistic camps promise is nothing but a momentary deletion of the absolute separation between individuals, and their equally momentary fusion in a sociospatial container with a fixed and presumably stable identity.

> Club Med: "No constraint, no obligation. Barefoot, dressed in shorts, a sarong, bathing trunks if you like, you completely forget so-called civilised life." As an "antidote to civilization" Club Med sells places "where one could strip off not just clothes but everything that locked one into a public role."
>
> (Littlewood 2001: 210, 211, cited in Diken and Laustsen 2004)

It is perhaps useful to return to Bataille here, when he affirms the "impossibility of the community," in the sense that a true, original, fulfilling, and self-sufficient community is literally impossible. The impossibility of community, maintains Esposito (2009: 140–148), can be explained also by the fact that all those "philosophies of decline" advocating some sort of return to the origins do nothing other than trying to historicize an ahistorical condition: community is neither an origin, nor a destiny, but simply a condition of shared subtraction. And it is precisely here that tourism shows its nihilistic face: the tourist community, that strange formation that brings strangers to spend together a week or so in apposite spatial arrangements, is a genuine expression of the nihilistic foundation of the post-historical condition. That community, in the village-resort or in similar spatial "enclaves," is a grouping of subjects who have in common the fact that they do not have anything in common beyond their very presence "there," as tourists. The best representative of this culture of togetherness is the smiling tourist surrounded by other smiling strangers and equally smiling staff in a holiday camp or "club." In the eternal smile economy of the tourist camp and in the reassuring healthy and "normal" look of these hosts and guests resides the *arcanum* of the biopolitical in post-historical tourism.

And yet community remains very popular in tourism;[4] it is presented as a model space associated with a specific set of expectations and related arrangements. It is a space of compensation – again, for the loss of a hypothetical past community – and of eternal youth: the end-product of a biopolitical reproduction of happy and healthy normalized bodies, a form of "pure existence," pure presence. The ultimate post-historical tourist community, as a form of pure existence, as temporary life for the sake of life, cannot contemplate death, and so cannot accept aging and the decadence of the body. Illness, unhappiness, imperfection, disability, ugliness are not supposed to inhabit this realm of pure immanence, as it is portrayed by the visual rhetoric of the industry and its popular literature. For this reason, in the newly born utopian community founded on a Thai island in *The Beach*, the illness and the death of a member is an unthinkable, and therefore unmanageable, event – since the tourist community as a utopian space of eternal youth cannot metabolize imperfection and disease, together with unhappiness and suffering: the answer to the irruption of the unexpected in the community – one member in need of medical care – turns into a machinery of death. Life sublimated in its instantaneous perfection must be maintained at the price of death. Death (or expulsion and invisibility in the case of regular enclavic communities) is the price to pay in order to maintain the performance of perfected life in the purified community.

This is nothing particularly new, since totalitarianism can be read precisely as an attempt to bring this sort of social project to realization. The perfected community is, in fact, constitutionally founded on a horizon of exclusion and invisibility – of the subject, of meaning, of difference, of the effects of time on the body. This is the abyss, according to Esposito, that stands before those who look for the ultimate origins of community. The imagined community of the origins, and its future utopian projections, in tourism and beyond tourism, is not to be found for the simple reason that it was never lost. What the tourists have in common, then, is precisely the very impossibility of the community that is promised to them. And this perhaps explains the post-historical abandonment to "the rest" that Kojève had in mind: pure pleasure, hedonism, sex, the glorification of the "instant," the aestheticized celebration of the body in its biological terms – that is, the ultimate outcome of the caesurae operated on the tourist-subject in its negotiation with his presumed animality, the ultimate desubjectivation produced by the biopolitical in tourism.

Zombies

> Why should I go to a museum if I live in one?
> (student in Fez, cited in Pieprzak 2010, Ch. xi: 1)

The biopolitical in tourism operates in another important way. In her 1998 book *Destination Culture*, Kirshenblatt-Gimblett (1998: 1) shows how in modern cultural economies, the museification of "local" subjects has gone a long way since the first forms of objectification and how the tourist gaze has played and continues to play an important role in this process. The awareness of some representatives of what we normally define as "local" or "traditional" culture is a sign of the deep penetration of the biopolitical in the production of what she defines as the "political economy of showing".

The interest (desire?) within tourism for the experience of otherness provided by travels in and to foreign lands has by now a long history. Colonialism and modern science, especially social science, have indeed prepared the field for an understanding of culture, of the culture of others, which has taken a biopolitical form in many of its manifestations. The "political economy of showing" that has driven, and still drives today, many "presentations" of culture for the visiting tourist has indeed deep roots in Western modernity, and often consists, even today, in the reiteration of performances in which the idea of culture is mediated by the use of bodies, of real and imagined desubjectivized bodies. In addition, the rhetoric of authenticity, often associated with the reasons for actually-traveling-to-places-to-see-things-in-the-real, is also sometimes accompanied by a paternalistic language aimed at giving meaning and ethical flavor to the penetration of the living spaces of others. The "Care for Children in Goa" project is a case in point (Responsibletravel.com 2011). Tourists are offered the opportunity to take part in a volunteer project in Goa with a charitable trust dedicated to working with underprivileged children. The aim of the project is

> to help the poor and needy children of the area by giving them free shelter, clothes, food, education and health care – all aiming to provide the kids with a bright and better future. [. . .] Many of the children come from very

tough and challenging backgrounds and you will play a part in really brightening up their lives. In your free time the whole of Goa is yours to explore – from stunning beaches and fascinating markets to the bustling main city and incredible food.

The anthropotouristic machine is in motion here again, and operates with strategic caesurae/cuts on/in the bodies of the objectified subjects of culture. The culture of "others" is often presented with specific arrangements of bodies on display, either in the form of spectacle – in a theatrical performance of selected and orderly elements of the culture in question – or in the form of an actual penetration (again, selectively operated) of the "drama of the quotidian."

Brochures promising cultural travel experiences in faraway lands are populated by the smiling faces of unnamed people, often accompanied by abundant exposure of their bodies, especially if young and sexualized, and by more or less sophisticated folkloristic images[5]; the promise here is of unmediated (often articulated in the language of "authenticity") contact with the local population, of a learning experience about their deep culture; of penetration, in a respectful but nonetheless deep way, of their living spaces. Those very spaces tend to be presented as if they were a sort of open-air museum, populated by smiling people waiting to be visited and performing a reassuring idea of difference.

> Gecko's grassroots adventures are all about authentic travel – small groups, local leaders, inspiring destinations and real experiences.
>   Gecko's grassroots adventures are about getting to the heart and soul of a country. [. . .] Local leaders are the grassroots of Gecko's grassroots adventures. Gecko's clients come back time and time again for the knowledge, passion and personality of our leaders. Our leaders are all born and raised in the regions we travel to, have strong connections with local communities and have a great understanding of your culture as much as their own.
>
> (Gecko's Grassroots Adventures brochure(s) 2010–2012)

The question remains: why is cultural tourism today still so strongly deter-mined by this disturbing economy of zombies? For these are indeed zombies, since "presented" as if they were deprived of any subjectivity – a sort of bridge between an essentialized idea of culture and the corporeality of an actual human being, whose body is disposed and put on display as part of that very distinct political economy.

Kirshenblatt-Gimblett (1998: 3) describes in detail the process of becoming an ethnographic object, a process that "brings together specimens and artifacts never found in the same place and at the same time and shows relationships that cannot otherwise be seen". This often results in "the paradox of showing things that were never meant to be displayed, 'exhibitions' whether of objects or people, display of artifacts of our disciplines. They are also exhibits of those who make them" (Kirshenblatt-Gimblett 1998: 2). Curiously, she continues, "live displays, and especially the display of humans" (1998: 4) seems to be still central to the political economy of showing that drives the anthropo-touristic machine. Tourism is, in fact, deeply involved in this process, "which not only compresses the life world, but also displaces it, thereby escalating the process by which a way of life becomes heritage" (1998: 7). People/ individuals subjected to this form of colonization thus become the medium of ethnographic representation: they perform "themselves" while the tourist often tries to establish some sort of "connection" with these ever-smiling "locals," revealing, right in that gesture, the non-relational nature of the tourist "contact zone," the void at its very inception (on this, see also Ewen and Ewen 2006).

In tourist sites, these performances are often repeated many times in one day, hundreds of times in a single month. What is interesting here is the relationship between the present culture of display in tourism and the eugenic tradition that Kirshenblatt-Gimblett recalls in order to explain how human specimens happened to become objects of curiosity and, indeed, display. She starts from the International Eugenics Conference held in 1927 in the USA (1998: 27), where ideas of normality were discussed along with a selected display of a set of "nature's mistakes." Since then "bines and mummies, body parts, plastic death masks [. . .] living human specimens have been displayed in zoos and exhibitions" (1998: 28). The objectified nature of these exhibits raises a question that is crucial for the understanding of the biopolitical in tourism: "where does the object begin, and where does it end?" (1998: 18). Every time we put people on display like fragments, "we do indeed produce fragments," biopolitical ones. We all know, at this point in history, that "humans are also detachable, fragmentable and replicable as a variety of materials [quote] morbidity, living specimens . . ." (1998: 34). This speaks directly to what Kirshenblatt-Gimblett defines as the semiotic complexity of exhibits of people: "ethnographic displays are part of a longer history of human displays in which the themes of death, dissection, torture and martyrdom are intermingling." We are, in other words, used to a culture of display "exhibiting the dead as if they were alive, and the living as they were dead" (1998: 35).

We can still experience some of these exhibits, albeit often in a reinterpreted version – in the tourist products that are sold and arranged as if they were part of a sort of "gallery of nations," or, even worse, when fragments of a globalized (but highly selective) "great human family" (1998: 37) are presented as local culture and "experience." Racial typologies of the past are re-enacted via the cultural geographies of a globalized market selling the experience of prima facie contact with their either smiling or hieratic representatives. The "theatrical" and the "zoological" intermingle in these colorful performances of the local self (Ewen and Ewen 2006).

The anthropotouristic machine is thus deeply affected by a sort of "museum effect;" that is, by a widespread tendency on the part of the industry and of the tourists themselves to convert the quotidian into a spectacle, through the hubris of penetrating the living space of others (Dicks 2003). For instance, a Kenyan excursion company takes tourists

> to the slums of Kibera by car, [where] driver Jeremiah will be the whole day with you. [. . .] Visit the compound of Emily. Walk around in Kibera, visit a family, Emily will explain the way of living in the slum. It is very safe living there, she will show how people take care of each other. Walking through the slums is like a hike, adventurous, children will like it.[6]

Displays thus populate tourist destinations as well, where specimens are often displayed and asked to "explain" the landscape, as if they were an organic part of the visited scene. This, again, is *no country for old men*. These cultural geographies of display, in fact, are often translated into in a scary geography of zombies, where the threshold between animality and humanity is constantly reproduced and negotiated: a zombie culture elected to relational model, the relational model of "cultural tourism" in remote and not so remote areas. Especially when in contact with putative primitives and their living spaces, post-historical travelers can literally touch and test the persistence of the monkey-men among us; that is, of subhuman objects of observation and inspection deprived of subjectivity. These desubjectivized figures occupy the threshold between their body – a real and present body – and the equally real presence of a putative primitive/local, an idealized and normalized other on display.

Not too surprisingly, tourists are invited to visit those contact zones via the perfomative display of other zombies as well, tourist zombies this time around: the smiling and happy tourists in the brochures are also presented as normalized traveling objects, as abstract referents for the potential travelers still at home with whom they are invited to relate and identify – for example, with the eternal smiling Indiana Jones lookalike traveler–anthropologist. *Zombies meeting other zombies* – this seems to be the by-product of the anthro-potourist machine. Its biopolitical regime is an imagined timeless land of perfected encounters driven by the logic of deferral. In their practice, tourists and locals in fact transgress "the script" all the time, but what is interesting here is the fact that, despite the endless deferral of its promise and the degree of disbelief that is often expressed by the real people populating tourists places, this biopolitical model of zombies remains at the core of most presentations of cultural tourism, especially when difference and adventure are emphasized by the industry. What is then at the root of this obsession for normalized bodies and the related representations of static cultural types in tourism? Perhaps it is time to turn to our last move, and explore the question of care and control in relation to the biopolitics of tourism.

Care and control

> Travel widens [one's] view [. . .] the best patriots are people who like to travel
> Adolf Hitler (in Semmens 2005: 27)

In *Seeing Hitler's Germany*, Kristin Semmens (2005) argues that, for what is often considered the ultimate biopolitical regime (Agamben 1998), the organization of leisure and pleasure had to be taken seriously. Tourism was considered important by National Socialism for a number of reasons: first, it was perceived as a useful means to consolidate and experience the greater unity of the national community (Semmens 2005: 12). Second, the democratization of travel offered the possibility of a better appreciation of the national landscape and of its more traditional inhabitants, as was the case for the tours of the Black Forest (2005: 89). Perhaps more importantly, however, tourism was a necessary expression of controlled transgression, since it included a degree of promiscuity associated with its unavoidable intense sociality but, at the same time, allowed for the exercise of benevolent and normally well-received authority, discipline, and propaganda (2005: 17).

A key player in the democratization of travel in Nazi Germany was certainly the *Kraft durch Freude* (KdF, "Strength through Joy") organization, led by Robert Ley and concerned with the provision of leisure for the masses, especially for the working classes. From the relevant literature emerges that tourism was given a more political than economic value by the regime (Semmens 2005: 147), since not only did these (carefully selected) leisurely travels allow many Germans to witness the achievements of the Third Reich, but also to connect their experience to the ideology of *lebensraum* – that is, the need for more vital space for the German people (Bassin 1987). Even German soldiers, during the first successful campaign of the war, reported experiencing something similar to what had been offered for some time by the KdF initiatives. Conquered lands became lands to be visited also with a tourist eye (Semmens 2005: 178; for the relationship between tourism and imperialism, see Chapter 5 in this volume). But there was also a genuinely biopolitical preoccupation at the basis of the emphasis given to the tourist experience for the selected master race: there was indeed a clear sense on the part of the regime that Germans could be regenerated and gain increased working capacity and morale through the experience of traveling.

This aspect deserves further enquiry. In his book *Immunitas*, Esposito (2002) reflects on what he defines as the immunitary paradigm at the basis of modern politics and biopolitics. Particularly relevant here are his considerations on the question of the "conservation and protection of life itself" as a key biopolitical principle. The contemporary emphasis on the biological dimension of the body – the individual body, but also the body politics – according to Esposito, is part of an increased attention placed by the state on the protection *and* the control of the reproduction of both individual and collective life, a strategy that pays a high tribute to the principle of "contamination" and to the myths of "preservation" and "perfection." My claim is that the immunitary paradigm has direct influence on what we have so far presented as the biopolitical in tourism; on a culture of travel and leisure often driven by – and promoted through – ideas of immunization and purification, and by the desire for a distant but ever young and healthy body.

One crucial passage of Esposito's analysis is his comment (2002: 32) on how the modern juridical incorporation of life was conceived in ways that ended up sacrificing what he describes as "the intensity of life" in the name of its conservation. The juridical normalization of life also implied the definition of a "just life", which immediately produced a *scarto*, a gap when compared to the actual life of people (2002: 37). This brought two important corollaries: first, the idea of a "just life" became a hypothetical referent and a political horizon; second, life, from that moment onward, had to be protected by anticipating potential threats. This is what the immunitary logic prescribes: to inject a fragment of the potential threat into the "body" to be protected; that is, a preventive, controlled intervention in order to preserve the integrity of the life (2002: 58). What is clearly at stake here is the well-being and the happiness of the governed body politics, which is also a biological body, or at least conceived as such.

Once the centrality of life is established, reaffirms Esposito in *Bios*, it is precisely politics that is awarded the responsibility for saving life and the responsibility of its government, involving all aspects of individual and collective life, from justice to finance, from work to healthcare, to even pleasure and leisure (Esposito 2008: 57). Andrea Cavalletti (2005) maintains that the police itself, initially, was conceived as an organization preoccupied with the happiness of their citizens, as famously suggested by van Justi in his classic text on the same topic (see also Esposito 2008). What we find here is the affirmative character of biopolitics, as highlighted by Michel Foucault on several occasions, a biopolitics conceived as a project for the conservation and the expansion of life itself (Rose 2001). What we are facing here, according to Esposito, is a biopolitics supported by an immunitary paradigm with the declared aim of protecting life for life itself, in which control and protection are the two faces of the very same process.

How does this reflect on our biopolitical reading of tourism? First, it allows us to think about the ways in which tourism injects fragments of difference (i.e. the hospitable zombies) into the experience of travel, precisely in order to protect, reproduce and control the threshold that keeps "the-animal-and-the-human-in-us" (Giaccaria and Minca 2011) separate, but in a mutual relationship. The "inspection" of the putative primitive on the part of tourists can be read as part of an immunitary process that aims at normalizing and containing difference. By traveling like tourists to foreign lands and by penetrating according to a very specific modality other people's lives, they inject a monitored dose of difference in their projection of the self, in their experience of the post-historical. Second, the search for an aestheticized difference is part of a process of cultural prophylaxis that promises to compensate a perceived absence of difference in our quotidian.

In the post-historical, how can we differentiate, wonders Esposito (2002: 96), what subverts and annihilates all identities – and therefore all differences – in a sort of endless post-historical metonymic contagion? How can we reintegrate the lost order? The endless reproduction of communities, origins, orders, mappings that we are witnessing today, Esposito maintains, tends to express nostalgia for something that has never existed, something that cannot return. The myth of the origins, of an original order of difference, is indeed a myth, a horizon, *something that can be perhaps represented but never presented*. This explains why this kind of cultural politics inevitably turns into a politics of pure representation; that is, of absence. This explains also why it can be performed only in theatrical terms (Esposito 2002: 117), with every actor becoming a copy of himself, a metonymic arrangement of an imperfect original. This is the nihilistic stage for the performance of the (bio)politics of compensation that determines very often the ways in which we travel and we enter contact zones of cultural difference.

Compensation here means also response to a sense of loss. But what is lost and potentially reconstructed by the tourist experience *in situ*? According to Esposito (2002: 125), again, what the nostalgia for community (in tourism and in politics) produces, is the sense of a void, a cultural and biological void, for a unified subject able to sublimate his individuality into a greater, collective self. In other words, for the (only theoretical) possibility of reconstituting the whole of life separated precisely by the same biopolitical regime that yearns for its loss. This is also, in many ways, the constitutive aporia of the biopolitical in tourism. It is biopolitical because it tends to complicate the co-implication of life and body politics (2002: 137), but also because it reacts to this sense of loss with interventions aiming at the biopolitical production of an immunitary horizon of comfortable geographies, populated by people and landscapes *all in their proper place*. But these people and landscapes are never in their proper place, since they constantly move and change; they need to be tamed and "cut" by endless caesurae in order to reproduce the desired order and control. In tourism, this is translated into the calm waters of the cultural geographies of the anthropotouristic machines, that is, into a world intended as an orderly patchwork of different cultural types. These geographies are disturbingly similar to the classifications operated by Nazi geopolitics and their cultural geographies of tourism intended as true geographies of the *anthropos* – that is, as a "container of radically diverse biotypologies that move from the superman (Aryan) to the anti-man (Jew), passing through the average man (Mediterranean) and subhuman (Slavic)" (Esposito 2008: 129).

Esposito reflects at length on the homeopathic overtones of the Nazi therapies generated by the anthropogenic machine. This biopolitical *dispositif* was indeed based on an organicist model of culture and society, and was driven by an obsession for the separation of the healthy parts of the body politics, but also of the actual people, from the unhealthy bits. As a consequence, it implemented a series of prophylactic arrangements focused on the idea of public health, intended in the general sense of the well-being of the nation (Esposito 2008: 164). This imagined co-implication between health and well-being, on the one hand, and space, on the other, has been at the origin of many biopolitical formulations about "life worth living" on the part of the Nazis – formulations that have still some currency today when the relationship between life and space is discussed.

Nazi tourism was deeply implicated in this. Journeys to exotic lands were conceived as ways to justify German ambitions for the construction of a greater *lebensraum*, while the exploration of the *heimat* provided the traveling masses with images of a racial community in the making. More importantly, National Socialist propaganda was quite explicit about the political (or, more aptly, biopolitical) implications of tourism: "Strength through Joy testified to the Nazi regime's desire to convince its racially 'valuable' citizens that it enhanced their well-being" (Baranowski 2004: 2). The overall idea, as brilliantly shown by Baranowski, was that of constructing the conditions for a "good life" for the master race, a good life corresponding to dreams of future prosperity according to which work and leisure were seen "as complementary aspects of the workers creative lives" (2004: 6). The joy of work *and* pleasure, together with ideas of individual self-improvement, was to promote the racial community through tourism. KdF intended to embrace "the totality of workers' creative lives" in order to cultivate "the whole person" by emphasizing the beauty of labor and the construction of creative lives for the ordinary German worker – a new, non-alienated human type (2004: 10, 48, 82). The Strength through Joy movement "exposed Nazism's fusion of pleasure and violence" by means of a typically biopolitical set of caesurae – selecting who should have a good life and at the expenses of whom. In particular, the physical appearance of German tourists had ethical meaning, since Nazi tourism was about the biopolitical management and control of normality, purification, transgression and even "joy of living" (2004: 72). At the same time, agents, mixed up with tourists and behaving like tourists, were deployed to observe the travelers, especially women and their public behavior, while the quasi-militarization of the tourist spatialities was accompanied by the deliberate recreation of the racial(ized) community in miniature (2004: 138).

Tourism under Nazism became then a biopolitical experiment, the characteristics of which, however, are not entirely absent from many forms of contemporary tourism, especially when cultural difference and community are at the core of the promised experience and seem to re-enact many of the arrangements that were fundamental in the organization of mass tourism under the Third Reich. The point here is not to claim that tourism today is similar in any possible way to a Nazi regime, or any similar nonsense. What these three articulations try to suggest, instead, is that questions of community, culture, and care in tourism have deep biopolitical implications that speak to a broader understanding and interpretation of the principle of immunity and its related management of bodies – real and imagined bodies.

Conclusions

Today, in tourism, it is enough to browse through a specialist magazine to realize that we are constantly presented with, and invited by, a crowd of objectified smiling and typified bodies. Breezes Resorts shows a happy "lawyer transformed into another person";[7] at Sandals Resort it seems that "all you need is love," as reflected in the relaxed bodies of the young couples acting as unnamed testimonials;[8] Thai Airways, among many others, display a set of anonymous beautiful women, a timeless smiling crew, dressed in folk-lore; in an extraordinarily sensual pose, a half-naked young faceless female body is the visual vehicle for the promotion of a set of resorts in Cancun, where "ME Cancun becomes you";[9] the Body Holiday campaign instead promises: "Give us your body for a week and we will give you back your mind";[10] and the list can continue.

Bodies, bodies, and more bodies. Bodies are exposed, are photographed, are trained, are promised, bodies are located in the virtual horizon of perfection(ing) that every good packaged holiday tends to promise. In holiday camps, on beauty farms, on cruises, on culturally sophisticated tours, in hedonistic camps and in spas, in themed hotels and resorts, etc., what we find again and again is the same biopolitical imagination, albeit with different arrangements from the past. The link between tourism, health, politics, care, fun, hedonism and controlled transgression therefore needs to be analyzed also in biopolitical terms, and the most recent emphasis placed by the academic literature on emotional and affective labor in the tourist industries seems to offer robust support to this idea.

This chapter is a first attempt to look in that direction. Let me conclude, then, with a few considerations on the biopolitical in tourism that may point the way to an entirely new field of investigation. We are faced today with the proliferation of spaces of care, offering personal regeneration based on a specific hypothetical body, normally the body of the smiling tourist/guest on the cover. Who is that person in the picture and why does (s)he smile? What is our relationship with her/him? Should we look like her/him during and after our holidays? If we think carefully, nobody actually ever looks like those hypothetical bodies; they represent indeed a sort of pornography of health and eternal youth. Their promised horizon of "regeneration" of the *bios* appears as a sort of strategy of immunization – from disease, from aging, from getting fat, from looking tired, etc. – against the abyss produced before our eyes by time, and discussed in depth by Martin Heidegger. These eternal bodies seem to address the question of a timeless happiness based on a "normalized" and controlled bios, which, because of its normative and "normal" charac-teristics, can be nothing but a manikin, an unreachable biopolitical horizon. It is precisely in this sense that I identify in the zombie a key figure of the anthropotouristic machine. The zombie here is a figure that literally "embodies" a self that never dies, but which, at the same time, is neither completely alive, since it does not age and does not get sick – the perfect inhabitant of a country with no old men. The zombie of the tourist promotional material is the biopolitical transfiguration of the monkey-man so dear to Linnaeus and, especially, Haeckel (Agamben 2004).

This kind of body is a referent for both the tourist and the local – hosts and guests are placed on the same biopolitical plane/plain. They are smiling zombies facing each other in a bizarre political economy of display. They also constitute an important threshold between a horizon of total immunization – a fully biological destiny or a "new man," something that was certainly part of the Nazis' ideology of total life – and the everyday lives of both the tourist and the local residents dealing with the tourist. This threshold is home to the biopolitical in tourism, since it is in this hypothetical no man's land that the illusion of transparency for a renewed community or for a timeless regeneration is accompanied by intense forms of control and tamed transgression – sometimes even planned transgression (think of holiday camps for swingers, or for singles).

This is a hypothetical body that, while offering a land of protection and compensation, also responds to what Bataille – and Esposito with him – would define as the "excess of life," an excess that often translates into a need and a desire for a life as a form of pure immanence, pure presence. This "form of life," as we know it at this point, can find expression only in instants, in events, in the carnivalesque and the erotic. Tourism is there to offer, in an organized and communitarian way, the spaces where to experience these monitored Dionysian glimpses of real life.

Utopian communitarianism, hedonism, temporary suspension of the rules, zombie-like experiences of otherness, regeneration and rejuvenation in timeless spaces; these are all aspects of a biopolitical *dispositif*, in which the principle of immunity plays an increasingly important role. Esposito indeed shows how, in order to become the/an object of politics, life must be separated and closed in spaces of progressive desocialization, so that it can be immune from any genuine communitarian drift. This requires and justifies the arrangement of endless defensive walls (Esposito 2002: 168, 183). The smiling zombie-tourists of the promotional camp are indeed the inhabitants of a threshold where separation, closure and protection, in the form of immunization – from aging, from difference, from the lack of a community of the origins, etc. – are what is offered: that is, a biopolitical horizon populated by a new kind of man, a horizon that is nothing but a form of eternal deferral. This land of the zombie-men is, in fact, nowhere to be found; it can only be promised, never realized. As French philosopher Luc Nancy would have it, there is nothing behind what we are now.

The biopolitical in tourism can thus be described, perhaps, as a process of progressively intensifying immunization from otherness, difference, contamination, from the abyss of time that lies open before us. This process of immunization operates via the incorporation of a negative that must be recognized, incorporated and neutralized. This is the function of the supposed-to-be-hospitable silent monkey-men, presumably waiting for the tourist *in situ* with their eternal smiles and open to inspection. The contact zones produced by these forms of tourism are spaces in which a reassuring difference is incorporated by the trembling subjectivities of the post-historical traveler. At the same time, the tourist her/himself is incorporated into a strange political economy of display of zombies, where her/his hypothetical smiling mate (on the front cover) is also waiting for her/him *in situ*, a tourist Dorian Gray, promising eternal youth and protection from the contaminations of the real. The result of all this is a land populated by ghosts of real and imagined bodies, which are neither too alive nor too dead, neither too animal (in their biological fixity and permanent youth) nor too human. This is *no country for old men*.

Notes

1 Responsibletravel.com (2011) "Philippines community based marine conservation." Available online at www.responsibletravel.com/holiday/1486/philippines-community-based-marine-conservation (accessed April 26, 2011).
2 See, for example, South Seas Island Resort. Available online at www.southseas. com (accessed April 26, 2011). Also, Temptation Resort Spa Cancun, "An adult experience". Available online at http://temptation.originalresorts.com/cancun/en/index.asp (accessed April 26, 2011).
3 Africa Albida Tourism, for example, is "all about giving back! [. . .] all about creating opportunities [. . .] and enhancing living standards, to share our passion for Africa's treasures: culture, wildlife and its immense physical beauty." Available online at www.africaalbidatourism.com/givingback.html (accessed April 26, 2011).
4 See, for example, Fair Trek's Community Based & Responsible Tourism in Laos. Available online at www.trekking-in-laos.com/why-fair-trek (accessed April 26, 2011). Or Mara Gates Safaris "Masai Mara Safari." Available online at www. maragates.com/safari/safaris.php?keyword=Masai_Mara_Safari&gclid=CN7B0tXn wqgCFYYXzQodfh6BqA (accessed April 26, 2011).
5 See, for example, Go Native America. Available online at www.gonativeamerica. com (accessed April 26, 2011). Or Original World's "Ethiopia Tour." Available online at www.originalworld.com/travel-to-ethiopia/ (accessed April 26, 2011).
6 Brendafrica.com (2011) "Income generation project. 'This is Kaloleni'." Available online at www.brendafrica.com/downloads/kibera_en_kaloleni.pdf (accessed April 26, 2011).
7 The advertising campaign for Breezes Village Resort do Brazil in 2004. Available online at www.advertolog.com/village-resort-do-brasil/print-outdoor/lawyer-6585555 (accessed April 26, 2011).
8 See www.americanexpressvacations.com/offers/sandals_promo.htm and www. waterbike.com/press/sandals_resort.jpg (accessed April 26, 2011).
9 ME Cancun (2010) "ME, it becomes you," Resort Advertisement. Available online at www.scribd.com/doc/13683866/Me-by-Melia-Hotels-and-Resortspdf (accessed April 26, 2011).
10 Thebodyholiday.com (2011) "Give us your body for a week and we'll give you back your mind." Available online at www.thebodyholiday.com (accessed April 26, 2011).

3   Time to hostess

Reflections on borderless care

Eeva Jokinen and Soile Veijola

Introduction

In our early writings, just as in many other scholars discussing tourism in the field of social theory, we have focused on *the tourist experience* as one that materializes the generalised subjectivity of our time. What we often found lacking in these discussions, however, was the body, and thereby also the gender, of the agency of the mobile social figure. Later, having already concluded that there is perhaps not so much to add to the topic of the body in tourism (e.g. Swain 1995; Johnston 2001; Macnaghten and Urry 2001; Ateljevic *et al.* 2007), we ended up, through different routes, at the same crossroads again, but this time it was the alleged opposite of tourism: *the working life*. It did not take much effort to see how the work performances called for in Western societies are constituted by corporealities, affectivity and emotions, and how fittingly the – formerly strikingly invisible – figure of the *tourism worker* epitomizes the processes and agencies involved in the production of the tourist experience (Veijola and Jokinen 2008; Valkonen and Veijola 2008; Haanpää *et al.* 2005).

Nevertheless, whether the issue has been the tourist or the tourism worker, or something in-between, such as the au pair (Jokinen and Veijola 1997), we have been consistent in arguing that tourism can never be fully grasped without a broad and subtle conception of gender, nor without acknowledging the role that gender plays in organizing life and symbolic orders in today's societies (e.g. Jokinen and Veijola 1990, 2003; Veijola and Jokinen 1994; Jokinen 2005; Veijola 2009a). In the context of mobilities, the most common theoretical or ideal type of the tourist – and likewise of the migrant and the vagrant – is implicitly a *male* figure (e.g. Cresswell 2011), which implies *someone else* going on tour with him, serving him in the destination, or staying at home – while missing the wanderer, keeping things going or waiting for remittance (see e.g. McDowell 2008). In other words, this (usually male) figure presupposes a caring, cooking, and catering female or feminized figure. A similar gesture of turning women transparent in the accounts of human action is witnessed in tourism-related work: even if attracting or entertaining the tourists is habitually linked to women, being good at the job tends to be conceived of as expertise and a skill worth a raise in salary or social respect only when men perform it. When women excel in creating an amenable and comforting atmosphere, this is considered to be part of their nature (to please others), not of their professional know-how. The lack of systematic knowledge production of tourism-related jobs and workforce, and their gender divisions both globally and locally, could partly be explained by the presupposition of the occupational field in question being dominated by women, and thereby somehow marginal (read: transparent) to economic production (see e.g. Veijola and Jokinen 2008).

As for the future, it does not seem likely that gender will lose its prevalence in working life, nor in family life or the spheres of leisure and vacation, all four being deeply embedded in one another. While societies all over the world have experienced ample transformations of economic and social life over recent decades, gender has been in the very center of these changes. Labor-force participation rates of women have risen or stabilized at high levels; jobs taken up by men and women have been restructured, with the result of an increasing number of service sector jobs with higher skill requirements, but also with higher demands.

Despite the rearrangements of labor in society, however, industrial and occupational sex segregations, as well as earning differentials, persist (e.g. Vosko *et al.* 2009: 1). On a statistical level, women earn less than men even if they have equal or better education. Furthermore, migration, mobility, and traveling have been feminized in the sense that there are more women on the move than before (Sinclair 1997; Ehrenreich and Hochschild 2003) – which does not mean that they travel in the same conditions and formations as men (e.g. Veijola and Valtonen 2007). There is thus a largely under-examined "arrangement between the sexes" (Goffman 1977) throughout the new global economies, involving "a highly mobile yet, in various ways, vulnerable feminine and/or foreign-born workforce" (Zampoukos and Ioannides 2011: 28; see also Bianchi, 2000; Ehrenreich and Hochschild 2003; Baum, 2007; Pritchard *et al.* 2007).

The main factor in the reorganization of gender liaisons is, however, the *porosity of late modern societies*. In the wake of the modernization pro-cesses of Western societies, there appears to be a blurring of the borderlines and divisions that seemed self-evident at the time of the birth of modern tourism. The public/private dyad, along with the parallel coupling of men's and women's spheres, no longer stand on their own (e.g. Haraway 1999; Virno 2002: 23–24). Correspondingly, the imaginary "insides" and "outsides" of nation states collapse: borders that were supposed to protect (and patronize) those who live "inside" are melting, due to, for example, new technology, migration, diasporas, terrorism, and global wars. The global economic systems prompt free movement of capital, products, services, knowledge, and people. It is no longer easy to tell the guests from the hosts.

People have, of course, traveled throughout history for labor, to gain subsistence and freedom and to escape unlivable conditions. Yet currently the range of experiences of traveling is wider than ever. While some receive good service and luxurious meals, others starve or are killed by gunshots when trying to cross borders (see e.g. Gibson, S. 2003; Germann Molz and Gibson 2007; Lynch *et al.* 2011).

Timewise, in the "global present," the division of life into working hours and free time, or productive time and reproduction, has dissolved. Gadgets and computer screens go *bling-bling* at all hours. Turning the new technology off, shutting the mobile phone or refusing to up-date one's Facebook status are maybe the contemporary *rite de passage*, marking a shift from labor to vacation – at least for those who can imagine or afford an exit from the circuit of economic value production (see e.g. Valtonen and Veijola 2011).

Leaving home, traveling, and being on the move are not only privileges of the well-educated middle classes and aristocratic cosmopolitans, but also the obligations and possibilities of those who are not equally well off. "Immobility," for its part, is not merely about feeling stranded or stuck due to temporal inconsistencies of transportation (see Birtchnell and Büscher 2011), but (more grimly) a fact of being tied in place – for instance, in neighborhoods for the poor. Then again, a more amiable version of immobility is reserved for those who can afford to live spaciously in the scarcely populated, aesthetically pleasing or generationally treasured countryside, even if social and labor market policies, in their quest for creating a flexible workforce for economic growth push people to move to cities after jobs.

Tourism, a modern mixture of institutionalized practices of visiting places and receiving visitors, for its part, has always been a mix of labor and free time, even if the fact is usually ignored by analysts, who tend to focus on either tourism *or* working life. Vacationers are hosted and the "reproduction" of the workforce of the tourists is being taken care of by people at work. Moreover, many middle-class people in knowledge-intensive occupations do not draw a line between free time and work even when on holiday. In the age of globalized care (e.g. Robinson 1999), those who travel by migrating often take care of children, the elderly and others in need, in terms of sending money home and by doing care work in the public and private spheres of the wealthier nation. Should a more prosperous family leave for a vacation, say, to Thailand, their less affluent migrant nanny might get a chance to travel and see how her family is doing back home (e.g. Precarias a la Deriva 2004, 2009).

In this chapter, we shall focus on the intersecting and transforming acts of moving and staying, and laboring and caring, as part of contemporary arrangements of gender and hospitality. Our claim is that tourism (as well as the tourist experience) *is* care: tourism is engendered as a common production of both the tourists and their host(esse)s, both of whom are simultaneously subjects and objects of care, and cannot be distinguished from one another. Tourism, in the sense of the tourist experience, is born only in this particular instance of "commons."

In order to maintain close contact with "what people know" (Foucault 2004a: 7; see also Valtonen 2009: 129–130), we weave our discussion into the conversation of a group of women who embody, in more than one way, the discourses of tourism, mobility, migration, and labor market. These women have moved from different areas of the former Soviet Union to North Karelia in Finland. In focus group discussions arranged for Russian-speaking migrant women in spring 2009, they collectively produced their narratives on various kinds of mobilities. We shall listen to one of these women especially: Larissa, who lives in a small village in the Finnish–Russian borderland in Finland, as her experience of a mobile agency is being articulated in the conversations in more length and detail as that of the others. All names in the data have been changed to pseudonyms.[1]

Having previously explored the ways in which "gender, skill, and tasks are interpolated into individuals and the institutionalized relations between them" (Veijola and Jokinen 2008: 170), our aim now is to expand our analysis on the nature of hostessing as a practice that interweaves the figures of the tourist and the host, blurs the distinction between tourism and migration, contests the conventional modes of temporalities, and reorganizes arrangements of gender. We do this by way of two reconstructed narratives depicting the redivision of care work between affluent and not so prosperous women, on the one hand, and female and male tourism workers, on the other. How do acts, habits, temporality, and transformation affect gender in hostessing? How does the act of gender – that is, the machinery each individual has to pass through in order to have access to her intelligibility (Foucault 1978; Butler, J. 1999) – affect mobile practices? More specifically, from the point of view of women, what role does "the invisible hand" of "the maid of the global economy" play in the accumulation of wealth in societies?

The geographic context of our treatise, North Karelia, is a borderland between Finland and Russia, but also between the European Union (EU) and non-EU. The region has a complex and partly traumatic history as "a periphery of all directions." First, it is a periphery of "the West" (as western Europe and Nordic states); second, that of the south (the metropolitan area of St Petersburg); third, that of the north (as regards the new EU idea of a Barents region); and last, but not least, it is a periphery of the east, of the area of Karelia that was formerly a part of Sweden and later of Russia. After World War II, Karelia was divided into two areas split by the border, one side in Finland and the other one in Russia. In line with the aim of the book *to articulate real tourism* (see Chapter 1 in this volume), our conceptualization of borders refers most of all to everyday life as a lived experience when living in a borderland between east and west, rather than on geopolitical aspects of the area. In everyday life, the checkpoints channel, formulate and control the movement of people crossing the border as well as life on both sides of the border, while also being the link and the line from one country to another, thus blurring the strict divisions ("insides" and "outsides"; e.g. Davydova and Pöllänen 2010).

Care in the hostessing society

The hostessing society argument put forward earlier (Veijola and Jokinen 2008) claims that we are about to enter an epoch in which the grounding facet of production is the human capacity to relate, take care, and coordinate – in other words, the core skills of a good hostess or a housewife. The outcome is often called "new work." Conjugating the apparently genderless term of hosting into an explicitly gendered version (adding a feminine appendix) of hostessing alleviated the roles that gender plays in the acts and images of hospitality and care-taking: "hostessing is an act and a performance that both 'genders' work performances and separates the very same performances from the gender of the actor;" it is "a *qualification, competence, skill, appearance, offering*, and sometimes a *vocation* – in process – that new work requires *from both women and men*" (Veijola and Jokinen 2008: 170). Managing multiple tasks, chronological intermingling, and spatial overlapping simultaneously, while keeping up the good mood and high spirit for all, is the basic skill in both managing a domestic household successfully and new work (Veijola and Jokinen 2008: 170).

Hospitality and caring are profoundly gendered issues, but not in a simple manner. Women hostess more and more often than men do. Caring for other people, whether they are family members, friends, strangers, or tourists, is conceived of in Western culture as feminine activity and labor. Yet men can and do perform acts of hostessing as well, and many contemporary jobs in all sectors of employment and entrepreneurship require "skills of femininity" from all employees irrespective of their gender: amiableness, considerateness, warmth, empathy, affectivity. It is easy to list jobs in which workers sell dreams and identities with the help of "people skills": hairdos in barber shops and bank loans for buying a home are more or less in the same ballpark. The phenomenon has been called *feminization of work and economy* (McDowell 1991; Adkins 2001; Morini 2007; Gutiérrez-Rodrígues 2010). All kinds of relational work (i.e. work based on the human capacity to create and maintain human relations and to be taken care of through them) is gaining more and more significance in the global economy. Thereby, we can refer to the feminization of economy in a radical sense: both the feminine skills and gendered habits sedimented in female bodies, and the affects and corporeality (tissue) of women as such, become an essential part of production (e.g. Waldby and Mitchell 2006; Cooper 2008; Skeggs 2010). The contrast between it and the formerly dominant industrial Fordist production is remarkable since, in the latter, women and femininity function(ed) outside of production, reproducing the labor power of men, and gradually also women as they entered working life (e.g. Adkins and Jokinen 2008).

Our notion of the hostessing society is based on understanding "gender as a contingent habit, hostessing as an act, and domestication as a process" (Veijola and Jokinen 2008: 176). Gender arrangements are taken for granted and habitualized during a lifetime, and even before that: we act as women or as men because it is comprehensible and makes life easy (for those who pass the heterosexual matrix), not simply because we are men or women in the very beginning (Butler, J. 1999). However, there always are potential ruptures in the logic of habit. Gender is not inevitable, although it is predictable. The logic of habit, or the *inertia of habit* (Bourdieu 1990; Adkins 2003) in particular, explains why the division of work and power between women and men changes so slowly. Change – contingency – is a far more difficult question and task; yet "the elements of variability and potential creativity immanent to even the most mundane and habitual of action" (McNay 1999: 101) pinpoint the importance of temporality in the analysis of change. Thus, following the idea of Judith Butler (1999: 191), we approach gender as a *constituted social temporality* in its performativity, as "not a singular act but a repetition and ritual, which achieves its effects through its naturalization in the context of a body, understood, in part, as a *culturally sustained temporal duration*" (Butler, J. 1999: xv; emphasis added).

The main transformations in terms of *social* temporality and duration have been labeled both as feminization of labor and economy, and as the general precariousness of life (e.g. Foti 2004; Gill and Pratt 2008), which pertains especially to women. In these frameworks, both work and the entire life situation of women are symptomatic of the new global order. The Madrid feminist collective Precarias a la Deriva (2009), for instance, in their provocative methodological initiative, searched for the experiences of feminized precarity in the early 2000s "drifting" among Madridian women: students, migrants, domestic workers, sex workers, freelancers, trainees, workers in low-paid social and healthcare work. For the task, they revised the conventional map of work and private life, with both spheres "in their right place at the right time." As the "axes" of the new map they used time, space, income, relationships, conflict, hierarchies, risks, and bodies. By time, for instance, they referred to stress, excess, instability, and impossibility to plan; by space, to mobility, porous locations of life and borders, increased migration, and problems in settling down; by income, to badly paid jobs, lack of resources, and new formations of support through family and friendship networks; and by relationships, to new constellations of working groups, social structures, and affective relations (Precarias a la Deriva 2003).

One of the major interests in this research endeavor is *care:* care as a threshold where the global economy meets the lived precarity.[2] Care connects the axes mentioned above with everyday negotiations and reconciliations, and it is this link that provides us with methodological insight: by looking at care we may grasp key facets of precarious lives in porous societies. In contrast to being "fixed" to home, motherhood, and being poor, which have characterized the situation of women earlier, women have now become mobile. While new positions are created for them, it is – again – care that acts as the fluid oiling this change. Even if care has been ignored by the majority of social theorists and economists, this does not mean that it would not be "an *arche* of human existence and social relations" (Precarias a la Deriva no date), making life possible by generating, nourishing, and healing it. Care contributes to happiness by creating relations of interdependence among embodied beings as well as to making life more interesting by way of generating exchanges and flows of knowledge and affect. Women have been culturally associated with care-giving, and have in practice taken care of caretaking, and, indeed, divided care work largely among themselves. This is not, however, the result of a real free choice for individual women; ethical codes tend to require that "someone" takes care of children and those who are ill or fragile with age (Precarias a la Deriva 2009.)

It is not only the current mobility that makes care more visible than before. The existential notion of precarious life imposes on us an obligation to think of care. Judith Butler (2009) insists that to be a body is to be exposed to social crafting and form, and to others; the persistence of the body depends on social conditions and institutions. In order to be and to persist, the body must rely on what is outside itself (Butler, J. 2009: 3–23). In other words, the more precarious life is, the more we would need to be taken care of, to take care of, and to rely on the continuation of care. To rely on someone means that one anticipates good care and perhaps has vivid memories of it. Thereby care, as well as gender and transformation, seems to link with temporality and time. Care taking requires time, and there has to be time to care and to host. Caring is a relation, a continuum, and a maintainer of life; "a politics of comfort that applies not only to the host's and guest's ontological security but also to their embodied well-being" (Lynch *et al.* 2011: 15).

In the following two sections, we will "walk our talks" with Larissa, our main protagonist in these migrant tales of precarious mobilities. First, we feature her as a *tourist* in her former homeland, Russia (see also Veijola 2006), and then as a *local* in her "new" homeland, Finland. Both perspectives provide the alternative "generalized subjectivity of our time" – of the tourism worker – with new shades (see e.g. Veijola 2009b).

The guest situation revisited

The precarious nature of "the guest situation" (Berking 1999) has occupied the human mind since primordial times. Encounters with strangers have brought along the risk of losing one's life, as the joint etymology of the two terms, guest and enemy, suggests (e.g. Gibson, S. 2003: 376; Lynch *et al.* 2011). After the pivotal social invention of hospitality, and the historical transformation of ceremonial hospitality shown to the stranger into the varied contemporary forms of commodified hospitalities, the attention of tourism scholars has focused on the means of detecting authentic or profitable performances of attracting and serving tourists and travelers. The precariousness of the tourist experience and its dependence on both the visited environment and the tourism workers have been, in other words, central to both critical theorizing and the applied business studies of tourism. Could the stories of Larissa add something to understanding the contemporary and future guest situation based on global movement of people?

Larissa and the other women in the focus group are extremely mobile. Not only have they migrated from the former Soviet Union, but also many of them have changed places in Finland from one municipality to another. Moreover, they travel a lot; having parents and relatives living in Russia, they visit them often and also take care of them in many ways: they bring things over, deal with bank affairs and check up on their housing conditions. Many of these women have grown-up children who live elsewhere in Finland or abroad. A few are already grandmothers, and taking care of grandchildren is a motivation for traveling. The labor market situation of all women in the group is, to say the least, precarious;[3] but that very fact, paradoxically, enables them to be mobile and to provide care, and also to be cared for: meeting one's mother in one's homeland is potentially a reciprocal source of nourishment, happiness, and reconciliation. Besides, these trips are not merely for care; the women combine having fun, meeting friends, and experiencing cultural events in their journeys. The story of Larissa's life, reconstructed from the group interviews, includes three episodes describing her travels in Russia: Larissa visits St Petersburg with her husband, takes her older female friend on a charter trip to Sortavala (a small village in Russia close to the Finnish border), and goes with another female friend to shop in Viborg.

The first episode starts with the group discussing whether it is possible to travel to St Petersburg by car. The public transportation between North Karelia and Russia is almost non-existent, except for a few seasonal connections; the only collective means of traveling is using a group taxi, which is reasonably cheap, but complicated to organize. Moreover, it requires adjusting to other people's timetables and itineraries. On top of everything, the roads on the Russian side are in very bad condition; several participants described the repairs their cars required after visits to Russia. According to Larissa, driving in St Petersburg would be all right if it were not for the constant "rush hour" there. (At this point in the data, the Russian transcriber has added a note, "Homeric laughter," indicating loud and heart-felt laughter, which, according to Homer, is what God's laughter is like.)

Having thus established the context of cruising in Russia, Larissa begins to recount her second-last driving experience in St Petersburg: "Well, no sweat. Oleg [her husband] is sitting next to me, drunk. But I drove from Hattsina to Finland, that is, through the entire city. It was one o'clock in the afternoon." Hattsina is a suburb behind St Petersburg (from the perspective of Finland), and Larissa is actually quite heroic in managing the endeavor. The role of the drunken husband sitting beside her remains unclear, but it appears that Larissa also comes out clean from a visit to another suburb in a tough corner, since her father-in-law lives there, "really on his own and is already over 80 years old." Larissa has lived in St Petersburg for nine years so she knows her way around in the city, yet when she finally pulls up next to her father-in-law's house, her legs will not carry her, "and I could not get out of the car." Another woman, Vera, in the group exclaims: "Crazy woman!" Larissa seems to accept the assessment by confessing: "As a matter of fact, I was terrified but I simply had to get back to work [in Finland] on time." Here the issue is care; Larissa chauffeurs her husband and confronts the famous traffic congestion of St Petersburg in order to take care of her father-in-law and hurries back home to take care of other people as her job. The travel narrative, in all its banal everydayness, witnesses the point made by Precarias a la Deriva (no date) that care is a continuous, omnipresent *line* or threshold, which varies in its intensity. It is indeed this very line that is getting blurred in current societies; the line that links and demarcates the spheres of private and public, informal and formal, as well as the margins and commodities of the marketplace (see e.g. Guiver and Jain 2011: 48).

Another tourist episode combines taking care and having fun. Larissa begins: "I have one granny [in the municipality], Olga. Olga is now 76 years old. She migrated six years ago." At Olga's request, Larissa had joined her on a Christmas trip organized by the Finland–Russia Friendship Society to Sortavala. The other charter tourists were mostly retired Finns. Straight after the checkpoint, bottles started to clink in the bus already on the way to Sortavala. "Some had long drinks, some had cognac." Larissa was surprised since she had imagined this to be more the practice of younger people. "And we, Olga and me, were also given cognac and plastic mugs right away. It was so fun, and everyone starts chatting and talking about what one can see from the window on the right and on the left." The rest of the evening was hearsay: "They danced and sang until nine o'clock in the evening. It took only some hours, because everyone got tired." Larissa was not there since they spent the night in Olga's daughter's place.

Olga is Larissa's *ottomummo* (in Finnish), her "adopted grandmother," whom she had met when working at a restaurant. Despite her age, 76 years, Olga came to the restaurant to dance by herself. Larissa explains: "I tried, I took care of her all the time." This account shows how even mundane and banal small events contain several layers of care and precariousness. Larissa took care of Olga in a restaurant in which she was paid a salary for hosting as a waitress, not for "adopting" Olga. Simultaneously, Larissa nourished herself and established a bond that extends into the future. She has learned, for instance, to know Olga's daughter, whom they visit in Sortavala. As Precarias a la Deriva (no date) state, this kind of affective virtuosity, inter-dependence, transversality, and everydayness constitute the key ingredients of caring know-how, which is the fruit of collective and corporeal knowledge, fracturing the walls of fear and precarity.

The third episode does not deal with the travel destination at all, only with car trouble on the way. The windshield wipers broke and Larissa bought new ones at the petrol station on the Finnish side, only to discover that she could not figure out how to install them. The "young man at the station" helped her to do this and noticed that there was not enough windshield wiper fluid in her car. He helped by adding some and, when opening the hood, saw that the brake fluid had run out as well. "Everything was taken care of, and I left." When the young man at the station checked Larissa's car, he took care of her safety and well-being as well, even if it was the car that was tended to with attention and anticipation. The incident underlines the evasiveness of the very concept of care. What counts as care? Whose care counts? Surely the work of lifeguards, night guards and janitors, as well as firefighters and soldiers in rescuing or searching operations, is about care? Or do care and hospitality equal "woman", even if this cannot be said aloud? All human intercourse houses care – or at least potential for it.

Precarious contours of equality

By turning the tables and listening to Larissa talk about the times when she works *for* the tourists, we can study the ways in which the clearly demarcated map of education, skills and jobs breaks down as the basis of a welfare society that promises and requires work from everyone with a potential and capability to learn and labor.

Larissa moved to Finland in the beginning of the 1990s. She was born in Estonia, migrated to St Petersburg to study, married, gave birth to three children, and spent nine years in St Petersburg before migrating to Finland. According to Larissa, the move to Finland was slightly accidental: she is an "ethnic Finn," and there is a law concerning ethnic Finns who live in the former Soviet Union that gives them the possibility to migrate to Finland (with the same rights as those who are married to Finns). The move was indeed suggested to her by a worker in Inkeri Liitto, an organization of Ingrian Finns in Leningrad. The family moved first to western Finland, to a small community of about five thousand inhabitants, of whom they only knew one person beforehand, and even this person was an acquaintance of an acquaintance. The community had almost no practical know-how in ways of encountering migrants, but Larissa managed to gain access to a language course almost at once and learned to know other Russian-speaking migrants there. Larissa says "everyone wanted to help." The ideal of universal equality of the Scandinavian welfare society got hold of the family: "I have never had more money than what I had then." Yet she was extremely dependent on other people, on strangers:

> I was taken by the hand. I did not understand anything. I really did not know what to do, where to go. First I was taken to the police station, then to employment office. Then I was told I have to go to "social". I did not know what that was.

What Larissa had left behind was the collapsed Soviet Union, where women had formerly been "married to the state," and the paradox of the official Soviet ideology of emancipated women in the traditional nuclear family, upon which equality, citizenship, and the sustainability of life were based (Liljeström 1995). The post-socialist gender policy was even more shaky and unstable (Rotkirch *et al.* 2007), making women's life more precarious than it had been before. The emergence of women's unemployment pushed many women to migration, but it has become evident that it is impossible to separate this push from the will to change one's life, to see the world and improve one's conditions of living.

The ideal of universal equality of a welfare society in the Nordic countries differs from the liberal ideal of egalitarian and liberal equality linked to the rights and responsibilities of individuals. (At the end of the day, it does not differ so much from the former Soviet ideal of formal equality guaranteed by the state.) Nordic equality was negotiated as a contract between groups, not between individuals, and the participants of these negotiations have been trade unions, employers' organizations, and the state. The welfare system was created during the stable economic growth after World War II, and notably based on relations of paid labor, including for women. The flagship of the Nordic welfare state is indeed the equality between genders: women perform paid labor principally in the same terms as men, and via this paid labor "hinge," they are socially and economically secure in various precarious situations (e.g. Julkunen 1990, 2010). This kind of equality has been criticized for the fact that, while being based, on one hand, on the ideal of gender equality and, on the other, standards of welfare and the principles of how to share it, it has been negotiated between the labor market parties; thus, it *ignores other differences* such as those linked with sexuality, ethnicity, and citizenship.

This is also apparent in the story of Larissa when we follow her "work career," which is the central mechanism of distributing equality and well-being between individuals. Larissa was educated as a midwife in the Soviet Union. When living in Finland and undertaking various practical training periods at working places during her language course, she sought out a health care center and worked there, according to her own estimate, "quite actively." She received a reference stating that she fitted the line of work extraordinarily well. She applied for a position of midwife, but was told that she did not have the "corresponding education" – which meant Finnish education. They proposed that she should educate herself as a practical nurse, which she started to do, but soon had second thoughts about "studying again something I have already studied, so I dropped the course."

Next, she experimented with being an entrepreneur, but found out that she was far too naive for it (women who knew her exploited her sentiments of loyalty), and survived the debts only by way of restructuring them. Then she moved to a small municipality by the border (where she still lives) and got a permanent job contract in a hotel. However, times suddenly got worse and the employer noticed that they could do without a fluent Russian speaker in reception. Nevertheless, they still needed a workforce with this qualification in the restaurant. The employer offered an apprenticeship in the restaurant. "Of course, I agreed, I always do," says Larissa, but adds: "I was quite an inexpensive worker." After two and a half years she got a permanent contract again but her working hours began to decrease "somehow." Larissa managed to survive for nine years, at which point the restaurant was sold to another entrepreneur, who "does not like Russians."[4] After recovering from being sacked, Larissa went to the employment office, which happened to need her for translating jobs until a post opened up for a position in a holiday center. This is where, at the time of the interviews, she had worked for a year as a receptionist, cook, and cleaner. "I can also go to travel expos. In addition, I am sent to do interpreter's work at the factory." Larissa's employer, in other words, turns a profit by leasing her out.

The welfare states described here prevent precarity but protect most vigilantly those who fit into the ideal on which it is based: people living in families with two breadwinners who have permanent labor market contracts, are preferably born in the country, have received their education there, and have grown up into the language. Ruth Lister (2009) calls this version of equality a "Nordic nirvana," one based on dual-earner and gender-inclusive models, which tends to ignore other differences (such as ethnic diversity) and differences among women. In the state of nirvana, we are lulled into the delusion that everything is fine for all, but we only need to scratch the surface of that equality a little to notice that this welfare state does not equally take care of all who live within its territory (see also Keskinen *et al.* 2009).

Larissa's current job as the all-round handy-woman of a hotel is a paradigmatic example of the so-called new relational work (see e.g. Adkins and Jokinen 2008; Veijola 2009b). She opens the door when clients ring the bell, even in the middle of the night: "We don't have any timetable [for work]." As for secure employment, "there is this sort of an absolute insecurity." Larissa does not trust the employer "in the sense that I would, for example, get my salary paid." The global crisis of 2008–2009 had reached the community where she lives: "This might kill us."

Both the expansive, ripe welfare state and the post-expansive, post-welfare global labor market (in Finland), as well as individual employers, have treated Larissa in a discriminating manner at times, and she has encountered sexism and racism at work. Her Russian education has not been acknowledged; instead, she has repeatedly been returned "back to the factory settings" (Vähämäki 2011). In her current job, she uses precisely her most embodied, personal and gendered capacities: language skills, flexibility, and the capability to "behave well;" as she herself phrases it, "I always yield to everything," "I do not get upset. I manage" (see also Davydova no date). Despite managing and knowing how to do her work, it is "absolutely uncertain" and "there are no timetables." Her long-standing dream of becoming a doctor has not come true. "Of course I would like to find a decent job, but I would like to like it. I would like to enjoy, to see the result. I would like to hear the words of thanks."

Larissa expresses the "feelings of being stuck" (see Hage 2009) not only in terms of her work career but also in terms of dwelling. She lives in a small village in Finland and reflects upon moving to the Helsinki area: "One always finds reasons not to leave. But to be honest, if I were on my own, I would leave. My daughters live there, my mom would be near." However, her (new) husband is not keen on moving; besides, it is expensive to live in Helsinki. "I would need a really good job to pay for my life there. This is why I live here." In another meeting, Larissa says that she appreciates the convenient conditions of living and housing; in the place where they live now, they have four rooms and reasonable rent, but should they move to the Helsinki area they would have to settle with only one room for the same price.

The previous example illustrates the ways in which living and dwelling have temporal and political dimensions, not merely geographical ones. Indeed, the most heated discussions in the group dealt with the question of leaving or staying in North Karelia. Permanent, full-time labor contracts – a link to a less precarious life – are scarce in the area, but the inertia of habit (lack of stamina to move again), as well as various care relations, hold them in place. Conversely, the women are pushed to "stay on the move" by the competitive labor market policy, by the imperative to be reflective and free. Larissa and the other women are forced to ponder whether, where, and for how long they could expose their bodies to further social crafting and form (Butler, J. 2009: 3); whether they can rely on the social institutions for their survival in the future; and whether, in real life, they can mobilize their "constitutive human powers" to subvert and resist the conditions for their living "as political subjects" (e.g. Minca 2009: 106; Reid 2011). Indeed, the same condition features everyone being born within the Nordic nirvana state; the fate of the migrant worker only crystallizes it best.

Conclusion

For Judith Butler (2009: 3), social being *is* precarious. Her own analysis is centered on the phenomenon of the vulnerability of some people being worth grief while that of others is not. The logic of this is as follows: what we feel is in part conditioned by how we interpret the world around us. Affect is structured by interpretive schemes that we do not fully understand. These schemes limit our understanding about what is thinkable, and thus a grievable life to the ones included in "us" (Butler, J. 2010: 2). Here the critical question reads: who belongs to "us?" How does this "we" welcome the "stranger" (Germann Molz and Gibson 2007: 2)? Or, actually, how will the politics of life and labor market policies adjust to the current post-host/guest situation?

The flipside of the Finnish welfare (or workfare) state reveals itself in its tendency to push migrant women (Larissa certainly is not the only one) to educate themselves as practical nurses, regardless of their previous degrees or their individual hopes and dispositions. In the framework of the arrangements between the sexes, one of the cornerstones of Finnish (and other Nordic) welfare states has been the high education of health and social care personnel, which has created possibilities for (and forces) women to educate themselves without competing with men and to earn money of their own. Furthermore, publicly organized care has shortened women's "second shift," their private reproduction work at home. However, it appears that only those who belong to "us" are offered this opportunity. Practical nurse – the care job with the lowest pay in the health sector (albeit being very important work and also experienced as such by patients) – is the proper role for migrants, according to this educational and occupational racism (Jokinen and Jakonen 2011). The migrant care workers can be seen as the au pairs of an entire society, not merely of a domestic household, to paraphrase our earlier analysis of an explicitly sexed tourist; they are baby-sitting an affluent nation state that obediently plays its part in the global economy (Jokinen and Veijola 1997: 48–49). The social temporality embedded in gender performances at work is not the same to everyone living and staying within the Finnish territory.

The other possibility offered to migrant women and men is to find work in the just-in-time employment offered by the tourism industry, with its institutionalized practices of intersectional oppression along the lines of gender, class, and ethnicity. The use of low-paid – on the basis of defining it as "low-skilled" – labor as the basis of profitable business management of the tourism industry further intensifies the social effect of contemporary policies on future societies (see e.g. Wilkinson and Pickett 2010), and on the generational memory and experience of migrant families of the political hospitality of affluent societies (see Germann Molz and Gibson 2007).

According to Butler, gender can be understood as "not a singular act but a repetition and ritual, which achieves its effects through its naturalization in the context of a body, understood, in part, as a *culturally sustained temporal duration*" (Butler, J. 1999: 191). In the narrative of Larissa, we cannot decipher "a cultural" that would sustain since cultures melt into one another in her life, without, however, engendering a new temporality that would be shared by all in her life. Larissa's gendered acts of caring consist of incongruous lived temporalities: driving in the St Petersburg traffic jam incorporates the rhythm of a metropolis, the ethics of care, family habits, and the demands of the Finnish employer. Moreover, her language skills are exploited by her (several) employers, leading to a situation in which she "translates at nights," both when awake and in her dreams. Translating – which is, of course, a form of care (Könönen 2011) – has become an inerasable part of Larissa.

To sum up our reflections, we have discussed the post-host–guest relationship between two neighboring countries, epitomizing the borders between (former) East and (former) West. In our treatise, the experiences of a group of migrant women embody the borderless care on which the global economies and individual lives depend. Having been stirred by the vivacity of Precarias a la Deriva, we have borrowed their idea of care as a transversal continuum in porous, precarious life. On a structural level, care that has been located, conventionally and implicitly, in the sphere of privacy and women, is currently leaking and flowing over the borders, and is, indeed, turning into a line that *unites* rather than separates. Daily acts and relations of care witness the lived and livable realities of people; care is the lived continuum that integrates the new "axes" of precarious lives.

Larissa's stories of migration, tourism, and work give further evidence of the fact that women tend to distribute care among themselves rather than among men. For accessible testimonies of the latter, see, for example, *The Nanny Diaries* by Kraus and McLaughlin (2002), or the film *Mammoth* by Lukas Moodysson (2009). This is also the situation in the porous, precarious society. Care is not something one can choose, or decline to choose, or even *plan* extensively in advance; we cannot know, for instance, how Larissa's mother or father-in-law would get along if she chose not to visit them. Yet care is not only a burden or an obligation, but involves joy, communality, and reciprocal streams of affects – as we realized when meeting Larissa's "adopted granny." Care is a relation that necessitates continuity and predictability, and, until today, it has been based on the assumption that women take care of both. We might thus ask for how long women are able to do this in the precarious conditions assigned to them in the global economy? And what will happen to the *time* to host and to hostess (see, for example, Urry 2000)?

Beyond that, we (the authors of this chapter) need to ask whether it is possible at all to separate hostessing from being a guest. After all, when walking and talking with Larissa and the group of migrant women, they were hosting and visiting at the same time – all the time. Then again, if hostessing and traveling as mutually incompatible activities are replaced with the perhaps more accurate notion of care as a reciprocal and renewing relation, as we have suggested, the ideological premise popular today in the Western world, of care work as unproductive labor that burdens *proper* economic production and prevents the latter from prospering by way of increasing the costs of the public sector, will be deservedly dismissed. Then the migrant maid of the global economy – as well as of the domestic household – would no longer carry the weight of unjust division of labor and care in the post-host–guest society.

Acknowledgments

For valuable comments on earlier drafts of this chapter, we wish to thank the editors of this volume, Tim Oakes and Claudio Minca, as well as Anu Valtonen, Pirjo Pöllänen, Turo-Kimmo Lehtonen, Suvi Alt, Jussi Vähämäki, Zoë Koivu, and Maartje Roelofsen.

Notes

1   The data used in the chapter is produced in the research project "Fourth Shift: On the Borders of Home, Labour and Affects" (Academy of Finland 2008–2011, no. 121754) directed by Eeva Jokinen. The project studies precarious work and life conditions in the regions from the angle of everyday well-being and survival. The research team consists of Olga Davydova, Katri Heikkilä, Mikko Jakonen, Eeva Jokinen, Jukka Könönen, Iiris Lehto, Heidi Meriläinen, Tiina Tikka, Juhana

Venäläinen, Jussi Vähämäki and Leena Åkerblad. The data is also extensively consulted in Davydova (no date) and Jokinen *et al.* (2011).

Three focus groups were organized: one involving Finnish-speaking white-collar Precariat, another with women migrated from the areas of the former Soviet Union, and the third by Social Policy MA thesis students. The Russian-speaking group's discussions were conducted and transcribed in Russian, then translated into Finnish, and further, for the purpose of research texts such as the one at hand, into English. Some aspects of narration may have been lost in translation. However, we used the English transcription as it was narrated: being engendered in an atmosphere of humorous sessions, providing information on what happened to these women, what kinds of experiences and thoughts they had, and what took place in the situations of interaction. Out of nine discussants, one was in the position of a researcher. All women had migrated to Finland from Russia; some were originally from the territories of the former Soviet Union (for example, the Baltic countries). They had a relatively high education: among the group there was a lawyer, an economist, a biologist, two doctors and a teacher.

2   The research on care, one of the most flourishing areas in feminist and gender studies, can be divided into several streams of thought. Some researchers emphasize the ethics of care, the moral value that care presupposes, and the gendered bias of care ethics (e.g. Tronto 1999; Sevenhuijsen 1998), while others zoom in on the urgent need to recognize and to make care-related issues, such as women's invisible care work, visible and politically relevant (e.g. Fraser 1994; Dahl 2010). Materiality, practices, and embodiment of care are the focus for others (e.g. Tedre 1999; Mol 2008).

The discussion that has particularly inspired us here, however, deals with global movement, border crossing, and global chains of care (e.g. Ehrenreich and Hochschild 2003), as well as comparisons of care regimes (Bettio and Plantenga 2004). Precarias a la Deriva (2003, 2004, 2009 no date) combine many of these discussions, and develop the idea of care as transversal and all-around potential, while depicting the biopolitical dimension in the politics of care. As Foucault (2008) has shown, the ideological roots of current neoliberal biopolitics replace the ideals of equality, planning, and controlling competition by inequality, free competition, and enterprising selves. Although he does not explicitly discuss ethics or the logics of care, neoliberal politics replaces the ideal of a universal right to be cared for by demands that everyone should take care of him/herself – which, for its part, is a very old idea in Western thinking (Foucault 1990; 2005). Gutiérrez-Rodríguez (2010), for her part, elaborates on materialist feminist theories of domestic work in the context of care work by migrants at households, and develops, being likewise inspired by Precarias a la Deriva, a decolonialist approach on the value of unproductive labor.

3   Larissa was the only one in the group with a permanent (tenancy at will) labor contract, which is the assumed norm and cornerstone of the Nordic welfare system. The others had freelance or temporary contracts, or were unemployed. One was on a parental leave and one was a small business entrepreneur.

4   Larissa is not of Russian origin, but Estonian, and an "ethnic Finn." She is a Russian citizen as she was born in the Soviet Union.

4 The rhythms of tourism

Tim Edensor

Temporality and tourism

As others have noted, the multiple forms of tourism do not constitute a bounded sphere of activity (Franklin 2003). Tourism is a modality of social life, not apart from it, and yet by confining tourism to a specific academic ghetto, analysis has been starved of ideas from the wider social sciences. In tourism studies the focus is often on the place-making qualities of the production of places as tourist venues and their continuous reproduction through tourist practices, while notions of the timings and temporalities of tourism have been neglected. However, brief consideration reveals that tourism is replete with temporal structures, phases, and paces at a range of scales. Since explorations of time are as innumerable as those investigating space, in this chapter I confine my focus to the particular temporal element of rhythm to explore how, in tourism as an aspect of social life, humans are "rhythm-makers as much as place-makers" (Mels 2004: 3). I follow Barbara Adam's assertion that we need to investigate particular formations of "tempo, timing, duration, sequence and rhythm as the mutually implicating structures of time" (1998: 202), and utilize the concept of rhythmanalysis, a field of investigation initiated by Henri Lefebvre (2004), to explore how the rhythms of tourist places, mobilities, bodies and mundane routines provide an important constituent of the experience and organization of tourist time.

Lefebvre's *Rhythmanalysis*, first published in English in 2004, is concerned with investigating how rhythms shape human experience in timespace and pervade everyday life and place. It has proved to be a stimulating resource for current thinking about timespace, place and everyday life. Though brief, it introduces richly suggestive ways for thinking about rhythm, but as an unfinished project, *Rhythmanalysis* also allows scope for wide interpretation and provides a basis for further exploration, as part of a broader context of time-geography. The cultural experience and social understandings of time are dynamic, multiple, and heterogeneous, rather than "a singular or uniform social time stretching across a uniform social space." May and Thrift draw attention to "various (and uneven) networks of time stretching in different and divergent directions across an uneven social field" (2001: 5), and Barbara Adam identifies "tempo, timing, duration, sequence and rhythm as the mutually implicating structures of time" (1998: 202). Rhythmanalysis is particularly useful for investigating the patterning of a range of multiscalar temporalities – calendrical, diurnal and lunar, life-cycle, somatic, and mechanical – whose rhythms provide an important constituent of the experience and organization of social time. And besides developing analyses of the synchronic practices identified by Hägerstrand's (1985) space–time paths, rhythmanalysis can develop a fuller, richer analysis of these in space, while also accounting for spatial qualities, sensations, and intersubjective habits. Rhythmanalysis is thus a useful tool through which to explore the temporal processes that (re)produce connections between individuals, society, and space.

Crucially, while Lefebvre maintains that there is no "rhythm without repetition in time and space, without reprises, without returns, in short, without measure," he also insists that "there is no identical absolute repetition indefinitely . . . there is always something new and unforeseen that introduces itself into the repetitive" (2004: 6). This then allows for the imposition of powerful temporal norms and unreflexive accedence to them, but also for the ways in which these rhythmic conventions might be sidestepped and resisted.

Here, as well as initiating a more considered analysis of the temporalities of tourism, I extend and apply notions of rhythmanalysis by discussing how we might conceive of tourist rhythms. Tourism is a realm in which the "when, how often, how long, in what order and at what speed" are governed by "norms, habits, and conventions" about temporality (Adam 1995: 66), a host of implicit, embedded, and embodied forms of social knowing that regulate tourist practice and space. As in other social realms, spatio-temporal patterns are laid down through a mix of social ordering and disordering, and in this chapter I identify some of the regulatory rhythmic conventions that shape tourist experience while acknowledging the other rhythms that intrude to disrupt these, the moments of arrhythmia and the ongoing proliferation of less hegemonic tourist rhythms and counter-rhythms.

The complex interplay of social rhythms and the great range of scales and contexts within which they occur can be summarized by identifying institutionalized rhythms, marked by national festivals, religious occasions, hours of commerce, television schedules, and bank holidays (Edensor 2006a). These mesh with locally organized rhythmic conventions, following particular hours of work and play, celebrating local festivals and customs, and synchronized practices whereby people eat, play, and work together. And these routinized social rhythms, which consolidate a sense of the ways that places feel as well as are practiced, intersect with numerous "natural" rhythms, including the embodied rhythms of humans and animals – breath, heartbeat, and biorhythms – and the diurnal and lunar rhythms of the sun and moon, the hours of daylight and the flow of tides (Jones 2010), seasonal rhythms of the year and the larger astronomical cycles that pervade a larger temporal scale (Edensor 2010).

By highlighting the social rhythms through which rituals, habits, timetables, schedules, the conventional order of events, and notions of appropriate timings that inhere in the arrangements that reinforce normative ways of understanding and experience, we can identify particular tourist rhythms. For instance, the notion that we need an annual break, a convention supplemented in the West by ongoing claims for more holiday-time, is part of the social rhythm of the year. However, though in the era of mass tourism huge numbers of working-class holiday-makers synchronized their trips to seaside resorts en masse, holidays now tend to be more individualized and specialized, although many collective endeavors still take place. The year is now rhythmically punctuated by time off work, including Christmas and Easter holidays, and weekend breaks. This is further complicated by life-cycle rituals, such as honeymoons, stag and hen parties, holidays arranged to celebrate exam success, gap year travels, and retirement and birthday occasions, all of which add to the rhythmic composition of the year and of the whole life-cycle. Yet the idea that tourism represents "time out" or a liminal movement to another time is one I critically interrogate.

At a smaller level, the temporal structure of particular tourist holidays and travels reveals rhythmic reiterations. The daily rhythmic shape of the short package holiday spent in a resort may comprise a late breakfast, a leisurely afternoon by the hotel pool or on the beach, and an evening spent dancing, being entertained, and eating and drinking according to a fairly predictable schedule, often punctuated by occasional day trips to visit surrounding attractions. This rhythm contrasts with the longer structure of backpacker tourism, where pace may be more fragmented, but nevertheless, a routine emerges where travel via local transport is complemented by wandering around unfamiliar cities and villages, permeated by periods of attentiveness and reverie, and evenings spent hanging out with fellow backpackers in hotels, bars, and cafés. Tourist schedules and routines thus vary in pace, duration, degree of synchronization and regulation, predictability, and familiarity, but all except the most improvisational are undergirded with a degree of rhythmic regularity, as discussed below. However, so diverse are the various manifestations of contemporary tourist practice that it makes little sense to talk of *a* tourist rhythm. Rather these are multiple, ever-changing, and place- and time-specific. Accordingly, a recognition of the multiplicity of tourist rhythms can further decenter the ethnocentric figure of "the tourist," a universalist construction of a white, middle-class male that has emerged out of highly specific Western forms of tourist practice (see Jokinen and Veijola 1997; Edensor 1998; Winter *et al.* 2009 for critiques).

In order to try to make sense of this rhythmic multiplicity, I confine myself to four general intersecting themes. First, I discuss the ways in which rhythms and flows (re)produce different forms of tourist space and place; second, in contributing to the "mobilities turn" (Sheller and Urry 2006) in the social sciences, I focus upon mobile tourist rhythms; third, in accordance with Lefebvre's particular focus on somatic rhythms, I look at the embodied rhythms experienced and produced in different tourist endeavors; and fourth, I use rhythmanalysis to argue that tourism is not merely an extraordinary temporal event, but also echoes the mundane rhythms of everyday life in possessing its own quotidian characteristics.

The familiar and unfamiliar rhythms of tourist space

In conceiving of rhythmanalysis, one of Lefebvre's premises is that "[E]very-where where there is interaction between a place, a time, and an expenditure of energy, there is *rhythm*" (2004: 15). In identifying the spatio-temporal specificities of place, he further contends that "every rhythm implies the relation of a time with space, a localized time, or if one wishes, a temporalized place" (Lefebvre 1996: 230). All places can thus be distinguished by their particular and invariably complex mix of rhythms.

A focus on rhythm and space is useful because it emphasizes the dynamic and processual, and thus circumvents the reifications of place and culture, which purvey geographical notions of place as static, or as a spatial envelope with borders. This sidestepping of overarching conceptualizations of space and place is thus able to highlight the multiple, fluid characteristics of tourist space and the sensual, volatile, immanent, and embodied experience of the world as experienced by the tourist. These contentions have been particularly useful in demolishing dominant versions of landscape and space whereby what is beheld by the human observer appears passive and inert. Tourism studies has been particularly culpable in reiterating notions of space that confirm this reified passivity, notably with the emphasis on the imperializing tourist gaze as it is mobilized to look upon historical attractions, scenic rural views, and archetypal cultural scenes. Tourists – as sightseers – are conceived as beholding landscape as a motionless vista available for distanced visual appreciation. However, no space is fixed; each is always immanent, in process, fecund, and decaying. Lefebvre asserts that there is "nothing inert in the world" and, using the example of the garden, which though it may at first seem quiescent, is suffused with the polyrhythms of "trees, flowers, birds and insects," an "apparent immobility that contains one thousand and one movements" (Lefebvre 2004: 17). Space and place are thus replete with rhythms, flows, and becomings, seething and full of life, contrary to appearances glanced at on the move or represented in tourist guidebooks. Like other realms, we can identify the distinctive charac-teristics of the tourist place according to the particular intermeshing of different rhythmic processes of varying regularity and irregularity. More broadly, we can consider the regular movements to and fro, the repetitive work and play patterns of the city, the "openings and closing of shops, the flows of postal deliveries, bank deposits and coffee breaks" (Labelle 2008: 192), as well as the schedules of public transport, shop and pub opening hours, and lighting up times.

This rhythmic mix becomes more evident if we think about how, in familiar space, the rhythms and interactions of a multitude of social actors intersect. Consider how suburbanites, young, old, shopkeepers, dog-walkers, the reli-gious and the festive, drug addicts and alcoholics, the homeless (Hall 2010), migrants (Conlon 2010), schoolchildren, shoppers, workers, traffic wardens, students, and tourists collectively constitute space through their rhythmic and arrhythmic practices, producing distinctive temporal qualities. For instance, the rhythm of urban life varies within cities, with their hectic rush hours, quiescent mid-afternoons, vibrant early evenings, and low-key nights, and may strongly contrast with the rhythms of other cities, villages, or rural settings. In the latter case, awareness of a host of non-human actors may come into focus. For instance, some years ago I stayed in a Gujarati village for one month. The beginning of the day was marked by the voluminous racket of frogs calling from the village pond, and twilight was heralded by flocks of large fruit bats that flapped over the houses in leisurely fashion and contributed to the rhythms of place.

As with this case, tourists may find themselves in environments in which the rhythms of place contrast greatly with those of their home and other familiar places. The Gujarati frogs and bats were scarcely noticed by the villagers at a daily level, but to me, a first-time visitor to rural India, they were more momentous events because of their unfamiliarity. A Gujarati tourist visiting Europe for the first time would likely notice equally unfamiliar rhythms, perhaps the British "dawn chorus." In this context, then, what conditions the rhythmic shape of the tourist experience is the extent to which local social rhythms are part of the mix of place, for in many venues, tourism is part of the jumble of activities that flow through place.

I have written previously about backpacker venues, particularly those settings that contain a complex of small hotels, internet cafés, and bars among a plethora of other, non-touristic enterprises and institutions. These "honey-pots" serve as temporary stopping points where backpackers congregate and socialize with each other. In doing so, they imprint their own particular rhythms on place, alluded to above, with a mix of sightseeing, wandering, socializing, shopping, eating and drinking, going online, hanging out, relaxing, and planning further travel, activities that are mostly carried out at a leisurely pace. But such rhythms are also accompanied by a plethora of other rhythmic practices carried out by local inhabitants in this "heterogeneous" tourist space (Edensor 1998, 2001), a realm that contains tourist activities and businesses but is not determined by them, and in which tourism is one of numerous practices that shape that space. In such settings, tourists cannot be insulated from ordinary everyday activities but must accommodate themselves to, and improvise around, these regular rhythmic practices that occur in work places, schools, cafés, extemporized leisure sites, transport termini, bathing points, offices, administrative centers, houses and flats, and places of worship.

In non-Western backpacker settings, in Indian, Moroccan and Thai cities, for instance, the interplay of diverse rhythms may be rather overwhelming to those who seek a relaxing holiday destination, although such spaces are often sought out by backpackers for a complex of reasons associated with quests for authenticity, cultural challenge, cultural capital, and difference. The proliferating activities may confound familiar, comfortable rhythmic experience, producing rhythms far more variegated than those generated in single-purpose tourist spaces. Such rhythms might include the multidirectional movements of different bodies and vehicles across and along roads, and the juxtapositions of activities, people, and things that disrupt a contemplative or romantic gaze, and this may thwart the usually unreflexive sensual and rhythmic attunement to place and familiar space, producing a tourist body that feels "out of place." In such circumstances, spatio-temporal patterns may quickly be reinstalled to reconfigure ordered existence in unfamiliar space and regain a sense of security.

In contradistinction to these movements into a rhythmic otherness, much tourism depends upon the reproduction of highly regular rhythms where rigorously managed timetables and routines are followed and tourist spaces are organized to reinforce dominant rhythms and reduce arrhythmia. These tourist rhythms are reproduced by a spatio-temporal ordering that seeks to minimize external intrusions and cultivate relaxing atmospheres, particularly in the space of the "other," where life is apt to move to a different beat. Timetabled activities, selective routes and sights, and the reiteration of potted narratives strain toward rhythmic repetition and predictability. As enclavic spaces (re)emerge, so do the grounded routines – lounging, eating, shopping – that make space homely through the sensual and practical engagement with familiar material textures and affordances (Edensor 2006b).

This rhythmic ordering fosters a sense of being in place, whereby regular routines constitute patterns of "social practices, coded gestures, metaphorical styles, technological applications and experiences" (Mels 2004: 6) that globalize notions of dwelling. Tourism thus constitutes a particular rhythmic way of "being-in-the-world," unreflexive, habitual performances that reproduce another kind of everyday, a home-from-home. Accordingly, a relaxation-inducing predictability re-emerges, which follows regular routines of eating, traveling, working, sleeping, and socializing.

In the same way that familiar places form unquestioned settings for regular patterns of walking, driving, shopping, and other routinized practices, so enclavic tourist space fosters the following of regular paths and points of spatial and temporal intersection that routinize action in space and collectively constitute the "time-geographies" (Gren 2001), within which people's trajectories separate and cross in regular ways. Hotel shops, bars and restaurants, beaches, pools, and games rooms are meeting points at which individual paths congregate and around which social activities are coordinated and synchronized. These repetitive, collective choreographies in such spaces of interaction, rest and leisure produce rhythmic "place ballets" (Seamon 1980). As I will shortly discuss, the accumulation of repetitive events also becomes sedimented in bodies that become unreflexively familiar with the textures, routines, and practices of these rhythmically regulated environments. As in other habitual, everyday environments, such rhythmic systems are rarely apparent except when they break down or no longer pertain, when tourists violate the expected order of events or other intrusions occur. Vitally, these regularized rhythms also depend upon tourism workers – the guides, cleaners, waiters, hotel receptionists, drivers, and performers who work continuously to ensure the smooth running of tourist routines and timetabled activities. Repetitively, according to temporal orders, hotel beds are made, food cooked, tours undertaken, and stage shows produced by these workers.

These examples only hint at the diverse habits, routines, and conventions that constitute tourist rhythms. And this is complicated by the advent of a global scenario in which increasingly heterodox tourisms move from numerous points of origin toward different objectives, but also toward common destinations, wherein certain sites are stages for the practice of varied rhythms, where timings, paces and ways of moving clash and contrast with each other. This rhythmic variation can be used to conceive of the varied tourist practices that I identified at one global tourist attraction: the Taj Mahal (Edensor 1998; see also Degen 2010). Backpackers linger at the site, often for hours, strolling at leisurely pace across and around the whole area, lying on the grass, writing diaries and chatting. Western package tourists, following a timetabled itinerary that involves a limited stop at the Taj (usually of around one hour), tend to hurry individually around a rather prescribed pathway, taking photographs and gazing at the mausoleum. Large Indian family groups amble around the central causeway, taking photographs, laughing, and talking. Western package tourists are apt to express irritation at the slow-moving crowds of Indian domestic tourists who to them seem to manifest insufficient reverence for this world wonder, while to the Indians, the intensity and seriousness of the photographic compulsiveness on display is perplexing. The backpackers are also apt to be disrupted in their serene progress by requests from the Indian family groups to be included within photographs of family groups. Here, then, a rhythmanalysis foregrounds the multiplicity of often contesting tourist practices that take place at one site, decentering any notion that there is an archetypal tourist. Instead, the globalization of tourism is producing numerous forms of tourist praxis whose temporal conventions clash and intersect.

Place and the mobile rhythms of tourism

While by staying somewhere initially unfamiliar we may become aware of the different rhythms that incorporate us and flow around us, and thus experience a sense of place, much tourism is also concerned with mobility. Indeed, the tourist might appear exemplary of the modern mobile subject. Here I investigate the ways in which mobility is productive of a variety of tourist rhythms.

First, the mobile rhythms of tourism can produce an embodied, material and sociable "dwelling-in-motion" (Sheller and Urry 2006). Since many forms of tourism are characterized precisely by extensive mobility between home and away, and between attractions, hotels, and airports, for instance, it is important to consider the mobile experience as part of the tourist experience, not a merely functional event that allows engagement in other places. The stop-start rhythm of passages of rapid mobility and periods of relative stasis are productive of the broader temporal shape of tourist ventures. This is akin to a daily routine, where breakfast is followed by a coach trip, a subsequent visit to an attraction followed by lunch, another period of travel, a visit to another attraction, a spell spent shopping, tea, and then the evening spent within the confines of the hotel. More specifically, the interior of a mobile vehicle is a different sort of place with its own rhythms. The packaged travel itinerary that uses a tour bus is a notable example of a particular mobile rhythm. The machinic pulse of the engine can produce a eurhythmic consistency, a comfortable mobile environment from which the passing scenes are apprehended, a homely and relaxing setting within which the body is enfolded and lulled into a state of kinaesthetic and tactile relaxation. The steady pace in a cushioned interior, perhaps interspersed with commentary about the space in passing, allows an intermittent drifting off and tuning in, a mixture of attention and inattention (Edensor and Holloway 2008).

Second, intensive and regular travel even over a limited period can engender a more expansive sense of place. It has been asserted that "places marked by an abundance of mobility become *placeless*" (Cresswell 2006: 31; see also Augé 1995) realms of detachment. However, the apprehension of serial features through a mobile gaze enacted on repetitive bus and train journeys allows passengers to develop a sense of place, even if they are unable to feel at home in it. For instance, regular travel on the roads of Greece reveals a succession of encounters with stone or wooden roadside shrines, or *kandylaki*, based on platforms and comprising small glass doors, flickering candles, an image of a saint, and Greek lettering, standing out against the Mediterranean vegetation. Here there is a visual rhythm through which the characteristics of place are absorbed in successive rapid transit, highlighting that although the mobile experience of place may be fleeting, it can also be associated "with prolonged or repeated movements, fixities, relations and dwellings" (Merriman 2004: 146).

Third, the mode and style of travel also produces distinctive kinds of tourist rhythms. For instance, travel by car, bicycle or foot produce an array of different sensual experiences of time and space. Further, Jennie Germann Molz highlights the distinctions between slow and fast mobilities, showing how these are not mere modalities but that "certain values come to be associated with stillness, slowness or speed" (2009: 271). The quest for different rhythms can be located in tourist promotions that emphasize the slower pace of life in both rural settings and non-Western destinations. A widespread, common-sense notion persists that tourists may escape to the rural settings to "wind down" away from the "rat race," away from the faster pace of "modern" urban living. In the West, the rural has long been produced as a realm within which slower rhythms pertain, an assignation that emerged during nineteenth-century industrial growth and the expansion of urban areas with a concomitant, nostalgic desire to revert to a romantic, imaginary rural idyll. Such ideals continue to motivate second-homeowners, retirees, and tourists, although whether the expansion of urban lifestyles and practices into the rural means that distinctively slower rhythms endure is questionable. Different conjugations of a slower, more traditional, idyllic rurality are currently invigorating the diversification of Chinese (Chio 2009) and Japanese (Graburn 2009) tourism after decades of the rural being conceived as "backward" in these countries.

It is not only the rural in which slower rhythms are promoted, but also the postcolonial site, construed by the Western tourist industry as a venue for the antithesis of the fast-moving, pressurized pace, and speedy lifestyles of Western, "sophisticated" urban living. Such realms are typically represented as those in which "time still goes slowly" and in which "nothing has changed for centuries." As Germann Molz declares, slow travelers are drawn to "a particular backdrop of cultures and people who are required to play along in this anti-modern, slow motion drama" (2009: 281; see also Jordan 1995). These sentiments about slow rhythms and unchanging time recur throughout advertising literature, and are exemplified by journalist Laurence Marks (2002) who, in discussing how one should properly spend tourist time in the Maldives, advises:

> I also learned another lesson by which I abide to this day: you don't need a watch. When I arrive I put mine in my suitcase and get up when it gets light, go to bed when it gets dark. I have no need to know what time it is. Who needs a watch in Paradise?

Germann Molz draws particular attention to the Slow Travel movement, which recommends would-be tourists to "spend a week in a vacation rental and see what is near you" (Slow Travel no date). Slow down, immerse yourself in the local culture and avoid the fast pace of rushing from one guidebook "must-see" to the next, while further suggesting that tourists stay at least one week in a particular place and investigate that which is close at hand, imploring them to "live like a local: shop at the local stores, go to the same café every morning, take the time to see the things that are near you." Particular kinds of mobilities and space are championed in the quest for a slower rhythm. Walking, cycling, and canal cruising are all recommended, along with sites such as "remote" cottages and country hotels. Associated with these slower ventures are a bundle of ethical imperatives, including spiritual health, environmental sustainability, and deeper, more authentic cultural and social engagement. This moral disposition is also apparent on another website, the School of the Seasons, where the upfront advice is to "align yourself with the rhythms of the earth" and thereby escape the "frantic pace of modern life" and celebrate those local, time-honored festivals based on moon lore, pagan rituals, saints days, and seasonal world holidays that embody "slow time, sacred time and seasonal time."

Germann Molz also highlights how in that particular mobile tourist endeavor, the round-the-world year-long adventure, travelers consciously combine slow and fast rhythms during their global journey. She argues that for these tourists "difference and contrast are essential features of a global itinerary" (2010: 340). One way of distinguishing places is through their differentiation by time and rhythm, a distinction that seeks out rhythms that contrast with their own culturally informed understandings of time, and also with the rhythms of the other places they visit on their journey, mixing, for instance, the fast rhythms of cities such as Bangkok and Tokyo with the different pace of beach resorts and rural settings.

Finally, and in contrast to the quest for slower rhythms, a more kinaesthetic engagement with mobile rhythms can be located in the expanding sector of adventure tourism, where tourists place themselves in, or try to steer through, boiling torrents, toiling seas, rough terrain, and turbulent air. The rhythms of waves and the flow of rivers, the jarring passage caused by rapid transit across rough terrain on quad bikes, or the smooth journey navigated by yachters and windsurfers constitute the quest for rhythmic or arrhythmic pleasures through intense spells of mobility that contrast with the usual pace and rhythm of moving across and through space. Here tourists confront the rhythms of nature, placing their bodies and the mobile technologies they utilize to enliven somatic experience, as I discuss below.

Crucially, although the kinds of mobilities cited above have been institutionalized and form part of the mobile conventions of travel, they can never wholly shape tourist experience. On the contrary, an exploration of rhythm can capture the always emergent possibilities of tourist experience, which may well be the regular reproduction of what is expected and familiar, but also reveals the diverse other rhythms and arrhythmic experiences that decenter a timed and controlled experience. For travel also "involves reverie, an imaginary drifting to elsewhere and moments of giddiness, distraction and boredom" (Edensor and Holloway 2008: 499), and features discomfort and disruptions, roadside surprises, and revelations. For mobile flows and rhythms invariably intersect with other flows and rhythms that may interfere with their smoothness and regularity or provide a point of contrast. For instance, and to return to the example of the tour bus cited above, the bus is but one mobile, rhythmic element in spaces that are themselves seething with numerous flows and rhythms, with intersecting trajectories and temporalities. Where flocks of livestock cross the road, gusts of wind shake the bus, and rivers flow underneath the road, we may suddenly become conscious of a world in motion.

Embodied rhythms: decentering the tourist gaze

Lefebvre puts much emphasis on body rhythms, with their "respirations, pulses, circulations, assimilations" (2004: 5), and hence he argues that the regulated "rational" rhythms of industrial and bureaucratic life are constantly in contact with "what is least rational in human being: the lived, the carnal, the body" (2004: 9). Accordingly, we sense rhythms through our bodies rather than standing objectively outside rhythm.

As I have asserted, many tourists are apt to search for different and distinct rhythms, and, like all rhythms, this multifarious array invariably enfold tourist bodies within them. I have already alluded to the embodied rhythms of coach travel, to moving through heterogeneous tourist space and the comforting environments of enclavic tourist space. The desire to immerse the body in environments where regulated, comfortable, and familiar rhythms persist contrasts with urges to insert the body in enlivening situations, where normative somatic experience is challenged, where the body opens up to new sensations, paces, and rhythms. Yet the bodily rhythms of the heart, breathing, digestion and excretion, sleep and wakefulness, and longer biorhythms and bodily processes such as menstruation and growth patterns intersect with rhythms of work, play, and relaxation. These somatic rhythms may be accommodated with and attuned to the particular rhythms of specific tourist spaces, or they may be disrupted and made irregular, producing bodily arrhythmia and a consequent discomfort.

In investigating tourist immersion in predictable and pleasurable rhythms, consider the beach holiday, where a routine engagement with sun, sea, and sand is composed of regular and anticipated rhythms. The timetabled laying down of the towels, the occasional bursts of activity on the beach with the playing of ball games, swimming in the sea, and paddling at the water's edge punctuate the relaxed somnolence of sunbathing. The sensual rhythms of the beach experience, the sound of the waves, the cries of children and seabirds, the passage of the sun across the sky, and the emergence of sea breezes also produce specific diurnal rhythms composed of stages that include settling down at an established spot, the post-lunch nap, and the greater propensity to engage in physical exercise towards day's end. All provide a familiar sensory realm, which is impressed upon memory and remembered upon reacquaintance as a collection of familiar rhythms that are not principally shaped by visual apprehension.

Indeed, the notion that the world is primarily perceived through the tourist's gaze has recently been critically decentered, with a growing awareness about the diversity of sensory experiences that constitute tourist experience (Veijola and Jokinen 1994; Saldanha 2002; Edensor 2006b). I have already mentioned how this search for bodily deconditioning also occurs in an immersion in the environmental confrontations of adventure tourism (Cloke and Perkins 1998; Wheaton 2004). In considering the tactile and haptic experience in certain kinds of heterogeneous tourist space that may initially immerse the Western tourist in unfamiliar rhythms, this visual imperialism seems particularly inappropriate. Unlike the linear progression experienced on guided tours and in highly organized forms of tourist space, in backpacker Indian honeypots, for example, where tourism combines with a multitude of everyday social functions, it can be difficult to move in a straight line. Instead, tourists must weave around obstacles and be alert to other people, traffic, and animals, an arrhythmic situation that requires attunement and adjustment to the irregularities of other moving bodies. In jostling amid other people, maybe some animals and a variety of mobile forms of transport, across rough surfaces, tourists, along with other users of the space, must participate in a "sensual dance" (Buie 1996: 227).

Similarly, the regulated, predictable soundscapes of intensively regulated space contrast with the arrhythmic, atonal, shifting combination of noises generated by practices of worship, play, and work, and with the symphony of different vehicles and performed or recorded music. Again, such environments may be sought to jolt the body out of its habituated rhythms. Yet this arrhythmia is not merely a condition deliberately sought out by tourists but is also part and parcel of their travel experience, waiting in the wings to disrupt smooth rhythm and harmony. Somatic rhythms may generally become accommodated to temporal procedures, but the body is also apt to find discord with delineated rhythms according to chance and event. An obvious rhythmic realignment comes when long-distance travel produces jet-lag and the subsequent adaptation to a different time. The usual rhythms of sleep and eating are disrupted and we feel "out of synch." Moreover, the unfamiliarity of the rhythms of place, for instance, in the earlier and louder dawn chorus that one may be used to, the calls of the muezzin throughout the day and night in Muslim settings, and the lengthier, noisier, livelier urban nights of many Mediterranean urban environments, where economic and social activity extends into the early hours of the morning, are all apt to disrupt habitual somatic rhythms.

These embodied rhythms may also be disturbed by the kinds of practices tourists engage in. Most obviously, excessive drinking or drug-taking may lengthen the nocturnal hours of wakefulness and invert the usual diurnal patterns of sleep, and lying uncovered for too long in the sun is likely to result in sunburn or sunstroke, with illness fracturing the regular pulse of life. While hedonistic practices and sickness may produce arrhythmia, the experienced tourist is likely to cope with such eventualities, minimizing their impact on the body. Emily Falconer (2009) discusses how Western female backpackers manage these embodied arrhythmic effects and deal with the regular rhythms of the body in organizing their tourist experience. She exemplifies how one Western tourist in India was resentful of the disruption to her budget bus travel caused by her heavy periods, which restricted her capacity to endure a long journey without toilet facilities. She also points out that many rather loosely structured backpacker routines are organized around regular eating and drinking to provide structure and rhythm to life "on the road." Food breaks up the day and provides temporal goals. After a while, Falconer reveals, travellers tire of local fare, which gradually affects their habitually attuned digestive systems, and routines of eating local food are replaced by a more anxious quest for familiar fare, often fast food that will restore digestive harmony. Accordingly, backpacker discussions often revolve around the "phases" of travel charac-terized by eating "local" and eating "Western," and the consequent effects on their bodily constitutions. Of course, a feature of much backpacker travel (along with other tourisms) is attuning the stomach to local food, and the ways in which this is often thwarted by digestive ailments and food poisoning. Here, the usual rhythms of digestion and excretion are thoroughly disrupted, and tourists aim to alleviate these processes through medicine and careful food consumption to achieve a semblance of somatic rhythmic order once more.

Tourism and everyday rhythms

As I have implied, one approach is to think about tourism not only as movement to a different space but also to a different rhythm – to a realm in which one can slow down and chill out, or where difference is marked by different temporal ways of being. This quest for rhythmic alterity appears to constitute a break from everyday routine and immersion in another temporal state. John Urry posits that tourism comprises a "limited breaking with established routines and practices of everyday life and allowing one's senses to engage with a set of stimuli that contrast with the everyday and the mundane" (1990: 2). Normative cultural and academic understandings thus underpin the notion that tourism is a time of escape from the "stresses and strains" of mundane, everyday life. Normal conventions are suspended within this extraordinary period as tourists search for a "liminality" (Turner and Turner 1973) or "authenticity" absent from their ordinary lives (MacCannell 1999 [1976]). Diurnal and weekly routines are replaced by a plenitude of self-directed time and opportunities are available to transgress ordinary temporal order.

However, along with others (Franklin and Crang 2001; Larsen 2008), I suggest that, on the contrary, tourism is replete with rigid conventions of its own, habits and routines that shape the particular practices and experiences of tourists, and it is therefore also somewhat mundane (Edensor 2007). Tourism, then, while often initially resembling a break from banal rhythms, very often quickly reorganizes itself into regular practices that imitate those of the non-tourist everyday. Urry (2002) also points out that much of the time we are tourists whether we like it or not, for tourism is part of everyday perception: "a way of seeing and sensing the world with its own kit of technologies, techniques and aesthetic sensibilities and pre-dispositions" (Franklin and Crang 2001: 8). Accordingly, rather than transcending the everyday, most forms of tourism are fashioned by culturally coded escape attempts. Moreover, although suffused with notions of escape from normativity, tourists carry quotidian habits and rhythms along with their luggage. Tourism thus involves unreflexive, habitual, and practical enactions that reflect common-sense understandings of how to be a tourist, including the embedding of rhythmic norms about when practices should be performed and what the temporal structure of the day should be like. These cultural norms, grounded in kinds of tourist habitus, inform largely "common-sense" and unreflexive ways of being (Bourdieu 1984), whether these concern package holidays, backpacking, adventure tourism, or beach holidays.

Modes of traveling, walking, consuming, listening, gleaning information, relaxing, and socializing as a tourist reveal persistent and regular forms of bodily hexis and embodied praxes. The accumulation of repetitive events becomes sedimented in the body to condense an unreflexive sense of being in tourist space. This intimate and unreflexive praxis about how to get things done in place is grounded in the everyday home, but also, so familiar are certain tourist settings, successively encountered over a tourist career, that the multitude of habits, schedules, and routines that lend to home an ontological predictability and security can similarly be enacted at the home-from-home that is the recognizable tourist realm. In such common spaces, a particular "structure of feeling" (Williams, R. 1961: 63) is reproduced by collectively shared practices, through which, as Frykman and Löfgren put it, "cultural community is often established by people together tackling the world around them with familiar manoeuvres" (1996: 10–11). These collective practical rhythms reproduce a familiar timespace of being on holiday.

A useful example is provided by O'Reilly's (2000) study of a British expatriate community in Spain who consolidate a shared identity through enacting repetitive social rituals of Britishness. While this group has moved more permanently to a space of otherness, in which a heightened sense of Britishness is repetitively performed to continuously reinscribe identity, we can see this occurring at a shorter time-scale through the practices of British holiday-makers who visit the Costa del Sol, who similarly instantiate a shared rhythmic structuring of the day, a synchronized hedonistic routine.

This tendency to collectively reproduce shared rhythmic practices on holiday intersects with the more established rhythms laid down by tourist businesses. Lefebvre argues that "political power knows how to utilize and manipulate time, dates, time-tables" (2004: 68), and the capitalist enterprises that organize tourist packages shape the temporal structure of holidays so that they commercially optimize business, controlling the provision of a regularized "product" that minimizes scope for accident and disruption. If we consider the much stereotyped British mass holiday camp experience, the popularity of which peaked in the 1950s, the instantiation of organized, timetabled activities for the campers serves as a prototype for more sophisticated and less coercive schemes to involve bodies in collective sporting, dramaturgical, and other leisure practices at distinct times of the day. As I have mentioned, the highly structured rhythms of guided tours, coach trips, shopping (Kärrholm 2009), and sightseeing excursions highlight the organization of predictable and familiar routines that also provide a sense of security and familiarity for tourists. More recent forms of distinctly organized travel include the provision of mass tourism in China that includes scenic, nationally iconic, modern, and playful sites, and remains decidedly scripted, replete with shared conventions and "heavily enmeshed with the state" (Nyiri 2009: 168).

These home-from-home activities are part of what Lefevbre describes as "*dressage,*" or the breaking-in of the individual to (re)produce "an automatism of repetitions" (2004: 40), rooted in what he calls "the military model." By enmeshing the body within a conventional assemblage of instructions, supervisions, architectures, narratives, timetables, and technologies, military exercise served to correlate the soldier's physiological rhythms with the requirements of the wider system and produced an efficient, docile body. Similarly, the immersing of the tourist's body in the timetables and rhythms of the tour, with their well-rehearsed enactions involving travel, narration, photography, consumption, and sport, for instance, means that it becomes trained to anticipate and unreflexively know what it should do, and how. For numerous forms of tourism produce a rhythmic repetition "of movements, gestures, action, situations, difference" (Lefebvre 2004: 15) through a practiced knowledge of what, how, and where to act – how and where to photograph, for example – that is part of the tourist repertoire through which "something passes as *natural* precisely when it conforms perfectly and without apparent effort to accepted models, to the habits valorised by a tradition" (Lefevbre 2004: 38–39).

In addition to these distinctive tourist rhythms, the notion that tourist time is filled with novelty, unfamiliar practices, and unusual experiences also denies the rhythmic regularity of the ways in which familiar social, cultural, and religious enactions that are carried out at regular intervals during everyday life outside a tourist context also continue to be practiced while *in situ* or on the move as tourist. Larsen (2008) points out how much tourism is concerned with carrying out ordinary convivial relations with family members and friends, or visiting relatives, a point exemplified by Charles Carroll's account of the typically dense sociality involving obligations to friends and family in contemporary Laotian tourism (2009). These everyday familial interactions are increasingly accompanied by the role that the expanding reach of new technologies has in facilitating the sustenance of habits, such as routine texting and telephoning to those with whom one is familiar, sending and checking emails, and accessing the internet to contribute to blogs and find out about the latest news and sporting results. Such practices require synchronized engagement with distant others irrespective of time-zone differences. The compilation of individual travel blogs has replaced or complemented the daily writing of the travel diary as part of the rhythmic routine of tourism. The rhythmic interspersing of virtual and physical space is also part of the conventions of an emergent Chinese backpacking, in which strict conventions are discursively and practically reiterated in both realms (Lim 2009).

Many popular and academic critiques of tourism point to these unreflexive habits as emblematic of the banality of tourist praxes. However, this tourist mundanity is better conceived as a submission to the desires to dispense with responsibility, for one's own travel arrangements and enter a familiar, comfortable, and relaxing realm. The embodied state of "unwinding" is part of the common-sense understanding with which tourism is conceived, and is the antithesis of what a middle-class disposition might regard as an "improv-ing" activity (on this, see also Chapter 6 in this volume). Moreover, although tourism is another kind of everyday practice, with its distinctive and regular rhythms, and the everyday may be the site in which commerce and the state attempt to install predictable rhythmic practices (Potts 2010), this does not mean that the everyday is inevitably a dystopian cage of unfreedom.

Michael Gardiner argues that the everyday possesses "transgressive, sensual and incandescent qualities" (2000: 208). Likewise, Paul Harrison argues that "in the everyday enactment of the world there is always immanent potential for new possibilities of life" (2000: 498). Quotidian practice is open-ended, fluid, and generative, concerns becoming rather than being, is a sensual experiencing and understanding that is "constantly attaching, weaving and disconnecting; constantly mutating and creating" (Harrison 2000: 502). Thus, the immanent experience of the everyday – the daydreams, disruptions, and sensual intrusions – constantly threatens to undermine the unreflexive routines and rhythms laid down by habit. This is also the case with mundane tourism, for it is a period when, through relaxation, intoxication, discomfort, and sensual experience, there are openings for thinking otherwise, occasions when fantasy colonizes the mind and unbidden desires spring forth. Tourism offers great potential for these moments of relaxation and "tuning out" that Lefebvre calls "'appropriated' time, periods during which 'time no longer counts' due to unreflexive absorption in creative activity, dreaming or contemplation" (2004: 76).

In identifying the contrasting urges to seek out arrhythmia, different rhythms, and highly predictable rhythms, tourism can be conceived as a process through which a greater diversity of temporal experience is sought, though with an abundance of safety checks to prevent things becoming too arrhythmic. Thus, the flow of tourist experience includes a succession of temporal and rhythmic experiences, offering what David Crouch describes as a "potential fluidity" between repetitive performances that secure a stable sense of being and those that "reach forward . . . going further in sensation and desire" (2003: 1949). In any case, as I have emphasized throughout this chapter, all sorts of regular rhythmic patterns are apt to be disrupted or even curtailed by moments and periods of arrhythmia and dissonance, even in the most temporally and spatially regulated contexts. As Germann Molz remarks, "anyone who has been delayed in an airport, endured a long-distance bus trip, or waited for a photo to upload in a tourist Internet cafe knows that travel involves speeding up, stopping, slowing down, hurrying and waiting" (2009: 272). Additionally, while rhythm is always concerned with recurrence and reiteration, it is crucial to acknowledge, as Lefebvre does, that while there can be no rhythm "without repetition in time and space, without reprises, without returns, in short, without measure" there is also "no identical absolute repetition indefinitely . . . there is always something new and unforeseen that introduces itself into the repetitive" (2004: 6).

It is important therefore, to avoid assumptions that managed normative tourist rhythms possess an overarching force that compels individuals to march to their beat. Instead, tourists, like those in other social contexts, are apt to attune themselves to the rhythmicity of the moment through breathing, gestures, pace of movement, and speech (again, see Chapter 6 in this volume). And, as Labelle declares,

> To locate one's own time is to derive a personal spacing within the built; it is to cut into the standardisations of daily routine an interval by which to fashion perspective, according to the mutations and nuances of time.
>
> (2008: 193)

Conclusion

This chapter is an attempt to investigate the extraordinarily varied, complex and contesting rhythms and temporalities that are produced and experienced in tourism. In developing Lefebvre's ideas, I have used rhythm to interrogate broader issues about the distinct mobilities of tourism, the qualities of tourist place and embodied tourist experience, and the mundane, everyday qualities of much tourism.

Two issues arising from this discussion are worth briefly elaborating upon. First, it is important to take far more seriously the extent to which tourism as a product and an experience is constituted by multifarious approaches to time and to the modern discipline of time management. This involves the external regulation of tourist space and timetabled activities in accordance with organized and regular rhythms. In one sense this absolves the tourist of making decisions about what to do and how to arrange a routine, often in the larger space of the "other," providing a familiar temporal structure within which comfort and predictability are produced. Here, it is important to honor the legions of tourist workers who ensure that such rhythms are continuously reproduced (Crang, P. 1997; Veijola 2009b). However, tourism also involves the *self-management* of rhythm, routine, and other temporal conventions. This management operates at various temporal scales, ranging from the ways in which tourist ventures are carved out of broader time, such as the annual schedule, to the plotting of itineraries, visits, and daily routines while on holiday. Such planning may involve a mixing up of rhythms; alternatively, a highly structured, repetitive set of rhythms may be sought. In contrast, much tourism entails the desire to enter diverse temporal frames and become immersed in spatial difference, a search for rhythmic variation that moves away from normative temporal experience. Overall, then, we may ascertain how tourism mixes desires for rhythmic regularity, rhythmic difference, and arrhythmia, a process of negotiation that is particularly evident in tourism but extends across collective and individual social life.

Second, tourism is exemplary of an industry in which global collective rhythms and synchronicities are produced by an increasingly sophisticated global capitalism (Edensor 2010). Consider how travel agencies and other key managers and businesses temporally coordinate the collective routines of visitors who arrive at destinations from multiple points of departure. Systems of transport, accommodation, sustenance, and entertainment fashion globally synchronic rhythms. More broadly, strategies to establish global simultaneity use tourism as part of a mix to market places as sophisticated cosmopolitan venues and catch hyper-mobile capital, as exemplified by the projection of Singapore's image as a world-class city, which includes the promotion of boutique hotels (Teo and Chang 2009). On the other hand, global mobility also opens up the melding, clashing, and merging of a host of different rhythms, and again tourism is exemplary in highlighting this temporal clashing and harmonizing. The playing out of diverse tourist rhythms is expanding as Asian, African, and South American tourists who perform and expect culturally specific temporal and rhythmic experience are increasingly participating in global tourist adventures, and these may synchronize, collide, and contrast at particular tourist sites, producing arrhythmia, asynchronicity, and synchronicity. While I have only been able to allude to certain non-Western tourist practices here, and recognize that more studies that point to their diversity and dynamism are necessary, they highlight the inadequacy of over-general and ethnocentric theories of tourism that are applied across the globe without acknowledging the cultural contexts in which they emerged, as Raewyn Connell (2007) argues is the case with most theories originating in Western academia.

Finally, this chapter highlights how investigations of tourism are useful for revealing larger economic, political, social, and cultural processes, and for providing a specific focus for exploring particular trends. With questions of temporality, we can see that the themes of rhythm that I have discussed above highlight much wider processes about the complex ongoing reorganization of space–time under conditions of globalization, a still-dominant neoliberalism, and a general context in which both homogeneity and extraordinary diversity are being produced.

5   The rime of the frequent flyer

Or What the elephant has got in his trunk

Steven Flusty

"What am I missing?" This is perhaps the most uncomfortably nagging question to colonize my head whenever I find myself sealed into an aluminum can and hurled across the troposphere. Wedged into four square feet of space, at most, for untold hours as I excrete my own personal quarter ton of carbon onto the world below, I find myself obsessively wondering if I remembered to lock the stove, pack the front door, and turn off my passport on the way out. I know there is something I must have forgotten, as does every other traveler shoehorned into steerage class here with me. No procession of slightly outdated movies, truncated and miniaturized to accommodate our friable sensibilities and seatback screens, can assuage the anxiety.

The question, however, is neither so simply pragmatic nor so existentially limited to the prolonged moment of transit – that homogeneous bardo of seat pitches and overhead bins suspended outside the space and time of home and destination, interrupted only by occasional bouts of turbulence that viscerally recollect the precariousness of our present disposition. Rather, I believe the question permeates touring itself. I do not mean by this to imply that I have derived a single, universal explanatory algorithm of optional travel. While it is unlikely there are as many rationales for travel as there are travelers, given that persons setting out upon similar ventures must have motivations that are at least congruent to some degree, my conversations with my fellow in-seatmates have certainly elicited a broad range of explanations for our shared confinement. Some are en route to relaxation, others to excitement, yet others to the different, to the unexpected (but not too unexpected, most – although not quite all – of us hope), to the new, or to the long lost. Such variation leads in turn to a variety of tourisms. To sun-and-cocktail-drenched tropical paradises nestled within perimeter fortifications of razor-ribboned chainlink and aerosolized insecticide. To "olde townes" saturated with Taylorized handicrafts and tourist police. To charnel scenes of memorialized atrocities retrofitted with restrooms, snackbars, understated purveyors of mementos of mass mori, and interpretive placards thoughtfully arrayed along pedestrian paths.

However, despite their diversity, a collective discomfort cross-cuts the lot – we are all missing something, something we believe we must be able to find somewhere elsewhere. We pore through libraries of unceasingly updated guidebooks that instruct us where to find it. We purchase package tours that promise to lead us straight to it. It would, after all, be a shame to go all that way and somehow miss it. And whatever it is we believe we are missing, it must be something vastly important and irresistibly attractive. Otherwise, why would we subject ourselves to imprisonment in four square feet of imperceptibly yet inflammably propelled space to begin with, let alone pay for the experience?

Sightseeing, or But what, then, is it?

"Whatever it may be, ironically purpled verbiage will get you no closer to it" my traveling companion mutters condescendingly, reminding me that I have thus far missed mentioning him at all. We have traveled together off and on since I was very young, and he is prone to addressing me in this tone. It is the tone of one accustomed to authority, but also a tone I have heard gradually soured by his long years in exile following his deposition from his rightful throne. Or so he accounts for his present disposition, although he has never struck me as particularly royal in his battered derby hat and his threadbare suit, faded from what must once have been a becoming shade of green. Not to mention the sizable trunk he carries with him at all times, although this is to be expected given that he is an elephant. One might think this would strike onlookers as odd, but nobody seems to notice. In fact, nobody but me ever much acknowledges his presence at all, although this too is unsurprising – it is common practice to ignore an elephant in the room.

Or, in this instance, an elephant in the Kodak Photo Spot. "If you are at a loss for just what is missing, why not try to infer it from what you are doing – and rather incessantly, I might add – to find it? Think about what you are doing."

So what am I doing? Browsing shopfronts and surveying store contents. Amassing postcards. Composing photographs of the Flavian Amphitheater (open daily from 9am; entry fee 15½ euros), of weathered triumphal arches, of more than a dozen pilfered Egyptian obelisks, of a centurion in full armor chatting on his cellphone. Enlisting others to photograph the same, but with myself included in the foreground. I protest that what I am doing is hardly representative, as my motivations for these seemingly touristic behaviors are different. I, after all, am not engaged in common tourism but in assaying commodity landscapes and gathering evidences toward learned ends. My companion is clearly unimpressed, and, in a souvenir shop a mere pilum's throw further on, it becomes apparent why.

The shop consists predominantly of row upon row of waist-high bins, each displaying upright reams of antique images in heavy cardboard mattes. Many are engravings that faithfully reproduce my photographs, but in black linework on white. The amphitheater, the arches, the obelisks, pedimented temples, domed cathedrals and ruined tumuli are all there, although most admittedly

Figure 5.1 A state of considerably worse repair (photo: Steven Flusty).

in a state of considerably worse repair. And while there is not a single cellular-toting legionnaire in sight, many of the engravings include other human figures in frame, dressed in culottes and tricorne hats. They marvel and point at the landmarks and, in at least one instance, a figure even seems to be posing for a portrait sketch in front of a triumphal arch. The shop's proprietor laughingly proclaims these "snapshots before cameras," and adds that Giovanni Piranesi made his living peddling them to the Grand Tourists of England.

He then lifts additional prints, color reproductions of oil paintings, out of another bin and introduces me to those English. Depicted here by their favorite portraitist, Pompeo Batoni, they are a sumptuous lot in their satin knee-breaches and waistcoats, their velvet cloaks and fur trimmings. Young, mid-eighteenth-century jetsetters such as Charles Crowle, Richard Milles, and Gregory Page-Turner, fortunate scions of their time's most up-and-coming superpower, posed among what look to be personal collections of classical busts and frieze fragments, invariably with books and scholarly documents immediately at hand (Page-Turner being a particularly apt moniker under the circumstances). They seem as keen to be witnessed as worldly-wise as they are to witness the world, immersing themselves in ancient glory gone to ruin while immortalizing their immersion, all to show they are now equipped for the attainment of greater glory still. And they seem nearly identical in their pursuit. They are all men, all similarly and splendidly dressed, all in possession of classical artifacts. Chuck, Dick and Greg even pose identically, right hand on hip and left resting on field notes or route maps.

My companion fixes me with a maddeningly wry stare as if to say, "looking uncomfortably familiar, are they?" I pointedly elide the barb by grabbing another print from the bin. This one is a reproduction of Johan Zoffany's *Tribuna of the Uffizi*, in which a veritable package tour of Georgian era aristocrats cluster in discussion about various, predominantly nude, *objets d'art* in an ornate salon lined wall-to-wall with paintings. These gentlemen are older and even more sumptuous than Batoni's, my eye drawn particularly to a nobleman in a dark velvet waistcoat encrusted with ornate gold embroidery across the chest, surmounted by a bejeweled breast star and sash. A painting is being held up for display before him, with a solicitousness suggesting that the art is not merely being presented for study but offered for acquisition. As with Batoni's, Zoffany's composition enlists assemblages of a classical past to serve as a backdrop against which knowing travelers stand illuminated in the foreground, rendering them simultaneously masters of a static antiquity and its living opposite. "And the opposite of antiquity . . . ," my companion prompts, and there is no eliding his insight no matter how maddeningly pedantic its delivery. These are paintings of tourists inventing modernity, making themselves modern by touring.

Getting there, or The hitchhiker's guide to modernity

"Successful travel, after all, relies upon timeliness. If you run late you will never be where you should be when you should. You wouldn't want to be left behind, would you?" The elephant reaches into his trunk and withdraws a timetable, waving it at me to emphasize his point. The timetable is yellowed with age, depicting the route of a weekly flight from Amsterdam to Batavia – present-day North Jakarta – with only a mere two dozen stops along the way. Its cover proudly announces "14,350 kilometers in 10 to 12 days," this conquest of space and time illustrated by a graphic of the Westerkerk towering high above a thatched hut nestled in the shade of coconut palms.

As we meander between the Prinsengracht and the Singelgracht, I try to focus my attention on what is immediately in front of me, and, of course, to photograph it before it recedes behind me again. I am leery of the proposition that what we now seek through travel is our own modernity. If anything, isn't touring supposed to be a respite from the mundane routinization of modern life? My eye moves from one narrowly elongated centuries-old canal house to the next, the hoist beams of their gabled rooftops reaching out above us to the waterway beyond, their windows populated by ceramic curios in blue and white, curtain lace, and in one instance a cadre of exotically ornate wooden puppets. The effect is quaint, like stepping back in time, which I reluctantly begin to acknowledge would necessarily suggest that, in relation to the concrete everyday reality I am touring, I myself must therefore be visiting from somewhere forward in time.

Figure 5.2 Dissonant imagery (photo: Steven Flusty).

More improbably still, the imagery of my companion's timetable seems to be somehow proliferating in ever more peculiar forms along our path. It begins innocently enough, a postcard on an outdoor rack depicting the Westerkerk rising adjacent the Prinsengracht's banks, but upon closer examination this Prinsengracht proves to be thickly lined with coconut palms, flocks of parrots and pink flamingos, while tanned swimmers cavort with wildly leaping cetaceans in the canal's water. And as we proceed, similarly dissonant imagery appears wherever we look. Stamped tin novelty placards, greetings cards, and posters combining mechanical conveyances with wild animals, savage people, and even mythological beasts. I purchase them as we go, harvesting souvenirs on the fly, and finally pause at a brown-bar's canalside terrace for a break, a beer, and a less frenzied assessment of my acquisitions.

The very first one confirms and compounds my suspicions. A vintage advertisement for Royal Dutch Airlines, it depicts a twin-propeller-driven airplane, no doubt the high technology of its day, aloft above a massive seventeenth-century sailing ship at sea, accompanied by the slogan "The flying Dutchman, FICTION becomes FACT." The juxtaposition of the antiquated and then-modern vessels in use suggests a process of progressive evolution somehow inherent to travel technology itself, a hereditary lineage of machines whereby travel makes even itself modern. And this evolution, we are instructed, is a marvelous and perhaps even miraculous thing, whereby the mythical becomes the material. At the same time, though, something feels ominously amiss. The legendary flying Dutchman, after all, is a skipper – christened Hendrik van der Decken in most versions of the tale – who sets out from home for the colonies but, in mid-journey, wrathfully refuses to submit to insurmountable headwinds. For this stubborn pride, he is condemned to sail forever at top speed, only to remain trapped perpetually in place between home and destination, never to make landfall or even headway, plying the seas until Judgment Day. An odd mascot for an airline, and indeed I recall my long-ago hesitancy to enroll in KLM's old "Flying Dutchman" frequent-flyer program for fear that it might curse me with insurmountable departure delays or, perhaps, being imprisoned forever in some transit lounge. So the celebratory advertisement seems to have inadvertently subverted itself. Or perhaps, conversely, it is on to something, although I am not yet certain what.

This theme of contrasting modern technology above with antitheses below proves a constant in my new cache, albeit with distinct typological variations. Two old Air France advertisements, for instance, depict a god's-eye view of propeller-studded passenger liners high above an "Extreme Orient" – stylized blank landmasses from which sprout the upturned eaves of toy pagodas. Here too the modern realizes the mythological, as in one situating the airplane in the tail of a soaring phoenix. And perhaps there is some unintended ambivalence here as well, given that the life cycle of the phoenix entails bursting into all-consuming flame. But the principal depiction is one of sleek, silvered mobility gliding swiftly over the tans and jewel-tones of immobile edifices rooted timelessly in the exotic place below.

Four additional advertisements – one each for Air France, Air Afrique, Sabena, and Pan Am – invert the perspective with ground-level views, looking skyward at modernity in flight. In one of these, it is a trio of elephants grazing obliviously below. My companion harrumphs irritably at this. In another, it is west Africans staring up in astonishment, with what is evidently intended to be a shaman (although I suspect the illustrator would have been thinking something more akin to "witch doctor") raising his arms toward the plane as though welcoming a deity. In the third, there again are those same raised arms of welcoming supplication, although here they belong to a lone Bedouin beside his camel in the desert sands. And finally, Pan Am shows us a hulking passenger liner cruising above a palm-lined tropical lagoon while, in the foreground, a reclining woman in a floral *kikepa* and *lei* welcomes the arrival with a more odalisque greeting. So it is not just edifices immobilized in exotic places but their inhabitants as well. The antithesis of the aircraft aloft is no longer yesteryear's technology, but peoples depicted as living still in yesteryear, and the year before that, perhaps reaching backward through time immemorial.

Of course, those aircraft are no less inhabited than the landscapes above which they soar, as another advertisement for Air Afrique illustrates. In this one, a passenger reclines luxuriantly in a wicker chair, gazing out the window at the palms and plantation houses arrayed beneath him. His overview of this landscape is twofold, the view out the window augmented by the map of his aerial route across Africa in his hand. While he can see all below him, we can see no more of him than the pinkness of his chin and hands. His wide-brimmed pith helmet, coordinated to match his white bush jacket, conceal his face completely.

The story told collectively by my new stash of souvenirs is revelatory. It delineates a genealogy of the modern constructed by Europeans in continually accelerating conveyances situated at ever greater heights above the past. And above others perpetually mired in that past who are, at most, able to traverse it only at the speed of a camel's trot. Another route to modernity seems to be revealing itself here, but I am thrown off-course by a trumpet of alarm sounding from across the table. My companion stares aghast at the tinplate printed with the pith-helmeted passenger, snatches it up with his trunk, and hurls it into the canal. "Wicked hunter," he cryptically utters a few moments later, seemingly by way of embarrassed apology.

A final pair of stamped tin placards stand out in that, unlike the other images, they place the traveler and the local in direct contact. One bears a sepia-toned illustration for the steamship company Rotterdam Lloyd's bimonthly service between Amsterdam and Batavia. It depicts a single-funneled steamship looming over a twig-roofed sampan in the background, while in the foreground a Javanese woman kneels over a basket of fruit at the feet of a binocular-wielding European woman in tailored white traveling clothes. This self-lionizing encounter with supplicant exoticness is reinforced on the second plaque, depicting a phalanx of mustachioed men in forage caps bicycling out of a palm forest while a gaggle of bare-footed Javanese villagers look on from the side-lines. When I had grabbed this particular item, I had thought it was some sort of antique advertisement for bicycles, or perhaps even for an early organizer of bicycle tours, and in a way it was the latter. A closer inspection reveals the cyclists to be dressed in blue uniforms, with rifles slung over their shoulders, and the accompanying text an offer of five to thirteen guilders per week for service in the Dutch Indies Legion. These cycling tourists are occupiers.

My shopping binge, it seems, has amassed a compendium of tourists making themselves modern, and tourism making the modern, by means of manufacturing contrasts. In this instance, though, modernity is attained not by contrast with "classical antiquity" but with "living tradition." This contrast is enabled by developments in logistical technology that afford tourists opportunities to sightsee others they can position within hierarchical degrees of putative barbarity, or even savagery, and to proclaim themselves civilized by comparison.

This ordinal social positioning, then, depends upon mobile geographic positioning – the itineraries that relate airlines to destinations, for instance. As depicted by my souvenir reproductions, these would include Pan Am to the South Pacific, Air France to Indochina, Sabena to sub-Saharan Africa, and of course KLM to Java. Each flag carrier to its own territorial possession, expediting administration of, and extraction from, the colonies. And tourism alike, for these are routes that clear the way for leisure travel, routes to

Figure 5.3 No longer so quaint (photo: Steven Flusty).

modernity that over time intersected and entangled to weave the network of airways we travel across today. This is certainly a thing we miss, and even prefer to miss, in our travels: the awareness of their imbrications with colonial dispossession. And if this realization is what I was missing, I am already beginning to miss missing it.

But once I have recognized this has been missing, the more pervasively it presents itself, the harder it is to miss, and the less our own touristic culpability is plausibly deniable. I lift my beer for another draught, and now notice the label: a seventeenth-century Dutch sailing ship, over the brand name "Batavia," and the additional note "produced by PT Delta Djakarta TBK Bekasi, Indonesia." We set off again along the waterways, past canal houses that are no longer so quaint. Now they have become donjons for the plundered wealth of distant shores. Even the charming puppet collection in the lace-curtained window resolves into a chain-gang of acacia-wood deities and heroes abducted from *wayang golek* puppet shows some 14,350 kilometers away.

Eventually, we find ourselves drawn to the sheer mass of the Bushuis Library (open Monday through Friday 9am until 6pm; entry is free of charge), a brick building in the Dutch Renaissance style, large enough to fill a city block entire. We are pulled through its courtyard, beneath a Baroque lintel inscribed with an interlocked "VOC," into what at first glance is an unassuming meeting room. A long table and a score of modest velvet-upholstered chairs cluster at one end, the white walls and exposed beam ceiling ornamented only with a gilt-garlanded and marbled fireplace set amid a handful of framed pictures: a map or two of Asia, and paintings depicting Couchyn (now Cochin) on the Malabar coast, Canton, and between the two the fortress of Batavia – all sites of Dutch merchant settlement. And, despite the unpretentiousness of the setting, what I had been missing overwhelms me in this room that once sat at the very center of it all, the boardroom of the United East India Company. The intimate and immediate place from whence routes were determined, sailors hired and dispatched (from the very courtyard through which we ourselves have just passed), native populations decimated, and ruling dynasties unseated half a world away, and everything from porcelain to pepper – and puppets – drawn the many thousands of miles back again.

Somewhere along our travels, seeing the world and experiencing its civilizations became stealing the world while excoriating its civilizations. Is it that travel is power, the power to *be* the modern, extracted from those one encounters along the way for distillation into the new, the next, and the latest? Is this where tourism begins, and its infrastructure originates? If so, might this give some clue as to why the term "tourist" is frequently used as an obloquy?

Dining, or Eat, prey, loathe

"Self-loathing is not particularly becoming in a tourist," my elephantine friend cautions me, "nor do I share in it. While I cannot for the life of me clearly recollect what initiated my own travel," an assertion I find astonishing given my companion's uncanny capacity to remember absolutely everything else, "I certainly recall both its pleasures and its efficacy in readying me for my . . . ahem . . . crowning achievement. But if you are so committed to your convictions, far be it from me to blacken your soul further with any more of this!" he adds wryly, placing another square of estate-grown single-origin chocolate into his mouth and savoring it dramatically.

We are exploring a cluster of chocolate shops (open daily 9am until 10pm; entry is free of charge but the chocolate most definitely is not) just south of the Grand Place, methodically journeying from Valrhona to Leonidas to Godiva and back again, simultaneously taking our taste buds on tour from Madagascar to Ecuador, with layovers in the Ivory Coast and Dominican Republic. Yet throughout it I keep thinking not "chocolate" but "chocoltl," and its violent expropriation by a typically high-spirited tour group of Spanish souvenir-hunters during their Mexican Riviera cruise's shore excursion nearly five centuries ago. My companion thinks my misgivings an unwarranted

Figure 5.4 Perfect summations of modernity (photo: Steven Flusty).

stretch, showily savoring another bite while exaggeratedly declaiming, "No, not a hint of blood, just the unadulterated flavor of fine Belgian chocolate. But if you can show otherwise, then lead on, Ferguson." Noting the jesting reference, I take up the challenge.

It is not far to the Cinquantenaire (open Tuesday through Saturday from 10am until 5pm; entry fee 5 euros), a pleasant monument-studded formal park that at the close of the nineteenth century was the site of a major national exhibition. The exhibition's central venue remains to this day. Its two wings of exhibit halls embrace us expansively, terminating on either end with façades that strike me as perfect summations of modernity's genealogy – classical stone temples of Doric stone columns rising from rusticated stone bases, topped with barrel vaults of industrial iron and glass, ornamented with ironwork crowns, shields, and bemedaled sashes. The two wings are centrally conjoined by the triplicate gaping portals of a towering triumphal arch surmounted by verdigris muses, angels blowing gilt trumpets, and a militant quadriga. The arch's coffered underside is embossed repeatedly with King Leopold II's mono-grammatic crowned double-L, the adjacent façades emblazoned with murals featuring militantly stylized soldiers on the march in steel helmets and greatcoats, while goddesses and mere mortal women look on in varied states of undress.

"Kings will be kings," my companion muses sympathetically, to which I respond, "That they will, Ferguson," and request his travel copy of Mark Twain. With some surprise, he reaches into his trunk and produces a volume of the collected works. As I expected, *Innocents Abroad* is particularly well worn, but I page through until I find *King Leopold's Soliloquy*, Twain's scathing critique of Leopold's rule over his personal private colony in the Congo, where (to paraphrase page eight of the second, 1905 edition) all the riches of the land were his – his solely – and gathered for him by the men, the women and the little children under compulsion of lash and bullet, fire, starvation, mutilation, and the halter. How that gathering was encouraged is made plain in accompanying photographs and etchings of men, women, and children each relieved of a hand or foot by Leopold's colonial agents. The volume even includes what could be an alternate design for the Cinquantenaire, more accurately reflective of its funding: forty 35-mile-long radial boulevards, each lined with 400,000 headless skeletons chained together, converging upon a 450-foot-tall pyramid of human skulls crowned at its apex with the taxidermied corpse of Leopold II himself, machete and manacles in hand. My case, however, is only half made.

A little further on, we arrive at the Royal Museum for Central Africa, previously known as the Museum of the Congo, and before that the Palace of the Colonies (although Palace of the Colony would have been more technically correct), an eighteenth-century French *palais* built towards the end of the nineteenth century, contemporaneously with the Cinquantenaire. We enter past a larger-than-life-size statue of a bull elephant ridden by three naked, spear-toting African hunters, eliciting from my companion a disdainful utterance of: "Not damned likely." The entrance rotunda displays gilded allegorical statues of evidently European missionaries, saints and women-at-arms providing succor and protection to African women and children. Beyond this are the exhibition rooms, featuring ritual and everyday artifacts along with taxidermied animals, all taken from the Congo Free State, and innumerable stone-engraved rolls of honor and busts celebrating the explorers and officers who took from the Congo Free State. And one room concentrates entirely upon colonial industry, describing in detail the Free State's production of rubber, cotton, tobacco, coffee, and, most significantly for my purposes, cocoa.

Unsurprisingly, the usual is missing from the exhibits, just as we all prefer to miss it. There is no mention of Congolese being compelled to plant, harvest and surrender cocoa, of the failure to do so in prescribed quantities costing them quite literally arms and legs, of how this provided a model of conduct for combatants throughout the region to this day, nor of how it is precisely

Figure 5.5 Larger than life, not damned likely (photo: Steven Flusty).

the heritage and continued practice of such violent expropriation that affords us our own leisure, leisure travel included. But I expect my case is made nonetheless. My companion's attention, however, is too riveted elsewhere to notice. He anxiously grasps at his tusks, and I follow his aghast stare to discover that ivory, too, was one of the colony's major exports. I turn him away, only to find us confronted by a television displaying a degraded black-and-white movie of Africans delivering their bundles of cotton, or perhaps coffee, or even cacao – the quality of the video is too poor to be certain – to a colonial agent for weighing and payment, again with no indication of the penalty for underproduction. What is clear is that the colonial agent is clad in a white bush jacket and matching pith helmet.

Somehow, my companion avoids shattering any of the museum's contents or fixtures in his panicked stampede out the nearest rear exit. I find him in the museum's back garden, his horrified gaze transfixed by a fountain decorated with Leopold II's bust, three legless Congolese warriors, and the decapitated head of a bull elephant.

Shopping, or Babaric splendors

My companion remains irritable and agitated, constantly craning his massive head as though expecting to find a pith-helmeted nemesis emerging from every

Figure 5.6 The wrong mode (photo: Steven Flusty).

shadow. I wonder what trauma might provoke this paranoia, and whether he perceives a pith helmet atop my head as well. I myself do not see any pith helmets donned in our vicinity but, then again, perhaps my perceptions are as flawed as those incapable of seeing elephants immediately before them. "You Americans never see the world's wickedness, too busy seeing yourselves and expecting the best," my companion vents. "Narcissistic optimists, thinking every voyage is one of self-discovery, everywhere you go a mirror to uncover your shining inner light. Pfah! Does it ever occur to you that mirrors can reveal things you would not care to see?" Far from disagreeing, I want to admit that, seen in relation to its past, all tourism is beginning to look to me like dark tourism. But my elephant friend needs cheering, and I know how to do it. Palaces always make him feel more at home.

Fortunately, we have at least two to choose from. Entering the eldest, we pass through a high, pointed-arch gateway thickly emblazoned with arabesques of flowing golden script across black stone panels, and enter the grounds of Topkapı Palace (open 9am until 7pm, Wednesdays through Mondays; entry fee 20 Turkish lira, plus an additional 15 for the harem). Wide greenswards punctuated by cypress trees and gurgling fountains alternate with labyrinths of deep colonnades, broadly projecting eaves, and pavilions tiled in ornate patterns of blue, white, and gold. The interiors are similarly ornamented, frequently lined with low divans, and stocked with artifacts sufficiently elaborate to be like miniaturized concentrates of the pavilions themselves. Bejeweled thrones and daggers, delicately damascened blades, even an imperial wardrobe displaying richly embroidered silken robes.

I move from one kaftan to the next, admiring a pattern of blood-red tiger stripes and leopard spots on one, silvered peacock feathers and warding eyes on another, but am brought up short upon encountering another unlike the rest. It is in midnight blue velvet, almost black, embroidered down the front and at hem and sleeves with wide bands of intertwined leafy vines in gold thread. And I am certain I have seen something very much like it already, worn by an English nobleman in Zoffany's painting of the Uffizi. Admittedly, here it is not a fitted waistcoat but a flowing kaftan. Still, the resemblance is uncanny. It is labeled merely as a robe in an antique style and dated to the second quarter of the nineteenth century, succeeding Zoffany by roughly half a century.

In a nearby room, I encounter a deluge of this gold embroidery upon midnight blue velvet. It is a portrait gallery, lined with depictions of Ottoman sultans more or less in chronological order of rule. Viewed one to the next it is impossible to ignore the transformation that occurs in the early nineteenth century, somewhere between Mustafa IV and Abdülmecid I. Voluminous robes and massive turbans give way abruptly and entirely to dark blue jackets, gold embroidered plackets and collars, shoulder boards, the glittering breast stars of imperial orders, and the simple fez.

I express my surprise at the sudden appearance of this seeming uniform to my companion, but evidently it strikes him as so commonplace that he scarcely noted it at all. "Court uniforms, embroidered coattees – the newest, the next, the latest thing. All the rage once King George IV put them on all his courtiers. No point to being à la mode," he muses, "if it is the wrong mode. The wrong fine clothes, the wrong handsome hat, and you are merely barbarous, decadent, or both. Fezzes, though," he winces, *"de gustibus non disputandum est.* And at least it is an improvement on those outré turbans."

Rummaging about his trunk, he removes an album of what he chucklingly terms "family photographs," and flips through it. On its very first page is a wizened and bespectacled bull elephant, resplendent in a dark blue jacket embroidered at placket and sleeves in gold and a matching, plumed cocked hat. "My closest adviser," he tells me. The next page is a photograph of a bronze-complexioned man with curly black hair and muttonchops, his dark jacket spangled with a shoulder sash, lanyards, epaulets, and an octet of breast stars, its collar and cuffs embroidered with gold fern and taro leaves. A cocked hat with plumes rests on a pedestal by his side. "King David Kalākaua of Hawaii, diplomat, legal scholar, and ardent ukuleleist." A few pages further along, a double-page spread. To the left, an elderly Asian man in yet another dark, gilt-embroidered jacket, albeit worn over a sarong. "King Mongkut, Rama IV of Siam, and for more formal portraits he did prefer knee-breeches. His son Chulalongkorn – Rama V – was more consistent," the elephant says. He points to the picture on the right of a mustached Asian man in an embroidered, bemedaled jacket and plumed pith helmet. I notice my companion retains his composure at this last, and he in turn notices my noticing. "Sometimes you must look like a hunter to evade a hunter," he mutters, although whether he is referring to Rama V or to the contents of the entire album I am uncertain.

Exiting back the way we came, I now find myself hunting for what could be termed "imported Baroque," and notice details I had originally overlooked. Harem chambers sporting Delft tiles and crystal chandeliers; ceiling coffers painted with *trompe l'œil* bucolic scenery; stone medallions carved with a coat of arms featuring the sultan's calligraphic *tughra* monogram in a sunburst and crescent over an encyclopedic array of swords, spears, revolvers, cannons, military medals, and battle flags, with a cornucopia, a scale, and a pair of books thrown in for good measure. A sunglasses-clad Janissary sets aside his walkie-talkie and briefly explains that the *tughra* itself was the true imperial coat of arms, but needed some radical augmentation in the late nineteenth century for the other European powers to make heads or tails of it. Evidently, donning the right coat and hat are necessary but not sufficient. Even then, something is missing still – there is more to the modern than just what is on one's head and chest.

"Of course there is more," the elephant tuts. "Don't forget what is beneath your backside!" He turns to a sepia-toned picture of himself in the album, a much younger elephant in a flawless derby and crisp new suit, posed in an ornate straight-backed chair atop an expensive carpet. I page through the album again and see what is pointedly, even strategically missing: there is not a divan in sight. In every picture, the pointedly modern monarchs are seated on finely carved and upholstered formal chairs atop fine carpets, or standing beside more-or-less empire-style side tables that seem to have been the universally preferred receptacle for cocked hats. Even the monarchs' poses are similar, the slightly casual lean to one side, left hand resting lightly on sword hilt, and familiar as well. They are roughly the same postures as Messrs Crowle, Milles and Page-Turner.

I flippantly ask my companion if his "family" was much for traveling, and elicit an enthusiastic, "Of course, commonly preceded by these very photographs as a kind of calling card." My companion proceeds to a list of tour itineraries: Sultan Abdülaziz, the first sultan to leave the empire in peacetime, from Istanbul to Paris and London, where he received the Order of the Garter from Queen Victoria herself; King David Kalākaua, the first monarch to circumnavigate the globe, from Honolulu to San Francisco, and from there back due west around the world by sail and rail, meeting with his fellow kings, queens, popes, kaisers, emperors, and presidents en route; and Rama V, the

Royal Buddha and Great Beloved King, who ventured throughout southeast Asia in his youth and, upon ascension to the throne, traveled from Bangkok to London. Every stop along his way was simultaneously a major media event and a coming-out party. And while his father never made the trip, Rama IV did beat a path by sending a Grand Embassy – although Grand Package Tour seems an equally apt descriptor – of two dozen nobles and attendants to Queen Victoria's court, to spend an entire winter shivering in their tropical silks.

"And speaking of Grand Embassies, let us not forget the one Peter the Great accompanied incognito from Muscovy a century and a half earlier," the elephant concludes. "Although I suspect the true identity of a 6-foot 4-inch Russian autocrat calling himself Piotr Mikhaelovich was never much in doubt." Recollecting my history, it occurs to me that Peter the Great also returned to update his court by compelling them to shave off their beards, over a century and a quarter before George IV would update his own by compelling them to don embroidered coattees.

So is it a universal predilection of elites everywhere, touring to make themselves modern and to make the modern along the way? And to display their modernity, and the authority it confers, for approbation both abroad and back home? Perhaps, but there are evident differences as well. For the Grand Tourist, modernity seems to be acquired through contrast with the antiquated and the exotic. But for what might be termed the Grand Ambassadors, it seems to derive more from breaking with ascriptions of antiquatedness and exoticness so as to erase the contrast, from basking (and being seen to bask) not in the rusticated ruins of ancient glories but in the precision-engineered and well-oiled machinery of their contemporary analogs.

But does not that latter entail conforming to the self-serving normative standards of another, and to spoiling one's own uniqueness in the bargain? Do entire traditions go missing in the process? These misgivings arise as we make our way through the chambers of Topkapı's mid-nineteenth-century replacement, Dolmabahçe Palace (open 9am to 4pm Tuesday, Wednesday and Friday through Sunday; entry fee 15 Turkish lira, plus an additional 10 for the harem and a further 7 for photography), a relentless pastiche of broken pediments and Corinthian columns, spiraled corbels and stone garlands, polychrome marble inlays and gold-leaf accents. The cavernous interiors are precisely the sorts of parlors in which my companion's family photos must have been posed. The rooms are liberally studded with Louis XIV furniture and fittings, the world's largest Bohemian crystal chandelier, and a central staircase with banister spindles made entirely of Baccarat crystal. Were it not for the occasional inlaid *tughra* or gold-leafed globe surmounted by a crescent moon and star, it would be difficult to determine just where in the world this palace is located. Even the mosques adjacent are concatenations of the neo-classical, the Baroque and the Romanesque, marbled walls and *trompe l'œil* ceilings all outlined in gilt.

I find my companion in a nearby gift shop, sampling the tracks on a compact disc of Ottoman classical music from the period. Like the palace itself,

Figure 5.7 The latest thing (photo: Steven Flusty).

they are European compositions with nods to local idioms – sonatas, fugues, marches, and even a "national" hymn composed with a surfeit of minor chords by palace conductors Giuseppe Donizetti and Callisto Guatelli, both Italian imports, both created pashas by their respective sultans. I sample a disc or two myself, Janissary *mehter* marches remixed as electronica, before expressing my misgivings. My companion bristles. "Remind me not to take you to Peterhof, let alone the Bang Pa In summer palace – you'd hate what Chulalongkorn did with it. Or to 'Iolani Palace; you would no doubt find Kalākaua's all-night après-surf poker parties dreadfully inauthentic. Why should you be the only ones 'spoiled' by broad streets, automobiles and buses, and fine clothes? You are somehow entitled to cocoa and ivory, but Peter the Great has no business with tooth-keys and wrung staffs? King Mongkut's emissaries must not be allowed to contaminate themselves with whatever . . ." – and here he fumbles in his trunk for an antique intelligence report to

Her Majesty from the Siamese Grand Embassy's British handler – "they can . . . 'thoroughly understand without the assistance of Europeans to work them' . . . 'portable machines of all kinds' . . . 'scientific instruments' . . . 'chronometers' . . . and 'arms from the best makers and of the latest improvements'?"

The act of sifting quotations calms him somewhat, but still he adds, "You may carry home anything we produce that strikes your fancy, but we are forbidden to return the favor. Would you prefer me a naked little calf riding his mother's back forever? And while we are on it," he concludes, taking on a tone of understated mischievousness, "just how are those twenty-first-century electro-mehter remixes you have there any less tainted than their nineteenth-century Italo-Ottoman precursors?"

Accommodations, or My plenipotentiaries went to the continent and all I got was this lousy embroidered coattee

By what criteria is authenticity to be measured, I wonder, as we arrive at the doorstep of Sirkeci railway station. Which is more authentic: the imported Baroquerie of Dolmahbaçe, envisioned and realized by a loyal Ottoman-Armenian subject of Sultan Abdülmecid the First, or this very station, its Orientalist archways and Byzantine crenellations designed and financed by imported German agents of Kaiser Wilhelm II? And by what standard, and by whom, can such innovation be declared innocuous and even inherent to the authenticity of one civilization, but poisonous to that of another?

My companion and I board the Orient Express, yet another Belgian venture from the time of King Leopold II, and take our seats. All the while the elephant regales me with how a modern, civilized demeanor is not merely a matter of putting the right thing on your head, your chest, or beneath your backside, not just the parlor in which they are arrayed, nor the palace that contains them all. "The sovereign traverses the broad streets no less than his subjects, his modernization is his people's." He invokes another long list of examples, proceeding from the same railway we are riding to those King Rama V stretched out from his numerous new German- and Italian-built palaces in Bangkok; expanding to include streetlight electrification and hydroelectric dams; reaching a crescendo with the construction from scratch of Saint Petersburg and "my own lakeside capital – admirable, practical and convenient – to each elephant his own house, employment from the Bureau of Industry, and entertainment at the Amusement Hall! If one is going to undertake a Grand Embassy, after all, one may as well make the most of it."

The elephant reopens his family album toward the back, to a pair of group photos. One, labeled "First European Mission, 1862" (followed by a handwritten notation "first in centuries, anyway"), shows a party of nine well-dressed gentleman immediately prior to their departure for an official state tour through Europe. They are resplendent in *kimono* and *hakama*, topknots carefully coifed and *katana* at hand. The other, labeled "Iwakura Mission,

1871," depicts a second party of gentlemen to tour Europe, along with much of the rest of the world, in an official state capacity. Of the party's five members, all but one are clad in fine black suit jackets and trousers, their hair parted to one side and slicked back, and all five carry top hats.

I am taken aback at such vivid evidence of a learning curve so steeply surmounted, to which my companion responds I am in good company – that of the Iwakura Mission itself. "They were just as startled to discover that their hosts were themselves *parvenus*, although, being gentlemen, the ambassadors kept the observation to themselves." Or, more correctly, kept the observation to the pages of their diarist Kunitake Kumio's illustrated travel journal, a copy of which the elephant withdraws from his trunk to recite:

> Most of the countries in Europe shine with the light of civilization and abound in wealth and power. Their trade is prosperous, their technology is superior, and they greatly enjoy the pleasures and comforts of life. When one observes such conditions, one is apt to think these countries have always been like this, but this is not the case – the wealth and prosperity one sees now in Europe dates to an appreciable degree from the period after 1800. It has taken scarcely forty years to produce such conditions . . . How different the Europe of today is from the Europe of forty years ago can be imagined easily. There were no trains running on the land; there were no steamships operating on the water. There was no transmission of news by telegraph.

"And there is some cause to suspect this mission knew it was not alone in the realization, either," the elephant adds, paging through the journal to Kunitake's carefully drafted illustration of the *Bronze Horseman*, the equestrian statue of Peter the Great at the center of St Petersburg.

My companion then returns to his family album, and points at what I take to be an example of the learning curve's summit attained – another pair of photographs. To the left, an intensely civilized young adolescent in a capacious *raifuku* robe and tied-on skullcap with a crest nearly half as tall as the wearer, seated on a low dais atop a tatami-covered floor. And to the right, the same refined adolescent, but now sporting the beginnings of a beard and moustache, dressed in a jacket encrusted with golden embroidery at the sleeves, hem, chest and collar (although, in all fairness, the embroidered patterns are in relatively Asiatic motifs). At his elbow is a side table bearing a cocked hat with plumes, and he sits in an overstuffed armchair with a thickly patterned carpet beneath. "The Emperor Meiji," the elephant announces, "before, after. No point to being civilized if it is the wrong civilization."

We disembark at the old Shimbashi railway station, designed in the neoclassical style by an American and built at the last quarter of the eighteenth century by otherwise underemployed samurai on the brink of seeing their caste abolished entirely. Our arrival is no mean feat given that the station's tracks would run directly into the sheer glass face of an adjacent high-rise,

Figure 5.8 A learning curve so steeply surmounted (photo: Steven Flusty).

were it not for the fact that while there is an arrival platform there are no tracks whatsoever. But then again, the Orient Express only ever traveled due westward from Sirkeci to Paris Gare de l'Est in the first place, rendering the Orient itself no less a mobile absurdity.

As is to be expected at any railway station, this one has a rack of postcards to facilitate tourists' reportage of their travels to audiences back home. And, as might be expected of any reconstructed late nineteenth-century railway station, were such a station to be expected at all, these postcards replicate imagery of the period. Being less expensive in bulk, I purchase a packet assortment of them, and flip through them as we walk.

Together, the postcards constitute something of a pictorial inventory of the souvenirs returned home by the missions. The topmost card in the stack depicts the station itself, with a topknotted engineer piloting his train toward awaiting passengers in kimonos. The next shows a quartet of affluent women by a lakeside, dressed in a mixture of kimonos and Victorian ruffled gowns, a woman in the foreground working a hand-powered sewing machine. A third displays a unique hybrid image – a graphic of a hand-cranked telephone atop a side table cloaked in a richly embroidered cloth, adjacent an inset roundel ornamented with cherry blossoms containing an early black-and-white photograph of switchboard operators lined up at their stations. Another portrays a cadre of imperial dignitaries in a profusion of dark jackets, gold-filigreed chests and cuffs, epaulettes, cocked hats, and tall straight-backed chairs. There is also a profusion of moustaches, luxuriant beards, and one truly prodigious pair of muttonchops – no mean accomplishment for a gentleman of Japan – and I cannot help but wonder which are more modern, Peter the Great's forcibly clean-shaven courtiers or the Emperor Meiji's conscientiously bewhiskered counterparts.

The packet includes a card bearing a portrait of the imperial family itself, the bearded Emperor Meiji in dark coat with gold embroidery and braid, his Empress in damasked Victorian gown, with the heir apparent between them in miniaturized black naval livery with brass buttons. They sit in upholstered gold-framed armchairs with a potted bouquet of chrysanthemums between them, a golden screen depicting pine forests and Mount Fuji as the background. In its poses and furnishings, this imperial portrait strikes me as familiar. It seems a variant on one in my companion's album, of Rama V in his parlor with his Regent Queen and their five royal offspring, some of whom are also dressed in scaled-down sailor suits. That latter portrait, however, is most telling for what it does not depict of the family: Rama V's three other queens, 20 consorts, and 72 additional children. This portrait, conversely, is more telling in the technique it uses to depict the Emperor Meiji's family – by means of the centuries-old technology of polychrome woodblock printing. In fact, all these picture postcards of newly imported mechanical, sartorial, and administrative technologies are produced with the same, centuries-old technique, perhaps as a means of rendering their subjects more apprehensible for the audiences of their time.

At the same time, the audience's apprehension is depicted as well. A postcard accredited on its back to Utagawa Yoshifuji and entitled *Imported and Japanese Goods: Comic Picture of a Playful Contest of Utensils* envisions two armies locked in combat. One consists of kimono-clad paper lanterns, palanquins, bamboo-ribbed *wagasa* parasols, and stacks of woodblock prints. The other is comprised of kerosene lamps, rickshaws and steam locomotive engines, umbrellas and framed photographs, all dressed in trousers and red military jackets. The latter army appears to be winning.

My companion and I pause at what may as well be the site of this battle, a bridge over the Nihonbashi river that constitutes the center of the country entire – the zero-mile from which all distances are measured. This bridge's wide, graceful wooden arch can be found in numerous Hiroshige woodblock prints. It cannot, however, be found spanning the river. In its place, we come upon a low neoclassical double archway of stone, rusticated at its base, supporting a flat asphalt causeway with wide balustered side rails. Along these rails are patinated cast metal lamp stanchions conjoined to sculptures of guardian lions and dragons realized in muscularly realist Victorian idiom – or, perhaps more correctly, muscularly realist Wilhelmine, as the architect, Tsumaki Yorinaka, had brought this latest style back with him from his extended stay in Berlin. And, more completely, Wilhelmine except insofar as the lamps are translations of paper lanterns into metal, the dragons seemingly crossbred between European and East Asian stock, and the lions more akin to what one might find in front of a Chinese temple than at the foot of Nelson's Column.

Figure 5.9 The form of modernity accomplished (photo: Steven Flusty).

The triumph of this early twentieth-century viaduct over its early seven-teenth-century predecessor, however, is now itself contested. The bridge and its protective beasts now lurk in shadows cast perpetually by the stripped-down concrete columns and steel beams of a multi-lane overhead expressway. This more recent battle between the new and the newer for the country's zero-mile, however, has not extirpated the original wooden bridge entirely. Its replica can be visited inside a museum some distance removed.

I ponder, with sharpening sardonicism, whether this is the form of modern-ity accomplished. The elephant hands me a stack of brittle newspaper clip-pings in silent answer, along with his collected Mark Twain opened toward the middle of *Innocents Abroad*. The top clipping is a yellowed copy of October 23, 1872's *Newcastle Daily Chronicle*, reporting disappointment with the Iwakura Mission: "[t]he gentlemen were attired in ordinary morning costume and except for their complexion and the oriental cast of their features, they could scarcely be distinguished from their English companions." But attached to this clipping is an editorial cartoon from a German newspaper of the period, captioned, "The Japanese, true to their mission of becoming familiar with European culture, get themselves an inside view in Essen," and depicting caricatures of grinning, topknotted samurai sticking their heads into the breech of a giant Krupp field cannon.

Nor, apparently, were the Japanese the only ones trapped between the rock of disappointment and the hard place of disparagement. Another clipping, from June 19, 1867's *Le Figaro*, acknowledges popular regrets over Sultan Abdulaziz's European enough appearance, despite his red fez: "without doubt, not as marvelous as we believed . . ." Conversely, upon seeing the Sultan in Paris during his own Grand Tour, Twain describes him as "stout, dark, black bearded, black eyed, stupid, unprepossessing," and reported:

> Napoleon III, the representative of the highest modern civilization, progress and refinement; Abdul Aziz, the representative of a people by nature and training filthy, brutish, ignorant, unprogressive, superstitious – and a government whose Three Graces are Tyranny, Rapacity, Blood. Here in brilliant Paris, under this majestic Arch of Triumph, the first century greets the nineteenth!

Critics of colonialism, it seems, are not immune to thinking like colonizers themselves. "Typically American, that. As Niebuhr said, frantically avoiding recognition of one's own imperial impulses, all the while turning Kalākaua into a figurehead and using the price tag for his modern palace as an excuse to do it!" the elephant snorts. "Gone too far, while somehow never having gone far enough, in the end you are still just a pachyderm in a suit, no matter how artfully embroidered your court uniforms, how opulent your palace, how many bureaus of industry and amusement halls you build, or how grandly you tour the crowned heads of Europe. And when they have emptied your treasury for palaces and railroads, or they have discovered you have more bauxite than you are willing to surrender . . ." he trails off bitterly.

In case of emergency, or Am I modern enough for you?

Noting that I was distracted by the prospect that no amount of mileage accrued or souvenirs amassed can ever acquire respect, my companion repeats the question: "I said, 'Am I modern enough for you *now*?'" I turn to find him posed like a hunter atop his trophy, a massive and wicked-looking assemblage of tubes and gears held crosswise in mock heroism across his torso. How he fits an entire Gatling gun into his trunk is beyond me, let alone how he has managed to carry it about unhindered. But of course, why would an elephant in the room suddenly attract notice merely because that room happens to contain a security checkpoint? "Upward of 400 rounds per minute at the mere turn of a handle can persuade even the most reluctant host to welcome you with open – or at least raised – arms. But relax," he chuckles, "nobody besides you egalitarian Americans would be so ungentlemanly as to use one of these on anything but lesser peoples. Not before the Great War, at any rate. A good reason to never be lesser, no? Sometimes it is not enough to look the wicked hunter. Sometimes, you must become the hunter."

"Remember," he adds, "those Siamese ambassadors went shopping for more than just chronometers and scientific instruments." Returning to his family album, the elephant turns toward the back and indicates paired photographs of rakish soldiers. One wears a fez and prodigious beard, but also a thickly bemedaled Imperial German dress uniform. The other is clean-shaven and young, a Blue Max and Iron Cross prominent upon his *feldgrau* dress tunic, all topped off by a tall lamb's-wool *kalpak* hat emblazoned with a dramatically winged crescent moon. My companion makes the usual introductions, "Gifts from the Kaiser: the Baron Bodo-Borries von Ditfurth, sent to reorganize the Ottoman army; Hauptmann Hans-Joachim Buddecke, an aerial ace to the Sultan." Apparently, the sultans ultimately took to complementing their Italian composers with Prussian tacticians.

Flipping through the last of my postcard pack, it becomes apparent the sultans weren't alone in this. The final card of the set, accredited as Toyohara Chikanobu's *Observance by His Imperial Majesty of the Military Maneuvers of Combined Army and Navy Forces*, displays a woodblock print of exactly that. The Emperor Meiji stands high atop a hill, field glasses in hand, while below him soldiers and sailors clad in uniforms crossbred from French and American acquisitions practice Prussian battlefield tactics with ordnance brought from Britain. "There is, in theory, no evident reason that colonies should be reserved for the itineraries of Grand Tourists, or that extracts of colonies should power the West alone with the new, the next and the latest," my companion observes. In response, I note that theory is not practice, nor necessarily lived experience. "You have heard of the Treaty of Sèvres, have you not? Or of Hiroshima and Nagasaki?" my companion mutters in agreement, disconsolately.

Unsurprisingly enough, my companion now suggests that another palace tour will do us good. The degree to which this predilection has begun manifesting as an obsession at times of unsettlement concerns me. I suppose, however, that it is to be expected in my present company, given what it is that a deposed monarch must be most inclined to miss. So I accompany him to the Yuanmingyuan, the Old Summer Palace (open daily 7am to 5.30pm winter, 7am to 7pm summer; entry fee 10 yuan, plus an additional 15 yuan for the concessions). The Yuanmingyuan is less a palace, though, than a deluxe resort for rulers. It is an 860-acre conurbation of palaces, pavilions, undulating colonnades, and shaded courtyards clustered around innumerable artificial lakes and canals. My elephantine fellow traveler waxes poetic about the site:

> Build a dream with marble, jade, bronze and porcelain, frame it with cedar wood, cover it with precious stones, drape it with silk, make it here a

Figure 5.10 A good reason to never be lesser (photo: Steven Flusty).

sanctuary, there a harem, elsewhere a citadel, put gods there, and monsters, varnish it, enamel it, gild it, paint it, have architects who are poets build the thousand and one dreams of the thousand and one nights, add gardens, basins, gushing water and foam, swans, ibises, peacocks, suppose in a word a sort of dazzling cavern of human fantasy with the face of a temple and palace.

He does then admit, with some slight embarrassment, that the description is not his own. Withdrawing a tied sheaf of correspondence from his trunk, he rifles through it until he finds the excerpt, in a letter signed by no less a personage than Victor Hugo himself.

Regrettably, though, we seem to have missed the place, and done so by a century and a half. Instead, we find ourselves standing amid a vast plain of ruins strewn out in every direction as far as the eye can see. Empty foundations and vast piles of broken stone, punctuated intermittently by a crumbling moon bridge or partially effaced and toppled frieze, rim the banks of reedy lakes and eroded canals. Further along, we encounter a dense cluster of shattered monoliths like the wreckage of a catastrophic collision between Chinese and Enlightenment-era European manor houses traveling at high speeds, a gigantic graveyard of Chinoiserie. Baroque pilasters and rococo columns with complexly faceted moldings jut up into the bare air in support of nothing; ornately medallioned porticoes topped by curlicued pediments grant entry to emptiness; long dry fountain basins in the form of massive stone seashells project from desiccated rubble.

As the occasional carved stone interpretive placard makes clear, in Chinese and intermittently idiosyncratic English, this is what one gets when one hesitates to receive repayment in opium from a well-armed debtor. My companion expands upon the story, paging through his sheaf of correspondence to locate a letter home from Charles Gordon (late of Khartoum), one of the 3,500 soldiers who spent a full two days looting the place and another two setting much of it ablaze:

> We . . . went out, and, after pillaging it, burned the whole place, destroying in a Vandal-like manner most valuable property which would not be replaced for four millions. We got upwards of £48 a-piece prize money before we went out here; and although I have not as much as many, I have done well . . . [y]ou can scarcely imagine the beauty and magnificence of the places we burnt. It made one's heart sore to burn them; in fact, these palaces were so large, and we were so pressed for time, that we could not plunder them carefully. Quantities of gold ornaments were burnt, considered as brass. It was wretchedly demoralising work for an army. Everybody was wild for plunder.

I am reminded of a T-shirt I encountered at a pirate supply store on a previous excursion, emblazoned with the slogan "pillage before plunder, what a blunder; plunder before pillage, mission fulfillage." In the same spirit, I find myself ruefully redacting the platitudes of ethical tourism into more historically accurate formulations along the lines of "take only valuables, leave only ruins."

Delving deeper into my companion's letters, we discover these sentiments stirred in us by the surrounding devastation are not ours alone. Victor Hugo's own narration of the palace continues:

> One day two bandits entered the Summer Palace. One plundered, the other burned . . . [t]he devastation of the Summer Palace was accomplished by the two victors acting jointly. Mixed up in all this is the name of Elgin, which inevitably calls to mind the Parthenon. What was done to the Parthenon was done to the Summer Palace, more thoroughly and better, so that nothing of it should be left. All the treasures of all our cathedrals put together could not equal this formidable and splendid museum of the Orient. It contained not only masterpieces of art, but masses of jewelry. What a great exploit, what a windfall! One of the two victors filled his pockets; when the other saw this he filled his coffers. And back they came to Europe, arm in arm, laughing away. Such is the story of the two bandits . . . [b]efore history, one of the two bandits will be called France; the other will be called England.

Little wonder, then, that my companion and I find little by way of souvenirs. And as per Hugo's commentary, ultimate responsibility for this must rest with Lord James Bruce, the Eighth Earl Elgin, successor to his father, Lord Thomas Bruce. Lord Thomas, one-time ambassador to Ottoman Sultan Selim III, is best known for his thorough tour of the Athenian Acropolis, pieces of which returned with him as souvenirs he had gotten for a steal. His son's latter scorched-earth shopping spree was similarly prodigious, yielding bejeweled and silken giftware for friends in high places back home: gigantic cloisonné vases, gilded jade scepters, richly embroidered imperial robes, elaborately carved thrones, even the first Pekingese ever to be seen in Europe – christened by Queen Victoria with the jocularly shameless name of Looty. Additional to this transfer of imperial regalia, bronze fountainheads wrought in the form of zodiacal animals seem to have been particularly hot commodities, periodically turning up to this day for auction at Sotheby's and Christie's. Postcards excepted, reproductions of these decapitated fountainheads in materials ranging from cold cast resin to verdigris bronze are the only keepsakes we find on offer in the interpretive center's gift shop, available in various sizes and assorted price levels. Perusing the shelves with my companion, I give silent thanks that the animals of the Chinese zodiac do not include the elephant.

Simultaneously perusing the elephant's collection of correspondence, however, we are startled to discover that the disgust we share with Victor Hugo over this triumphalist thievery is reiterated by none other than Lord James himself. We pore over dispatch after dispatch, and in each the Eighth Earl Elgin excoriates his empire's machinations, his fellow subjects for demanding them, his soldiers for executing them, and himself for commanding them. As to the Yuanmingyuan specifically, he writes:

> I have just returned from the Summer Palace. It is really a fine thing, like an English park – numberless buildings with handsome rooms, and filled with Chinese curios, and handsome clocks, bronzes, &c. But, alas! Such a scene of desolation . . . There was not a room I saw in which half the things had not been taken away or broken in pieces . . . Plundering and devastating a place like this is bad enough, but what is much worse is the waste and breakage . . . War is a hateful business. The more one sees of it, the more one detests it.

Yet, to use an Orwellian turn of phrase, he went ahead and did it just the same.

If the Yuangmingyuan embodies the tourist's ultimate nightmare, destinations entirely despoiled through ravenous acquisition, then Lord James in turn is both the prototype and the paradigm of the tourist's self-loathing: the cultural tourists revulsed by the impact of their own presence upon the peoples they tour, the ecotourists lamenting their own swelling carbon footprints midflight. Indeed, all of us who in our travels strain to think of others as tourists but not ourselves, to revile their presence alongside our own and to avoid their "tourist spaces."

All the while, we continue in our travels to avail ourselves of the acquisitions some very indelicate souvenir hunters brought back in their baggage, and the routes they established to make good their escapes. Tourism, then, is inextricably rooted in conquest, concealed beneath the traveling cloak of the new, the next, the latest; in short, the modern. Vaguely suspecting this, and repressing those suspicions, we nurture our contempt for the tourist who somehow is not, must not be, could not be us. It is the assiduously ignored elephant we prefer to miss that nonetheless accompanies us in our travels.

But it is just one in a herd of like absences, a grand ambassador for the willfully unseen pachyderm at the heart of the modern that manifests simultaneously within our own hearts as well. It is our inner king of all elephants, forever afraid of being a pretender to the throne of the now and constantly in danger of being dethroned by change. We are naggingly colonized by the constant absence of we don't and can't know what, an insatiable hunger for whatever is newer and next, and so does not even exist, yet to be had, conjoined to the absence of what we continually surrender to attain, what is always just beyond reach. So something is missing, and, of course, we can never apprehend what it is.

We have become the fiction of the Flying Dutchman made fact, all members of Van der Decken's crew. Whether we signed on voluntarily or found ourselves impressed by force, we are all sailors for a global imperium of discontent. The pasts we could never have experienced, irrevocably rendered and mummified as picturesque ruins and tourist attractions, the future fated to become the claustrophobic and inadequate present at every moment of arrival, our souvenirs melting into air within our grasp. Our perpetual travel in pursuit of what will always necessarily be missing dooms us to sail with all our might merely to remain in place, to stave off being blown backward and left behind, as the tantalizingly new becomes the intolerable now.

If we can make no headway, why undertake the voyage to begin with? True, there are some exquisite souvenirs to be netted along the way. But over the course of my own travels, I believe my companion has provided me with the answer we have been missing. Just as travel gives rise to the modern, the modern's travels give rise time and again to an indisputable object lesson: those who do not subject themselves to modernity's relentless and shifting winds are forever in danger of finding themselves subject to those who have.

Thus are we all (all who can afford the luxury, anyway) pulling geographics, as the recovering addicts call it, and playing Elgin all the while. Traveling from place to place in acquisitive search of idyllic paradises, unspoiled cultures, shining paragons of luxuriant technological utopias, or vicarious encounters with brutal mass mortalities past or ongoing. We transit through endless chains of departure lounges and arrival gates, passenger cabins and hotel lobbies, never to find rest until we have attained the irremediably unattainable.

Sources

Being over a year and a half in constant transit, with no fixed address or regular workplace, often alone in settings where one can barely speak the language (if at all), can do strange things to a person. The traveler starts to recollect widely separated locales as immediately adjacent, for instance, and have dialogues with traveling companions others cannot see. This latter can persist even on those occasions when accompanied by the best of plainly visible and entirely human companions, among whose numbers I thankfully acknowledge Heather Childs, Engin Isin, Timmo Kaupi, Claudio Minca, Shusaku Morinaga, Pauliina Raento, Evelyn Ruppert, Yangyang Sun, and, most especially, Pauline Chia-Wen Yu. Gratitude is also due to the Rikkyo Amusement Research Centre for encouraging, in multiple senses, many of these travels, and to Carol Borden for continually reviewing their reportage.

The effects of incessant dislocation can be even more pronounced when the dislocatee is an academic, deprived of the usual library sources in a familiar language even were there time to remain sedentary and read. The productive output of such circumstances can be exceedingly peculiar and highly idiosyncratic in its source material. In this instance, I have relied upon a range of sources not conventional to academic research in writing this traveler's tale, a good deal of it drawn from the collected contents and interpretive augmentation of multiple museums and venues *in situ*. The most significant of these include the University of California at Santa Barbara's University Art Museum (and especially their 2009 exhibition "Holiday: Nineteenth-Century Travel Photography and Popular Tourism"), the University of Amsterdam's Bushuis Library, the Royal Museum of Central Africa in Tervuren, the Topkapı Palace Museum, Dolmabahçe Palace, the Harbiye Military Museum, the Old Shimbashi Station Museum, the Edo-Tokyo Museum, the Tokyo National Museum, the interpretive centers of the Yuanmingyuan, the British Museum, and the Victoria and Albert Museum.

None of the above supplant textual sources entirely, as listed below by section.

Sightseeing

Black, J. (2003) *Italy and the Grand Tour*. New Haven, CT: Yale University Press.
Blaut, J.M. (1993) *The Colonizer's Model of the World: Geographical Diffusionism and Eurocentric History*. New York, London: Guilford Press.
Braudel, F. (1984) *Civilization and Capitalism: 15th–18th Century: Perspective of the World* (Volume III). New York: Harper & Row.

Getting there

Davies, J.Q. (2005) "Melodramatic possessions: The Flying Dutchman, South Africa, and the imperial stage, ca. 1830." *The Opera Quarterly* 21(3), pp. 496–514.

Dining

Clarence-Smith, W.G. (2000) *Cocoa and Chocolate, 1765–1914*. New York, London: Routledge.
Lindqvist, S. (1997) *Exterminate All the Brutes: One Man's Odyssey into the Heart of Darkness and the Origins of European Genocide*. New York: The New Press.
Twain, M. (1906) *King Leopold's Soliloquy*. Boston, MA: The P.R. Warren Company.

Shopping

Aracı, E. (2001) *European Music at the Ottoman Court*. Istanbul: Kalan Müzik.
Aracı, E. (2005) *Istanbul to London*. Istanbul: Kalan Müzik.
Çelik, Z. (1993) *The Remaking of Istanbul: Portrait of an Ottoman City in the Nineteenth Century*. Berkeley, CA: University of California Press.
Chief Clerk of the Ceremonial Department (ed.) (multiple years) *Dress and Insignia Worn at His Majesty's Court*. London: Harrison & Sons.
Kuykendal, J.S. (1967) *Hawaiian Kingdom 1874–1893: The Kalakaua Dynastism*. Honolulu, HI: University of Hawai'i Press.
Manich Jumsai, M.L. (2000) *King Mongkut and the British*. Bangkok: Chalermnit.
Peleggi, M. (2002) *Lords of Things: The Fashioning of the Siamese Monarchy's Modern Image*. Honolulu, HI: University of Hawai'i Press.

Accommodations

Jansen, M.B. (2000) *The Making of Modern Japan*. Cambridge, MA: The Belknap Press of Harvard University Press.
Kunitake, K. (2002) *The Iwakura Embassy, 1871–1873: A True Account of the Ambassador Extraordinary and Plenipotentiary's Journal of Observation Through the United States of America and Europe*. Princeton, NJ: Princeton University Press.
Niebuhr, R. (2008) *The Irony of American History*. Chicago, IL: University of Chicago Press.
Yonemura, A. (1990) *Yokohama: Prints from Nineteenth-Century Japan*. Washington, DC: Arthur M. Sackler Gallery, Smithsonian Institution Press.

Emergency use

Çelik, Z. (1992) *Displaying the Orient: Architecture of Islam at Nineteenth-Century World's Fairs*. Berkeley, CA: University of California Press.
Hugo, V. (1861) Personal correspondence in response to Captain Butler.
Twain, M. (1869) *The Innocents Abroad, or the New Pilgrim's Progress*. Hartford, CT: American Publishing Company.
Walrond, T. (ed.) (1872) *Letters and Journals of James, Eighth Earl of Elgin, Governor of Jamaica, Governor-General of Canada, Envoy to China, Viceroy of India*. London: John Murray.
Wong, Y. (2000) *A Paradise Lost: The Imperial Garden Yuanming Yuan*. Honolulu, HI: University of Hawai'i Press.

My companion

de Brunhoff, J. (1937) *Babar the King*. New York: Random House.

de Brunhoff, J. (1937) *The Story of Babar*. New York: Random House.

Dorfman, A. (1996) "Of elephants and ducks." *The Empire's Old Clothes: What the Lone Ranger, Babar, and Other Innocent Heroes Do to Our Minds*. New York: Penguin, pp. 17–66.

6 Touring modernities

Disordered tourism in China

Tim Oakes

The disordered tourist

On a warm summer evening in 2005, four middle-aged men drove a silver Volkswagen Jetta out of their city and into the Chinese countryside. Two of them were managers in foreign joint-venture factories. Another worked for the government. One was a middle-school administrator. Before they left town, they called their wives and told them they would be tied up all evening with meetings. They carried cigarettes in their shirt pockets, and rolls of pink hundred yuan bills. A couple bottles of distilled liquor rode between two of the men in the back seat. They drove to the village of White Crane Fort not far from the city. It nestled alongside a stream with lush rice fields on one side and wooded hills on the other – a beautiful and serene setting. The sound of a thousand croaking frogs greeted them as they opened their doors and stepped out of the car into the damp coolness of the rural evening. White Crane Fort was a tourist site for urban white-collars like them. A banner hung over the entrance, proclaiming it a state-level cultural heritage preservation site.

They'd all been there before. They had, on their previous visit, been marched through the village by pretty young guides toting megaphones and wearing long gowns. They'd seen the ornate courtyard homes, where village customs and rituals were performed for them. But on White Crane Fort's outskirts, where some new houses and shops had recently been built to cater to the developing tourist trade, they'd run into an older woman who cackled at one of them: "Come back tonight! Then you can have some real fun!" She opened the curtain to her room to reveal a gleaming new electronic mah-jong table. "It's brand new!" she continued, sensing their interest. "My son just bought it. Cost him ten thousand yuan. Come tonight and try it out! We have karaoke too!" As they peered in, she murmured her final enticement: "And we have other entertainments you might want."

So, a few months later, they went back. That evening, they gambled at the 10,000 yuan mah-jong table. And when they were done at the table, some girls came in and sang karaoke with them before leading them off to their rooms to perform those "other entertainments" for the men.

This was not the way villagers were supposed to perform for tourists. And it was not the way tourists were supposed to consume rural culture. Sex and gambling were neither the cultural heritage that the state sought to preserve, nor the products that discerning middle-class consumers were supposed to desire. Not that we should find their behavior surprising. Tourism shares with prostitution a certain cachet: the "world's oldest profession" and the "world's largest industry" simply cannot avoid each other. Tourism was supposed to have turned the village into a model for a new kind of enterprise, one that performed a healthy culture and a patriotic heritage. It was supposed to have turned the men into new kinds of citizens who consumed only quality products and experiences, and who regulated and disciplined themselves as was proper, given the new freedoms – a car, time off, wads of cash – afforded by their well-salaried professional lives. But there they were: drunk, out of cash, sprawled in bed with a girl who was herself probably also from the city and who, like the men, viewed rural tourism as a very different kind of opportunity from that advanced by its promoters. None of it worked out the way it was supposed to.

For the Chinese state, the tourist was an exemplary consumer, a model citizen for a nation seeking to reconstitute its modernization project around quality consumption rather than mass production (Figure 6.1). The village was an exemplary site for a new project of ordering, in which cultural performance and heritage preservation would compel villagers to improve themselves and govern their lives with discipline and civility, all the while ensuring the preservation of the national patrimony. Obviously, however, there were some bugs in the system. Villagers and tourists alike seemed to have lost the script.

Or had they? While the state had not planned this sort of behavior, things *did* work out exactly the way the men and the sex workers had intended. Tourism *had* introduced the village to a new form of enterprise, a new mode of ordering in which new kinds of performance skills, competences, appearances, and qualifications were valued. Soile Veijola and Eeva Jokinen (2008) have called this new kind of work "hostessing," and have argued that the proliferation of tourist modes of ordering are moving us toward a "hostessing society," where work and leisure increasingly resemble each other and where we can no longer order our daily lives around the distinction between the two. The gendered terminology is purposeful. It is not so much the mobility of the sex tourist that characterizes this tourist ordering, but the hostessing skills that have been honed by villager and sex worker alike to part the sex tourist from his cash.

Tourism, as many observers have found, is as much about deviating from the script as following it. For every account of the "masses" and "herds" of tourists bumbling along wherever they're led, and of tourism as a form of social control (Crick 1989; Morgan and Pritchard 1998; Dann 2003; Gregory 2007), there's another confirming the spontaneity, irony, and unintended discovery of the tourist experience (Horne 1992; Neumann 1992; Harrell 1995). Missives about tourists chained to their guidebooks (Turner and Ash 1976) are matched

Figure 6.1 Exemplary consumers, model citizens (photo: Tim Oakes, Vientiane, Laos, January 2009).

with fantastic tales of falling off the map, stumbling onto paradise, and discovering self and other anew (Seth 1987; Iyer 1988). While I do not mean to equate village sex tourism with the unexpected sublimity that travel is capable of producing, I do mean to emphasize that we cannot count on the tourist or the hostess to follow any script. If this is true, it also follows that we cannot put much faith in understanding "the tourist" or "the tourism experience" as some kind of distinct experience with particular hard-wired qualities. And yet, again and again, tourists and tourism are viewed in this way. The Chinese state has come to view tourism as a very particular kind of *quality*, with attributes that can be isolated and – more importantly – cultivated. Tourism in China is a vast ordering project, and as such depends on a stable set of qualities seen to be inherent in "the tourist." But those qualities were not on display in White Crane Fort that night.

And what are we to make of that? The expected answer from the state would be to claim that there is always some deviance from the norm, that with time and effort, the herd will be culled of its impurities. That answer betrays a stubborn faith in the tourist as a particular kind of person. While he may be a bumbling buffoon, an "ugly American" toting a camera and wearing Bermuda shorts, he is still a very *modern* type of person, one whose success in life is measured by his mobility, his global networking that over-rides ties and commitments to any locale (Bauman 1998). For the Chinese state, the tourist is the symbol of a new kind of modern subject, the kind China's citizens should aspire to become. As Chio (2010: 14) has recently noted, "ideas of national character and individual development are bound up in the moral discourses of tourism and travel as a means of governance" in China. While Veijola and Jokinen's "hostessing society" reminds us of the narrowness and, indeed, masculinist nature of equating the modern subject with the mobile tourist, there was something else going on besides "deviance" when those four men visited White Crane Fort that night. There was another kind of ordering project at work, something Foucault (2008) would have called "counter-conduct."

If we are to understand that ordering project as something other than deviance, it seems we need to first work against the temptation to view "the tourist" as a particular kind of (modern) subject. With the rise of tourism in China and other increasingly affluent Asian societies, this is more important – and in some ways more difficult – than ever. For with the rise of Asian tourism, it seems faith in "the tourist" as a modern subject position has been given a whole new lease of life. This is partly because the "Asian tourist" is increasingly called upon – by Asian states, intellectuals, and elites – to represent an alternative Asian modernity. As such, he represents an opportunity to challenge the Eurocentrism of our understandings of the modern experience. And what could be wrong with that? And yet, the tourist's role in this kind of postcolonial politics is not very distant from her role as an exemplary state subject. In that role, she is merely a reified category of difference.

In this chapter, I explore tourism in China as a project of ordering with unforeseen consequences. I argue that ordering projects rely on a kind of "expert knowledge" of tourists and tourism, one that conceives of tourism as a set of categorized behaviors and motivations. This, in turn, implies a view of tourism studies itself as an expanding field of faith in the "ever finer subdivisions and more elaborate typologies" that might "eventually form a classificatory grid in which tourism could be defined and regulated", and, I would add, ultimately understood (Franklin and Crang 2001: 6). In China, this expert knowledge of tourism is part of a much larger set of ordering projects seeking to shape modern Chinese society in very particular ways. But these projects are unable to account for the kind of actions displayed by the men and the villagers in any other way than to find them deviant from the norm. This is because they conceive of tourism and tourists as stable categories of knowledge rather than social processes. This chapter, then, explores both a critique of tourism as a modernist project of ordering and a reconsidering of tourism as a social process. I hope to suggest a productive alternative to our search for the Chinese tourist and what his "difference" might tell us about (alternative) Asian modernity and, indeed, our Eurocentric assumptions about tourism in general.

In search of the Chinese tourist

At a 2006 conference on Asian tourism organized by the Asia Research Institute in Singapore, presenters were encouraged to consider the ways that "tourism of Asian origin required an analysis which moves beyond certain themes – such as the traditional and modern, hegemony and resistance, local and global – which have often dominated the tourism literature in recent years." In the resulting 2009 volume *Asia on Tour*, the editors argued that Asia should "become the context from which theory emerges" rather than the location in which a presumably "universal" theory is tested (Winter *et al.* 2009: 8). It is certainly true that the rise of Asian tourism requires that we acknowledge the provincial nature of *all* theory, and move beyond the Eurocentric assumptions underlying much theory in tourism studies. And *Asia on Tour* is an important and well-received step in that direction. But I remain skeptical of the implications that continue to be drawn from the rise of Asian tourism. For, despite the volume's explicit call to avoid "falling into the trap of essentializing Asia as somewhere or something that is fundamentally 'different'" (Winter *et al.* 2009: 8), those implications seem nevertheless to be primarily drawn in terms of recognizing the "difference" that the Asian tourist makes, and what she might tell us about (alternative) modernity. While *Asia on Tour* seeks to dispense with "the Asian tourist" as an outdated conceptual category of "analytical stasis and intransigence" (Winter *et al.* 2009: 6), we remain burdened by an analytical legacy of assuming, from the beginning, that Asian tourists must somehow be different from Western tourists. That legacy is the ordering project of modernity itself.

After writing *Tourism and Modernity in China* (Oakes 1998), I had intended to begin exploring the ways the different modernities experienced by Western and Chinese tourists articulated with their varying conceptions of authenticity when they visited ethnic villages in rural China. In hindsight, it was a naive project. I was convinced that there was something to learn from middle-class Chinese tourists who came from a completely different cultural milieu from those observed by, say, MacCannell (1999 [1976]) in France, or Neumann (1992) in Arizona. My assumption, it turns out, was not unusual. Nyiri (2006) has argued that domestic tourism in China hues closely to a state-sanctioned model of canonical sites; his Chinese tourist explores not the Westerner's geography of personal experience and encounter, but rather consumes a highly regulated and controlled space of state-defined national identity.

On the other hand, Vasantkumar (2009) has found that Chinese tourists are embracing a Western adventure model as they increasingly pursue independent travel and embrace a cosmopolitan post-national identity. It seems that putting "the Chinese tourist" in conversation with our theoretical understandings and sorting out what difference he makes has been an irresistible move for many of us. Thus, Lim (2009) argues that Chinese backpackers have "Chinese characteristics;" Yeh (2009) argues that Taiwanese youth seek to travel in order to perform their (alternative) modernity; and Arlt (2006: 106–108) has claimed that Chinese tourists display group-oriented behavior and emphasize group harmony during their travels. Their weak conception of the individual, he continues, encourages a desire to go where everyone else goes, to do the typical thing and buy the typical souvenirs. Whether such "herd-like" behavior distinguishes, even rhetorically, Chinese from Western tourists is doubtful, but the observation that Asian and Western tourists might occasionally behave in similar ways has yet to put a serious dent in our collective premise that the "Asian tourist" somehow carries in her luggage the permanent imprint of cultural difference.

To be clear, I do not seek to dismiss the actual fact of cultural differentiation (though I do question the analytical ordering of such difference into neatly defined, if ambiguous, categories such as "Asian" or "Chinese" or "Western"). Nor would I deny the significant and important interventions of the contributors to *Asia on Tour* in establishing a new, less Eurocentric, and more "provincial" theoretical agenda for tourism studies based on the actual practices of tourists "of Asian origin." I view this chapter as building on their work. And finally, I am certainly not the first to view the sociology of ordering as a productive analytic for tourism studies (see, for example, Featherstone 1995; Franklin and Crang 2001; Franklin 2008). But it seems that if we are to take Franklin's (2004: 2) advice and approach tourism with a "theoretical pluralism," then we need more accounts of the various social ordering projects for which tourism is called to serve, and of the many contexts within which the social processes of tourism emerge and generate different outcomes. I thus view "ordering" as a kind of anti-theory, for, while it offers a guide for a contextually specific interpretation of tourism in China, it deliberately eschews any stable (or even unstable) structure upon which general patterns might be understood. Before proceeding with that particular context (i.e. tourism development in China), then, I discuss modernity as ordering and tourism as a modern ordering project.

Modernity, ordering, and tourism

So, once more about modernity. We might begin with an image of modernity as a Renaissance- and Enlightenment-inspired faith in reason, rationality, and the scientific process of peeling away, gradually, the contingencies of life to reveal the hidden order of the universe. Science and reason would, in turn, give humans agency over their own history, and an electrifying if not sobering responsibility over their own fate. Some have called this image "first modernity" (Touraine 1995; Lash 1999). They then remind us that there is "another" modernity that thrives in the shadows of "first modernity," which presents an ever-present sense of doubt, irony, skepticism, and anxiety over the unintended consequences, the pathologies, of modern life (Berman 1982; Bauman 1991; Heller 1999). The inherent tension between these "two modernities" has been interpreted in many different ways, but few would deny that they are in various ways mutually constitutive. Modernity churns away toward a dream of ultimate order and purification, building along the way its chaotic Other, the dystopian nightmare that serves, more than anything, as incendiary fuel for yet further iterations of ordering. As Featherstone (1995) has pointed out, this view of modernity generating and seeking out disorder to fuel its ordering project recasts the Schumpeterian idea of "creative destruction" as a kind of non-teleological dialectic. Referring to the work of Bauman, Featherstone writes, "Modern consciousness is governed by the urge to extend outwards, to map and classify, which means it has to discover or reveal ever new layers of chaos beneath its constructed order to feed its Sisyphean restlessness" (Featherstone 1995: 148). This, in turn, produces "endless disruption and social disorganization," resulting in ever-unfinished ordering projects of all shapes and sizes.

Such a view of modernity can be productively applied to colonialism, as a kind of assemblage of ordering projects that continuously generates its own justification. Colonization, then, comes to be justified as a project that promises to bring order to a disordered world and, in the process of ordering, generates the very disorders that legitimize the colonial project (Mitchell 1988). We can extend this logic beyond colonialism as well, to notice that much of our expert knowledge of the social world plays the same game. For example, conceptions of culture that have been generated within the context of colonialism seem to suffer from the same circularity. Culture, here, becomes a code for explaining an assumed underlying order to people's behaviors, practices, and beliefs. Featherstone (1995: 150), then, wants to consider "the impulse to generate a culture of order through the colonization and domestication of the world defined as disorder." This impulse, however, seems to easily predate the modern era of European imperialism and colonialism, for it seems to inform European conceptions of Asia that date to ancient Greece. As Said (1978) has famously observed, Asia has long served as a central figure in the stories Europe has told about itself. And two of these stories have figured with particular prominence: Europe's secularism contrasted with Asian spirituality, and Europe's democracy contrasted with "Oriental despotism." Asia, here, signifies the disorder of illiberal rule, coupled with reason, trumped by a surfeit of spirituality. This has been a well-trodden European narrative recycled again and again by Herodotus, Aristotle, Montesquieu, Marx, Wittfogel, and George W. Bush, among many many others (see Oakes 2009).

Asia, then, exists as part of the binary epistemology of Euro-American modernity, and has thus always been crucial to the formation of modernity as a European idea. Chakrabarty (2000) has argued that modernity gains its power by assuming a telos of progress and development over time and across space toward the utopia of a well-ordered world. Time and space have been conceived in this ordering project as "History" and "Asia." As Fabian (1983) pointed out, Europe's Other has long been denied coevalness with Europe itself. Leading intellectuals of modernity – Herder, Hegel, John Stuart Mill, to name just three prominent examples – all denied Asia its own History, seeing it rather as existing in a timeless stasis outside of history until Europe's arrival to force the issue. Modernity was always "not yet" in Asia. And, as Kerr and Kuehn (2007: 1–2) have noted in their overview of Western travel writing on late-imperial China, the immense weight and palpability of Chinese antiquity encouraged visiting Westerners to think of themselves as "specialists in modernity."

So it shouldn't be surprising that one of our first theoretical impulses in making sense of the rise of Asian tourism, and more specifically Asian tourists who travel to Europe and North America, has been to frame the phenomenon in terms of Asia as a place outside (Euro-American) modernity, looking in. The Asian tourist is "seeking modernity." This, at least, has been the case concerning recent reporting on Chinese tourists. In a 2004 BBC report on a small group of Chinese tourist–chefs on a culinary tour of California, we are told that:

> They are just not interested in exploring American history and culture, and they don't want to see spectacular scenery, they've got plenty of that at home. What they do want is to see how America measures up to the American Dream. They're all familiar with the stereotype of the United States as the richest and most advanced nation in the world, its lifestyle as the holy grail of development. And they want to see it in all its brilliant modernity, to understand how far China has to go to catch up, and whether the struggle will be worth it.
>
> (Dunlop 2004)

Modernity is also on display for Nyiri's Chinese tourists. But on a tour of Europe, they betray some disappointment at how the sights measure up to the dream of modernity. One tourist tells him, "Western and Eastern views are different. In the East, the newer the better. Here the older the better . . . The modern part is a bit blander, but the historical is very strong." "I'm a bit disappointed," another adds, at the lack of skyscrapers in Berlin; the city seems "backward" compared with Shanghai, or even Hangzhou (Nyiri 2005). The point here is not to deny that many tourists from Asia make sense of their travels by calling on the narrative of competing modernities. Part of Nyiri's argument, indeed, is that this narrative is a state construction meant to order the tourist's experience in deliberate ways. More will be said about this ordering below. But modernity as an ordering narrative that tourists at times adopt and adapt as they reflect upon their experiences – or as their experiences are reflected upon by "experts" (scholars, journalists, industry planners) – is quite different from modernity as an agentive social force that *structures behavior* in certain ways, instilling in Asian tourists, for instance, a motivation to travel. The latter approach presents itself as an explanation for what becomes a *type* of behavior assumed to exist as part of the structuring elements of some abstractly construed "Asian society." The tourist then becomes a reified abstraction, a carrier for "culture" conceived as the expression of an underlying but hidden social order. Just as MacCannell's tourist searched for authenticity in response to the alienation of Euro-American modernity, the Asian tourist searches for modernity in response to her alienation *from* Euro-American modernity. In both cases, the tourist serves as a proxy for abstraction and bears little resemblance to any actual tourist.

If we consider, instead, the other approach suggested above – modernity as a *narrative of ordering* rather than a pathway leading to order – we might be better prepared to appreciate what tourists actually do when they travel, rather than what we would expect them to do given our abstract structuring of the world according to an assumed order of things. As a narrative of ordering, modernity becomes a story about the dream of order, and a dream project that is never complete, is inherently unpredictable, chaotic, precarious, and full of "partial accomplishments that may be overturned" (Law 1994: 2). "Many of us have learned to want to cleave to an order," Law writes. "This is a modernist dream." While the dream of utopian order might be viewed as a kind of aspirational or progressive project, it is a dream that has had devastating consequences for those, for example, who have been on the receiving end of imperialism, colonialism, development, and even the "democracy" bestowed by the United States on Asian states such as Iraq. "It seems to me that we have spawned a monster," Law writes. He continues:

> the hope or the expectation that everything might be pure; the expectation that if everything were pure then it would be better than it actually is; and we have concealed the reality that what is better for some is almost certainly worse for others; that what is better, simpler, purer, for a few rests precariously and uncertainly upon the work and, very often, the pain and misery of others.
>
> (Law 1994: 6–7)

This precariousness and uncertainty marks what Franklin (2008: 31) has referred to as the sociology of ordering's "ontology of unintended consequences, failure, unforeseen agency, and promiscuous enrollment." By this, Franklin means to highlight tourism's unpredictable qualities, and in particular the networking processes that insinuate tourism into other realms of social and cultural life.

As noted earlier, the concept of culture has been productively framed as an intellectual ordering project. This can be rendered in several ways, according to the various complex derivations of the term itself (see Williams, R. 1983: 88–92). As a "whole way of life," culture emerged within a context of colonialism as an expression of coherent, distinct and pure systems of behavior and belief extant prior to the contaminations of modern European contact. But as an expression of civilization, culture also conveys a normative ordering of the world, of keeping chaos at bay, of marking the boundaries between order and disorder. Of this latter expression, Featherstone (1995: 138) notes a tendency "to present culture at one pole of a stark Manichaean choice between order and chaos. Culture, then, is often presented as a necessary corrective normative regulation to underlying violence and selfish egoism."

In a similar vein, Tony Bennett has called culture a "reformer's science." Culture, Bennett writes,

> entails a hierarchical ordering of the relations between different com-
> ponents of the cultural field, one part of which is defined as a lack, an
> insufficiency, a problem, while the other is viewed as offering a means
> of overcoming that lack, meeting the insufficiency, resolving the problem.
>
> (Bennett 1998: 91)

Thus, one component of the cultural field is strategically mobilized in relation to another, in order to (for instance) improve the morals and manners of the working class, civilize the tribal savage through the institutions of church and colony, empower communities through development, promote cultural diversity through affirmative action, or eradicate the corrosive effects of capitalist individualism by mobilizing the virtues of working-class community (this latter example being Raymond Williams's project for cultural studies). Such strategic mobilizations of culture have the whiff of governmentality in them, since they aim to develop techniques of cultural self-management, self-inspection, and self-reform. Bennett's museums, thus, are regarded primarily as institutions of governance in their deployment as halls of self-cultivation, with culture less important for its presumably enlightening content than for its properties as a medium for ordering narratives.

As our sex tourists in the Chinese village remind us, however, it is fairly clear that museums, and heritage villages for that matter, probably fail just as often as they succeed in generating the intended product: a self-governing and governable subject. That doesn't stop planners, of course, from continuing to mobilize culture for instrumental purposes, but it does lead us to ask a different sort of question about culture. Rather than ask why deviance occurs, or why culture might devolve into incoherency and chaos, the crucial question to ask about culture is what explains those instances when things actually go according to plan. What constellations of social power have managed to come together when we find self-disciplined tourists, or tourists who indeed embody the roles that have been laid out for them. A similar kind of question about culture was asked by Duncan and Duncan (2004), who argue that any cultural analysis must begin with the premise of cultural mixing, hybridization, and other forms of "contamination." If that is the case, they ask, what explains those moments when culture actually coheres around bundles of meaning and signification? If culture is enrolled in projects of ordering, in other words, how are cultural unities produced out of complexity and conflict? How are unintended consequences actually avoided? What this does is reframe our view of social process, as one seeking to explain not disordered deviation from an assumed stable order, but fleeting moments of order that emerge from projects that continuously churn out new disorders.

It is crucial to recognize, in other words, not just the governmental instrumentality apparent in Bennett's view of culture (see, for example, Barnett 2001; Yúdice 2003), but more importantly not to lose sight of these instrumental ordering projects as what Foucault called "permanent provocations" with unintended consequences. Tania Li's (2007) study of Indonesian development as an assemblage of improvement projects churning out unforeseen results maintains such a focus on this precariousness of ordering. She points out that when experts rule, the empirical question of what actually happens remains open: what kinds of push-back result from expert knowledge and programs? What kinds of challenges cannot be contained by expert knowledge? In this sense, governmental ordering itself responds to political provocations generated by earlier orderings. Li asks, "what happens when those interventions become entangled with the processes they would regulate and improve?" (2007: 27). Nothing ever happens the way it is laid out in planners' schemes (cf. Mitchell 1988).

What happens when we look at tourism in this way, as an assemblage of ordering projects churning out "unintended consequences, failure, unforeseen agency, and promiscuous enrollment"? A productive start in this direction was offered by Rojek's *Decentering Leisure* (1995), which argued that leisure is a fundamental component of the advanced capitalist state's social ordering and regulation. Viewed as an ordering project, leisure cannot be separated into an autonomous realm of experience, distinct from work. Rather than treating leisure as something separate from society, where the individual has control of her "own time," it becomes necessary to appreciate leisure's central role of keeping society in good order, as necessary to the stability of the whole system. Classic definitions of leisure miss this. Dumazedier (cited in Rojek 1995: 38), for instance, defined leisure as "the time whose content is oriented towards self-fulfillment as an ultimate end. This time is granted to the individual by society, when he has complied with his occupational, family, socio-spiritual and sociopolitical obligations." Gramsci's theory of moral regulation offers some insight into the limitations of Dumazedier's definition, for if we view leisure as a mode of regulation, in which historically and geographically specific forms of conduct are made normal, then we can no longer view it as some kind of extra-social pursuit.

But moral regulation tends not to emphasize the extent to which people negotiate this process of normalization. Nor does it see social regulation as an unfinished process always churning out other ordering projects with their own unintended consequences, failures, and disorders. The actual experiences of leisure require us to look beyond the ordering projects of modernity themselves to appreciate those ordering projects as provocations to disorder. Bakhtin's view of the carnival articulates something of this perspective, seeing in it "both a utopian reaction against the norms of individualism associated with the growth of the market and a licensed release from the hierarchical order of 'high' culture" (Rojek 1995: 85). Early amusement parks displayed much of this "licensed release," with their bawdy sexuality and vulgar exuberance. While one might see places such as Coney Island or Blackpool as spaces of exception, where temporary and limited breakdowns of the moral order are permitted, they need also to be understood as the unintended products and failures of moral regulation. Early amusement parks have been called truly democratic spaces, where

> A changing sexual code of conduct gave men and women an opportunity to partake in gaiety along the beach and within the many rides and attractions that literally threw them together. As people were propelled into further proximity with one another, the idea emerged that the amusement park itself could be a harbinger of democratic ideals.
>
> (Lukas 2008: 41)

Referring to Coney Island, Edo McCullough claimed that, "Nowhere else in the United States will you see so many races mingle in a common purpose for a common good. Democracy meets here and has its first interview, skin to skin" (cited in Lukas 2008: 41).

Disordered leisure has in turn spawned all sorts of new ordering projects. Disneyland was Walt Disney's deliberate project to bring some middle-class order to the working-class chaos of places such as Coney Island (Marling 1997: 31). A century earlier, the Rational Recreation Movement in England responded to middle-class fears of moral decay with "campaigns to clean up the leisure activities of deserving workers and to instill in them habits of thrift, industry, and self-improvement" (Rojek 1995: 13). This included building art galleries for the working class, promotion of sport and exercise, parks, and promoting youth organizations. The culture and leisure industries were thus viewed as central to ordering, because people turned to them during their own "free time," the time when they felt themselves to be acting only for themselves and not for the good of society. While this recapitulates, somewhat, the Frankfurt School's critique of mass culture – in particular Kracauer's mass psychology of bewitchment as embodied by the dancing Tiller Girls – it recognizes that the moral regulation of the state and the dominant classes is never complete and always generates new disorders as consumers negotiate the conditions by which their lives are meant to be ordered. This is something for which Kracauer never made an analytical space.

Franklin (2008: 32) has called tourism "a rhyzomic assemblage of technologies, governmentalities, texts and 'travel objects' on multiple lines of flight." Keeping in mind that ordering projects are always multiple, and operating at a variety of scales, Franklin views tourism as networking across scale. It is a global process, transforming more and more places into tourist sites and becoming a central social force in everyday life, "a key cultural form of translation across the world," rather than an industry limited to marginal enclaves, destinations, resorts. But on smaller scales, tourism also orders individuals as touristic, travel-oriented, world-curious persons. In all of these there are multiple unforeseen outcomes in everyday life that spin far beyond anything we might recognize immediately as tourism. And yet tourism has increasingly become central not simply to our practices of mobility, but of consumption more generally, as well as our bodily comportments, aesthetic tastes, senses of style, and our outlooks on the world as a collection of visitable places (whether we actually visit them or not).

Law (1994) identifies four modes of ordering – enterprise, administration, vision, and vocation – all of which can be implicated in tourism. In discussing tourism and Chinese projects of ordering in the following section, however, I am particularly interested in how enterprise, as a mode of ordering, helps us understand both the intended and unintended outcomes of tourism development in China. Law's modes of ordering can be thought of as narratives, aspirations for the ideal models of order toward which subjects cleave. The narrative of enterprise is particularly relevant to tourism, for enterprise depends on *creating an impression* of organization. A successful enterprise gives one the sense that the organization is not only well ordered, but ordered exactly as it appears to the outsider. A successful enterprise can be trusted by the outsider, the potential consumer. Enterprise thus depends on maintaining "a profound epistemological dualism" between a front stage of earnest performances and a backstage propping up those performances. The gap between the appearance of order and the underlying messiness compels enterprise to place a premium on performances: "These re-present the organization to others . . . they help define the boundary relations between institutions" (Law 1994: 178).

Similarly, tourism sells places by managing the impressions that tourists have of those places and succeeds to the extent that tourists trust that what they're consuming is, in fact, what it seems to be. This means trusting that there is no gap behind the performance, that the place is really what it appears to be, when in fact it is not. Because of this, Law identifies a *moral* dimension to the dualism of enterprise:

> For what goes on frontstage is also a form of impression management, and it slides easily into dissimulation, or suspicion of dissimulation. So it is that in enterprise the syntax of performance gets divided from the syntax of reality, and the need to perform starts to erode the possibility of trust.
>
> (Law 1994: 176)

Tourism performs this epistemological dualism; it is the business of impression management. It insists on carving out a gap between performance and reality, representing the ordered narrative of the tourist's world to others, maintaining the boundary between an image and the construction of that image. And that boundary is particularly crucial for tourism as an ordering project.

For, as Law points out, our need "to cleave to a single order" is answered by the performance of *artificial* worlds. And yet the tourism enterprise is always set up to fail, for the gap behind the performance will always reveal itself in unexpected and unintended ways. While Law's approach envisions an erosion of trust resulting from the artificiality of performance and the "suspicion of dissimulation," there are many other ways in which the enterprise mode of ordering can fail to produce its intended outcomes.

Tourism and Chinese projects of ordering

> While the primal chaos had vanished, it survived as a permanent background condition to human existence. First, it formed a constant reservoir of infinite potentiality accessible to the sage who thereby obtained power to alter the spatially structured present. Second, it remained as a constant menace of universal dissolution and chaos should the principles that had forged order out of nondistinction ever be abandoned. This is the source of the specter of 'chaos' that has haunted the Chinese imagination for millennia.
>
> (Lewis 2006: 2)

Mark Edward Lewis reminds us that keeping chaos at bay was a project of Chinese statecraft and spirituality long before European modernity had anything to say about it. Protecting the space of the empire from the descent into chaos required constant ritual vigilance. Ritual practice "maintained order through imposing divisions." It separated men from women, elders from juniors, rulers from subjects, and civilized Chinese from barbarian others. Ritual practice thus constituted properly ordered social roles and group boundaries. Not only has ritual in Chinese tradition been conceived as an ordering project of particular urgency, but it would not be a stretch to also suggest that the dynamic cycles of imperial and regional history in China have led to the conviction that social order has always been an unfinished project in China. Keeping chaos at bay with ritual is best viewed, like all ordering projects, as a process.

After the "permanent revolution" of the Mao era, the Chinese state has returned to maintenance of "social order" as its primary measure of legitimacy, most clearly articulated in its call for a "harmonious society" of "socialist spiritual civilization." While Mao Zedong still gets credit for laying the foundation for a powerful, modern China, his rule is viewed as one that unleashed primal chaos and abandoned the principles of order that keep chaos at bay. Having recovered from the Cultural Revolution and initiated an era of unprecedented economic expansion, the state's strategy for achieving social order has hinged on maintaining that expansion at all costs, along with minimizing unemployment, social divisions, inequality, and other potential sources of instability and upheaval. Consumption plays a role in this strategy, and leisure time has become a major consumer product. Two-day weekends, forty-hour work weeks, annual "golden week" holidays for professionals, and a loosening of consumer credit have all been deliberate state policies to stimulate "leisure culture" and consumption among the "exemplary" middle classes. Tourism has become a "pillar industry" of regional development, and a major generator of revenue for most local governments.

The promotion of leisure culture, however, has helped spur a popular culture revival throughout China that has often threatened to destabilize the state's plans for maintaining social order. Thus, while China's glorious traditions and cultural heritage are now celebrated, this has also opened up a space for activities regarded as "backward" or "superstitious." It has become imperative for the state to introduce ordering projects that guide popular culture in "healthy" directions. In the words of Wang Mingming,

> Constant effort is still made by government agencies to prohibit popular ritual activities. Although the government has generally permitted popular worship of ancestors, the system of territorial temples, the deity cults, and festivals are still defined as "manifestations of superstition" (*mixin de biaoxian*). Annually, around popular festival times, official campaigns against them are organized. These ideological and political actions are often not effective, but they have continued to convey the message that the cultural front (*wenhua zhendi*) should still be "fought for" (*zhengduo*) in the phase of reform.
>
> (Wang Mingming 2006: 3)

Wang examines the maritime city of Quanzhou, in Fujian, as an illustrative site of this struggle. Quanzhou has a long history as conduit of trade and diplomatic relations, particularly between China and Iran, and this has resulted in the establishment in the city of a great variety of religious and cultural traditions from throughout Eurasia. Quanzhou's rich tradition of religious festivals was viewed as a liability by local officials seeking to promote a modern, secular, and orderly image of the city. Their solution was to brand the city as a living "museum of world religions," and transform traditional festivals into commercial touristic arts fairs. Turning popular religion over to the exemplary consumption of tourism, it was believed, would dampen local superstitious zeal. As Wang Di (2003) has documented for early twentieth-century Chengdu, this is a municipal ordering strategy that has been around for a while. In Quanzhou, the traditional Lantern Festival became the "Grand Concert of Southern Music," the Universal Salvation Festival became the "Operatic Performances Festival," and the Mid-Autumn Festival became the "International Puppet Festival." As the Cultural Bureau director admitted, "our choosing such dates is based upon the consideration that there is a return of superstitious activities in these years." He added that "many Quanzhou people love festivity; so by way of creating festive events, we can reduce the opportunity for their superstitious practices – this is more effective than forcing them to stop their old habits" (Wang Mingming 2006: 13).

Locals tended to see these government orderings as heavy-handed and wasteful. One complained that "The government's festivals only entertain foreigners and overseas Chinese and have nothing to do with our lives. We ordinary people are still quite poor. However, the officials are not concerned with this. They are more concerned with the face of the state" (Wang Mingming 2006: 13–14). The city's attempts to intervene in local popular culture were matched by massive urban renewal projects, earning the municipal Party Chairman the popular title of "Doctor of Architectural Destruction" (*pohuai jianzhu boshi*). Many old houses were torn down and replaced with pretentious "traditionalized" concrete structures. This also gave the state the opportunity to destroy many of the city's neighborhood *pujing* temples, regarded as focal points of superstitious popular religious practices (see Abramson 2009).

However, the results were in many ways opposite those intended by the project's planners. Residents were adept at negotiating deals with developers to ensure that new, better-looking temples would be built later, after the state's gaze had turned away. Indeed, the state's secular ordering projects may have yielded even more *pujing* temples than before. The influx of tourists and invest-ment, particularly from Taiwan – where many Quanzhou emigrants lived – had the unforeseen consequence of helping finance what was amounting to a local "superstitious revival." Quanzhou's make-over resulted in residents' appeals to their Taiwanese relatives to return and invest in their old neighbor-hoods. This they did, by supporting temple festivals, temple refurbishments, and other popular religious and cultural institutions. "The amount of money donated to temple festivals had increased to such a scale that even the formal theatrical troupes controlled, but poorly financed, by the Bureau of Culture had become interested in making money from 'superstitious activities'." (Wang Mingming 2006: 20) In this case, every facet of the state's ordering projects had spun out of control, with even the professional troupes employed to displace traditional festival practices becoming dependent on those practices for their survival.

In the Zhejiang town of Wuzhen, officials similarly sought to secularize a traditional religious landscape by turning it over to tourism development. As in many parts of China, local governments – with an eye toward generating tourism revenue – have paid to rebuild temples and shrines destroyed during the Mao era. Tourists, as exemplary consumers, are expected to present a commercial, secular presence in these religious spaces that should keep chaos – in the form of backward superstition – at bay. Yet Marina Svensson's (2010) observations of tourists at temples in Wuzhen suggests that their practices cannot be neatly ordered into "modern," "secular," or even "commercial" categorizations. Svensson found that tourist visits to temples often included some element of either observation or participation in "superstitious" ritual performances. Tourists thus offered incense or asked the gods for advice and protection. Although fortune-telling is officially seen as superstitious, fortune-tellers were nonetheless often part of the attraction for tourists. The ordering project of turning over local shrines to tourists could not guarantee that the tourists themselves would not experience their own "religious revival."

Part of the reason for this might be found in the disorder of the market itself, where – as in the case of Quanzhou – superstition-related commercial activity offers a clear dilemma for the local state hoping to limit popular religion, yet finding itself dependent on the revenue generated by popular religious activities. This is not, by any means, a new dilemma for local Chinese government's, as Poon's (2008) study of Guanzhou's early twentieth-century efforts to modernize the City God Temple indicates. In Wuzhen, the Xiuzhen Daoist temple was rebuilt in 2000 and is run by the town tourism development company, which, since it is not a temple sanctioned and run by the state Daoist Association, makes it technically illegal. Nevertheless, the temple employs at least one ordained Daoist priest who tells tourist fortunes, and several other employees in quasi-religious roles, encouraging touristic ritual observances and purchases of incense and expensive amulets. Tourists have complained about "pushy guides," "tricky priests," and "fake Daoists" on various travel websites, spurring the company to post a sign at the temple that proclaims freedom of belief and tells the tourists that donations are voluntary. That such a sign is necessary betrays the disorder that can always be counted on to emerge from any touristic ordering project.

We might want to view the disarrayed ordering projects in Wuzhen and Quanzhou on a larger canvas, in which Chinese society views ordering as an ongoing project with unforeseen consequences, but also depends on particular sites to serve as models or exemplars of order realized. Such sites are usually labeled as "typical" (*dianxing*) spaces – a term that, as Bakken (2000) has argued, carries a connotation in Chinese more akin to an "ideal type" rather than the "average" meaning that it more often carries in English. Tourism development is always a project of creating, identifying, or developing "typical" sites for visitation and consumption. Such sites offer concrete instances of an "exemplary norm," and are fundamental components of what Bakken calls China's "educational" society, where the rule of morality based on learning by models has long been prioritized over the rule of abstract law. In an exemplary society, ideal – utopian, even – models provide mechanisms for social order and control that are not disciplinary in a Foucauldian sense, but which provide a powerful means of moral regulation by valuing behavior that complies with moral norms.

One of the most consistent spaces within which utopian models were conceived, as Bakken (2000: 32) points out, was the self-sufficient, so-called "earth-bound" rural comunity. The most obvious version of this comes in the form of Tao Qian's classic prose poem *Peach Blossom Spring*, where an isolated and self-contained village serves as a model for a stable social order. For classical Chinese intellectuals and officials, the village community always contained within it the seeds of this utopia, but the realization of this ideal community could only come about through cultivation, learning, or some kind of transformation. This is because the village also contained within it the seeds of chaos and disorder. Bakken argues that the exemplary society is always producing what the early twentieth-century intellectual Zhou Zuoren called the twin demons of order and disorder, the "gentleman" and the "hooligan." The exemplary nature of the village, then, is not a given, but always a *project*.

In a similar vein, Duara (2000: 25) has written of the early twentieth-century writer Lu Xun's impatience with what he saw as a growing nostalgia for the village community among China's urban elites. The village, for Lu Xun, was not a frozen specimen of tradition, but rather a site for reform, and a place where today's peasants would be transformed into tomorrow's citizens. Much of this sort of expert knowledge of the village as a project was inspired by the Japanese folklorist Yanagita Kunio, who made the vernacular village an object of investigation, invention, and recovery (see also Mitchell 2002). Duara (2000: 17–18) notes that Yanagita inspired Zhou Zuoren's "New Village Movement", which sought to model the rural folk as an alternative source of national identity. Fei Xiaotong's "earth-bound China" was similarly conceived as a project of recognizing that the enduring essence of Chinese civilization inherent in the village was important as an object of cultivation and transformation. Duara (2000) further writes of the seventeenth-century scholar Gu Yanwu, who saw the village not as a site of irreducible value, but as a place where customs (*su*) would have to be transformed (*jiaohua*) and revitalized by moral leadership (*feng*).

Part of the appeal of Bakken's exemplary society, then, is its emphasis on the ongoing tension between order and disorder, on the project and process of governing by models, and the fact that the outcomes of such projects are seldom predictable, nor are they always in the best interests of the powerful. Bakken writes:

> The exemplary society . . . is about willed consent as well as resistance and the erosion of control . . . People make of the rules, norms, rituals, and laws imposed upon them something quite different from the effects intended. A society simply resists being reduced to the exemplary discipline of its social engineers.
>
> (2000: 2)

There have been enough cases throughout rural China to suggest, as Mitchell (2002) has argued in the case of the Egyptian heritage site of Gurna, that villagers do not always simply accept the expert knowledge of their communities and passively fulfill their roles as actors in a strictly regulated morality play.

Perhaps the most well-known case of villagers refusing to play along is the Anhui village of Hongcun. A UNESCO World Heritage site since 2000, and perhaps best known as the setting for Ang Lee's film *Crouching Tiger, Hidden Dragon*, Hongcun's development as a heritage tourism site was turned over by the local government to an outside company. Local officials in Anhui felt that the heritage represented by Hongcun's landscape was too important to leave in the hands of the villagers themselves, who were, like all villagers, deficient in "quality", almost by definition (see Harwood 2009). The rights to Hongcun's tourism development were sold by the county government to Beijing-based Jingyi Company for thirty years. Villagers themselves were never informed of the deal. They were never consulted beforehand and were never informed after it had happened. By 2000, the Hongcun villagers were beginning to see that their government-arranged "marriage" with Jingyi was not a prosperous one, and they began to actively oppose it. Of the 1.3 million yuan in ticket revenues collected by Jingyi in 2000, the village received about 6 percent, or roughly 70 yuan (a little more than US$10) for each person. Few of the villagers were employed by the company, and they were prevented from opening their own businesses to profit from the throngs of tourists marching through their streets daily. So, in late 2000, the villagers began using their horse-carts to obstruct tourist pathways into the village. They made tourists pay to take pictures of the village; and when that didn't deter enough of them, they spread animal excrement on the walls of their own houses. They began to beat up any company personnel who showed up in the village. They stopped maintaining their houses – "Why should I fix up my house so that someone else can get rich?" The confrontation was the subject of a *Southern Weekend* exposé that sparked an unsuccessful libel suit from Jingyi (Zhai 2002; see also Ying and Zhou 2007).

As a result of their disorderings, the Hongcun villagers were able to negotiate a new, more favorable deal with Jingyi. While they still have little control over their own display, they have at least won better compensation. Villagers stressed that they have never been opposed to tourism development, just the terms upon which it was thrust upon them. They do not necessarily reject expert knowledge and ordering projects when they are foisted upon them, but will always insist on using that knowledge in the service of their own interests, which may or may not be aligned with those of the expert planners themselves. It is in this sense, then, that the village has been viewed as a project of continuous cultivation, where proper moral leadership would achieve alignment between local and imperial/national interests.

This alignment is now conceived more than anything else as a project of cultural enterprise, in which – as we would expect – performance now plays a central role. Enterprise, and its reliance on a performance of order, has become the transformative vehicle of moral leadership in contemporary China's exemplary society of tourists and tourist sites. Culture has emerged as a kind of technology of government in post-reform China, and cultural performance has become one of China's central mechanisms in managing the tension between order and disorder, for distinguishing civilization and quality from backwardness and ignorance. To turn your village into an enterprise, and perform its cultural order for tourists, is to turn oneself into a model of improvement, to claim status as an exemplary norm. And cultural enterprise serves as the framework for articulating the broader set of ideals exemplified by that norm.

Touring modernities?

Just what do we make of the role tourism now plays in China's ordering projects? Clearly, we can conclude that Euro-American modernity has no exclusive claim to ordering. Nor, of course, does any kind of modernity. But while it is tempting to draw from China's social and historical contexts evidence for ordering as some sort of "universal" principle by which we might organize – theoretically – our knowledge of tourism, I think there is a different, more subtle lesson on display here. Tourism as an ordering project in China performs that ordering in different ways, for different reasons, and in articulation with different social processes than tourism in other places. In pointing this out, I do not mean to suggest that tourism as ordering in China is significant merely as an alternative or different model of modernity from those we have been accustomed to analyzing in Euro-American contexts. Rather, I mean to suggest that appreciating tourism as ordering requires, as Franklin has also argued, a theoretical pluralism, provincialism, and modesty. Tourism is ordered for particular reasons in particular places, and universal explanations are likely to hide those contextual particularities to our detriment. Thus, at the risk of sounding obtuse, when Chinese tourists "deviate" from the norm, they do so for their own reasons, not ours.

I think we also learn that disorder is also always "local." As an ordering project, tourism generates its disorders according to specific geographical contexts. The sex tourists who opened this chapter cannot simply be written off as a predictable deviation or escape from the structural constraints of modern life, as if we were somehow hard-wired by modern life to respond to our workaday lives in such a way. Instead, they operated within a particular context of state-promoted leisure and tourism, of village improvement, and of cultural enterprise that generates particular forms of disorder, which make better sense as strategic engagements with social processes than as "escapes" or "deviances." We might even see them as forms of political practice, in the sense used by Tania Li (2007: 12), where the practice of politics is always that which "stands at the limit of the calculated attempt to direct conduct." Ordering projects always emerge *in response to* these practices, and as such must always be conceived as local, partial, limited, and (of course) doomed to failure. I do not mean to celebrate sex tourism as some heroic anti-governmental claim to freedom. That would simply ennoble another kind of "tourist" as yet another kind of modern subject position. Instead, I think that village sex tourism in rural China might point up a particular assemblage of social processes that help us make sense of tourism as an ordering project.

7 Practicing tourist landscapes

Photographic performances and consumption of nature in Japanese domestic tourism

Eriko Yasue and Kazuo Murakami

Introduction

Thinking about the relationship between tourism and landscapes has become more important in terms of investigations of the production of tourist places and spaces (Aitchison *et al.* 2000; Cartier and Lew 2005; Minca and Oakes 2006; Minca 2007; Knudsen *et al.* 2008). In particular, some scholars have paid attention to the multivocality of tourist landscapes, which may derive from involvement with several social actors in the practices of tourism. As Cartier states:

> Touristed landscapes, and as places, represent an array of experiences and goals acted out by diverse people in locales that are subject to tourism but which are also places of historic and integral meaning, where "leisure/tourism" economies are also local economies, and where people are engaged in diverse aspects of daily life.
>
> (2005: 3)

Multiple purposes, meanings, interests, and intentions elaborated by different social actors intersect in the processes of tourist landscape formation. This requires, then, that we consider the relationship between tourist landscapes and "three sets of actors: tourists; locals; and intermediaries including government ministries, travel agents, and tourism promotion boards" (Nash 1996, quoted in Knudsen *et al.* 2008: 4). Besides, Squire suggests that "tourism particularly trades in different groups of image makers and analytical interpreters" (Squire 1994: 6). In other words, tourist landscapes are "open to multiple interpretations – they are heterotopic" (Knudsen *et al.* 2008: 4). While the multivocality of landscape may complicate the understanding of landscape formation in tourism practices, it is necessary to take into consideration the intersections between social actors in order to understand the changing representations of landscape and its practice in modern tourism.

At this point, it seems crucial to pay more attention to the practice dimension of tourist landscapes where leisure/tourism economies take place at local and national scales. Löfgren points out that the "tourist gaze" and the making of the picturesque misses the fact that "the picturesque above all concerns sensibility: a search for atmosphere and sceneries that opened your senses and sent your thoughts flying" (Löfgren 1999: 21). We believe that the processes of reproducing landscapes through tourism practices do not solely involve the power of the tourist gaze. On the contrary, tourist practices themselves, such as searching and experiencing the new sensibilities, dynamically participate in the making and remaking of landscapes where "new" meanings and values are inscribed.

This chapter discusses the process of reproduction of tourist landscapes in contemporary Japanese tourism. By focusing on tourist practices at a natural landscape site in Asuke, one established destination in Japan, we aim at investigating how tourist landscapes are shaped by the local tourism authority while such constructed visibility and materiality are performed by contemporary individual tourists. Particular attention is placed upon the relationship between the materiality of space, touristic visual images, and photographic performances at landscaped sites. Using visual ethnographies, a variety of corporeal movements, gestures, and experiences enacted by tourists during photography are examined. The study aims to offer evidence for explaining through photography what Japanese tourists actually do and gaze upon. While research on photographic practices has paid attention to Western tourists' photography (Crawshaw and Urry 1997; Suvantola 2002; Bærenholdt *et al.* 2004; Minca 2007), empirical work that focuses on Asian tourists' photographic practices is still sparse (except Edensor 1998; Yeh 2009). We find that these tourist practices illuminate the multivocality of landscape formation.

Tourism, landscapes and practices

Denis Cosgrove defines the notion of landscape within the context of cultural geography as follows:

> Landscape has a complex history as an organizing and analytical concept within cultural geography. Its usage has varied from reference to the tangible, measurable ensemble of material forms in a given geographical area, to the representation of those forms in various media such as painting, texts, photographs or performances, to the desired, remembered and somatic spaces of the imagination and the senses.
>
> (Cosgrove 2003: 249)

Such variety seems to complicate our understanding of tourist landscapes. What we want to make clear here is: in which ways are these aspects of "landscape" reconfigured in view of modern tourism practices? Visual images play key roles in the practices of modern tourism (Crouch and Lubbren 2003). Meanwhile, tourist places and their landscape representations are also constituted, and new meanings and values are added through the practices of national and local tourist industries (Bærenholdt *et al.* 2004; Crang, M. 2004; Cartier and Lew 2005). Besides, tourists themselves are among the most powerful engines in the production of tourist places and their images (Edensor 1998). In this study, we will investigate the complexities of the reproduction of tourist landscapes, highlighting tourist practices themselves, namely photographic performances at popular landscape sites in contemporary Japan.

One aspect that the notion of landscape as a way of seeing has not paid much attention to is the "practices of seeing" of visual images (Crang, M. 1997: 360). M. Crang points out that this implication foregrounds "the limitations in looking solely at cultural products without looking at how they are taken up and used" (1997: 360). Similarly, recent landscape studies in cultural geography have shifted their focus from the notion of landscape as a representation to the practices of landscape, and in particular "the simultaneous and ongoing shaping of self, body and landscape via practice and performance" (Wylie 2007: 166). While landscape is regarded as a highly visual concept, removed from the subject, it seems useful to employ the notion of landscape as embodied practices in order to explore the ordinariness or the "banal seduction" (Obrador *et al.* 2009: 6) that the culture and practices of modern tourism convey.

Some studies have already shown that embodied practices such as walking, photographing, and narrating act as key factors highlighting the performative dimension of landscape experiences. Wylie discusses the process of distinctive articulations of self and landscape through walking along the South West Coast Path in the UK and narrating his walking experience (Wylie 2005). Moreover, Tim Edensor examines landscape as a space to be criss-crossed and imprinted on the bodily presence through tourist performances at the Taj Mahal (Edensor 1998). Bærenholdt *et al.* conceptualize landscape as a stage where people perform their vision through photography, highlighting a visual performance – photographing – at a "picturesque sublime" site in Denmark by stressing "the sociality, creativity and embodiment of tourist photography" (Bærenholdt *et al.* 2004: 69). We employ these insights and suggest that the practices of landscape in tourism, particularly tourist photography, are a diverse collection of performances, including visuality, movements, activities, sensuous experiences, and materiality.

While existing tourism theories tend to focus on images, signs, and discourses produced by tourism-related industries, the practice dimension of landscape experience helps deepen the understanding of tourist practices themselves. We believe that looking at the complexities of landscape formation and interpretation of tourist practices in contemporary tourism is helpful in understanding the practice dimension of landscape formation.

The notion of landscape as embodied practices needs to be complemented by the notion of landscape as a cultural image and text. This is because modern tourism always involves "the production of the local and the different" (Robertson 1992: 173) through a series of "cultural discourses that distinguish places in terms of particular values" (Edensor 1998: 121). In addition, images of place help shape people's practices and performances in sites. People's perception of places through place-myths may "impact on material activities and may be clung to despite changes in the 'real' nature of the site" (Shields 1991: 47).

The concept of practice and performance in modern tourism foregrounds complex relations between tourists, images, places, and experiences. A number of studies focus on the enactment of the bodily sense in the context of tourism (Veijola and Jokinen 1994; Jokinen and Veijola 2003; Crouch 2004, 2005; Edensor 2006a; Minca 2007). Tourist performances concern the diverse enactment and the conventions that are characterized by temporal, spatial, and social conditions.

Edensor mentions in his book on tourist performances at the Taj Mahal that "tourist performances are shaped by the constraints and opportunities that tour structures produce and are informed by beliefs about the symbolic meanings of the site, and they vary from the rigid enaction of tourist rituals and 'duties' to attempt to construct and transmit alternative meanings" (Edensor 1998: 62). Thus, tourist performances are intimately linked to specific social and cultural discourses and practices, while tourist sites are considered as stages where tourists encounter different social rules and improvise their enactments.

Gazing is actually performed with the help of photography (i.e. the use of cameras). Joyce Hsiu-yen Yeh considers photography as "a central touristic ritual, the recording and capturing of the moment of gazing" (Yeh 2009: 303). Photography is powerful in shaping tourists' movements and activities by indicating where to see and how to capture sights, while it is also evidence of what tourists see and experience (Crawshaw and Urry 1997). However, photography involves a variety of performances in and with tourist sites. In fact, photographic experiences are performed through gazing *and* other additional performances. It is a set of performances such as finding objects to capture, holding or setting cameras, looking into lenses and focusing. Besides, photography plays an important role in distributing new sensibilities among modern tourists. The invention and development of the camera in the nineteenth century had a considerable influence on the ways of experiencing landscapes. Picture postcards actually became very powerful tourist media in the late nineteenth century in terms of communicating feelings and experiences with others through the visual (Löfgren 1999).

Through the processes of production and consumption, photography and its materiality have become important factors in the production of imaginary landscapes as social worlds. They produce photographic performance in sites as well as semiotic and visual images. Photography is therefore useful for exploring the ways in which tourists create and reproduce "pleasures" in tourism through visual images. This chapter will attempt to clarify how photographic practices and performances are involved in the reproduction of imaginary and material landscapes that take place during people's travels.

We conducted an intensive "visual ethnography" of photographic performances at a flower garden in Asuke. By looking at the photographic performances at a natural landscape site, the dynamic process of reproduction of tourist landscapes in contemporary Japanese domestic tourism will be examined. Significantly, the materiality and visuality of the site is socially and culturally constructed. This investigation also enables us to undertake a more focused consideration of the meanings and experiences of nature-viewing practices for contemporary Japanese tourists. In order to capture photographic performances undertaken by tourists, we have adopted Larsen's way of observing tourist performances, namely "picturing/filming-while-observing" (Larsen 2004: 33).[1] A variety of activities, such as photographing, walking, viewing, posing, and chatting, which tourists performed in the chosen landscaped site, were photographed and observed.[2] Since the leisure activities of viewing nature are strongly linked with seasonality in Japan (Linhart 1998), the study was conducted during the garden's peak season (i.e. spring), when the dogtooth violet, the main attraction in the garden, is in bloom. The ethnographic research produced a total of more than 600 photographs and 22 short films (2–3 minutes each). To be able to acquire tourists' knowledge, insights, ideas, and experiences regarding photographing, 14 semi-structured interviews[3] were also conducted.

Tourism in Asuke

Located in the northeast of the Aichi Prefecture, central Japan, with a distinctive natural and historical landscape, Asuke is one of the most popular one-day destinations in the Chūkyō Metropolitan Area,[4] which includes several major cities. It is a rural "town" in a mountain area, called Asuke-*chō* – literally, Asuke-town – and has belonged to Toyota city since 2005. Its population was almost 9,000 in August 2009. The town covers almost 193km², 86.5 percent of which is forest. Most of the tourist attractions are situated in the town center and a valley called Kōrankei.

The scale of present-day tourism in Asuke – 1,296,485 visitors in 2007 (Aichi Department of Industry and Labour 2007) – shows its popularity as a destination.[5] Despite its rural location, Asuke is not a faraway place for tourists from the Chūkyō Metropolitan Area. Thanks to the improvement of road links over the past few decades, it is only a 1–1.5-hour car journey from most major cities to Asuke. In fact, cars are the most popular form of transportation for tourists coming to Asuke due to the lack of convenient train networks between the large city centers of the Chūkyō Metropolitan Area and Asuke.

The flower garden, on which we focus in our study, is situated in Kōrankei, a five-minute walk from Asuke's town center. Alongside the Tomoe River, almost 4,000 maples and other trees, such as cherry blossoms, attract tourists throughout the year. The flower garden, which was constructed for tourism promotion in 1986 under the Asuke Tourism Association (hereafter ATA)'s supervision, is situated on the east side of the Tomoe River, on a hill called Mt Iimori.

There is a community of wild dogtooth violets on one of Mt Iimori's slopes, the preservation and nourishment of which was organized by the ATA in 1986. The flower garden is one of the major features of Asuke as a tourist destination. It has charmed tourists in the springtime for over twenty years. The dogtooth violet (*katakuri*) is a small herbaceous perennial of the Liliaceae family, which is said to take seven or eight years to bloom its first flower. It produces a single small pinkish flower at the beginning of spring, and a pair of narrow, purple-spotted leaves grow at its lower middle. The flowering dogtooth violet is noted for its beauty, which represents the herald of spring. Every year, local newspapers and TV programs cover the flowering of the dogtooth violets in Mt Iimori in the early spring.

The aim of promoting the dogtooth violet as a new tourist attraction was clear for the ATA – to attract tourists in Asuke during the spring season. The difference in parking space usage between November (32,778, in autumn) and March (3,115) in 1986 urged the ATA to address the irregular distribution of tourist arrivals (Asuke Tourism Association 2005). One of the ATA's ways to deal with this seasonal imbalance was to create a new attraction by cultivating flowers. Together with experimental plantings and extractions of the bulbs with the help of local residents, the enlargement of the flowering area was put into practice under the supervision of the ATA in 1987. Thus, flower viewing as a recreational activity was staged by the local tourism authority, and clusters of dogtooth violets at Kōrankei were developed as a tourist attraction. The object of the natural landscape, portrayed by the flower garden, in this case is not wild itself, but instead a well-organized garden.

Similar to other items which are developed into tourist commodities at certain destinations, the clusters of dogtooth violets are described as Asuke's "regional" nature. Flower descriptions and photographs are found in a brochure compiled by the ATA in 1997 and including information on the history and cultural heritage of Asuke. The brochure, entitled *Shin* (new) *Sanshū Asuke*,[6] introduces the clusters of dogtooth violets as representatives of Asuke's nature and seasonal beauty. Currently, this pocket-size book is utilized as the 'textbook' for local guides in Asuke. Interestingly, an old version of the book, *Sanshū Asuke*, compiled by the ATA in 1979, did not have any articles on these flowers. This makes clear that the dogtooth violet was "rediscovered" and "approved" as an item to represent Asuke's nature in the context of tourism.

Production of tourist landscapes of dogtooth violets

Before moving on to consider the dogtooth violets' images, there are several points that need to be addressed with regard to the perception of dogtooth violets as nature by the Japanese. First, dogtooth violets symbolize spring and are employed as a seasonal word, or *kigo*, for spring. Seasonal words are essential to the aesthetics and forms of haiku (the Japanese verse form composed of seventeen syllables). *Kigo* is a fixed seasonal connotation, which indicates a particular season, and helps convey the proper meanings of a poem. Here, we need to consider the metaphorical meaning of dogtooth violets, which are commonly perceived as a symbol of spring. The use of Japanese traditional ways of seeing nature in poetry is also found in one of the *Shin Sanshū Asuke's* articles on dogtooth violets. The article describes an ancient poem,[7] composed by one of the most popular ancient Japanese poets, depicting dogtooth violet scenery and giving a general description of the flower:

> The eighty maidens,
> Busy at the officers at court,
> Bustle about
> Drawing water from the temple well
> Where this pink sweet-lily blooms.
> (Translated by Cranston 1993: 467)

The poem refers to eighty maidens drawing water from a well where the dogtooth violets are in bloom. Although natural imagery in classical Japanese poetry is used in a different context, it is possible to detect the influence and appropriation of the traditional perception of nature in relation to the construction of the tourist gaze. Thus, it can be argued that the dogtooth violet is considered not only as a flower that represents nature, but also a cultural artifact that conveys certain aesthetics.

The notion of dogtooth violet as an aesthetic object that reflects a way of seeing nature by the Japanese can be observed in the promotional tourism materials on Asuke. The visual representation of the dogtooth violet in clusters as a tourist natural landscape has been developed by the ATA. The ATA's tourism promotion has been actively involved in the popularization of this particular flower through visual materials. The oldest poster for dogtooth violet viewing at the archives of the Asuke Museum was produced in 1989 by the ATA, which has since produced tourism posters featuring the dogtooth violet almost every year. The posters are composed of four elements: dogtooth violets in clusters (and/or single flower), captions, the place name, and travel information, such as public transportation. Figure 7.1 is an example of a tourism poster produced by the ATA in 2000. The common visual representation of the dogtooth violets portrays the flowers in clusters while tourists or local residents are totally absent from the pictures. In some cases, a close-up of a single dogtooth violet is the only object depicted in the poster.

In fact, the size of the flower clusters constitutes the main appeal to the tourists. As the director of the ATA emphasized, "because we are not photographers, the least I want to show to people is the size [of the cluster]. Well, color and shape of dogtooth violets are important too, but one of the important things is the size of the cluster."[8] The uniqueness of the dogtooth violets in Asuke is linked to the spaciousness of the cluster. This is also reflected in the design of the tourism posters related to the dogtooth violet viewing produced by the ATA. Most of the posters depict dogtooth violets blooming in clusters, stressing the unique size these flower clusters have in Asuke. The

Figure 7.1 Poster of dogtooth violets in cluster produced in 2000
(photo: Eriko Yasue; reproduced by kind permission of the Asuke
Tourism Association).

local tourism authority is actually responsible for this new visual strategy of
dogtooth violet natural landscapes, which is currently becoming the typical
image of Asuke's dogtooth violets.

In addition, the solitary image of the dogtooth violet became another
essential figure in the flower's visual representations. Postcards sold in Asuke
portray close-ups of a single violet, or a couple of them, in unfocused and
blurred backgrounds. The fuzzy background generates soft impressions and
enhances the foreground objects, while rendering a fantastical and magical
atmosphere to the photographs. Similar to the images of the flowers in clusters,
the image of the solitary flower is entirely free of any tourists' depictions. Any
"noise," such as the busy tourists at the flower garden, is eliminated, and the
photographs of single dogtooth violets delight tourists and guide their eyes
toward the appropriate framing of gazing the flower; this way the dogtooth
becomes a metaphor of tranquility.

The posters' captions are also important elements in inscribing the cultural
meanings of dogtooth violets. The meanings of the photographs are determined
by related descriptions and the contexts in which these photographs are
employed (Price 1994). Descriptions not only provide further information about
the photographs, but, most importantly, they regulate how to look at them by
directing the viewers' practices of gazing and photographing:

Dogtooth violet smiling *sweetly* under warm sunshine.
(Poster of the year 1998; translation and italics by the author)

Dogtooth violet whispering *"spring* has come," its figure looking at the ground *prettily*, looks like a *maiden*. Now dogtooth violets in Kōrankei are in bloom.
(Poster of the year 1999; translation and italics by the author)

Do you know dogtooth violet? Its figure is like an *adorable maiden* whispering the herald of *spring* that would calm visitors' minds. Now *spring* has come to Kōrankei, dogtooth violets are in bloom.
(Poster of the year 2000; translation and italics by the author)

The resemblance of each caption used in the visual tourism materials of dogtooth violet is striking. The above captions express certain images of the dogtooth violet by employing specific words, such as "sweetly," "prettily," "adorable," and "maiden," all of which are linked to "spring." The dogtooth violet is often called the "spring ephemeral," a term used to describe early spring wild flowers coming into bloom and fading quickly. In these captions, the flower is personified as a "maiden" and becomes a metaphor of spring. Thus, the symbolic association between dogtooth violets and seasonality is reinforced in the process of constructing tourist landscapes by the ATA.

The resemblance of this meaning to the ancient poem that we quoted earlier is obvious. The symbolic meaning of dogtooth violets, depicted in the ancient poem, still influences the ATA's contemporary image-making activity for the promotion of tourism. In fact, an interview with the director of the ATA[9] showed that the ideas for the descriptions and captions of dogtooth violets in the promotional materials came from several books containing professional descriptions of the flower. Subsequently, it can be argued that the aesthetic conceptions that derived from the ancient poem are still actively utilized and frame contemporary tourist imaginings of nature.

The analysis of the tourism posters and postcards that depict dogtooth violets in clusters also reveal that photography not only helps to visualize the construction of idealized and beautified scenery, but also creates objects of tourist gaze. Professional photographers actively create idealized and aesthetic-ally pleasing images of tourist sites by excluding cars, people, and bad weather from their shots (Crawshaw and Urry 1997). The ATA has similarly con-structed the dogtooth violets garden as a beautiful and salable landscape by selecting pleasing objects, arranging natural elements, and captioning the cultural values of the flower. Such photographic techniques and strategies can be regarded as an attempt to create objects of the tourist gaze with specific reference to conventional aesthetics towards nature.

However, it is worth noting that the tourist landscapes of dogtooth violets are not only constructed visually and textually, but also developed materially. In conjunction with the popularization of dogtooth violets blooming in clusters at Asuke, the ATA's preservation and cultivation activities resulted in the gradual development of space. According to the director, the size of the dog-tooth flowering area is now approximately 5,000m^2, whereas before the commencement of the flowers' preservation action in 1985 it was only between 2,000 and 2,500m^2. As tourist arrivals increased, some "typical tourist behavior," such as plucking out dogtooth flowers in bloom and squashing the flowers when photographing, appeared. The ATA needed to pay more attention to the management of the flowering area. In response, the path across the slope of Mt Iimori was protected with rope banisters, and the flowering area itself became a no-entry zone. There are two wide clusters of dogtooth violets on the slope, and the path was arranged around them. Some benches are placed all over the garden for tourists.

In the next section, we will discuss the results of our visual ethnographic research in order to show how the dogtooth violet flower and landscapes are enacted, performed by contemporary tourists, and how their performances at the garden are regulated by material designs developed by the ATA.

Performing photography at the flower garden

Nearly all tourists travel to Asuke by car, and most tourists who come to see the dogtooth violets park their cars at the main parking spaces, located near the flower garden. The dogtooth violets flowering area is located across the north side of one of Mt Iimori's slopes. The typical spring tour includes strolling in the garden; a walk in Kōrankei lasts about ninety minutes, excluding the time for a break/lunch in the restaurants/cafés. Approximately thirty minutes are enough to go around the entire garden and take some photographs during a leisurely walk. Most of the tourists that have cameras will stop in front of the dogtooth violets clusters to photograph them.

Our ethnographic research at the flower garden showed that elderly tourists predominantly visit the site during weekdays, whereas families and young couples are more abundant during weekends. Tour buses also bring a large number of elderly tourists to Asuke during weekdays. They tend not to stay for long because they have limited time, based on tight bus schedules, to go around the garden and capture scenic shots.

Some tourists carry single-lens reflex (hereafter SLR) cameras while others have been observed with handy automatic digital cameras and mobile phone cameras. In particular, solo tourists were most likely to bring SLR cameras, often with tripod stands. It seems that the difference in the type of camera used is an important indicator of the tourists' photographic performances. The appearance of tourists often differs according to the camera types they hold. The clothes, bag sizes and shoes worn by solo tourists with big SLR cameras are often different from those of tourists with handy digital cameras. For instance, some tourists bring huge backpacks with tripod stands and wear comfortable trainers. Their equipment suggests that they have come to the garden to take photographs, not just to walk around the site or the town center without capturing the natural scenery. The time invested in changing lenses or finding better locations to shoot their photographs reflects passion and desire for "proper" shots of the garden. Additionally, the number of photos taken is also different between the two groups of tourists. The interviews with tourists with SLR cameras showed that an astonishing number of photos were taken, such as 500 in one day, while the other group of interviewees (those using handy automatic digital cameras) usually reported taking approximately 15 to 50 photos. It is clear that the camera plays an important role as a tool not only in creating memories (Crawshaw and Urry 1997; Yeh 2009) but also in shaping tourists' performances, behavior, and fashion.

Even though the camera types differ according to tourists' interests and purposes, the photographic performances by both tourists with SLR cameras and tourists with handy digital/mobile cameras take place in fairly similar ways and locations. Figure 7.2 shows a queue of tourists waiting for the best time to shoot the dogtooth violets. Specifically, they are eagerly waiting for the

Figure 7.2 Queue of tourist–photographers (photo: Eriko Yasue).

afternoon sunshine to appear along the path and in front of the dogtooth violet clusters. Irrespective of the kind of camera in use, it seems that it is essential to the tourists to photograph the flowers at this particular spot in order to produce "proper" images at the "right time." Actually, the path itself goes around the major clusters in the garden so that the visitors can never miss out on the flowers blooming "beautifully." This is where most of the dogtooth violet images are captured by tourists; some of them make only a brief stop to photograph while others stay for much longer. This "traffic jam" that takes place in front of the major clusters in the garden reveals the intensity of the tourists' photographic performances and how it is related to various factors, such as weather and time, in that limited space.

Some tourist–photographers occupy more space than others in their efforts to create "artistic" pictures using tripod stands. They often remain standing or sitting, and patiently wait to get the desired backlight that will give a pleasing effect to their dogtooth violet pictures. Clearly, these tourists know where and how to capture their shots so as to recreate their own images of dogtooth violets through photography. As Minca discusses in his study of European tourist–photographers at the world-famous symbolic landscape site Jamaa el Fna in Marrakech, tourists seem to be "aware of their 'appropriately' dominant position, of their choice of the right framing, the right perspective, at the right time of day" (Minca 2007: 442). Although the photographers' queue makes the path more crowded and creates a "traffic jam" in the garden,[10] it also provides us with evidence of the patience and tolerance that "waiting tourists with cameras" may have.

Figures 7.3–7.5 depict other performances of tourist photography that frequently take place within the garden. In these, tourists are bodily and materially involved in capturing the object. The experience of producing photographs here is not only through capturing the beauty of dogtooth violets, but also through actively engaging in certain body movements and postures. Our ethnographic observations in the garden revealed that tourists' postures and movements are particularly diverse and flexible. In order to get lower viewpoints and capture close-up shots of inside the flower, several positions are deliberately employed by tourists. Squatting and kneeling on the path are the most common postures of photographing, whereas lying down on the path, a seemingly "curious" and "excessive" posture, is also often observed. As Bærenholdt *et al.* note: "tourists invest time and creativity in producing pleasing images with pictures, in experimenting with composition, depth, choice of motif" (2004: 81).

Material spatial elements in the garden partially condition the photographic performances that can take place in the garden. Tourist performances here are not separated from the material design of places. Tim Edensor and Uma Kothari (2004) discuss how material design, regulation, and effects encourage tourist performances and experiences. They argue that performances in familiar tourist spaces are conditioned to "specific materialities and the ways in which embodied subjects physically interact with space and objects"

Figure 7.3 Photographic performances: "squatting" (photo: Eriko Yasue).

Figure 7.4 Photographic performances: "lying down" (photo: Eriko Yasue).

Figure 7.5 Photographic performances: "stretching" (photo: Eriko Yasue).

(Edensor and Kothari 2004: 197). In order to produce "proper" pictures, tourist–photographers try to reach the dogtooth flowers from beyond the ropes, and stretch their bodies and arms as much as possible, sometimes with half of their bodies beyond the designated areas. The ropes and wooden poles are partly responsible for the diversity of tourists' postures and movements in the flowering area (Figure 7.5). The path and rope fence are not merely architectural and spatial elements that may disrupt normative values and roles in tourist sites. They also condition and enforce tourists' curious bodily postures and movements. The photographic performances enacted in the garden are strongly affected by the "surfaces, textures, temperatures, atmospheres, smells, sounds, contours, gradients and pathways" of the place (Edensor and Kothari 2004: 197). Photographic performances are partially conditioned by the "affordance" between the environment and humans (Gibson, J.J. 1986; for a discussion on affordance and performance, see Urry 2002; Larsen 2004). Thus, the tourist performance that takes place in the flowering garden is enacted not only through the enthusiasm for landscaping nature in an appropriate fashion, but also through the interplay between embodied enactments of tourists and Asuke's tourism development, which have afforded particular constructions of the garden.

Figures 7.6 and 7.7 illustrate photographically "reconstructed" images of dogtooth violets through the tourist gaze at Asuke. According to our interview data, there are two most popular compositions for dogtooth violet photographs: one depicts dogtooth violets blooming in clusters, and the other focuses on a single or a couple of flowers. Note that these compositions of the photographs resemble those of the tourism poster and postcard images we discussed earlier.The distinctive appearance of the dogtooth violet also conditions the "excessive" body postures adopted by the tourist photographers. The unique marking that appears in the middle of the flower when in bloom attracts tourist photographers to look into the core of the flower. Some tourists have actually claimed that a dogtooth violet's relaxed petals and the markings on their inner side are considered as key objects to be photographed: "There is the marking inside the flower, right? I like that" (elderly male tourist with SLR camera, with his partner). One interviewee stated that he attempted to shoot from very low positions in order to capture the marking inside the flower. Some experienced tourist–photographers explain the importance of shooting the very center of the flower: "to capture the pistil and stamen is important in shooting flowers because it becomes the energy of the pictures" (elderly male tourist with SLR camera, with his two friends); and "[it's necessary to focus on] the whole flower, I mean, the center of the flower" (middle-age male tourist with SLR camera, with his family).

In addition, the downward-facing petals of dogtooth violets seem to charm tourists in the garden. For example, one interviewee said: "I photograph ones with downward-facing petals as much as possible" (elderly male tourist with SLR camera, with his partner). Another tourist suggested that the "dogtooth violet's uniqueness is its downward-facing petals" (elderly male tourist with

Figure 7.6
"Reconstructed" image of dogtooth violets (1) (photo taken by a tourist)

Figure 7.7
"Reconstructed" image of dogtooth violets (2) (photo taken by a tourist)

SLR camera, with his two friends). For the tourist–photographers, the flower's appeal lies in the "prettiness" and "sweetness" of its appearance. To quote an interviewee: "I think the color, purple . . . it looks pretty . . . and the way they bloom, isn't it? . . . For instance, their petals will be facing downwards in the end . . . there are kinds of markings in the middle of the flower, I like it . . ." (elderly male tourist with SLR camera, with his two friends). "They are definitely gentle flowers" (elderly female tourist with single-use camera, with her family). "My impression is they are pretty . . . they have a soft, gentle, and warm spring color and flower" (middle-age male tourist with SLR camera, with his family). "They are pretty . . . and the color is gentle" (elderly female tourist with her partner). Thus, the dogtooth violets' physical features are explicitly interpreted through sensibilities, which may derive from the traditional aesthetic conception of dogtooth violets.

The dogtooth violets are reinscribed as a symbol of "spring" through tourist photography. Obviously, shooting "spring" is one of the major motifs that tourist photographers can have. One experienced tourist–photographer describes his passion for the dogtooth violet's image in the following way:

> In short, this time, in the case of the ordinary spring flower, I want to photograph with macro lenses to show the image of growing flowers, what's called atmosphere of spring, which shows that spring will be coming soon, in April, and it'll be warm, I take close-ups of flowers to show that it's blooming and getting warm, which is my aim of photographing . . . I think we need to show sense of the season . . . Japanese cherry is beautiful though; dogtooth violet has a soft atmosphere, which their pinkish petals produce. It suits the image of spring I guess.
>
> (Middle-aged male tourist with SLR camera,
> with his family)

The above statement shows that producing images of spring or ones that represent a sense of season is important to this specific photographer. His aim is to depict "spring" through pictures of dogtooth violets, which means that to him shooting pictures is more than just documentation. Dogtooth violets are conceived as a visible reference to spring, or something that heralds the coming of spring. In other words, a dogtooth violet is a symbolic evocation that is assigned the value of "sweetness," "girl or maiden," and "spring." Through such photographic performances and interpretations, the cultural meanings of dogtooth violets are repeatedly inscribed. Thus, the traditional aesthetics of the dogtooth violets are photographically consumed and continually reproduced by contemporary tourists.

Producing images of dogtooth violets appears to be part of an "active signifying practice" by becoming "an amateur semiotician" (Urry 2002: 128). Similar to tourists in other destinations, here in Asuke's flower garden, every tourist becomes a photographer and amateur semiotician through the act of photographing. It is precisely an "attempt to construct idealised images which beautify the object being photographed" (Urry 2002: 128) and to create "undisturbed natural beauty" through photography (Urry 2002: 43). Such tourist performances at the flowering area are strongly regulated by the semiotic meanings of visual images represented through tourism promotion by the ATA. Inscriptions of cultural meanings of dogtooth violets are performed and reinforced through the repetition of photographing that involves active body movements and postures. In that sense, tourist landscapes are repeatedly reproduced in photography through tourist practices.

Consuming the aesthetics associated with nature has a strong effect on the manipulation of landscape in the context of tourism. The dogtooth violet landscapes are continuously framed by tourists with cameras. The practice of tourist photography is an attempt to reproduce "ready-made" aesthetics based on the traditional aesthetics of the dogtooth violets. It is also an endless process of inscribing aesthetics that have been manipulated by the local tourism authority and other tourism-related visual materials.

This discussion of consuming manipulated aesthetics can be linked to the concept of "postemotionalism," which characterizes contemporary late modern society (Meštrović 1997). Sociologist Stjepan Meštrović argues that emotions are the salient feature of mass industrial societies, and he discusses how the "mechanization of the emotions" is embedded in late modern social life. He further discusses how contemporary news is narrated by linking stories to emotions and manipulating what he calls "quasi-emotions," including "niceness" and "curdled indignation." Through the photos and narratives of the tourists and their bodily immersions in photography, new meanings are also added to photographs and photographic experiences. Tourists' enthusiasm for photography extends beyond the visual consumption of the manipulated photographic objects. In Asuke, "sweetness" or "prettiness", linked to "spring," inscribed into the dogtooth violet, are consumed by contemporary tourists through the act of photography.

Tourists with SLR cameras differ from those using handy automatic and/or mobile phone cameras, especially as far as their skills and passion for photography are concerned. Manual cameras, with their adjustable shutter speeds and lens diaphragms, indicate the desire for more "artistic" and "professional" photographs. Handling this type of camera requires users to have more skill, knowledge, and money, as well as a passion for photography not shared by automatic compact camera/mobile camera users. We suggest that for tourists the use of new forms of technology is an experiment, a creative activity involving interaction with nature and its representations. For example, one tourist said:

> Today, I want to try taking photos with wide-angle lenses. I want to know whether wide-angle lenses work well . . . I don't know how it works because this is the first time I have used it . . . Normally, I use macro or telescopic lenses; I just want to try photographing by approaching and using only wide-angle lenses.
>
> (Elderly male tourist with SLR camera,
> with his partner)

Furthermore, some tourists carry multiple lenses in their bags and use them to capture various shots of the flower. For some interviewees, this process reflects their passion for elaborating their own aesthetics through photographic skills and techniques. Their primary aim is not only to photograph dogtooth violets but to develop their own aesthetics. Experimenting with a range of lenses, different shutter speeds, and various compositions and framings becomes, in this context, a valid reason for a trip to Asuke.

As Dean MacCannell notes: "amateur photography permits the tourist to create his own touristic imaginary with himself and his family at the centre, or just off to the side of the great sight or moment" (MacCannell 1999 [1976]: 147). The point to be addressed here is that "just as the individual tourist is free to make his own final arrangements of signs and markers, the modernizing areas of the world are also free to assemble their own images in advance of the arrival of the tourists" (MacCannell 1999 [1976]: 142). There is some room to be filled by contemporary tourists' creativity. Such shifting interpretations and representations of tourist landscapes could generate different meanings, functions and images through practices, performances, and mobility.

In the process of tourist landscape production and reproduction, cultural values are repeatedly inscribed according to the producer's intentions and interests. Feelings, emotions, and sensibilities inscribed into tourist landscapes are recycled, simulated, and reproduced through the practice of tourism. Thus, tourist landscape can be understood as a space in which transformations and combinations of symbolism, desire, and social practice take place.

The visual ethnography on which this chapter has focused indicates that Japanese tourists seem very busy with practicing nature-viewing activities. They are constantly performing romantic gazing (Urry 2002) in diverse ways. I.M. Daniels's study on the practices of Japanese tourists at Miyajima in Hiroshima, Japan, suggests that Japanese tourists tend to travel at a fast pace, "without being particularly contemplative about their experiences" (Daniels 2001: 126).

We agree with I.M. Daniels's conclusion in the light of the Japanese domestic tourism practices. While Japanese tourists at the flowering garden are actively involved in performing romantic gazing, they are busy thinking about photograph compositions, finding locations, catching best moments, changing camera lenses. It seems justified that they invest time, creativity, and passion in performing the romantic gaze, as shown in the landscaped site of Asuke under investigation. However, rather than regarding romantic gazing as a contemplative act, we suggest that the act of looking at nature is the consumption of constructed visuality and sensibilities. Performing nature viewing is a consuming gesture that is regulated and ordered by tourism discourses and representations. Constructed natural landscapes do not merely shape tourists' preconceptions, but also guide the practices of viewing and consuming signs and meanings, which are partly composed of the traditional aesthetics, inscribed in the visual in determined ways. They hunt for culturally prescribed viewing spots without being contemplative, thoughtful, or serious.[11]

Conclusion

The tourist landscape we touched upon in this chapter is the interface where creative production and reproduction in a variety of fashions and actors occur. We have examined the construction of the "photographed" site by the ATA through their practices of producing visual images and their captions. The dogtooth violet in Kōrankei is deliberately constructed as a metaphor of "spring" and "maiden," and also represented as a unique regional product. By linking it to seasonality, idealized and beautified images of the specific flower are created. Furthermore, the tourist landscape of dogtooth violets is also developed materially. The development of material designs is one of the main ways to produce the stage for photographic performances enacted by tourists.

The investigation of tourists' photographic performances revealed that the reproduction of dogtooth violet images through tourist photography is conditioned by the symbolic meanings of landscape as proposed by tourism promotion. Producing images of nature in tourism sites appears to be part of signifying practices, inscribing nature and seasonality metaphorically. In other words, tourist experiences at the flowering garden are composed of corporeal movements and enactments of gazing and photographing performances. It is a playful search of signs visually and materially constructed. However, it should be noted that different aesthetics and values are also repeatedly added to the images and experiences that the ATA manipulated by the tourist photographers themselves.

The reproduction of tourist landscapes is shaped and reshaped simul-taneously by both visual and textual representations and embodied practices in tourist sites. It is an ever-changing process of intersecting imaginaries and experiences through corporeal movements in and with tourist places. While the inscription of meanings into the landscapes is regulated by tourist discourses, tourists' interests and intentions help frame tourist landscapes through photography. Tourist practices themselves perform an essential function in reproducing tourist landscapes in contemporary Japan. The tourists we focused on in this study are not only consuming signs and images, but are also participants in the reproduction of new images and meanings through tourist photography. Our discussion shows that the nature-viewing activity does not merely involve seeing/photographing nature and its landscapes. More than that, it is a set of relations of performances; walking, chatting, focusing, lying, stretching, kneeling, and smiling. We believe that the approach we followed in this study could advance the argument of tourist practices and landscape formations in contemporary society.

Notes

1 Since his research methods are inspired by Sarah Pink's photo-essays on bullfighting (1997), we also consulted her work for building our own research methodology.
2 The research was conducted during four weeks in March and April 2008.
3 The interviewees were placed into one of the four categories: couples; groups of three or four tourists; family tourists; or single tourists.
4 The Chūkyō Metropolitan Area centered in Nagoya city is the third biggest metropolitan area in Japan, following the Tokyo and Hanshin (Osaka) Metropolitan Areas.

5 The number of tourists visiting Kōrankei has exceeded one million visitors since 1989 (Asuke Tourism Association 2005).

6 The brochure, which contains geographical and historical information about Asuke town, is on sale at bookshops in Asuke at 500 Japanese yen. It targets both tourists and local residents in Asuke.

7 The poem was drawn from Manyōshū, the oldest compilation by imperial command in ancient Japan (around the eighth century), and composed by Yakamochi Ōtomono, one of the most famous poets and compilers of Manyōshū at the time.

8 From an interview in April 2008.

9 Interviewed in April 2008.

10 This created a serious problem for the ATA in terms of the management of the flower area. The ATA has received a number of complaints due to photographers staying in front of the cluster for a long time.

11 However, it should be noted that Japanese tourists are not free from a reflexive and contemplative attitude. The practices of international tourism, especially undertaken by individual tourists, are tightly connected with a sense of identity or identity construction (for instance, Takai-Tokunaga 2007).

8 Medical tourism, medical exile

Responding to the cross-border pursuit of healthcare in Malaysia

Meghann Ormond

Medical tourism may be a business, but that doesn't mean that it's solely for business purposes. It's still very much based on the very foundation that healthcare is for all, that healthcare should be affordable, equitable and of quality. We [Malaysia] are based on those kinds of premises.

(Malaysian Health Ministry representative, in Ormond 2011)

Introduction

Both travel (as bodily displacement) and health (as bodily ailment), as moments of corporeal vulnerability, have been intimately linked over time to the concept of hospitality – of "being moved to respond" (Barnett 2005b: 15) to the precarious situation of another. Premised upon the traveler's displacement from his/her home, hospitality entails a "guest" being temporarily welcomed across the threshold into the domain of a "host," with the host offering a mixture of tangible and intangible elements that ensure the guest's security and fulfill his/her psychological and physiological needs (King 1995: 220). While conceptual engagement with "hospitality" in the realm of tourism studies has largely taken place through the lens of business and management, with its focus on "commercial hospitality" (where "guest" and "host" become "buyer" and "seller"), the uneasy tension between "host" and "guest" at the heart of hospitality has long been at the core of social science engagement with tourism and its impacts (see Smith, V.L. 1989; Lashley and Morrison 2000). With this dichotomy growing blurrier by the day, as the question becomes not only *where* one is a "host" and a "guest" but also *when* (Crang, M. 2005), social scientists are increasingly mobilizing Kantian, Levinasian and Derridian conceptualizations of "hospitality" in order to critically explore the mediation and regulation of "relations among members and strangers" (Benhabib 2004: 27) in a mobile world in which conventional mobility categories (e.g. "tourist," "migrant," etc.) are rendered increasingly obsolete and new types of moorings grow ever more patent (see Barnett 2005b; Bell

2007; Germann Molz and Gibson 2007). Accordingly, much scholarly and mediatic attention has been given over to the question of "political hospitality" – that conditional invitation extended to a foreign Other across a sovereign threshold – at a moment in history when the contours of the modern nation-state are increasingly challenged, shifting, and adapting. In "developed" Western societies grappling with the dilemma of extending political member-ship within a "cosmopolitan" migratory context (Dikeç 2002; Benhabib 2004; Dikeç *et al.* 2009; Darling 2010), for example, we see the foreign Other having crossed that sovereign threshold often discursively constructed as a costly burden – the fruit of so-called "unproductive, disruptive hospitality" (Derrida 2002: 100). As such, while the hotel has become symbolic of the commodifi-cation of hospitality, the fortress has come to represent the "political ethics" of hospitality (Gibson, S. 2006).

   With this chapter, I seek to offer a reading of the nexus between "com-mercial" and "political" hospitalities to explore attempts at developing "productive hospitality" through the metaphorical space of the "hotel–fortress." Using the lens of international medical travel (IMT), I examine the respon-siveness of one of the world's prime IMT destinations – Malaysia – to the plights and needs of its foreign patient–consumer "guests," laying out some of the complex ethical, economic, and political logics shaping the recogni-tion of the corporeal vulnerabilities of different foreign patient–consumers and the correlate extension of hospitality to them. In casting "Malaysia" as a moral safe-haven free from many of the barriers that produce unsettlingly stark differences in access to healthcare throughout the world, the comments by a Malaysian Health Ministry representative at the start of this chapter point to an entrepreneurial medical solidarity being extended by the Malaysian state to international *consumers*, which envisions an "all" that departs markedly from earlier interpretations of the state's biopolitical scope. I advance that receiv-ing a foreign patient–consumer as a "Somebody, [and] not as a serialized nobody" (Barnett 2005b: 15) is part of a conditional "pact" between "hosts" and "guests" that insists on mutual recognition in order to "give place" to the claims of both parties (Derrida 2000: 23–25). Yet this reciprocity – speaking to the continuing significance of national borders in the accessing and provision of different regimes of care, medical expertise, and technology – is compli-cated, as it involves not only commercial but also political recognition of the legitimacy of certain groups' claims for "care" and, in return, the recognition of the expertise of the care provider to respond to them, serving to constitute "guesting" and "hosting" subjects, places, and moments.

   The chapter is organized into four parts. The first section situates IMT destinations within a broader temporal and spatial context of hospitality and well-being practices, tracing shifts and transformations in the ways in which places have come to be recognized as therapeutic and hospitable. The second analyses the politically charged language commonly deployed in distinguishing categories of medically motivated cross-border mobility in relation to their value to their "sending" and "receiving" contexts, and how specific mobile subjects come to be recognized as deserving of care. Section three identifies a disjuncture between IMT destinations' growing desire for patient–consumers from "developed" countries and their corresponding investments in spectacular "medical tourism" infrastructure, on the one hand, and the foundational role that "everyday" intra-regional medical travelers from nearby "developing" countries play in constituting these destinations, on the other. Seeking to draw attention to the relevance of these more "everyday" medical mobilities, the fourth section contemplates complementarities and solidarities imagined and performed in the extension of a commercial–political hospitality to regional patient–consumers by IMT destinations in Malaysia, which (sometimes defying conventional economic logic) hint at the negotiation of more nuanced allegiances. In the conclusion, I underscore the importance of considering how non-citizen mobile subjects' corporeal vulnerabilities are recognized differently by destinations seeking to harness IMT flows so that we may begin to consider what might be the consequences of such recognition.

International medical travel: from exceptional to everyday

"Hospitable" spaces respond to the anxieties of those who seek them out, with "new" arenas continuously being identified and proffered as havens for rejuvenation (O'Dell 2007: 115). For millennia, people have traveled long distances in hopes of restoring their spiritual and physical well-being, seeking out natural sites around the world perceived to be sacred due to their healing properties, around which places of worship and travel infrastructure were built to access them (Gesler and Kearns 2002; Smith, K. 2008; Connell, J. 2011). With the expansion of "modern" medicine, and in correlation with shifting conceptualizations and spatializations of disease and illness (Foucault 1994), health-motivated travel gradually extended beyond places endowed with natural morphologies held as therapeutic to include medical facilities in which the "specific geographical location [was thought to be] of less significance in its therapeutic role than the physical, social and symbolic organization of the space itself" (Smyth 2005: 488).

Today, "medical travel" constitutes yet another point on the broad spectrum of travel motivated by the pursuit of well-being, a "contemporary elaboration" on earlier pursuits of beneficial health outcomes – with the outcomes of modern medical intervention expected to be more substantial and long-term (Connell, J. 2006: 2; Smith and Puczkó 2009: 254).

Given medicine's privileged relationship to modern discourses of science and progress, it comes as little surprise that the "centers of the health care universe" (Toral, in MacReady 2007) have commonly been perceived to be located in the "developed" world. For decades, wealthy patient–consumers from far and wide have made "pilgrimages" (Wachter 2006: 661) to these modern medical "meccas," sites of "miraculous" achievements that "boast[ed] unrivalled medical facilities and funds to fuel research and innovation in many aspects of medical treatment" (Jenner 2008: 237). The last two decades, however, have seen an unprecedented proliferation of internationally renowned centers of medical excellence outside of the "developed" countries in which such expertise had been held to be concentrated. By the end of the 1990s, several prominent medical facilities in "developing" and former socialist countries (e.g. Thailand's Bumrungrad Hospital[1]), often backed by their national and provincial governments, began to launch programs both to attract specific types of foreign medical travelers and to retain their own domestic elite, complicating the presumed directionality of flows.

That which is identified by many as the *novelty* of the crossing of national borders for medical care, or international medical travel (IMT), today is rooted to its apparent gradual massification among middle-class Westerners and the emergence of non-Western spatializations of care corresponding to their growing demand (Carrera and Bridges 2006; Cortez 2008; York 2008). In recent years, media, policy-makers and the private sector have come to acknowledge a growing number of patient–consumers from "developed" countries who, faced with decreasing healthcare entitlement and access in their countries of origin, have begun to seek timely and more economical care in this new global constellation of private medical facilities (Carrera and Bridges 2006; Turner 2007a). With these middle classes – affected by welfare-state retrenchment and "frustrated by their own diminishing entitlements" (Sparke 2009: 11) as citizens – now involved, IMT could no longer be explained away as an escape valve for the few "exceptions" (Wachter 2006: 661) dis-satisfied with their countries' (more or less) functional healthcare systems. Rather, it came to be discursively reincarnated as a harbinger of social crisis wherein traditional care boundaries could not hold. With this movement of people redrawing the boundaries to the pursuit of care in order to sidestep obstacles perceived to inhibit their access "at home,"[2] IMT therefore has come to symbolize a shift away from what were previously imagined as nationally bound, locally based care settings to what are now increasingly conceived as "chaotic global networks . . . in an era of ever deteriorating national, technological, mental and physical boundaries in the delivery of healthcare services" (Jenner 2008: 242).

Articulated through this complex and emerging global healthcare assemblage, argues Whittaker (2008: 273), is "a range of new relations between capital and labor, bodies and the state, belonging and extra-territoriality, transformations in political governance, and realignments of medical citizenship and the meanings of public health." For the few able "to both circumvent *and* benefit from different nation-state regimes" (Ong 1999: 112; emphasis original), the crossing of national borders has the potential to produce significant shifts in political and socio-economic status that directly condition access to healthcare, such that care not accessible in one country may be within reach in another. As a result, IMT often gets cast as a "demo-cratizing" force for both healthcare consumers and providers (Turner 2007b; Jenner 2008) – a "'disruptive innovation' that can transform traditional processes and relationships" (Deloitte 2008; see Brooker and Go 2006; Wachter 2006; Bookman and Bookman 2007). With this "deterritorialization" of care calling into question and renegotiating the relationship between the pursuit of health and the assumedly "traditional" bounded settings of its provision, the globalizing healthcare "marketplace" thus becomes envisioned as a hopeful space of distributive justice for mobile "patient–consumers."

This neoliberal celebration of "deterritorialized" care provision constructs medical travelers as pioneering patient–consumer agents of their own emancipation, leaving behind healthcare systems that have somehow failed them for destinations envisioned as almost indiscriminate nodes of "world-class" care provision. Yet Benhabib (2004: 23) suggests that the resulting "disaggregated citizenship," wherein people "come under the purview of different rights regimes and multiple, nested sovereignties" through their participation in global markets, is not the same as "cosmopolitan citizenship." Cresswell (2001) cautions against the romantic gloss of "resistance" linking mobility and consumption: while some mobilities may appear transgressive, they also perpetuate existing power structures. International medical travelers' very presence and "needs" are recognized, received, attended to, ignored, disapproved of, or rebuked in accordance with their value to those sending, losing, abandoning, attracting, discouraging, filtering, or unified with them. There is therefore a need to critically examine the production of medical mobilities and the biopolitical distinctions drawn around medical travelers by their "sending" and "receiving" contexts.

What place for "medical tourism" in a world of "medical exile"?

Terms such as "tourism," "outsourcing," "migration," and "exile" are frequently employed in media, political, and academic coverage of a spectrum of health-motivated mobilities produced in the crossing into and out of national healthcare jurisdictions. They implicitly point to a host of social, cultural, political, and economic imaginings and interpellations of the subjects and spaces engaged in these cross-border movements (Germann Molz and Gibson 2007). To employ such terms is effectively to identify in IMT a profound challenge to sovereignty by "wandering peoples who . . . are themselves the marks of a shifting boundary that alienates the frontiers of the modern nation" (Bhabha 2004: 256) through their transgression of a political "care" relationship that, until recently, has been widely held as a decidedly national domain of action (Nye 2003). In line with Clifford's (1997) call for new representational strategies of and around mobile subjects, such a rich lexicon offers substantial material to explore complex dynamics shaping responsiveness to mobile health-seeking bodies that at once challenge and reassert the relevance of national borders in accessing "care" in ways that refuse "to place the emotion, the mess, and the softness of care in some prepolitical zone" (Staeheli and Brown 2003: 774; see also Raghuram *et al.* 2009).

Critically, only a handful of authors have begun to unpack the politics of IMT's semiotics. While authors such as Smith-Cavros (2010) and Kangas (2010) have adopted more "neutral" descriptors, such as "medical travel" and "transnational therapeutic itineraries," to step around the minefield of connotations linked to "tourism," "outsourcing," and "exile," Inhorn and Pasquale (2009), to the contrary, insist that we be careful to recognize the power relations that drive people across borders and to avoid their linguistic depoliticization in our work. Calling for greater acknowledgment of the breadth of influences that drive people across borders for health, Thompson (2008) distinguishes what she calls *medical tourism*, "with its emphasis on the movement of empowered, biosocial citizens . . . seeking medical care by traveling down scientific, regulatory and/or economic gradients," from *medical migrations*, those "movements across regional and national boundaries in ways relating to health status and care and to immigration . . . status and the freedom from various kinds of persecution" (Thompson 2008: 435). Her distinction between these categories of medical mobility draws attention to the less-than-elite nature of the vast majority of IMT, highlighting the nuanced influences that contribute to variably fostering and disallowing a range of mobile subjectivities. Crucially, however, the link that she draws between "tourism" and "migrations" superficially supposes a dichotomy separating the savvy self-regulating patient–consumer capable of transcending and rendering irrelevant the bonds of the nation state, on one hand, from the dejectedly displaced for whom those bonds constitute significant obstacles, on the other.

Alert to the plethora of value-laden judgments at various scales involved in deciding who may and may not receive treatment "at home," authors writing on "reproductive tourism" (e.g., Pennings 2002, 2005; Inhorn and Pasquale 2009; Smith-Cavros 2010) have produced some of the strongest critiques of the violence generated by the term "tourism." They argue that "connotations of the term are negative when considered in a medical context (recreation), thus devaluing the motivation for the journey, implying that the . . . tourist goes abroad to look for something exotic and strange" (Pennings 2002: 337). In theorizing the relationship between "reproductive tourism" and reproductive rights, Inhorn and Pasquale (2009: 904) specifically question "the language of tourism as an appropriate gloss." Contrasted with the real emotional, social, and financial costs shouldered by infertile individuals or couples, the use of "tourism" seems to mock their suffering. The authors endorse instead the term "reproductive exile" for its recognition of the legal, social, and economic barriers to their ability to access quality services "at home" and the pursuit of such services abroad. Exile becomes both forced migration and a sense of estrangement from one's "natural" community (Cresswell 2001; Kaplan 1996). In a similar vein, Milstein and Smith (2006) polemically describe American medical travelers as "refugees" escaping from an ailing healthcare system. "Refugee" here differentiates "real," urgent medical needs from discretionary ones: "This is not what is sometimes snootily referred to as 'medical tourism,' in which people go abroad for elective plastic surgery ... People are desperate" (Smith, in Ansorge 2006). With "tourism" widely held as an experience of leisure, hedonism, and escape in which everyday obligations are inverted (Urry 2002), therefore, IMT industry players are increasingly reshaping the terms of their practice by recognizing mobile patient–consumers' desperation, pushing for an industry-wide shift from "medical tourism" to "medical travel" to lend their services greater integrity (see Yap 2006; Woodman 2008).[3] Being driven – and limited – by "real" medical needs is held to distinguish "medical refugees" from "medical tourists."

Drawing from a predominantly Western base of concern with how health-motivated mobility categories get produced through "sending" contexts, these conceptual critiques and accommodations, however, fail to adequately address the constitutive role of "receiving" contexts. While acknowledging the role of "sending" contexts in countless medical travelers' suffering and desperation, I also want to call attention to what often gets obscured: "medical tourism" and "medical exile" are also produced by how these travelers get constituted as care-pursuing subjects by IMT destinations themselves. It is through processes of reterritorialization that different sets of values come to inform the contours of access to healthcare and form the relationship between medical travelers and care providers, "foreground[ing] the social construction of identity-in-place" (Dahlman 2008: 496). Rooted to their discursive deployment in dismissing or affirming what drives medical travelers abroad, the terms "medical tourism" and "medical exile" also indicate *destinations'* practices and expectations in sorting and relating to the categories of mobile patient–consumers to which they may or may not extend this commercial–political hospitality.

Destinations – frequently located within "developing" Asian countries – have embraced IMT as both a "passport to development" (Wood 1993: 48), via the "'trickle-down' of modern skills, new technology and improved public services ... imagined to follow in the wake of foreign tourists" (Enloe 1989: 40), and a platform for demonstrating that they can ensure "world-class" quality for foreign patient–consumers in "medical exile" from faltering healthcare systems in "developed" countries. This holds potent declarative value for destinations to improve their international visibility and prestige, since "becoming a tourist destination," suggests Urry (2002: 143), "is part of a reflexive process by which societies and places come to enter the global order." Indeed, throughout Asia, government authorities and IMT industry players focus extraordinary energy and investment on learning how best to appeal and cater to these prospective markets and their "disorders of affluence" (Jagyasi 2008). The term "medical tourism," therefore, often gets used to evoke the growing "world-class" commercial hospitality infrastructure and services catering to their demands and pocketbooks. In her work on IMT to Thailand, Wilson (2010: 138) retains "tourism" as a signifier to distinguish "a sector of the medical industry in relation to privileged foreign citizenship and currencies." That "the emblematic medical tourist" has been popularized as "a wealthy white Western or East Asian tourist" (Whittaker 2009: 323) reveals a commercial–political hospitality that is contingent upon "the differential capacities and dispositions" of destinations to be "affected by and moved to respond to certain claims and not to others" (Barnett 2005b: 20), hingeing on a distinction between invitation and visitation shaped by differences in national belonging, race, and class. "Tourism" here espouses a conditional hospitality, a politics of "care" that implies a return "home" by "guests" who cannot demand the same as local citizens from destinations' governments – a no-nonsense consumer relationship with the "hosts."

At the same time, IMT destinations offer a temporary haven for paying bodies recognized to be in "medical exile." Destinations do not thrive because they are "the best in the world" but because healthcare systems in patient–consumers' countries of origin are perceived to be somehow at fault – meaning that the success of an IMT destination is not merely a measure of its individual excellence, but, rather, is also contingent on an imagined geography of "care" that identifies perceived gaps and failures elsewhere. Take, for example, the conscious framing of Malaysia – a principal Asian IMT hub – as a "value for money" destination for a transnational bourgeoisie, where emphasis has been placed on the various plights that its prospective clienteles encounter in seeking healthcare in their habitual places: un(der)insured middle-class Americans are simply "priced out" of adequate medical care, while Middle Easterners have been turned away from their traditional IMT destinations in the West as a result of post-9/11 ethnic and religious discrimination. Malaysia is, in turn, marketed as capable of responding to these unmet needs through an auspicious combination of territorialized factors, including the material trappings of "world class" care, so-called "Asian hospitality," and the "peace of mind" assured through political and economic stability.

Such a strategy hinges upon a "magic" transformation of these patient–consumers who, "likely not part of the upper class within their own societies" (Smith-Cavros 2010: 472), can be temporarily cared for in relative luxury thanks to favorable exchange rates, low wages, and the "medical tourism" infrastructure built with them in mind. Medical travel agencies, top hotels, and serviced apartments are teaming up with private hospitals to attract foreign patient–consumers from "developed" countries to offer "seamless" door-to-door care services, and hospitals themselves have begun to redesign their patient quarters to offer exclusive international patient wards, guest lounges, and deluxe suites that allow families to stay with in-patients. Serving this "emblematic medical tourist" (Whittaker 2008) furthermore involves ensuring quality standards of treatment that meet or surpass those of Western benchmark facilities by investing in acquiring staff with internationally-recognized credentials and big-name accreditation (e.g. Joint Commission International, or JCI), perceived as key for attracting these "goldmine" patient–consumers.

What place for "medical exile" in destinations increasingly designed for "medical tourism?"

As a test-site for some of the world's most cutting-edge medical technologies and home to highly skilled foreign-trained medical professionals, the Malaysian context offers insight into shifting centers of "world-class" medical expertise and the varied manners in which newly recognized IMT destinations relate to the mobile embodied subjects they attract. Illustrative of the growing desire to tap into the potential of IMT, one of the country's most important IMT hubs, Penang, which made a name for itself as a destination for lower-middle-income patient–consumers from the nearby Indonesian island of Sumatra, is increasingly under pressure to "diversify" by opening facilities capable of attracting patient–consumers from "developed" countries. Committed to establishing Penang, one of Malaysia's richest states, as a "center of medical excellence" and "world-class getaway" (Emmanuel 2008c; NCER 2009), the state government is encouraging greater investment in "medical tourism" to help transform Penang's ailing tourism industry and foster growth independent of electronics manufacturing – its previous mainstay (Socio-Economic and Environmental Research Institute 2004). Key to this plan has been retaining, and improving on, Penang's share of non-Indonesian patient–consumers.[4] Yet responding to the urgent medical needs of lower-middle-income Indonesians looks very different from catering to "medical tourists." Accordingly, regional development plans prescribe the cultivation of spaces to attract higher-yielding (i.e. "big spender") patient–consumers. In addition to seven private hospitals in Penang endorsed by the Malaysian Ministry of Health for "medical tourism," there are proposals for turning a former island penal colony into a "medical tourism" resort, and for the construction of an integrated specialist hospital and wellness resort bringing together "Western" and "Eastern" medicines and homeopathy under one roof, complete with a nursing college, convention center, hotel, serviced apartments, and a herbal farm (Emmanuel 2008a). With such plans for upscale medical facilities, Penang officials are looking to boost overall prestige. "It adds to their résumé," observes one anonymous Malaysian medical travel agent (interview, 2008) about this general trend. "They can say, 'I get patients from the UK and Australia', rather than 'I've merely got patients from Indonesia'."

Whereas Penang may appear as yet another indiscriminate node on the map of "world-class" care for those from more "developed" countries, it assumes a different sort of relevance to Sumatran patient–consumers, who consistently generate the volumes that bulk up Malaysia's overall IMT figures and play a significant role in constituting the country as a destination (Ormond 2011).[5] Indeed, while Malaysia received only around 11 percent of its foreign patient–consumers from "developed" countries (6 percent of which hailed from "developed" Asian countries) in 2007, more than 83 percent came from "developing" Asian countries – and the vast majority of these from neighboring Indonesia (Association of Private Hospitals in Malaysia 2008). In spite of Malaysia's heavy reliance on these intra-regional flows, however, this reality has attracted little media, policy, and academic attention for simple economic reasons. The per capita expenditure of intra-regional flows from "developing" countries packs a significantly smaller punch than that of "medical tourists,"[6] leading Malaysian and other Asian IMT government and industry actors to increasingly invest in courting and cultivating Western, Middle Eastern, East Asian, and elite Southeast Asian "global health consumers." Still, as an inpatient myself in an upscale Malaysian hospital endorsed for "medical tourism" in late 2007, it seemed odd that my private room in the international wing, inaugurated only months prior by the Tourism Minister, was the only one occupied. The clamor for patient–consumers from "developed" countries has produced an infrastructure still largely devoid of "medical tourists" to use it, revealing a significant disjuncture with the real presence of foreign patient–consumers who are, by and large, *not* part of the IMT markets in which the private healthcare sector and government have heavily invested. These "real" IMT flows, due to the political and economic circumstances of the lower-middle-income Indonesians that by and large comprise them, have far more limited physical and economic mobility to access the exclusive "medical tourism" infrastructure being built.

The significant flows of patient–consumers out of Indonesia can be attributed to its substantial socio-economic polarities, political instability and overall poor access to healthcare, a reality that has long led middle- and upper-income nationals to seek healthcare in Singapore and Australia. Until the end of the 1990s, however, Malaysia was not recognized as a suitable IMT destination. This changed with the advent of the Asian economic crisis in 1997 when – contrary to neighboring Malaysia, Singapore and Thailand, whose nationals shifted from the private to the public healthcare sector due to reduced out-of-pocket health expenditure – Indonesia experienced a steep overall decline in the use of public sector provision and, correspondingly, of "Western" medicine more generally as real wages dropped by 40 percent at the peak of the crisis (Waters *et al.* 2003: 174–179; Pradhan *et al.* 2007).[7]

While health expenditure declined *within* Indonesia, however, it was precisely at this point in the economic crisis – correlating to currency devaluation that made Malaysian exchange rates attractive for those who could no longer afford to go further afield for treatment – that Malaysian private hospitals began to notice a rapid growth in the number of non-resident Indonesians turning to them for diagnostics and tertiary care. That this shift away from the wealthier IMT destinations and toward Malaysia was partly responsible for having kept Malaysia's private healthcare sector – which had been expanding at a rapid pace prior to the crisis – afloat during and in the wake of the economic crisis was not lost on the Malaysian government (Chee 2007). Its National Committee for the Promotion of Health Tourism identified early on the Association of Southeast Asian Nations (ASEAN) countries such as Indonesia, Cambodia, and Vietnam, home to emerging middle classes, as its core market (MOH 2002: 106). Even now, government rhetoric on the resiliency of Malaysia's IMT industry in the present economic crisis emphasizes the country's medical prowess within, and solidarity with, ASEAN, seeking out its patient–consumers "to cushion the impact of fewer arrivals from other markets" (*IMTJ* 2008).

With the Malaysian government's embrace of the IMT industry as a "National Key Economic Area" (Economic Planning Unit 2010), the territories and scales through which "national development" is pursued have effectively been rescripted to better link up with the foreign patient–consumer flows unevenly distributed across the 35 private hospitals endorsed for "medical tourism" by the Malaysian Ministry of Health.[8]

Recognition that this significant internal variation is largely attributable to IMT flows from neighboring Indonesia has made the national and state governments more active in their endorsement and fostering of greater cross-border regionalization. This can be seen with the Indonesia-Malaysia-Thailand Growth Triangle[9] (IMT-GT), whose role has been to identify and capitalize on "complementarities" both to benefit from and ultimately reduce disparities between the three countries' member areas by taking advantage of geographical proximity and improving cross-border mobility. Political leaders involved in the Triangle have suggested that cross-border patient–consumer mobility would be "the key for IMT-GT members to get through the current global economic crisis" (*Bangkok Post* 2009) for both "sending" and "receiving" areas. Indeed, "health without frontiers" has become one of the pillars of cooperation between ASEAN member states, in line with the notion that "[c]ooperation across borders may enable better use of resources, sharing of potential capacity and improving access of patients to quality care" (Pennings 2007: 506). The increasing focus on pooling resources and patient–consumers views this type of collaborative "outsourcing to other developing countries, especially for specialist, high-technology, diagnostic and rehabilitation services" as "a more cost-effective approach than attempting to develop national self-sufficiency" (Wolvaart 1998: 64; see McDonald *et al.* 2000; Morgan 2003; El Taguri 2007; Lautier 2008; Hopkins *et al.* 2009; Smith *et al.* 2009; Walraven *et al.* 2009).

The number of Indonesians traveling abroad for care during the Asian economic crisis did not decline after the end of the crisis. In fact, the Indonesian Medical Association (IDI) estimates that one million Indonesians currently go abroad for medical care annually (IRIN 2009). With quality health professionals, equipment, and facilities sparse throughout Indonesia, national commentators have suggested that "[l]ittle can be done to limit the practice [of IMT] as the government struggles to provide access to health care for average Indonesians who are financially weaker and generally in greater need" (Hulupi 2006). In light of these constraints, the IDI has admitted, "We cannot blame people for seeking treatment overseas" (Gunawan 2007). Industry commentators, however, caution against Malaysia's over-reliance on Indonesia, given the presumed volatility of intra-regional IMT and attempts at improving the quality of care in "sending" countries (Suwinski, in *IMTJ* 2010b). Efforts to curb the outflow of Indonesian patient–consumers include the 2010 reopening of Zainoel Abidin State Hospital (RSUZA) in Aceh. At its launch, the Aceh Governor announced:

> RSUZA is the most advanced hospital in Indonesia, and its facilities can match prominent hospitals in Penang and Singapore. I hope the new hospital will put an end to the practice of thousands of Acehnese going to Penang, Malaysia, or Singapore each month for medical treatment. Including myself, who had to opt for Singapore as a place to have medical treatment because the facilities there were far more advanced than what we have had in Banda Aceh. But with this new hospital, I am certain that the equipment we have now can rival hospitals abroad.
>
> (Irwandi, in *IMTJ* 2010a)

Despite the governor's optimism and the pundits' foreboding, however, the Indonesian healthcare system has a long way to go. The problem facing many hospitals in Indonesia is not necessarily the lack of technology but rather the persistent lack of trained specialists with the technical expertise required to operate the equipment.

Responsiveness to Indonesian patient–consumers' "exile" from their countries' healthcare systems has presented a series of challenges for Malaysian private hospitals, generating an "interdependency [that] is not cozy but . . . contested, complicated and productively unsettling" (Raghuram *et al.* 2009: 10–11). With the ability to respond to and attract these intra-regional flows contributing toward asserting Malaysia's broader regional relevance, medical professionals and political authorities throughout ASEAN have at times interpreted Malaysian private hospitals' extension of hospitality to mobile Indonesian *consumers* not as a collaborative act but rather as the patronizing flexing of political and economic muscle by a more "developed" country to poach their "rightful" patients instead of demonstrating "solidarity" with their *citizens* through more conventional humanitarian aid avenues that recognize nation states as the most appropriate venues for ensuring the welfare of their populace. Taking the provision of care to Indonesians away from the space of "home" has led Malaysian private hospitals to delicately reframe themselves as a "complementary" resource to regional medical professionals and not as competition. An anonymous Malacca private hospital marketing representative, whose institution's corporate social responsibility policy allocates funds for educating Indonesian health workers, explains:

> Many think that we are just being opportunists, going in and taking whatever we can from Indonesians. But we need to be a responsible corporate body, to show some responsibility and initiatives to help them. We say that we are always here to offer alternatives to your people. You should go to your doctor first. However, if you want a second opinion or a procedure that is not available in your country, then come here.
>
> (Interview, 2008)

With Indonesian political authorities doing little to improve healthcare conditions on the ground to stem their nationals' cross-border healthcare pursuits (Praptini 2007), this facility's active reinvestment in improving Indonesian healthcare delivery is indicative of a starkly different kind of engagement that is more intimate and sustained compared with that with "medical tourists," presumed to come from contexts where such aid is deemed less necessary or inappropriate.

"Complementarities" and "solidarities"

This section speaks to how globalizing concepts and ideals – such as the practice of "world-class" medicine – travel, as Minca and Oakes in this volume suggest, "through the production of new experimental tourist spaces but, once grounded, become something radically different in terms of practice and experience" by exploring components of a commercial-political hospitality taking place within the IMT-GT, a space of supposed "complementarities" and "solidarities" in which Indonesian Sumatrans enter parts of Malaysia more easily than other Indonesians to access "world-class" care. I draw upon in-depth interviews[10] with social actors engaged with IMT in the country's three main IMT destinations – Penang, Malacca, and the Klang Valley – in the scope of research undertaken on the material and discursive positioning of Malaysia as an IMT destination to relate how private Malaysian hospitals in Penang and Malacca, specifically, respond to mobile Indonesian patient–consumers in ways not frequently extended to the subjects of "medical tourism." Indeed, as we shall see, the sole overlaps with the spaces and subjects of "medical tourism" may be the "world-class" hospital staff and materials used for treatment.

Considered more within reach physically and economically than the national alternative, which entails a flight to Jakarta with care costs equal to or greater than in Malaysia, Penang and Malacca provide healthcare services critical for the Indonesian island of Sumatra. Nearly 88 percent of all Indonesians receiving private medical care in Malaysia in 2007 did so at the ten IMT-GT-endorsed hospitals in Penang and Malacca. Physical connectivity, therefore, has been key to overcoming "national" barriers, leading to the improvement of transport linkages across the Straits of Malacca. Among the most significant measures taken to facilitate Indonesian mobility was exemption from the one million Indonesian rupiah (€84) exit tax (*fiscal*) for departures from Indonesian parts of the IMT-GT to other areas of the Triangle, rendering more frequent travel across the Straits to nearby Malaysia economically feasible for larger numbers of Sumatrans and, in turn, fostering greater intra-regional trade, healthcare, tourism and educational "complementarities" (ADB 2007a, b; Emmanuel 2008b; *Mathaba* 2008; Suhaimi 2009).[11] Consequently, multiple regional airlines set up routes between Sumatran cities selected for their IMT "sending" potential (e.g., Djambi, Medan, Padang, Palembang, and Pekan Baru), and Penang and Malacca, to bolster their status as "regional" IMT hubs

(*NST* 2008; D-8 Secretariat 2008). Symbolic of the growing functional alliance between low-cost regional airlines and hospitals, Riau Airlines – whose 50-seater plane makes its daily 30-minute flight from Pekan Baru in Sumatra to Malacca with an estimated average of 30 patient–consumers on board – has a ticket counter in Malacca's Mahkota Medical Centre, allowing travel arrangements to be made within the hospital itself (Lim interview, 2008).[12]

While some "health-conscious" travelers use Penang and Malacca for preventive diagnostic screenings and first opinions before ultimately turning to Singapore for second opinions and treatment, many tend to put off seeking care in Malaysia until their illnesses have grown irreversibly chronic or acute. Regional airlines are adapting their fleets in order to transport Indonesian patient–consumers on stretchers, and authorized ambulances can now meet aircraft on the tarmac to transport emergency cases without the need for passing through conventional immigration controls (Emmanuel 2008d). Such emergency transport measures hint at the gravity of conditions and immediacy of treatment required by Sumatran patient–consumers crossing into Malaysia. "This means that it's very hard to treat some people because of the advanced states of their illnesses," observes an anonymous Malacca hospital marketing representative (interview, 2008). A Penang hospital public relations officer concurs:

> It depends on their [Indonesian patients'] financial ability – if they are financially secure. For those with less funds, it's quite restrictive, though they may come here for serious illnesses ... We have to screen them [remotely] before they arrive because otherwise there will be a big shock when you see the patient. Really! Sometimes they report that they have this [degree of medical problem,] but when they come in, it's usually worse than they described – people are a degree worse than they actually tell us. And sometimes the results aren't so great. We just have to deal with that when the patients come in.
>
> (Interview, 2008)

Although patient–consumers with particularly urgent needs may be denied admittance by airlines and hospitals if their conditions are too acute to be transported safely, this "open-arms" approach to Sumatrans in need contrasts with private hospitals catering principally to a "medical tourism" market that, concerned with cultivating their reputations for untarnished success rates, turn away patient–consumers who risk yielding negative medical outcomes.

Traveling to Malaysia involves significant financial planning and investment for many Sumatrans. Unlike the luxury inpatient suites and hotels geared towards "medical tourism," budget accommodation is sought by Indonesian patient–consumers with limited funds. Inpatients tend to stay in shared hospital rooms for MYR70 (€17) per night, leaving the single-bedded rooms (MYR200 [€48]) and VIP suites (MYR500 [€121]) for wealthier inpatients, while private hospitals receiving many Indonesians will work directly with local hostels and long-stay accommodation to secure affordable rates for outpatients' and inpatients' family members. A Penang private hospital public relations officer explains:

> Most of them [family accompanying Indonesian patients] don't stay at a hotel, unless they are super-rich . . . Most of them will stay at apartments where, it's like – can you imagine hospitals? – they sleep on cots. And I think that it's not easy to get that in Kuala Lumpur, where it's, of course, very expensive . . . It very much depends on the patient. There are apartments with or without attached bathrooms, with or without air-conditioning . . . They just need to tell us the budget.
>
> (Interview, 2008)

Indicative of the growing institutionalization of Malaysia as an IMT destination, some hospitals have begun to pair up with select Indonesian banks and credit card companies to provide credit facilities to account holders. Yet, given the extent of Indonesia's informal economy, some patient–consumers – uninsured and without credit – carry suitcases of Indonesian rupiah (IDR) to pay for treatment in cash. Francis Lim, CEO of Mahkota Medical Centre in Malacca, notes:

> Generally, they [Indonesian patient–consumers] are middle-class people. They normally would be able to afford to pay for their treatment . . . But sometimes we do have cases where, after the operation starts, the procedure becomes complicated. When that happens, the patient's family is liable for the full amount. In such cases, the doctors usually understand. We'll talk about how to help the patient, and we normally charge less. We want to do this business from the heart. We're not just here to make money from providing a service. Of course, we must be profitable because we have shareholders and we must pay competitive salaries. But we do this because we understand that it's more complicated than what was expected.
>
> (Interview, 2008)

With medical travel insurance covering complications largely out of reach to non-Western markets, private Malaysian hospitals acknowledge that uninsured foreign patient–consumers – particularly from "developing" countries – may not always be capable of fully covering their medical costs.

While the steady stream of Indonesian patient–consumers crossing the Straits of Malacca for care in Malaysian private hospitals more than compensates for any shortfalls, the pervasive "business from the heart" rhetoric in facilities in Penang and Malacca identified here hints at a certain flexibility and willingness to provide care to patient–consumers whose healthcare "needs" are placed against the backdrop of Indonesia's poor socio-economic circumstances. The ways in which these private facilities cater to the perceived requirements of quality and comfort of their predominantly Sumatran patient–consumers is powerfully indicative of providers' simultaneously political and commercial negotiation of responsible engagement with patient–consumers who appear to require very different regimes of support from those that are extended through "medical tourism."

Conclusion

Narrow focus on the seemingly "novel" spectacle of the "developed" relying on the "developing" has filtered how we have come to understand the extension of hospitality by contemporary IMT destinations, leading to an impoverished awareness of IMT destinations' multifaceted "care" relationships with an array of foreign patient–consumers and their implications. By drawing attention to responses to lower-middle-income regional patient–consumers who – in spite of comprising the bulk of IMT flows today – too often pass below the mediatic, political and academic radar locked onto the spectacle of "medical tourism" from "developed" countries and its associated trappings, I have sought to contribute to contemporary mappings of the wide "range of new relations between capital and labor, bodies and the state, belonging and extraterritoriality, transformations in political governance, and realignments of medical citizenship and the meanings of public health" (Whittaker 2008: 273) being produced through the international pursuit and provision of healthcare.

IMT destinations are held to have the potential to derive considerable benefit from profiling themselves as capable of responding to the "needs" of patient–consumers in "medical exile." "Care," as "the response to a need" (Tronto 1999: 170), undertakes fundamental political work. Through entre-preneurial attempts at harnessing IMT flows, foreign patient–consumers' "needs" get assessed, measured, and subsequently framed as motivated by discontent with healthcare "back home," conveniently repositioning foreign patient–consumers as "'cases' for the state and the development apparatus" (Escobar 1995: 225). Via claims to IMT destination status, we have seen Malaysian authorities try to accomplish this by promoting a commercial–political hospitality that seems to transcend national belonging by playing into biosocial claims to universal access for *consumers*, from wherever they might come. The provision of "care" through this extension of hospitality constitutes both international patient–consumers and IMT destinations in new ways in relation to the political, social, cultural, and economic barriers to "care" in patient–consumers' countries of residence.

My reading of the Malaysian IMT context has sought to present some of the dilemmas faced in the metaphorical space of the "hotel–fortress" evoked by an ever-larger number of IMT destinations throughout the world as they promote themselves (Ormond 2011). Government- and industry-sponsored

IMT campaigns with taglines such as "Korea: Hospitality in healthcare," "Malaysia Healthcare: Quality of care for your peace of mind," "Philippines: The heart of Asia," "Singapore Medicine: Peace of mind when health really matters," and "Taiwan cares for your health" increasingly welcome patient–consumers across the globe. Contrary to Lawson's (2007: 5) assertion that neoliberalism has "effectively privatized responsibility rather than politicized it," we see here that markets are not necessarily "exempt from an ethic of care" (Smith, S.J. 2005: 15). Yet, if recognizing courted patient–consumers as being in "medical exile" implies recognizing their dignity and the gravity of their unmet needs "at home," then IMT destinations are entering into an ethical playing field in which they are challenged by the political consequences of market-based recognition of the "needs" of their foreign markets. As Benhabib (2004: 19) suggests, there may be an "irresolvable contradiction ... between expansive and inclusionary principles of moral and political universalism, as anchored in human rights, and the particularistic and exclusionary conceptions of democratic closure." While "tourism" frequently gets deployed to designate an IMT destination's recognition and reception of patient–consumers from "developed" countries, as well as its deflection of extended responsibility toward them, what becomes of the largely ignored intraregional IMT flows from "developing" countries – so fundamental to forging and sustaining many Asian IMT destinations – that rely more significantly on these destinations? Important work remains to be done to explore the ethics of market-mediated responsiveness to "medical exile" in the context of IMT.

Notes

1 Medical travelers from over 150 countries have sought medical care at Mayo Clinic in the United States (Mayo Clinic 2009), while Bumrungrad Hospital, alone responsible for 31 percent of all international medical travel to Thailand, has hosted patient–consumers from 190 countries (Bumrungrad 2010).
2 Four categories of obstacles are most often cited in the literature. First, prohibitively high medical care costs and inadequate insurance coverage may keep essential and elective treatment financially out of reach (e.g. invasive surgeries, dental and cosmetic work; Connell, J. 2006; Rajeev and Latif 2009). Second, scarcity of supply of human resources and/or materials may significantly delay treatment (e.g. waiting lists for joint replacements or transplantations; Scheper-Hughes 2000; Katz *et al.* 2002; Turner 2007a, 2009; Hadi 2009). Third, states' regulatory controls may deny access to treatment on moral grounds (e.g. gender reassignment, IVF procedures for single women, pre-implantation sex selection of embryos, commercial surrogacy and abortion; Pennings 2002, 2004; Whittaker 2009) or due to their experimental status (e.g. stem cell therapies and fertility treatments; Blyth and Farrand 2005; Horowitz *et al.* 2007; Kiatpongsan and Sipp 2008; Whittaker 2008, 2009; Clarke 2009). Finally, care providers may be perceived to lack sufficient sensitivity to linguistic, cultural, and religious needs (Bergmark *et al.* 2008; Lee *et al.* 2010). Each of these categories provides evidence of the multiple ethical issues being worked out across the regulatory and economic patchwork of a globalizing healthcare "marketplace."

3 Furthermore, while a "conventional" tourism component (e.g. "post-op" safaris, Taj Mahal tours, and recuperation at tropical beach resorts) may be used in place-imaging techniques to attract patient–consumers and their families to long-haul destinations, the "recreational value of travel" is held to decrease in importance the more serious the condition being treated (Horowitz *et al.* 2007), whittling it down to little more than "long-distance migration for surgery" (Connell, J. 2006: 6).

4 Some 73 percent of Americans, 56 percent of Europeans, and 53 percent of Australians receiving care in Malaysia in 2007 did so in Penang. However, these comprised only 1.22 percent, 2.7 percent, and 1.12 percent, respectively, of the overall foreign patient–consumer population (Association of Private Hospitals in Malaysia 2008).

5 This is, in fact, the case throughout the region. According to an influential 2008 McKinsey & Company industry report, some 93 percent of Asian medical travelers are estimated to seek out IMT destinations also within Asia, an overwhelming figure compared with the relatively meagre 27 percent of North Americans, 10 percent of Europeans, and 2 percent of Middle Easterners who stay within their respective regions for care (Ehrbeck *et al.* 2008: 5).

6 While Singapore brings in US$2,111 per capita by using cutting-edge medicine to lure wealthier patient–consumers, Malaysia, with its reliance on higher volumes of lower-middle-income Indonesians, attracts little more than one-tenth of that amount per capita (Association of Private Hospitals in Malaysia 2008; *IMTJ* 2010b).

7 This was due to a significant increase in the cost of treatment and scarcity of basic medicinal products and supplies caused by a crippled tax base and the system's heavy dependency on imported pharmaceuticals.

8 In spite of efforts to portray the Klang Valley as the national anchor for the IMT industry, with no less than 17 MOH-endorsed hospitals for "medical tourism," the capital city's metropolitan region was responsible for treating only 11 percent of all foreign patient–consumers in 2007. The bulk pursued care elsewhere: 61 percent to Penang, with seven endorsed hospitals; 19 percent to Malacca, with three; and the remainder to the states of Kedah, Johor, Sabah, and Sarawak (Association of Private Hospitals in Malaysia 2008).

9 Having expanded significantly since it began in 1993 as part of a broader ASEAN development policy, it currently encompasses 100 million people across the Indonesian island of Sumatra, 9 Malaysian states, and 14 Thai provinces.

10 From late 2007 to early 2008, 49 interviews were held with respondents in top-level executive and administrative positions (e.g. CEOs, directors, senior managers, board members and advisers) for governmental, private, and not-for-profit bodies; research, business development, marketing, policy, public relations, and customer service executives and officers; medical travel facilitators; and medical professionals. The aim was to better grasp how they conceptualize IMT flows and responses and act to influence the course of the industry's development within Malaysia.

11 The *fiscal* was enforced upon exit from Indonesia everywhere else outside of the Indonesian part of the IMT-GT until 1 January 2009 when the Indonesian government's reformed regulation came into force. By showing their tax identity cards at border crossings, Indonesians can now travel abroad from anywhere in Indonesia without paying the tax. However, if they are without the card and not exempt from taxation, they are required to pay IDR2,500,000 to leave the country (*Jakarta Post* 2008). Paradoxically, this policy change now adversely affects Indonesian IMT into Malaysia. With many Indonesians unwilling or unable to acquire tax identity cards due to the pervasiveness of the informal economy, some Malaysia-based IMT facilitators have begun to pressure private Malaysian hospitals

that are popular among Indonesians to discount the cost of the penalty exit tax from high-ticket procedures in order to ensure that the Indonesian patient–consumer flow continues.

12 Similarly, with some 100 people departing daily from Medan to seek healthcare overseas, for instance, an estimated 80 percent of passengers on a daily 40-minute flight to Penang are thought to be seeking treatment (Gunawan 2007; anonymous Penang private hospital public relations officer, interview, 2008).

9 Post-ethical tours

Corporate social responsibility in tourism

Harng Luh Sin

After a 5.5 hour turbulent plane ride and waiting 25 minutes for a taxi (I got an eco-cab!) in the 101 degree F [38 degrees Celsius] heat, I finally stumble into my hotel room. I open the door and a heat wave hits me. I don't know the last time I was inside and it felt this hot. The thermostat in my hotel room is off. When I turn it on the it tells me it's 86 degrees F [30 degrees Celsius] in the room. It takes a full hour for the room to get to a manageable temperature. I climb into bed a little later and go to turn on the bedside lamp. It doesn't turn on. I check for a light bulb – that's not the problem. I reach around the back and the cord isn't plugged in. I have to blindly grope behind the bed to find the outlet. "What's the deal with this hotel?" I ask myself. "Don't they know I expect things to work?"

Then it occurs to me – the hotel is making an effort to save electricity.

(Elizabeth Sanberg 2008)

This example shows how easy it is to misunderstand efforts geared towards responsible practices in tourism, where underlying intentions may not be immediately apparent, and tourists may instead be frustrated at the seemingly poor standard of services provided. This was the case with Elizabeth Sanberg, founder of the Go Green Travel Green website – one who is clearly championing idea(l)s of eco-conscious travel. So would a typical tourist realize the hotel's effort at all?

Indeed, set amid numerous calls for consumers and corporations alike to assume larger responsibilities – whether this is toward the environment, the less privileged, or in addressing social injustices, as one of the largest industries in terms of economic revenue and labor employed, the tourism industry has too responded with a whole plethora of "ethical tours" that are increasingly marketed to mass consumers. While standards and definitions of ethical or responsible tours vary, of course, between different operators, one example, Exotissimo Travel, describes it thus:

Calling Vietnam, Cambodia, Laos, Myanmar and Thailand our homes, we love to showcase the beauty of the region through our tours and inspire in guests a genuine interest in responsible travel and sustainable tourism. We are fully committed to conserving natural resources, preserving cultural heritage and making positive impacts in the communities with which we come into contact. We work with local charities and encourage our guests to tread as lightly as possible during their travels.

(Exotissimo Travel 2009–2010)

The website continues with a list of tours one could join – tours listed as responsible/ethical. Such a listing is not uncommon, and within the same website and framework, then, are other possible tours to join – those *not* listed as responsible or ethical. It is the purpose of this chapter to question such binaries, suggesting that instead of seeing tours (or other tourism-related services such as hotels and transport) as ethical or not, there is a need to realize the implicit morality in all forms of production and consumption, and that "consumers do not choose between ethical and unethical consumption, smart and stupid shopping; they instead negotiate multiple and sometimes contra-dictory moral demands" (Foster 2008: 225).

This chapter therefore calls for a "post-ethical" approach, where beyond looking at the practices of so-called "ethical tourism," it is suggested that such binaries have less to do with actual ethics and more to do with the serving industry's interests. Indeed, the actual plurality of real and localized tourism practices – like all forms of production and consumption – is filled with the complex moralities and ethics with which we already navigate our everyday lives.

At the same time, neoliberalism and the privatization of "development" has meant a greater role for, and greater expectations of, corporations to behave "ethically," while "ethics" has emerged as a new marketing and accumulation strategy for these same corporations. The focus of this chapter is hence on the role of the private sector, especially in terms of their corporate social responsibility (CSR)[1] policies and practices, while acknowledging CSR and ethical consumer activism as two sides of the same coin. Corporations have an incentive to take on CSR as a means to create value and brand loyalty through attempts at aligning themselves with what they deem to be consumer pers-pectives (e.g. carbon offsetting programs to show consumers that they are equally conscious of their environmental footprint); on the other hand, "consumers use the commercial value of their brand loyalty to lobby corpora-tions for a variety of goods and services, the delivery of which was once presumed to be the obligation and function of elected governments in promoting social welfare" (Foster 2008: xvii). As such, notions of CSR will continually be contested, while terms and concepts such as ethical consumer-ism, CSR, and responsible tourism will all continue to stay with us (even though these are often at loggerheads over what is considered responsibility), and in many situations these translate into very real practices on the ground.

Also, when responsibility or ethics increasingly become what is sold as the "attraction" in tourism, one has to question – does place still matter? Does it matter where one is being environmentally conscious or where one is helping the "locals" overcome poverty? Or is it all the same whether one is saving rainforests in Brazil or in Thailand? Indeed, this chapter argues that focusing on broad idea(l)s such as ethics or CSR has detracted from realizing that intimate relationships and practices are often formed on the ground, and that the need to appreciate contexts of responsibility has become all the more evident – especially as we move beyond seeing tour(ism) as ethical or not, and toward realizing that ethics is indeed involved in all sorts of economic and personal decisions anyway (Micheletti 2003).

This chapter therefore explores the role of corporations when discussing ethics and tourism, especially in Asia (as one of such contexts we should pay attention to), as a space in which CSR tends to be enacted between "First World" ideals and "Third World" realities. An overview of the performances of ethics as observed in tourism is provided, followed by the corporation's role in enacting such ethical responsibilities. While such responsibilities are mostly undefined and can refer to a myriad of concerns from poverty alleviation to environmental awareness, this chapter focuses on one aspect – namely, the ties both CSR and ethical tourism have with developmental objectives – and suggests that critique toward development and postcolonialism should be better understood and integrated into how corporations construct and practice their supposed ethical responsibilities. Specifically, it argues for the importance of contextualizing CSR in a post-ethical manner, rather than discussing it in abstract terms. In tourism's case, then, the contexts of it as a service industry with no tangible "product," as well as one that is dominated by small-scale companies (in contrast to tradition CSR studies with corporate giants), are discussed. Also, more generally, looking at how notions of ethics and responsibilities differ from place to place and from people to people, highlights the sometimes highly charged contestations between what sorts of practices come to play, and how indeed CSR should be managed. Empirical excerpts in this chapter are drawn out from fieldwork (personal interviews) conducted from 2009 to 2010, for a broader research project on social responsibilities in tourism in Thailand.

Ethics and tourism

The prevalent view today is that "mass tourism" has all but failed to deliver the promised benefits of economic development in "Third World" countries (see also Chapter 10 in this volume), where multinational companies such as large hotel chains profit at the expense of cheap local labor, even as many countries continue to be heavily dependent on tourism for incomes and employment. Tourism has been criticized for causing more problems in terms of income inequity, sociocultural issues (such as loss of traditional practices in host destinations), and much environmental damage. Cleverdon and Kalisch elaborate that of the ills of mass tourism, "eviction and displacement for construction of tourism resorts, rising land, food and fuel prices, and commoditization of cultural assets are just some examples" (2000:172; see also de Kadt 1979; Scheyvens 2002; Smith and Duffy 2003; Mowforth *et al.* 2007). Since the emergence of a series of pieces severely reproving impacts of tourism from the 1980s (Britton 1982; Cohen, E. 1987; Leung 1989; Richter 1989; Butler, R.W. 1990), many have sought to develop new ways of conducting tourism to reform the industry of its ills – which met with varying success.

To start with, the key areas of alternative tourism (Weaver 1991, 1995) and sustainable tourism (for key initial pieces, see Cohen, E. 1987; Pearce 1987), of which many other areas can be considered a subset, reflect initial efforts to incorporate social and environmental responsibilities in an attempt to develop a form of travel that is more benign to the local community and the ecological environment. These developed alongside the popularization of the concept of sustainable development through the Brundtland Report, *Our Common Future* (WCED 1987), and together brought about an era of tourism development where discourses of responsibility are prevalent in both academic and popular observations. Since the late 1980s, works have frequently featured notions of ethics and responsibility, and this, in the initial stages, was seen to be represented by:

> tourism which is developed and maintained in an area (community environment) in such a manner and at such a scale that it remains viable over an indefinite period and does not degrade or alter the environment (human and physical) in which it exists to such a degree that it prohibits the successful development and wellbeing of other activities and processes.
>
> (Butler, R.W. 1993: 23)

Central to these is the idea that tourism ought to consider ethics, morals, and responsibility, as earlier discussed, where implicit morality is accepted in all aspects of life (including consumer and corporate decisions), and that the distinction between what is social or ethical and the economy is but an artificial result of the larger "historical transformation that disembedded the market from social life" (Foster 2008: 225; see Polanyi 1957 [1944]).

Within the popular discourse of responsibility in tourism development, however, there is often an underlying (but not always specified) assumption that the origins of tourists, travel agencies, and multinational corporations owning hotel chains, airlines, and other tourist services were from the developed world. The host destinations and "locals" were often regarded to be of the developing countries, many of which are in Asia. Responsibilities here are thus seen to be that of the "privileged" toward "others," and the overwhelming imperative to be responsible was also due to the great privileges accorded to the developed world (see Massey 2004, 2005). Smith and Duffy, for example, highlight this notion of the responsibility of the privileged toward the less privileged in some basic questions about ethics in tourism:

> is tourism all about the egoistic satisfaction of those paying for the privilege or should ethics play a part? What does it mean to say that a certain way of behaving, or a particular kind of tourism development, is wrong? Can the tourism industry "afford" morality?
>
> (2003: 7)

The privileged – namely, the paying tourists who can afford travel and the large tourism companies who earn profits from their travels – are all pictured to have great responsibilities in ensuring ethical tourism developments. And it is indeed in line with this view that this chapter focuses on social responsibilities of tourism corporations. Kalisch, for example, suggests that:

> We live in a world where largely unaccountable transnational corporations, whose main aim is profit maximisation, can wield tremendous economic power over national state governments and international trade agreements. Consequently, the calls for corporate ethical business practice and a fairer trade system are gradually increasing. Ever since Greenpeace confronted Shell over its environmental and human rights record, corporations are beginning to consider ethical policies and social and environmental audits to improve their public relations image.
>
> (2000: 1–2)

Ethical forms of tourism have therefore surfaced both in academic literature and popular consumption, with increasing numbers of tours offering "ecotourism," "just tourism," and "pro-poor tourism" (as discussed in Chapter 10 in this volume). While initial efforts were largely biased toward incorporating environmental responsibilities in tourism development, since the turn of the century, increasingly calls have been made to refocus on social responsibilities. Mowforth *et al.* state this clearly: "countless instances of the exploitative nature of tourism developments in the Third World have been documented over the last two decades. The new forms of tourism, however, are intended to overcome such exploitation" (2007: 47). Referring specifically to sustainable tourism development, Briassoulis comments that the key discourse is in:

> the central issue of how to manage the natural, built, and socio-cultural resources of host communities in order to meet the fundamental criteria of promoting their economic well-being, preserving their natural and socio-cultural capital, achieving intra- and intergenerational equity in the distribution of costs and benefits, securing their self-sufficiency, and satisfying the needs of tourists.
>
> (2002: 1,065–1,066)

However, the popularity of attaching ethical responsibilities to tourism development has not come without a dose of cynicism and skepticism. Most significantly, many have since questioned how different (if at all) these new forms of tourism are. Butcher, for example, argues that such "moral" forms of tourism are but a superficial sense that tourism development is achieving the "moral regulation of pleasure-seeking [that] is necessary in order to preserve environmental and cultural diversity" (2003: 7). Furthermore, research has shown that even though so-called green consumers may claim to support pro-poor or fair-trade initiatives when polled in surveys, many continue to disregard such notions of responsibility when booking holidays, and instead choose holidays based on financial considerations and convenience (Balooni 1997; Cleverdon and Kalisch 2000).

For example, "ethical tours" have been criticized as being nothing more than a marketing gimmick to make tourism development appear responsible, where a change in rhetoric has not necessarily meant a change in practices on the ground. New terminologies of alternative tourism products are continually introduced to the market, including: ecotourism, responsible tourism, fair trade through tourism, volunteer tourism, pro-poor tourism, green tourism, cultural tourism, soft tourism, ethnic tourism, sustainable tourism, and so forth. "The question is, are these just new names for old products that have ultimately been repackaged to appear more attractive to consumers, or do they indicate a fundamental change in approach to tourism?" (Scheyvens 2002: 11). Khun Eng, Director of a local tour agency called Let's Tour Bangkok, for example, shares this experience from the ground:

> I think we don't have a green business to proclaim on sale . . . But as I know from other suppliers and our vendor in America, they have responsibletravel.com to sell their product, and [so] they ask us to create a package so they can sell. So I notice that this is the trend. But you explain many things in the website about your responsibility this and that, and the product, it doesn't feel very green. How can we distinguish ourselves from the regular product and green product? They look the same . . . so far I have looked into many many companies that proclaim that they are green, and I also have the same question, I talk to the agent in America – how do you distinguish, the product looks like a regular tour that we service. How green, how do you know that it is a green product for real? We also have a question for that.
>
> (Personal communication, January 19, 2010)

Indeed, what makes it even harder to establish whether a particular tour or tourism company is ethical or not is its lack of a physical and tangible product whereby researchers and activists can trace similar efforts made for fair-trade coffee. While it is possible to identify "products" in particular sectors of the tourism industry, for example accommodations provided in the hotel sector, or local handicrafts produced as souvenirs for tourists, the tourism industry as a whole lacks physically tangible "products" in the traditional sense. Crouch *et al.* (2001) and Chris Gibson (2010), for example, have argued that tourism is instead an encounter, something that can be created and sustained by rhetoric, and it is indeed such ambiguities that make it hard to define what should or should not be considered as impacts and responsibilities tourism as an industry needs to acknowledge.

At the same time, given its broad scope, the tourism industry is necessarily implicitly linked with all sorts of "irresponsibilities," whether one is consciously cognizant of it or not. For example, transport provided in tourism – whether air, sea, or ground transport – continues to be highly reliant on petrol fuel, and thus even as a tourist may opt to take up one of such "ethical tours," as described earlier in the chapter, he or she can still easily be implicated in many petroleum companies' irresponsible corporate activities – whether this refers to Shell's exploitation of fuels in fragile areas such as the Arctic National Wildlife Refuge (cited in Chatterton and Maxey 2009), or BP's lack of decisive action to stop environmental damage caused by the massive oil spill in the Gulf of Mexico. While some may argue that this is too far removed from a tourist or tourism corporation's decision-making process to attribute moral agency and responsibility, this situation highlights the connected nature of production in today's globalized world, where ethical responsibilities cannot be separated between one industry to another.

Tourism further complicates matters for many would-be ethical or responsible consumers, for unlike many other (especially product-oriented) industries, the two "worlds" (for example the "First" and "Third" worlds, if they are indeed separate) are brought together into a shared space as tourists act out of their "care" and "ethical responsibilities" in their travel destinations. In comparison, in most other industries where fair trade or ethical consumption is strongly promoted, be it tea, coffee, or eggs, most at the consumer end will never personally encounter the farmers or even the chicken that they are supposedly responsible for. In a typical "fair" product, for example:

> the concrete application of the Fair Trade principles by companies is something that cannot be observed directly by the consumer. Since the beneficiaries of the fair characteristic (the producers in the South) are located far from the ones who finance it (the consumers in the North), there is an information asymmetry that requires a certain level of trust from the consumers.
>
> (Becchetti and Huybrechts 2008: 735)

Similarly, despite having bought The Body Shop's products for many years, I have never personally seen, felt, or assessed the effects of its charitable initiatives through community trade.

Ethics as observed in tourism is therefore a rather unique situation since, as end-consumers, tourists actually do personally see and engage with the "other" that he or she had committed responsibility to when he or she opted for "ethical tours." In fact, Korf has even suggested, using the case of philanthropic giving after the 2004 Boxing Day tsunami, that "[i]n the 21st century, spatial distance has become much more fluid: life-styles have become more cosmopolitan, global tourism has brought large numbers of Westerners into remote places where they personally experience an encounter with distant others," (Korf 2007: 371) and this in turn encouraged a vanishing of distance between what was "proximate" or "at home," and what was "distant" or "away" (for responsibilities across distance as argued in the subfield of geographies of care and responsibility, see Smith, D.M. 1998; Massey 2004; England 2007; Lawson 2007; Popke 2007). Through such an encounter, then, tourists are able to assess and judge in person whether what has been done is "ethical" or not, and in some cases, tourists may even be able to observe that the "local" or "cared for" may not always be receptive of the care and responsibility enacted, and this can immediately be observed by the "carer" since they are in direct contact with each other (see Sin 2006, 2010). Indeed, while many supposed responsible tourists could possibly desire to be ethical in all respects, in reality, varying aspects of tourism are within or out of their control, and what is considered ethical and responsible itself is also highly debatable, as the rest of this chapter elucidates. As such, instead of simply looking at the individual perspectives of enacting such ethical or responsible encounters, some have suggested that it is equally important, if not more important, to negotiate the broader structures of tourism as an industry – and especially the ways in which corporations enable or default on such supposed ethical and moral responsibilities.

Turning to corporations

If we put aside skeptics' frequent questioning of whether corporations can truly behave in a responsible manner (for example, Frankental 2001; Munshi and Kurian 2005), and accept that such contestations are part and parcel of (re)defining corporations' moral obligations, it is encouraging to note that most works make strong claims that there is indeed no good reason why corporations should not assume social responsibilities. A.B. Carroll, for example, provided a significant review on the evolution of the concept of CSR up to the 1990s, suggesting that CSR is quickly gaining ground both within academic literature and more importantly, within corporations themselves (1999; see also Garriga and Mele 2004 for a more recent review).

From as early as 1979, it was already noted that many *Fortune 500* companies included a section on CSR in their annual reports, mostly covering the five main categories on environment – equal opportunity, personnel, community involvement, and products (Abbott and Monsen 1979). A more recent study also highlighted that CSR issues and concerns were addressed in more than 80 percent of the *Fortune 500* companies, "reflecting the pervasive belief among business leaders that in today's marketplace CSR is not only an ethical/ideological imperative, but also an economic one" (Hobson 2006: 9).

The popularity of CSR can also be observed by the large range of publications, conferences and organizations dedicated to the subject, as well as the increasing numbers of consultancies providing CSR solutions, with large firms such as PricewaterhouseCoopers and Deutsche Bank having entire units dedicated to the comprehensive management of CSR within their corporations.

At the World Economic Forum in New York (February 2002), for example, chief executive officers (CEOs) from the world's largest corporations signed a joint statement on "Global Corporate Citizenship – The Leadership Challenge for CEOs and Boards" (see discussion in Matten and Crane 2003), which starts on the note that:

> leaders from all countries, sectors and levels of society need to work together to address these challenges by supporting sustainable human development and ensuring that the benefits of globalization are shared more widely. It is in the interests of business that these benefits continue both for companies and for others in society.
>
> (World Economic Forum 2002)

As seen here, the keen adoption of CSR, then, is not always purely ethically motivated, as it is equally "in the interests of businesses" to ensure that "benefits of globalization are shared more widely" (see also Hopkins 2003; Hawkins 2006; Vogel 2006). Many other works have also since drawn attention to the importance of CSR initiatives as a branding and marketing tool, or as a competitive edge in a company's long-term strategies, especially in the current-day context of increasing consumer pressures toward responsible corporations (Burke and Logsdon 1996; Dentchev 2004; Zadek 2004; Husted and Allen 2007).

The same has been observed among large tourism corporations – Manfred Pieper, General Manager of Conrad Bangkok, for example, states that CSR in the hotel business "has almost now become a necessity, because there are companies who very much base their decisions on where to hold their meetings and conferences on the reputation that the company has in supporting the environment" (personal communication, February 8, 2010). Similarly, Oliver Colomès, CEO of Exotissimo Travel Group, an inbound travel company focused on southeast Asia, highlighted that one of its main clientele, MICE (meetings, incentives, conventions, exhibitions), travel from France, which is increasingly abiding to the United Nations Global Compact and European Union CSR policies, and that "if we are ahead of the others, if we are already committed to this CSR issue, that will be a big selling point also for us" (personal communication, December 14, 2009). This is in line with what Bonini *et al.* have argued for – that companies "must see the social and political dimensions not just as risks – areas for damage limitation – but also as opportunities" (2006: 21), since companies are in the business of creating trust relationships between themselves and their customers (see Foster 2008), and as such, if CSR concerns addressed sufficiently ahead of time, it will put their businesses in good stead.

In more recent studies, it has been further argued that companies today have become so massive in size (in terms of revenues generated, employees hired, and markets served) and transnational in nature that they have also become powerful social institutions that can at times be more influential and/or effective than states or civil society organizations in dealing with social issues such as eliminating discrimination in employment, putting in place "fairer" trade practices, as well as improving environmental quality and standards (Davis *et al.* 2006). S.L. Hart, for example, states that the

> sustainable world falls largely on the shoulders of the world's enterprises, the economic engines of the future. Clearly, public policy innovations (at both the national and international levels) and changes in individual consumption patterns will be needed to move toward sustainability. But corporations can and should lead the way, helping to shape public policy and driving change in consumers' behavior.
>
> (1997: 76)

To this end, then, many civil society organizations (CSOs) and non-governmental organizations (NGOs) have since taken to collaborate with private sector corporations, including many instances of large corporations providing direct funding for civil society programs (Heap 1998; Bendell and Lake 2000; Warren 2005). What has received considerably less attention, then, is the role of smaller-scale companies, something that is especially important to note in the tourism industry where typical operations cannot compare in size with "corporate giants" such as Shell or The Coca-Cola Company. Such modest tourism set-ups often remain transnational in operation (especially when considering the nature of the tourism industry), and many have considerable tie-ups with CSOs and NGOs in niche initiatives, such as supporting rural schools and orphanages. For example, Exotissimo Travel and Khiri Travel (interviewed in this research) both regularly organize "responsible tours" and fundraising events in support of rural villages and schools. Indeed, a simple search in comprehensive portals such as responsible travel.com would pull out numerous options for tourists to support all sorts of civil society programs in their holidays – most of which are conducted by small-scale niche companies rather than corporate giants, as most often discussed in works relating to CSR.

The inclusion of such smaller-scale companies, and at times even family-run businesses and niche initiatives, then throws in additional dimensions to CSR that have been discussed less – for example, are there any differences in smaller-scale companies carrying out CSR, as compared with large and highly visible multinational corporations (MNCs) that are also easily targeted for consumer activism campaigns? And considering how widely dominated tourism is by smaller-scale companies, is it right then only to hold large corporations to standards of moral obligations while neglecting "responsibilities" that smaller companies may also have? And finally, what are the implications of considering corporations of various scales in tourism – in contextualizing CSR, how does size matter?

For example, Khun Eng, Director of Let's Tour Bangkok, shared difficulties in incorporating CSR, noting that:

> if the company is small like us and you run around doing everything, there's no way to think of something out of it. But for the big company, the owner or the management they have more time, they are able to manage that if they really want to, I think it's doable, it depends on how much they want . . .
>
> (Personal communication, January 19, 2010)

As such, CSR appears to be optional because a company is small and lacks resources or the power to change policies or trends. This is similar to what Chatterton and Maxey described as the self-rhetoric of the Universities Superannuation Scheme in the United Kingdom in its claims that "it is not big enough to really make a company such as Shell change its policies" (Chatterton and Maxey 2009: 434). However, if this argument were taken, then almost all of the tourism industry, with perhaps the exception of large airline companies and multinational hotel chains, would then have no need to adhere to ethical and moral obligations in their business operations. A quick look at the popularity and emergence of numerous eco, pro-poor, or responsible tourism initiatives would suggest that despite being dominated by smaller-scale operations, the adoption of notions similar to CSR (whether or not they are named as such) is indeed prevalent. Among the need to contextualize moral responsibilities in business operations, then, is not only that corporations have moral responsibilities, but also the need to consider the size and scale of corporations, and what this means to responsibilities as enacted on the ground.

Responsibilities as development

As alluded to earlier, it is common now to state that "[b]y following socially responsible practices, the growth generated by the private sector will be more inclusive, equitable and poverty reducing" (DFID 2004: 2) than that generated through traditional means of international aid and development loans. This line of thought is echoed by several state and inter-state development agencies – for example, Antonio Vives, consultant at the Inter-American Development Bank (IDB), goes further by stating that "CSR, by its very nature, is development done by the private sector, and it perfectly complements the development efforts of governments and multilateral development institutions" (2004: 46). Major international institutions such as the World Bank and the United Nations are also involved in promoting CSR as development, through the World Bank Institute and Global Compact respectively. The launch of the Global Compact in 2000 at the World Economic Forum was itself seen as "a means of getting corporate involvement in CSR worldwide; it urged business to embrace universal principles in the areas of human rights, labor standards, and the environment as a means to a 'more equitable global marketplace'" (Mitra 2007: 3; see special issue on tourism as work in *Tourist Studies* 2009). Following this, the European Union also joined the call for CSR in 2004, with the development aspects of CSR as one of its main agendas (European Commission 2004).

The parallels between a good and moral corporation's CSR practices and the bid to work towards international development and the related goals of poverty alleviation and sustainable development are evident (at least to some development practitioners) and CSR is increasingly intertwined with the rhetoric of universal human rights, equity, and economic growth (see Blowfield 2005; Blowfield and Frynas 2005). This is largely based on the assumption that large corporations not only have the financial muscle to pull off developmental projects, but such development can also be more sustainable in the long run (as compared for example to donor generated or government sponsored international aid). Indeed, some authors, while critical of what CSR has achieved to date, have suggested that the private sector or businesses have been left out of development thinking for far too long – foreign direct investments have always been seen as a major contributor to increasing wealth and providing employment in developing areas. It is now argued that large corporations can and ought to play a bigger role in development initiatives (see Blowfield 2005; Jenkins, R. 2005). Indeed, CSR as development can be placed within the larger context of a "globalizing era dominated by discourses of neoliberalism and privatization [where] it has influenced the displacement of various social, political and regulatory functions from traditional governmental institutions to the corporate realm" (Hughes *et al.* 2008: 351).

Since the early 1980s, neoliberalism has increasingly decentered the state as the monolithic source of power, while pointing to governance in a multiplicity of other agencies, such as NGOs and private corporations (Hart, G. 2004; Sadler and Lloyd 2009). Such deregulations were on the basis of the neoliberal belief that "the state cannot possibly possess enough information to second-guess market signals (prices) and because powerful interest groups will inevitably distort and bias state interventions (particularly in democracies) for their own benefit" (Harvey 2005: 2).

However, instead of viewing neoliberalism as simply a retreat of the state from the market, it is useful to explore literature on neoliberal governmentality (see Binkley 2009; Tellmann 2009), where a transformation of politics leads to the restructuring of power relations in society; that is, "[w]hat we observe today is not a diminishment or a reduction of state sovereignty and planning capacities but a displacement from formal to informal techniques of government and the appearance of new actors on the scene of government"

(Lemke 2000: 11) – actors such as NGOs and private corporations. G. Hart emphasizes that:

> Rather than *less* government, neoliberalism in this view represents a *new modality* of government predicated on interventions to create the organizational and subjective conditions for entrepreneurship – not only in terms of extending the "enterprise model" to schools, hospitals, housing estates and so forth, but also in inciting individuals to become entrepreneurs of themselves.
>
> (2004: 92; emphasis original)

In other words, the traditional binaries and categorizations of state and society, politics and economy, or society and economy cease to function, as governments increasingly acknowledge various stakeholders' involvement and commitments. As such, social campaigns for greater governance in corporations, for example, emerged as a check on the ethics of transnational trade. Similarly, the lack of global enforcement of International Labour Organization (ILO) conventions led to one of the earlier CSR movements that brought about the largely voluntary corporate codes of labor conduct (especially in developing countries) to ensure minimum standards in working conditions and prevent labor exploitations (Barrientos and Dolan 2006).

Neoliberalism therefore grounded the role of CSR in development (favored over state interventions), as echoed in the earlier quoted statement made by the UK Department for International Development (DFID 2004). Indeed, Sadler and Lloyd argue that while CSR reinforces the processes of neoliberalization, "[t]here is a quality to the onset of neo-liberalizing corporate responsibility which reflects and reveals the disjointedness of social life" (2009: 615), where neoliberalism itself is not a "coherent hegemonic project" (Barnett 2005a: 9), and instead "attention should turn to the pro-active role of bottom-up sociocultural processes such as changing consumer expectations, the decline of deference, the refusals of the subordinated, the politics of difference, and contested inequalities" (Sadler and Lloyd 2009: 614).

At the same time, ethics and responsibilities in tourism have long been positioned along the lines of developmental aims in the "Third World." For example, Peter Weingand, Managing Director of a small-scale inbound tour company in Thailand, Arosa Travel Service, shared his opinion on tourism in Thailand:

> Of course it [tourism] would be good. One example I've just mentioned is that the people benefit from it [economically]. In another perspective, the country benefits from it, because all the people who were here, let's say 99 percent they go back and they have a positive remarks and positive memories of the country, so they spread the word about the country and it benefits with a good image [e.g. through foreign investments] . . .
>
> (Personal communication, January 12, 2010)

He adds, specific to the case of organizing tours to Myanmar:

> When I send the tourists to Myanmar they are so, like the same in Thailand and any other countries, they go and eat in small restaurants, they go and use a minivan which we rent from somewhere and then the driver has the job. So it also filters down, and you cannot say just because some generals also own the hotels or whatever that you cannot send – that the whole – let's say a client pays you 2000 dollars to go to Myanmar – the whole 2000 dollars is not benefiting the military. I would say the major part of it is benefitting the little community here and there. Again it helps.
>
> (Personal communication, January 12, 2010)

Indeed, here the ability of income from tourism to reach the ground level and create income for the poor is highlighted and used as a key reason for developing tourism, even in the case of Myanmar, where many have since argued to boycott for the unethical/undemocratic practices of its junta or military regime.

Luzi Matzig, CEO of Asian Trails, further adds:

> There you have the poorest population of all the countries around here, in Burma. Because of these stupid boycotts . . . My God. Do-gooders, never been to Burma, but know everything about Burma and know and pressure the others not to. Why? I have my right to travel where I want to travel, so why they pressure me not to travel here or there? I mean, honestly, totally misguided. We have nothing to do with the Burmese government; we are 100 percent private enterprise. We employ lots of people, without us they wouldn't have a job and their children wouldn't have food . . . we can't change the generals from one to another, but the more you open up tourism, the more free information flows in there . . . So then, if tourists flood the country, if they do have prisoner working the new roads, then they will make them disappear because they don't want the tourists to go and see the chain gangs. So it will help.
>
> (Personal communication, December 22, 2009)

Inherent here is also the key notion that one should not judge (especially from afar) what responsibilities in the local context should entail, as criticisms are made toward "do-gooders, never been to Burma" who are "totally misguided." Indeed, this echoes ideologies similar to postcolonialism and development (which will be discussed later), where an emphasis on plurality and heterogeneity of voices is called for.

The role of private corporations in tourism, however, has received considerably less attention. In the existing literature, corporations have tended to assume a passive yet pervasively present role as targets for governments' sustainable development policies, or by reacting to consumers' demands for ethical practices. However, the agency of corporations has been little discussed. How do corporations indeed set and influence trends in ethical tourism? How do corporations understand their own ethical responsibilities? While it is not within the scope of this chapter to empirically unpack these issues, understanding CSR in tourism and its close associations with developmental objectives can contribute greatly to uncoding the commercial language of "win–win partnerships" and pushing engagement with corporations beyond the rhetoric.

Postcolonialism and ethics in tourism

At the same time, in considering ethics in tourism, especially as it is enacted in Asia, it seems strange that postcolonialism as a strand of scholarly works has so far been little considered. Set out to expose binaries of the "West" and "the rest," postcolonialism has contributed greatly to the decentering of forms of knowledge and social identities authored and authorized by colonialism and Western domination, and instead reveals plural societies in their complex heterogeneities (for comprehensive volumes discussing postcolonialism see Said 1978; Young 2001, 2003; Sharp 2008). While it is not within the scope of this chapter to dwell fully on the theories and debates put forward by postcolonialism, it is useful to examine here how postcolonialism has informed development theories and practices, and how these have in turn made their way into discourses of moral responsibilities. As elaborated by Schech and Haggis (2000), postcolonialism, under the broader umbrella of poststructural theory, calls attention to "the value of approaching culture as a social process rather than a static or immutable entity or ensemble of facts, material objects and rituals" (Simon 2006: 14). Many works have since highlighted how concepts developed in postcolonialism can be applied to development (McFarlane 2006; Power *et al.* 2006; Sharp and Briggs 2006; Simon 2006). Central to these works is the focus on a nuanced understanding of "locals," human agency, and subjective knowledge and perceptions, and moving beyond a supposed ideology of development based on Western contexts that has been imposed on to different parts of the "Third World" as if it was homogeneously understood (see Young 2001; Sharp 2008). Indeed, "going local" is most prevalent among almost any responsible or ethical travel credo. On Responsibletravel.com, one of the most successful travel agents focusing on responsible travel, the notion of the "rebellious tourist" was recently introduced that best encapsulates this fascination with all things "local." On its website, it states:

> When you think of Rebellious Tourism think of how Michael Palin travels – with a sense of humour, local guides, using local transport. Real-life characters such as Palin, Bruce Parry and Simon Reeve get their confidence from a curiosity to discover and learn about new places and people. It's clear to see it pays off and they are consistently rewarded with acceptance, laughter and wonderful travel experiences.
>
> (Responsibletravel.com 2010)

The plurality in the voices of the "subaltern" was thus advocated, and examples of localization and locality-based anti-globalization agendas became pivotal in de/reconstructing notions of development (see, for example, Escobar 2001; Escobar *et al.* 2002). The postcolonial approach stressed in a spatial genealogy that highlights the multiple sites and heterogeneity of knowledge, space and politics, resulting in an emphasis on "the role of circulations in constituting networks and bringing some sites and forms of knowledge together while distancing others. This circulation is generally not one of seamless travel, but of contested travelling discourses and knowledges" (McFarlane 2006: 40). This, perhaps, is a more theoretically informed way of saying what has also been observed in CSR, where "what constitutes good CSR practice in one country or sphere of operation might not be regarded in the same way in other countries" (Roome 2005: 331), and indeed the same holds true for ethical tourism. What is regarded as the norm or absolute rule of the game in one geographic locale or time period may not necessarily hold in another (for a discussion on this, see Roome 2005; Bremer 2008).

This means that tourism as an industry that is transnational in its nature will have to contend continually with differing expectations of social responsibilities. Indeed, this is not unlike broader observations of transnational corporations "localizing" their brands, advertising, and production, as Foster (2008) observed was the case for The Coca-Cola Company's latest corporate mantra, for example. However, the tourism industry is dominated by much smaller-scale corporations, where even multinational hotel chains would typically see themselves as small players that cannot make a significant differ-ence on their own. For example, Nelson Hilton, Marketing Director at Four Seasons Bangkok, described their operations thus: "We only have 300 rooms, that's not very mass [tourism]" (personal communication, January 14, 2010).

So, using the previous example of developing tourism in Myanmar, while some larger companies such as Intrepid Travel and Gap Adventures have pulled Myanmar out of their tour itineraries on account of the violation of human rights by its military regime, these are the minority. Instead, it is indeed easier to find tour companies that continue to organize tours to Myanmar, justifying their responsibilities on account of economic development on the ground. The different expectations of social responsibilities is thus not only one that exists between who is considered "local" or "foreign," but here is also among foreign-managed tour companies that adopt differing idea(l)s and priorities in practicing their responsibilities. The dominance of smaller-scale corporations in tourism thus challenges traditional ethical consumerism campaigns, where boycotts or buycotts are aimed toward corporate giants, and instead forces a re-evaluation of CSR that has so far tended to focus on large, visible, multinational corporations.

Indeed, the tensions of enacting responsibilities in tourism are not only encountered between different expectations of various stakeholders, but also on the larger scale of ever-changing societal norms based in differing geographic locales. The active deconstruction of sites and forms of knowledge and the contestations of such are therefore useful in serving as an academic backdrop from which real observations that are made in the corporate world (within CSR literature) can be explained. As Bebbington suggests, "[c]onsideration, for instance, of where, how and why economic decisions [especially those related to CSR] are made and structured, by whom, and with what geographical consequences is too often absent or underdeveloped in these analyses" (2003: 300), and the consideration of development and postcolonial theory, together with the often very practically worded corporate literature on CSR, can be helpful, broaching both theory and real-life observations in tourism.

Much has also been said on the importance of incorporating or engaging "indigenous knowledge" in development (Sylvester 2000; Briggs and Sharp 2004), especially in the need for researchers to "speak for" subalterns. It is noted, though, that equal volumes of literature have also critically questioned the representation of our "subjects" and contemplated our positionalities and reflexivities between the possibilities of doing research "for" or "with" our "subject." In the case of corporations promoting ethical tourism, then, one has to wonder – how much of such "going local" translates into heightened reflexivities or plurality of voices as advocated by postcolonialism? It is thus important to consider similar criticisms toward neocolonialism in development and international aid projects, as CSR in tourism, and/or responsible tourism is also largely consumer and/or donor driven. As Spivak (1988) suggested, such practice is "promoted as benevolent, but forecloses various complicities and desires. It is championed and propagated by development institutions, which nonetheless seek to obscure their own participation" (cited in Kapoor 2005: 1206). This is to say that, as a middle-agent, a corporation tends to seek responsible practices toward one party, such as the locals in tourism destinations, because of its desire to appease another party – tourists or consumers. This perhaps explains why, despite claims of inclusive and participatory objectives of CSR, little critical empirical data has actually focused on social responsibilities as perceived by the very people tourism attempts to be responsible toward, since consumer/tourist indicators are more immediately relevant and are therefore shaping CSR strategies. It is important, therefore, to bear in mind Spivak's point (1988) that while postcolonial theory asks us to incorporate the voices of the "Third World"/subaltern, our representations

> cannot escape our institutional positioning and are always mediated by a confluence of diverse institutional interests and pressures . . . If professional motives dictate, at least to a degree, what and how we do (development), we cannot pretend to have pure, innocent or benevolent encounters with the subaltern. To do so, as argued earlier, is to perpetuate, directly or indirectly, forms of imperialism, ethnocentrism, appropriation.
>
> (Kapoor 2004: 635)

Simon, for example, illustrates the importance of "scholars seeking to maintain active and constructive practical, but theoretically informed, engagement have sought diverse ways of promoting non-paternalistic North–South collaborations and deploying participatory and mutual learning research methodologies" (2006: 15).

In tourism, then, it is vital to appreciate that tourist destinations are indeed places that congregate the tourist, the corporation, as well as locals, places whereby each party is able to observe first-hand what is practiced in the name of ethics and responsibility, even as attempts by corporations to conceal any irresponsibility may continue to exist. Much as Massey suggests, in tourism, "'place' [all the more] must be a site of negotiation, and that often this will be conflictual negotiation" (Massey 2004: 7). For example, on a single issue of whether it is ethical to domesticate elephants and offer elephant rides and shows to tourists in Thailand, different parties indeed have diverse opinions.

Samantha Clarke, a British lady managing the volunteer tourism aspect of an elephant camp[2] near Pattaya, for example, shares her views:

> If we felt that a mahout was mistreating the elephant, then we would say that we wouldn't work with them, although we would probably do it in a way of not completely cut off the work with them, but say we would work with you but these are the kind of codes of conduct that you've got to stick with and we would probably pay them in installments rather than upfront. So if we saw improvements then they would get financial rewards as well.
>
> Other things we want to try to do is obviously improving the lives of the elephants is the number one thing, but as part of that, what we also want to try to do is try to show the mahouts that there is another way that they can treat the elephants. Because many of the mahouts have been brought up to believe that aggression is the way of controlling the elephant, and so a lot of them have been trained to use their sticks, to use their hooks, and we are pretty lucky here that none of them actually mistreats their elephants, but sometimes they get a little bit lazy and then they use the hooks out of laziness, so we're also just trying to re-educate them with that as well, and say you don't have to do this.
>
> (Personal communication, November 16, 2009)

Anne (pseudonym), one of the volunteer tourists at the same elephant camp, adds:

> I think they have achieved quite a good balance here, between having the elephants work in the afternoon, with giving them enough free time, time to go and drink water when they need it, time to graze when they need it, so I think they have achieved a reasonable balance between the economic necessity of making enough income for the families to live with the welfare of the elephant . . . [but] some of the elephants are mistreated

and we've seen that they have the economic carrot to say, OK, we're not trying to change your livelihood, we're not trying to say not to take rides, but there are ways and ways to do it, and you see some will make sure that their elephants drink, some will give them commands that aren't overly violent, and with that economic carrot you will get more money if you treat your animal well . . .

(Personal communication, November 25, 2009)

Both examples clearly show the desire to "teach," or at least provide some form of economic incentive to change what is deemed as the irresponsible behavior of using violence to domesticate elephants, while the next examples reflect a rather different point of view.

Yan, a Thai mahout at the same elephant camp, remarks:

Normally, every mahout, or even I, love elephant. Don't want to do [referring to hitting elephants], but sometime the people come here don't understand . . .

(Personal communication, November 25, 2009)

Lee, another Thai mahout, adds:

When tourist come here and see some mahout hit elephant, should he tell volunteer [to] understand [that every] elephant is different . . . When mahouts hit normally all of them [still] love elephant. They [mahouts] buy [elephants] very expensive and take care every day, but if they don't hit [to train the elephant], [this might] mean [being in] danger for mahout, for tourists, for anyone . . . Because elephant is wildlife.

(Personal communication, December 2, 2009)

Indeed, Noi Kwanjai, the Thai coordinator at the same elephant camp, comments that:

[Hitting and training elephants to perform tricks for tourists is] to teach the elephant how to be clever, because not every elephant can do, just only some elephant . . . this is just very very easy for elephant. But difficult life for elephant is mean working in the forests [for lumbering work] . . . if you are owner of [elephants], if you have your son, you love your son, so you have to teach them, why somebody go be doctor, why somebody cannot be doctor, because the same, elephant the same, son or daughter, so some elephant cannot, some elephant can be that, can be this, same same.

(Personal communication, November 18, 2009)

This string of differing opinions thus shows how, despite being brought together into one locale, in this case, within one particular elephant camp, each party continues to see ethics and responsibilities in a different manner, and the elephant camp then becomes the place of negotiation between such diverse opinions – where in a bid to appease the tourist (or consumer or donor), it is of utmost importance to show on site that locals, or in this case elephants (the subject of responsible practices), are indeed benefiting or at least receptive of such responsibilities (see also Sin 2010). While postcolonial development and the attendant calls for participatory methods are not without criticism, it is therefore useful to incorporate such debates and critical insights within research on CSR to further our understanding of the complicity of transnational corporations in the production of "responsibilities" in tourism.

Conclusions

Tourism as a space in which social responsibilities are enacted between "First World" ideals and "Third World" realities demands closer scrutiny. While the fluid constructs of CSR and responsibilities in tourism are indeed among its strengths in adapting and being malleable toward ever-changing social expectations and norms with regard to moral responsibilities, this also complicates the use of CSR in practice, as has been discussed in this chapter. This chapter therefore highlights the importance of contextualizing responsibilities rather than discussing them in abstract terms. Specific to our discussion in tourism, then, are several key contexts to consider. Namely: 1) As a service industry with no tangible "product," how does CSR in tourism then play out? 2) How can CSR also include smaller-scale companies, especially in an industry where traditional corporate giants are far and few between? 3) How do notions of ethics and responsibilities differ from place to place and from people to people? And finally: 4) When different parties – consumers, producers and locals – are all brought into the same sphere, what sorts of practices come to play, and how then must CSR be managed?

These are all important questions looking at tourism with respect to the larger field of CSR, and indeed, it is argued here that the existence of tensions between differing priorities in CSR, as well as, at times, conflicting responsibilities toward different stakeholders, should be assumed. An example of how this could be achieved is through a fairer trading structure that involves paying local producers higher rates that often equate to higher prices which consumers have to pay, and this in turn marginalizes certain segments of consumers. This chapter hopes to set the stage for further works delving into such tensions and how they are being actively negotiated on the ground, while highlighting the urgent need to go beyond abstract binaries of being "ethical" or not, and instead take on what is here argued to be a "post-ethical" approach.

Through identifying the parallels of CSR in tourism with developmental idea(l)s and "responsibilities," this chapter has also highlighted how tourism is also seen as part of the development agenda, and how looking at corporations in tourism (and their CSR strategies) can bridge an existing literature gap within tourism, while informing CSR through complicating notions of distance that has often been assumed in existing literature. Herein lies a need to understand critiques toward development and postcolonialism, so as to ensure that social responsibilities as enacted and practiced in tourism do not repeat the "failures" or neocolonial nature of the development project. Indeed, the underlying assumption that responsibilities (and tourist/tourism companies) originate from the "First World" and are then practiced in the "Third World" itself needs to be examined, as tourism today increasingly features mobility between and from supposed "Third World" countries (see Winter *et al.* 2009). All these observations complicate typical notions of ethics in tourism based largely on classical ethical theories, and by focusing on issues of development, this chapter hopes to have begun the process of unpacking some of such problematic assumptions.

Notes

1   While CSR typically refers to social citizenship and responsibility assumed by large multinational corporations, this chapter argues that it is important not to neglect smaller-scale businesses and their adoption of CSR-related practices, especially in an industry such as tourism where small- to medium-scale companies dominate. This will be further discussed in the section "Turning to corporations" (page 169). Corporations as referred to in this chapter therefore also include smaller-scale businesses.
2   Volunteer tourists at this camp will take up an informal "mahout training course," which includes learning how to ride and care for elephants as Thai mahouts do. Most volunteers have so far been from Europe, North America, and Australia.

10 Tourism and the question of poverty

Saithong Phommavong

Introduction

The idea of distributing tourism benefits to the poor has basically derived from mainstream development theories. Consequently, as development theory has shifted over the decades, so too has the thinking on the role of tourism in development (Clancy 1999; Turegano 2006). Reflecting shifts in dominant development thinking from modernization to neoliberalism, for instance, the concept of pro-poor tourism (PPT) has emerged as a market-based approach to a more equitable distribution of tourism benefits (Kabeer 1994; Bennett *et al.* 1999; Chok *et al.* 2007). However, PPT has been criticized for mainly serving to maintain the status quo (Mowforth and Munt 2003; Harrison, D. 2008; Goodwin 2010). The benefit of tourism for the poor has not been evident and support for PPT may repackage conventional development approaches rather than offer a solution to the unequal relations inherent in market-based exchanges. As Mowforth and Munt (2003: 273) have argued, "in the long run . . . the cumulative effect of supporting (through multilateral and bilateral aid programs) the expansion of capitalist relations . . . may undercut 'sustainable livelihood' and exacerbate, rather than alleviate, poverty."

While debate over the benefits of PPT continues, there is a lack of convincing empirical evidence to justify the claim that increased tourism development will lead to significant benefits for the poor, particularly in developing or transitional economies (Chok *et al.* 2007; Harrison and Schipani 2007; Manyara and Jones 2007). Conventional development approaches still emphasize a Eurocentric perspective and largely ignore the local political conditions of many developing countries, which are substantially different from "Western" models (Steiner 2006). In this context, some studies have adopted more empirical and descriptive approaches to analyze tourism impacts on poverty reduction (Clancy 1999), demonstrating the potential merits of empirical studies generated from small case studies in developing countries, rather than studies based on the local application of broader, abstract theories regarding sustainable tourism development.

The actual practices of PPT have varied according to the development approaches of different states. In much of Southeast and East Asia, the neoliberal approach has been rejected in favor of a more state-led approach (Schuurman 1996; Clancy 1999; Telfer and Sharpley 2008). Chinese and Vietnamese approaches maintaining strong government control over the tourism sector have demonstrated the importance of public sector involvement when tourism is promoted for poverty reduction (Bowden 2005; Suntikul *et al.* 2008). Similarly, in Lao PDR, the new economic mechanism (NEM) introduced during the 1980s marked the transition from a central planning system to a market-based economy, while maintaining the central role of the Lao People's Revolutionary Party. Tourism has been identified as one of eight priority sectors potentially contributing to national growth and poverty reduction (LPMO 2004). This was first manifested in the national tourism strategy for 2005–2015 (Allcock 2004). A further elaborated position was seen in the Lao PDR Tourism Strategies (2006–2020), which stated that "tourism can [. . .] contribute to poverty reduction of all ethnics groups" (LNTA 2008a: 13). The Nam Ha Ecotourism Project (NHEP) was the first aid-led project aiming at the protection of nature and wildlife in the National Protected Area and the eradication of poverty for the people living in the area (Schipani 2008). However, Harrison and Schipani (2007) have argued that the private tourism sector is doing better than aid-led tourism development projects in contributing to poverty reduction. Also, competing development interests such as rubber plantations still challenge ecotourism development as a tool for poverty reduction (Schipani 2007). International nature conservation interests, in other words, complicate the promotion of tourism for poverty reduction in Lao PDR. This is often reflected by the market penetrations of the global ecotourism industry, by the ambiguous role of the state as both promoter of development and guarantor of welfare for the poor, and in general by the inadequacy of broader models of pro-poor tourism to account for the social realities of actual tourism development places.

This chapter provides a case study of tourism development promoted as poverty reduction in Lao PDR, focusing on precisely those complex social realities "on the ground." While discussing the Lao PDR state's promotion of tourism development as a means of poverty reduction, I analyze some of the conflicts that have emerged between the state's general rural develop-ment policies and current ecotourism developments for poverty reduction, and explore the alternative development options intended by different stakeholders at different scales. A key problem we face when using tourism as poverty reduction in Lao PDR lies in the state's attempt to mediate the articulation between global and local scales of tourism development. International donors promoting nature conservation and ecotourism fund state projects that produce conflicts for locals pursuing their own livelihood strategies. I argue that tourism cannot be viewed as a particular kind of development model, but must instead be approached as a social process through which development is being practiced. As such, there is no particular model of PPT, since tourism cannot be simply categorized as an "industry" with particular characteristics, be these market-capitalist, state-led, or non-governmental. Rather, viewing tourism as a social process requires us to derive solutions directly from local social contexts, approaching tourism as poverty reduction in pluralistic ways that derive from actual social practices rather than a particular theoretical apparatus.

Methodologically, this study is inspired by thematic analysis (TA) (Boyatzis 1998). The study design for TA is not necessarily based on any pre-existing theoretical framework (Braun and Clarke 2006) and therefore it can be used both in different theory-driven analyses and in more data-driven approaches. My research is mainly based on primary data collected from fieldwork in the Luangnamtha and Champasak Provinces in Lao PDR from 2008 to 2010. Interviews were held regarding rural development and poverty-reduction goals, tourism strategies implemented within tourism for poverty reduction, benefits and constraint experienced by tourism stakeholders, and future implementation mechanisms. Key informants included villagers, government staff, private tourism operators, and staff of international non-governmental organizations (INGOs). The villagers included both people involved in tourism activities and people not involved in those activities in nine villages in Luangnamtha and in five villages in Champasak.

Rethinking state intervention in tourism as poverty reduction

Viewing tourism as a social process in which broader-scale processes are linked with local contextual specifics suggests a crucial role for the state in the regulation of tourism. The potential role of tourism development for poverty reduction based on a capitalist-market model has been contested for developing and transitional economies. The rise of tourism in Southeast and East Asia compels us to rethink the role of the state rather than debate its presence or absence in tourism development as poverty reduction (Harrison, D. 1994). This rethinking of state interventions in general, and for tourism development in particular, is stimulated by the rise of a new development paradigm in which the state figures prominently (Schuurman 1996; Clancy 1999; Telfer and Sharpley 2008). Often the role of the state has been to enable the private sector to lead economic activities, implying that state activity should be market-friendly (Kiely 1998). Glinavos (2008) quotes Stiglitz (2007), who sees the state as important for the functioning of the market, but also the market mechanisms as important for the effective functioning of the state itself. An "enabling state" protects a set of private rights and creates framework conditions for a flourishing market.

In this context of rising debate on the role of the state and market, some scholars have, in fact, already promoted this idea for government intervention in tourism development (Harrison, D. 1994; Brohman 1995, 1996; Jenkins, J. 1997; Clancy 1999; Dieke 2000; Hall and Jenkins 2004; Williams, A. 2004; Hall 2008).

In general, the debate on the role of government in tourism management focuses on coordination, planning, legislation, and regulation, but government can also have the role of entrepreneur, tourism promoter, and public interest protector within the tourism sector (Jenkins, J. 1997; Hall and Jenkins 2004; Hall 2008). Apart from these roles, there are a number of ways states influence tourism as mediator, regulator, national macroeconomic policy-maker, intervener in local and regional development, contributor to the reproduction of the labor force, social investor, and provider of a climate of security and stability for tourism (Williams, A. 2004: 68). Drawing from the political economy of tourism development, Dieke (2000) argues that tourism is multifaceted and regulated by more than one government ministry, and that the distinct role of government is to regulate the allocation of scare productive resources.

In tourism development, an option for the state is to provide more sustainable forms for distributing costs and benefits generated by tourism. Market forces alone seem incapable of resolving this, and thus they have to be complemented with specific regulations designed by the state (Brohman 1995, 1996; Dieke 2000). State intervention in tourism as poverty reduction is often viewed as a choice between neoliberalism and protectionism. Schilcher (2007) highlights this and argues that promoting the role of government to favor the "poor" is questionable in terms of policy and practice. Such a policy conflicts with the promotion of market liberalization underlying neoliberal approaches.

However, for countries such as Lao PDR, there is a clear need for strong political institutions to regulate market forces and allocate scarce financial resources to help people below the poverty line. Government redistributive strategies for the poor can already be seen in the form of primary education and healthcare policies. The direct distributive policy provided by the government can also take the form of local ownership and compulsory local sourcing where the poor can access assets of land, credits and skills (UNDP 2004, cited in Schilcher 2007: 181). Government interventions in tourism development have similarly been promoted in cases of market failure to distribute income among the poor.

Government intervention for poverty reduction highlights different roles of the state. Chok *et al.* (2007: 153) call for a role of government in planning to "recognize travel and tourism as a top priority" that "must balance economics with people, culture and environment to ensure the industry's long term growth and prosperity" for the poor's benefit. In a similar vein, government support for education, coordination, regulation, and implementation would be important if tourism is to become a tool for poverty reduction (Zhao and Ritchie 2007). Lack of knowledge is a key problem among the poor and there is no doubt that the government is central in the provision of education for the poor (Nadkarni 2008). The government has to tackle barriers to tourism-driven poverty reduction, for instance in addressing insufficiency of knowledge for providing tourism service and strategies (Jamieson and Nadkarni 2009). Government authorities must also address regulatory bottle-necks and loopholes that may obstruct the process of policy and planning, as well as, for instance, preventing adverse effects of (re)settlement programs (Mowforth and Munt 2003; Mbaiwa 2005; Wang and Wall 2005; Chok *et al.* 2007; Nepal 2007). At a local level, the role of government is to maintain a sustainable livelihood framework for poverty alleviation (Rakodi 2002; Tao and Wall 2009) by reducing vulnerabilities (Chamber 1995; Chok *et al.* 2007). To achieve poverty reduction, appropriate policies have to be designed to enable better access for poor people to land, shelter, markets, sources of income, information, education, healthcare, and other essential services, rather than merely raising incomes above the poverty line (Rakodi 2002).

Another task for government strategies targeting poor groups, and particu-larly ethnic minorities, is to build up necessary social, environmental, financial, human, and physical capital in order to utilize tourism resources soundly (Rakodi 2002). The "exoticism" of ethnic cultures is potentially of interest to the tourism industry, and poor local ethnic groups often find themselves promoted as tourist attractions (Belhassen *et al.* 2008). Attention is thus paid to the preservation and commodification of ethnic minority cultures as they are "assets" of the poor and part of their livelihood that can serve to generate income from tourists (Wahab 1974: 15; Briedenhann and Wickens 2003).

In planning for tourism development as poverty reduction, governments could take into account tourists' preferences for this kind of "authenticity." Governments might find themselves in a position of choosing between promoting this kind of tourism or offering concessions for resource extraction to foreign investors, which often means relocating ethnic groups (Mowforth and Munt 2003; Mbaiwa 2005; Wang and Wall 2005; Chok *et al.* 2007). Promoting this kind of tourism for poverty reduction has the risk of an "aestheticization and enjoyment of poverty" (Mowforth and Munt 2003) or "poorism-exploitation" as tourist attraction (Baran 2008, cited in Goodwin 2010). Promoting ethnic culture while reducing poverty is a challenging task. While tourists' satisfaction may decline if traditional culture is changed (Mbaiwa 2005), governments have the responsibility of directing and regulating tourism to manage these risks.

The role of government in aid-led tourism development in Lao PDR

Generally, the role of the government of Lao PDR (GoL) has been decen-tralized since the commencement of the "open-door policy" in 1986, which marked the transition from a central planning system to a market-based system. The role of the government was decentralized from central to local levels with the "province as strategic unit and district as planning unit" (Kaisone Phomvihane 1986: 54–55). As part of this general decentralization, reforms also encouraged the growth of a privatized tourism sector. For example, visa restrictions were relaxed and exempted for tourists in the late 1980s (Allcock 2004), and privatization of the majority of state-owned tourism enterprises, including hotel and tour operators, was realized both at national and provincial level. The Tourism Law promulgated in 2005 permitted foreign ownership in tourism (LNTA 2005). These changes contributed to an increase in the number of inbound tourists from 14,400 in 1990 to 737,200 in 2000 and 1.7 million in 2008 (LNTA 2008b).

In 1992, the National Tourism Authority of Lao PDR was established. It was renamed as Laos National Tourism Administration (LNTA) in 2005 and upgraded to ministerial level within the prime minister's office. The main duty of LNTA is to take the leading role in regulating tourism and coordinate between government and other stakeholders in forming and implementing strategies and policies on tourism. Provincial tourism departments (PTDs) were established in all sixteen provinces, and were given responsibilities for tourism planning and cooperation, licensing and legal affairs, marketing and promotion, and training (Harrison and Schipani 2007). This marked the intention to increase the role of government regulation in the increasingly privatized tourism sector.

Given the relatively high rates of poverty in Lao PDR – estimated between 33 percent (Epprecht *et al.* 2008) and 39 percent (Kakwani *et al.* 2002) – the LNTA, in 2001, adopted a poverty-reduction strategy in its formulation of tourism policy (LPMO 2001). Tourism was also clearly identified as a tool for poverty reduction in the National Growth and Poverty Eradication Strategies (LPMO 2004) and was further prioritized as one of the eleven development programs (LCPC 2006). Poverty eradication is also on the agenda of the Tourism Strategy for Lao PDR 2006–2020:

> [T]ourism strategies are to strengthen and develop tourism to become an industrial sector that generates foreign exchange revenue for the country; provides more employment; promotes the cultural conservation and preserves the nation's good norms and customs including the protection of abundant natural resources; promotes sectoral products in order to contribute to poverty reduction of all ethnics groups.
>
> (LNTA 2008a: 13)

Even though the LNTA was set up to direct tourism development in the country, it is still questionable whether tourism benefits are distributed to all provinces equally, particularly in the case of poor remote regions. Tourism income has ranked in the top three of total foreign exchange earnings for Lao PDR since 1999, and tourism was the top-earning industry in 2000 and 2005, bringing in US$114 and US$147 million, respectively (LNTA 2008b). At a regional level, tourism has brought about great benefits mainly to well-developed and accessible destinations such as Vientiane and the two world heritage sites of Luang Prabang and Champasak, whereas the number of visitors to other poor provinces remains relatively low (LNTA 2008b). So far, no research has been carried out in terms of the regional impact of tourism development for poverty reduction in the country.

To implement poverty reduction through tourism at a local scale, the LNTA sought financial and technical support for aid-led projects directed to poor areas. Nam Ha Ecotourism Project (NHEP) in Luangnamtha Province (Figure 10.1) was supported by international organizations such as UNESCO, International Fund Cooperation (IFC) and New Zealand Official Development Agency (NZODA). The first phase of the NHEP (1999–2002), however, focused on environmental protection rather than poverty reduction. Thus, the objective of the project was mainly "the conservation of natural and cultural heritage" (Schipani 2008: 71). Despite the claim that tourism activities should help the poor in targeted villages (Eshoo 2008), the expansion of the NHEP model to Champasak in the south also followed a similar pattern. This aid-led project [in Champasak] aimed at preserving forests and wildlife in the area, and received financial support from the ADB and World Wildlife Fund (WWF) during 2003–2007, and from the Du Puy de Dome and the French government during 2007–2009. Despite involving local people, these projects were not really initiated and fully owned by the local people, leaving their benefits questionable.

The LNTA and the PTDs still play a strong role in regulating and running tourism development and pilot projects in the cases of the NHEP and the expansion project in Champasak Province. Government staffs were recruited as project team members both at national and local level. After setting up the project, the government still has an active role in implementation. In all case study provinces, a so-called tourism service unit (TSU) has been set up to manage tourism packages, which means that the PTD maintains direct control. TSUs operated, for instance, two-night, three-day trekking tours to Samyord and Namtalane villages, in Luangnamtha (Figure 10.2C), and trekking tours to Kietngong and Taong villages, in Champasak (Figure 10.2E). The TSU primarily functions as a gateway to deal with marketing and selling trekking permits and to provide tour guiding. Phase 2 of the NHEP (2005–2008) focused on capacity building to ensure the participation of ethnic minority women in the operation and management of tourism, and in the promotion of the private sector. This project was supported by The Netherlands Development Organization (SNV), which provided a handicraft production and marketing adviser, and by the ADB, which granted low interest loans for tourism infrastructure and activities (Harrison and Schipani 2007). Thus, local people were given the option to choose to work with privately owned businesses parallel to TSU. All had to follow the rules set up by TSU, which were that the earnings were distributed in various degrees for the national tourism tax and a forest protection fee. Participating communities were entitled to receive as much as 72 percent of the earnings derived from visitors'

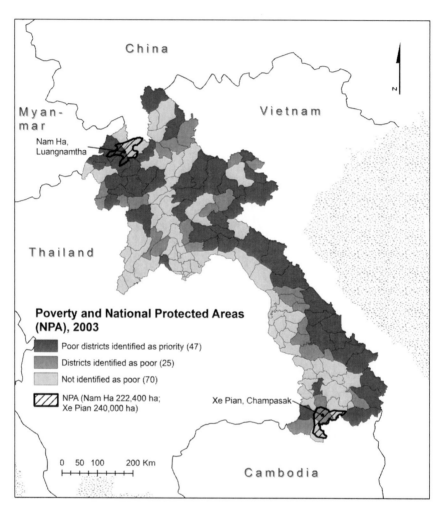

Figure 10.1 Poverty and National Protected Areas (reproduced by kind permission
of the Government of the Lao PDR, 2004, Department of Statistics,
Ministry of Planning and Investment, Vientiane, Lao PDR; map design:
Saithong Phommavong and Dieter Müller).

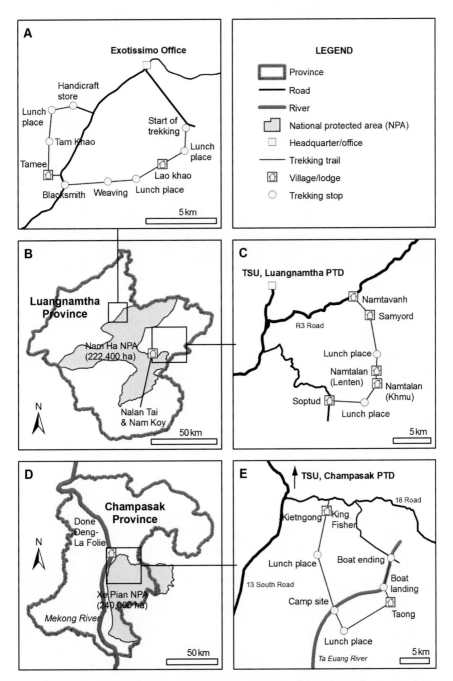

Figure 10.2 Study areas in Luangnamtha and Champasak provinces (reproduced by kind permission of the National Geography Department, Vientiane, Lao PDR, 2010; map design: Saithong Phommavong and Magnus Strömgren, based on the author's GPS survey).

"trip expenses," including fees for communities and merchants selling food and water, accommodation in villages, transport, guide services, handicrafts, and village service fees (Schipani 2008).

Thus, the role of the government has been directed toward privately owned tourism operators as it is believed that they can yield higher benefit than aid-led tourism projects (Harrison and Schipani 2007). But the government's relation to private tour operators is different in the north and in the south. In the north, local government gives priority to private sector enterprises to develop their own trekking trails. For instance, the Exotissimo Travel received fifteen-year concessions for two village lodges constructed by a GTZ Project and is now running trekking tours to eight Akha villages (Figure 10.2A). In contrast, in the south the local government allows both TSU and private tour operators to share a trekking trail and to allow overnight stays in the same Taong lodge (Figure 10.2E). The privately owned lodge can invest in the same village where the TSU village lodge already exists, as in the case of La Folie Lodge in Done Deng and King Fishers Lodge in Kiet Ngong (Figure 10.2D and E).

Aligning goals in tourism and rural development strategies: improvement and resettlement

When considering the main focus area of the general rural development strategy and tourism development as poverty reduction, their potential conflicts and interdependence become evident. The main focus of the rural development program has been to resettle people practicing shifting cultivation in remote or protected areas into "development clusters" (LPRP 1994; Baird and Shoemaker 2007). The resettlement of ethnic minorities is known as a central feature of this development strategy (Evrad and Goudineau 2004). The Instruction No 09 enacted by the Politburo of the Central Party Committee of Lao PDR provides guidelines for the "development cluster and village consolidation", or *kum ban phattana*, strategy.[1] A development cluster is defined as an area that gathers two or three villages and has a population of at least two hundred people. It aims at reducing poverty, promoting cash crop production, controlling shifting and opium cultivation, and constructing basic infrastructure including roads, clean water, electricity, schools, and healthcare centers (LPRP 2004; Baird and Shoemaker 2007). Similarly, village consolidation aims to combine scattered smaller settlements by reseting people into larger permanent villages (Baird and Shoemaker 2007).

The main focus region of tourism development as poverty reduction features similar ideas, since it also targets people living in remote and protected areas. The idea underlying tourism development is mainly environmental protection, resulting in a focus on National Protected Areas (NPAs), encouraging villagers who are living in core and buffer zones to participate in forest and wildlife preservation (UNESCO 1998; Schipani 2008). Income generated from trekking is regarded as a form of poverty reduction. Like rural development strategies in general, income generated through trekking aims at replacing opium, shifting cultivation, and wildlife hunting in the NPAs (interview with head of LNTH PTD, June 27, 2008). However, in practice, some tourism projects also seek to encourage local people to stay inside NPAs to help preserve the forest and wildlife, thus conflicting with resettlement policies aimed at relocating people from those same areas. The ecotourism taking place in NPAs is thus challenging the village consolidation programs. Even though one of the objectives of the NHEP project is to integrate with rural development, in practice they are not well harmonized.

Soup without salt: involuntary resettlers (move) out of the tourism cake

Although rural development programs have been presented to the villagers, not all communities follow the ideas promoted. Promises of better living conditions brought by permanent jobs and improved infrastructure have not been enough incentive for the villagers. In theory, resettlement is voluntary and improves service provision (interview with head of LNTH PTD, June 27, 2008), but that is not always the case. Ideally, participating in NHEP should exclude those from the core zone, which are targets of resettlement (Schipani 2008). However, tourism development projects have, in fact, been targets of resettlement. In some cases, resettlement was initiated in the villages prior to the beginning of tourism development. Resettlement in these zones thus affects tourism development projects, since they target the same local people.

We find examples in the villages of Nalan Tai (Khmu tribe) and Nam Koy (Lenten tribe), Namtha district (Figure 10.2B), which are both part of the trekking trails within a pilot project managed by TSU and the private tour operator Green Discovery. The villagers belong to two main ethnic groups: Khmu belongs to the Mon-Khmer ethno-linguistic group and Lenten belongs to Hmong Iu-Mien (Chazée 1999), and they have different spoken languages. The national Lao language is used to communicate with each other. Resettlement was proceeding during my first visit in May 2008. The villages were encouraged by the district governor to merge together at a new settlement site between their old villages. As compensation, the villagers were promised new facilities, including a road, a school, and clean water. Moreover, a new village lodge was also planned. However, after resettling, the government's commitment had not been fulfilled, causing an outrage among the villagers:

> the road access from town to the village was the greatest constraint for us when someone was ill, they had to be carried along narrow trekking paths to hospitals in town and sometimes during the night . . . the transport of products to the market was done along the same trail . . .
>
> (Mr Phoumy, Nalan Tai, May 31, 2008)

[A] road, clean water, a school and a healthcare center have to be provided to us at the resettlement area as promised; otherwise we have to move back to the same place . . .

(Mr Sivone, villager, Nam Koy, June 1, 2008)

After my second visit in February 2009, Nam Koy people had returned to their old village:

we have difficulty living without clean water, the road is not constructed as promised, the school has just only two classes, the ground for housing is not flat . . .

(Mr Dee, villager, Nam Koy, February 9, 2009)

Both villages had ecotourism lodges at their old sites and this encouraged them to return. The relocation resulted in lost opportunities to benefit from tourism development (Wang and Wall 2005). The resources for new housing, access to water, gardening, and NTFP collection were less abundant in the consolidated village, and even some relocated Khmu villagers mentioned that they would return to their old settlements to plant vegetables and rice (interview with villagers, Nalan Tai, May 31, 2008).

The villages of Namtalan (Khmu) and Namtalan (Lenten) offer another example (Figure 10.2C). They merged administratively some years ago, but still maintained a different culture, language, and village locations about 500 meters from each other. Khmu village was somewhat better off than Lenten, a Lao Huay village. Given their different socio-economic development levels, merging was meant to enable one to help the other (interview with head of LNTH PTD, June 27, 2008). But the result was different. After merging, at first they harmonized their tourism activities. Later, however, a conflict occurred regarding the transparency of the village tourism fund. The Lenten group disliked the perceived non-transparency and suspected the village tourism manager from the Khmu group. At last the Lenten group withdrew from participation in the tourism lodge situated in the Khmu zone. The fund was actually divided, but that was not the end of the problem; a piece of forest was cleared in the area of a trekking trail adjacent to the Lenten village. Here, the incentive to protect the forest was reduced since the benefit did not reach the local people in the area.

These two situations reflect the simple idea of eating soup without salt – something that is easy to do, but the taste is not so good in the end. Local government involvement in setting up village consolidation programs could not be harmonized without the participation of villagers in decision-making processes. Local community leaders were in a rather weak position in both cases and could not make decisions to find better solutions to the conflicts between resettlement and tourism projects. There seemed to be negotiations between villagers and local government but with few practical results. The solutions for the villagers seemed not to come from state intervention in either resettlement or tourism, but were rather related to the power of negotiation of local community leaders and villagers' own livelihood strategies.

The village consolidation policy reflects the idea of national unification, which aims for cultural and economic harmonization in line with the dominant Lao culture (Baird and Shoemaker 2007). National unification thus has an impact on "authenticity." Suntikul (2007) argues that the very remoteness of communities and the perceived "authenticity" of their way of life are important attractions for tourists interested in ethnic minorities. Resettling these villages would in this sense compromise their attractiveness to tourism. The main interest of tourists coming to Luangnamtha, for instance, is visiting ethnic minority villages (Focken 2007). As such, the village consolidation policy does not support "cultural tourism," which uses minority ethnicity to attract tourists. The unification of two different ethnic groups in a new resettlement area may thus pose a threat to tourism businesses focusing on "traditional culture." In fact, the number of tourists decreased during 2008–2009 in several cases, including the Namtalan trekking trail (interviews with Namtalan village managers, July 21, 2010; TSU officers, Luangnamtha, July 22, 2010; TSU officers, Champasak, August 10, 2010). This might partly result from the conflicts that emerged in relation to the merging of villages and the process of national cultural unification.

Nikhom Lieng Sad and Ban Phatthana: enjoying the tourism cake?

In contrast with the conflict situations described above, there were other resettlement examples that indicated an awareness and intention to rethink rural development programs and tourism development. A common issue brought up in two successful cases of resettlement was that community leaders have to be educated and learn from previous experiences.

Samyord in the north and Done Deng in the south (Figure 10.2C and D) are considered successful resettlements because of their strong community leadership, good integration of local potential resources from both tourism and non-tourism, and voluntarily movements. Instead of directly following the instruction of resettlement, the villagers made an effort to compromise between rural development and tourism development. The resettlement of Samyord (Hmong tribe) started in 2000 and the majority of the villagers followed the program. However, about nineteen families remained in the mountain location during my first visit in early 2009. The new resettlement area is located along the R3 road, the northeast corridor linking Thailand, Laos, and China. In 2005 PTD and NHEP project staff decided to build a lodge in the mountain village as the first night stay for a trekking trail (Figure 10.2C). The project sought to maintain the settlement of the remaining villagers. To achieve this, a suspension bridge to cross the river between the mountain village and the new settlement was built and a lodge and a water tank were provided. The community leaders and the village committee had received higher education and working experience with the government, which played a strong role in letting the villagers remain in their old village:

> Firstly, we are afraid of not having enough land for cultivation. Secondly, we have many cattle, including cows, goats, pigs and chicken, which are very important assets for us, so we do not want to leave them. Thirdly, a tourist lodge is already built for us by the department [PTD],[2] so we can earn some money from tourist services; it is only a project appropriate for a mountainous village . . .
> (Mr Tongyang, manager, Samyord, January 20, 2010)

A headman of the settled village who moved down ten years ago added that:

> local government allocates some plots of land for the villagers left behind and proposes that the highland village might not relocate all families, some might stay there to look after the tourism lodge and the cattle, promoted as *nikhom lieng sad* [place for cattle rearing] . . .
> (Mr Sichanh, headman, Namtavanh, January 20, 2010)

The voluntary migration is seen as a possibility to combine potential resources in the area, the "*nikhom lieng sad*," and income from tourism. During my last visit in July 2010, all sixteen families were constructing second homes in the resettlement area. Some acquired land under the resettlement program while others bought new houses and land from other villagers. The second home in the resettlement area was mainly for their children so that they would be able to continue their studies after primary school, whereas parents were staying in the mountain village (interview with village tourism manager, Samyord, and headman, Namtavanh, July 20, 2010). At this stage, tourism provided an option for them to support the resettlement in a voluntarily way.

> I combined the income derived from the tourism lodge, from selling animals and from NTFP to buy a house in the resettlement area, to where I will send my daughter to continue her study after primary school. Because I did not have the house there, she [her daughter] had to drop one year from school . . . this year I will send her there for study [school is started in September]; without money from this work, her study is difficult to support . . .
> (Mrs Vanh, villager, Samyord, July 20, 2010)

Another example is from Done Deng, a resettlement project on an island in the south where there are both TSU and privately owned tourism businesses. As in Samyord, the community leadership seems to play a key role in harmonizing resettlement with tourism projects:

to follow the Instruction No 09 of the Politburo of the Central Party Committee of Lao PDR and Notification No 13 of Prime Minister of Lao PDR in terms of merging small villages into a larger village, we merged Bang Say and Done Deng villages together several years ago . . . to fulfill the rural development goal, particularly the so-called "Ban Phatthana," we give priority to the poor to work in La Folie, a privately owned lodge to earn more income and reduce poverty . . . on June 2009, our village could fulfill all 13 village development certificates and declared as "*ban phatthana*" . . .

(Mr Vieng, vice-headman, Don Deng, August 4, 2009)

"*Ban phatthana*" literally means "developed village," a specific Lao concept, which refers to the supreme goal of rural development. To fulfill the "developed village" goal, a village has to surpass a set of criteria, including poverty reduction, basic education, healthcare, no criminality, and "good morals" of youth and women (LPRP 2004). Together, thirteen certificates are required (LPMO 2009; see also LPMO 2008). Based on these criteria, the committee leaders made use of local tourism resources to help poor, households. In this case, the villages belonged to the same Lao-Tai group, sharing language and sociocultural traditions, which facilitated the merging process. The merger was only administrative, and the two villages remained situated in their old locations. Poverty is reported to have been eradicated, but inequality is still evident.

I have worked for the lodge for three and half years. My salary has increased by about 100,000 Kip per year; currently I receive 700,000 Kip per month, plus bonus 180,000 Kip per month . . .[3]

(Mrs Boua, head of gardening section,
La Folie Lodge, August 2009)

This provides an example how the villagers earn from working with a privately owned tourism lodge. However, only fifty to sixty people can work in the lodge during high season (interview with Mrs Boua, August 3, 2009). Villagers who are not able to work in the lodge still rely on agricultural work as their main source of livelihood.

I do not know how I can benefit from tourism because I never worked with that . . . because I am not in the roster house, only the headman's and other families were called, I was never called except for communal work, I never missed that . . . I always work and stay in my paddy field to look after my chicken and make wood charcoal . . .

(Mrs Phim, villager, Done Deng, August 3, 2009)

Thus, the "developed village" is still questionable, despite the village committee's claim that all poverty is now eradicated. The TSU operates under a rotation system, which aims for equal distribution to all villagers, but not all households can become members. The power of local elite groups is still strong; the headman and manager benefit the most from TSU. Although poverty is eradicated, the challenge related to inequality remains. Nevertheless, this example reveals a situation where village consolidation was integrated with tourism development and took advantage of both the TSU and private businesses.

The two cases above highlight the role of local political party members intervening in tourism and resettlement. The headmen of the villages in both cases are members of Lao People's Revolutionary Party at the village level (interviews with headman, Samyord, January 20, 2010; headman, Done Deng, February 16, 2008), and they have the power to take action to help the poor. This is unique in the sense that the community leaders were both political party members and local government staff. Top-down state intervention seemed not to be enough for poverty reduction, and the role of local political party members appeared to be crucial in both Nikhom Lieng Sad and Ban Phatthana.

Trekking in rubber gardens

Numerous stakeholders consider alternative development options as complementary to or as a replacement for tourism development. Rubber plantations are one major example. Rubber plantations have been established prior to tourism projects to consolidate villages. The initiative of rubber plantation in Luangnamtha was identified in the Fifth Provincial Party Congress beginning in 1991, and the rubber was planted in 1994 with the goal of alleviating poverty and stabilizing shifting cultivation (Shi 2008). Plantations were established by different parties, for example as concessions to foreign investors, often from China, and by local villagers. The Khmu site of Namtalan is a case where the income from tourism is not sufficient and rubber plantations are used to fill the gap. Local government might consider benefits of tourism to be too small, and thus seek for other approaches to eradicate poverty. Also, the local government might not want villagers to stay in the rural area and be a target of the tourists' gaze of "enjoying poverty" (Mowforth and Munt 2003). This view contrasts with the idea of promoting tourism for poverty reduction and the new trend of tourism.

The allocation of land for rubber plantations in the area of trekking trails is part of the so-called *yad din* [land seizure] (interview, LNTA, June 18, 2008) between rubber investors and tourism projects. Because of limited cooperation between agents in the allocation of the land for rubber plantations, they are viewed as a hindrance for ecotourism projects. Although rubber plantations are silently viewed as a quicker way for poverty reduction (Suntikul 2007), the benefits can hardly reach the poor if the land does not belong to them (Boupha 2007). The idea of combining ecotourism and trekking in rubber gardens was proposed by an agricultural officer in the south, who foresaw the opportunities and different points of view over ecotourism development (interview Head of Champasak Provincial Agricultural and Forestry Department, June 27, 2008). However, it was argued by a former Natural Eco-Tourism Project Adviser that the attraction for tourists would be low in such cases (interview with Xe Pian Eco-Tourism Project Adviser, June 30, 2008). In this sense, the combination of these competing approaches cannot be harmonized. This also reflects how changes in landscape might impact on tourists' preferences. Economic benefits from ecotourism are higher for villagers than those from rubber plantations, and also have less environmental impact (Schipani 2007). Nevertheless, rubber plantation might be preferred by the government as an alternative option for poverty reduction.

Cardamom planting: no need to clear big trees, only small bushes

At the village level, not all agreed with the idea of rubber plantations. Rubber plantations require at least six to eight years of nurturing before harvest (Peters and Achilles 2007; Cohen, P.T. 2009; Singkeo 2009). Some villagers were reluctant to grow rubber and they returned to other livelihoods while waiting for the harvest. As shifting cultivation is prohibited they might plant another cash crop, make wood charcoal or hunt, in addition to normal agriculture such as upland cultivation and animal rearing. Actually, various cash crops, including cardamom, were introduced by the GTZ (Cohen, P.T. 2009). In the short run, cardamom is considered more competitive in terms of yield, forest protection, and price:

> Cardamom was introduced to the village, and it seems to be a competitive crop with no need to clear all forest, just bush and small plants; it can be harvested after 3 years; the harvest time is short, just twice per year, one month each and normally from July to September. Its price is 50,000 Kip per kilo for raw and 80,000 Kip per kilo for dried; so many households focus on planting this crop instead of rubber plantation . . .
>
> (Mr Ka, former headman, Namtalan, July 21, 2010)

It seems that this is a better way of compromising between agricultural production and ecotourism compared with rubber plantations, especially as the price of rubber decreased after 2007 (Singkeo 2009). This kind of agriculture is a "mosaic" pattern in a way that preserves biodiversity and minimizes soil erosion (Cohen, P.T. 2009: 5). Planting this intercrop can be harmonized with trekking trails in a better way than trekking in rubber plantations, since the natural forest landscape can be maintained. Villagers in the north pursue this idea, and some mentioned that not all of them wanted to plant rubber as they foresaw the opportunity of planting cardamom, with better yield (interview with villagers, Namtalan, July 21, 2010).

Some villagers turned to other livelihoods, which also had shorter cycles, including wildlife hunting and logging, which directly posed a threat to current and future ecotourism. A privately owned tour operator suffered from wildlife hunting as touring wildlife inside NPA was advertised as a selling point. She complained that "some nights, the sound of rifles was heard around the NPA; tourists would ask what the rifles were for, was this the NPA?" (interview with private lodge owner, February 15, 2008). Actually, local villagers with traditional hunting rifles could be observed during the trekking in both Nam Ha and Xe Pian NPA (observation, July 2010).

The importance of the tourists' gaze for landscape authenticity can be observed in this case and partly explains the decline in the number of tourists. Clearing of the scenery surrounding villages for rubber plantations, coupled with breaking into small hills for road construction, demonstrate the physical change of the landscape. Local government interventions from departments other than tourism thus pose threats to ecotourism. Opportunities might be seen in the long term in the case of rubber plantations, but these do not harmonize well with ecotourism. Community leaders and villagers play strong roles in decision-making for rural development, including resettlement and tourism development. Traditional knowledge of cardamom can be a better solution for harmonizing resettlement and ecotourism than large-scale industrial tree plantations.

Conclusion

Poverty reduction through tourism is not an easy business for a society in transition. Without a proper coordination policy, outcomes can conflict with each other directly, and even risk eroding the attraction base for successful tourism development. Government interventions are partly contingent on external stakeholders whose donations steer development in the directions they desire. The aims of these development projects do sometimes target issues relevant to donor countries rather than the society in transition (Mowforth and Munt 2003; Shi 2008). Protection of nature certainly fulfills the Western wish of sustaining ecological values, but sometimes aligns unsatisfactorily with local livelihoods, particularly if related tourism development does not occur to the anticipated extent.

Moreover, it appears that rural development programs largely fail to acknowledge the existence of traditional community structures and livelihoods. Ideas favoring private ownership collide with a strong Lao tradition of local organization. Thus, local social structures condition tourism development projects, resulting in widening income gaps within the local community rather than contributing to a general improvement of living conditions for all villagers. Hence, to poor people, tourism development does not always mean a blessing. Instead, they are required to navigate within a complex framework set by national and international interests between conservation and small-scale pro-poor development on the village level, and industrial resource use and income growth on a national level.

This applies also to the government. In the absence of its own funding resources, external stakeholders influence the agenda. This certainly contributes to diverging and poorly integrated development strategies and concrete actions. Moreover, this study also indicates that preconditions for tourism development vary within countries with regard to location, natural resources and alternative development options in place. The bottom-up approaches in this case are rather different in that local community leaders play important roles in harmonizing rural development with tourism development. Thus, a "one policy fits all" approach is unquestionably a thorny way forward. Instead, the examples from this study suggest tourism development in articulation with alternative sectors that share resources with tourism in order to reduce poverty. In this context it is less important whether development is achieved in public or private forms, as long as the traditional knowledge of villagers is acknowledged. This local knowledge can be decisive, as was demonstrated in the case of cardamom cultivation. Here, tourism resources were maintained successfully at the same time as a cash crop was introduced. These two actions together probably make a greater contribution to poverty reduction than many policies and projects.

Recognizing the local pluralism inherent in tourism development, then, suggests that we view tourism less as a particular development model – as implied by the concept of "pro-poor tourism" – and more as a social process characterized by local social conditions *and* broader scales – here represented by the state and the agents of international development, and their particular agendas of nationalization, nature conservation, and poverty alleviation. As practiced, tourism cannot be easily characterized as any particular kind of (capitalist) industry or (state) project, but must be viewed as an assemblage of processes whose characteristics are highly contingent and contextual.

Acknowledgments

I would like to thank Professor Dr Dieter Müller and Associate Professor Dr Aina Tollefsen of the Department of Social and Economic Geography, Umea University, Sweden; Professor Dr Tim Oakes, Department of Geography, University of Colorado at Boulder; and Professor Dr Claudio Minca of Wageningen University for their valuable comments and linguistic improvements on this chapter. This study was financially supported by the Swedish International Development Agency (Sida). I thank the staff of the Faculty of Social Sciences, National University of Laos, for their contributions to the fieldwork. Thanks to Dr Magnus Strömgren and Professor Dr Dieter Müller for help in mapping the study sites.

Notes

1   The definition of *kum* is "group," the definition of *ban* is "village," and *phattana* means "development." Literally translated, *kum ban phattana* therefore means a "group of development villages."
2   Three people trekking from France stayed overnight at the lodge during the visit on January 20, 2010.
3   The exchange rate was 8,755, 8,522 and 8,265 Lao Kip (LAK) per US$1 in 2008, 2009 and 2010, respectively.

11 Post-war tours

Jamie Gillen

Vietnam Vietnam Vietnam, we've all been there.

(Michael Herr, *Dispatches*, 1991)

Introduction

This chapter follows two groups of people – American tourists visiting Vietnam and the Vietnamese tour guides who serve them – as they create relationships out of their experiences of the Vietnam War. I argue that for as much as these groups share common experiences and sentiments of the Vietnam War through contemporary tourism encounters, and that these encounters dissolve the separation between American tourist outsider and Vietnamese guide insider, the rootedness of these tours in the American–Vietnamese conflict ensures that reconciliation is never fully possible. In this chapter I wish to show that this contradiction between shared experiences and enduring divisions has consequences not only for tourism practices, national identity, and the commodification of war, but also for geopolitical, diplomatic, and post-war relations.

The first group under scrutiny, American tourists visiting Vietnam, has been conditioned to American culpability in Vietnam largely through Vietnam War movies and more recent engagements in the American media that recall the war when describing contemporary military incursions in Iraq and Afghanistan (Laderman 2009). They are acutely aware (following Alneng) of "the crucial role the American War plays in promoting Vietnam as a tourist destination" (Alneng 2002a: 462), because movies and other representations of Vietnam correspond closely to the violent imprints left behind by American forces and on display in tourist sites throughout Vietnam. For these tourists, representations of the Vietnam War consumed at home – when inscribed in their trips to war tourism sites in Vietnam – aid in and inform their understandings of the pain and violence suffered by Vietnamese. This point challenges the notion that the Vietnam War in the American imagination is reduced to the image of the Vietnamese as inscrutable, savage, Other (Alneng 2002b; Laderman 2002). Upon arrival in Vietnam, American tourist groups often use leisure to offer symbolic gestures of reciprocity and respect, and material currency, to Vietnamese people in order to pay retribution for the sins of previous generations.

The first part of the chapter argues that many American tourists read the American invasion into Vietnam largely through the lens of contemporary media forms, and use these engagements to buttress their interest in resolving the Vietnam–American conflict through their predisposition as one of the world's most mobile and high-consumption class of people. Put another way, American tourists are playing a part in amending grievances and settling their debt to the Vietnamese through their tourist excursions there. By highlighting how leisure travel does not necessarily conform to typical nationalist discourses, which revolve around a newfound friendship built on economic trade as well as concern over human rights, this section casts daily tourism encounters between Asian hosts and American guests in a different light from traditional state- building exercises between two former enemies (Hayton 2010). This point also adds to the volume's goal of distancing tourism theory from its Western bias by decoupling tourist–tour guide relations from broader assumptions about enduring American hegemony in Southeast Asia.

With post-socialist Vietnam experiencing unprecedented levels of national economic growth, a corresponding sense of financial opportunity has enlivened the country's population (Kim 2008). The global financial crisis notwithstanding, Vietnam's "open door" policies have specifically focused on travel as a pivotal national economic engine (Biles *et al.* 1999; Hall and Page 2000; Suntikul *et al.* 2008). Central to Vietnam's tourism industry is the presentation of "American" war sites. Aware that the scenes depicted at these sites may upset and stigmatize American tourists, and in an effort to offset the graphic atmosphere surrounding them, Vietnamese tour guides commonly emphasize the tropes of a mutual pain surrounding the war and contemporary friendship as they direct tourists through these sites. The second section of this chapter, which follows from the first, argues that Vietnamese tour guides use discourses surrounding the American war as building blocks to solidify their relationships with American tourists, who use similar links to share in the pain of the war with guides. Their nascent relationship is complemented by the adoption of Western and non-Western forms of financial exchange, such as the acceptance and encouragement of tips, third-party involvement in the tourist–tour guide relationship, and the celestial benefits of offering monetary wealth to the altars of war dead, either directly or through Vietnamese intermediaries.

In ways symbolic (in the forms of regret and sharing in the pain) and real (in the form of currency exchange), American tourists and Vietnamese tour guides use the Vietnamese–American war as a platform to press forward in the labor of healing through bilateral economic development. The shared meanings of the war encourage alternative understandings of the processual nature of the shared history of the United States and Vietnam, thereby challenging some of the basic assumptions about tourist–host relationships as clearly dichotomized between foreign outsider consumers and local insider producers. Indeed, the unequal relationship between "First World" tourists and "Third

World" hosts is a key criticism of contemporary excursions into "needy" countries, for example through pro-poor tourism, philanthrotourism, or volun-tourism (Hall 2007).

The Vietnam War acts as a binding agent between two groups of people who have long understood their countries to be in conflict with one another. However, the war also invokes different, more solitary elements of pain and loss of the sort that irrevocably distance the two groups from each other. If the opportunities of leisure bring Americans and Vietnamese together, it is also an axiom of war tourism in Vietnam that travel experiences clarify and develop the differences between Americans and Vietnamese. What exemplify these differences are the presentation and narrative behind the war sites them-selves, which in harsh and unequivocal terms take account of the evil of the Americans and the resilience and unity of the Vietnamese. The most popular war sites in Vietnam, which are operated by the Communist Party of Vietnam, balance American practices of evil with the compassionate treatment of the Americans during the war. These stories shadow tourists and tour guides in their journeys through Vietnam, haunting their encounters with a history that ensures lingering disparities between the two groups. An inability to reach full reconciliation has broader implications for political and post-war relations between countries, and asserts the blurriness between tourism practices and other social relations (Urry 2002).

Therefore, this chapter offers three interventions in how we understand post-war relations between the US and Vietnam by looking at these relations through the tourism experience: first, by showing that the localized and interpersonal relationships between American tourists and Vietnamese tour guides diverge from commonplace understandings of the reconstruction of the relation-ship between the two countries (Rama 2008; Schwenkel 2009); second, by rethinking the distinctions between "First World" traveler and "Third World" host (Tucker 2009; Winter *et al.* 2009); and third, by focusing on tourism as a mediating force in broader global relations between former "enemies."

In the next section, American travels to Vietnam provide both tourists and tour guides with the opportunity to investigate the extent to which the war shapes both groups today.

On second chances: American tourists and the search for the Vietnam War

"Where's Charlie?"

In 2002, 2004, and 2006, I was in Ho Chi Minh City, Vietnam, conducting dissertation research on the changing face of the Vietnamese tourism industry during the reform era. One of my methods included participant observa-tion on tours of war sites in southern Vietnam. In May of each year I accom-panied study abroad groups from Virginia Tech University (USA) on their annual tour of the Cu Chi Tunnels outside of Ho Chi Minh City. The tunnels

– an underground system of paths and rooms built to be the temporary home of displaced Vietnamese and Viet Cong fighters during the war – are now Vietnam's most popular tourist attraction and a requisite stop for tour groups traveling from overseas (Schwenkel 2009). The weather during the visit in 2006 was nasty, with a penetrating downpour that dampened student interest in crawling through the tunnels as the American "tunnel rats" and Viet Cong had done in the 1960s and 1970s. Instead of having the students follow the normal tour itinerary, now impassable, the Vietnamese tour guide decided on an original alternative: march the group through a heavily forested area near the tunnels in search of a large crater created by an American bomb during the war.

Led by their professors, the group of approximately 35 students began walking into the wet darkness. Initially in disagreement over the prospect of ruining their clothes and shoes in the rain and mud, the soon began to enjoy the uniqueness of the adventure and recognized that the walk epitomized similar representations of the Vietnam War that they had seen. "We're in the real Nam now buddy!", I overheard one male student declare. "Where's Charlie?", another student stated, laughingly, if haltingly. A few began debating the "best" English language Vietnam War movies, beginning with *Platoon* and *We Were Soldiers*, and settling on *Full Metal Jacket*. The tour guide, a man named Thanh, continued silently leading the group without pausing. "Wow," a female student near me said offhandedly, almost to herself. "I can't imagine having to walk through this weather every day." Later on, as we arrived at the crater and were standing around it, peering inside, another student pulled me aside and said, "It must've been a terrible war," and stared back into the hole before him.

The group was more quiet on the walk back from the crater and pressed on to the main entrance to the tunnels, completely waterlogged. As the rain let up and the air became even thicker with humidity, softer, more concerned voices began to shift gears and whisper about the consequences of the war on the Vietnamese. Sprinkled with comments about which Vietnam War movies fared better in telling the "real" story of the Vietnam War, the tourist group began assessing how many Vietnamese "actually" died during the war. Others seemed unsure what to make of the crater and what it represented. One student asked two questions in rapid succession: "Did the US drop that bomb? Were people living here when that bomb was dropped?" The conversation grew more heated. A few students who said that the bomb was mere "Communist propaganda" and that the US wasn't to blame for trying to "help the Vietnamese" were outnumbered by students who were verbalizing the contrasts and compatibilities between their previous experiences with Vietnam War movies and the hostile mix of rain, humidity, forested environment, and the larger consequences of the bomb's destruction of Vietnamese soil and lives.

To be sure, not all of the tourists took part in these discussions, some preferring instead to walk in silence or focus on the more mundane moments of their trip, such as discussing the food they had eaten the night before or the poverty they had seen in Ho Chi Minh City (cf. Edensor 2007). However, for many, the combination of the weather and the "off the tourism path" bomb crater trip seemed to confront some in the group with the realization that for them and their generation, Vietnamese history began the first time they watched *Full Metal Jacket*, *Apocalypse Now*, or *Platoon*. For some, the trip marked the moment when they first began to connect their movie viewing with the violence and anguish for the Vietnamese people during and after the war. For the students, Vietnam War losses up until that moment meant the death of an American soldier (Kwon 2008: 14), or, for some, the temporary loss of most-favored-nation trading status (Gainsborough 2007), or potentially the death of American hegemony (Buzzanco 1999). For many American tourists, casualties in Vietnam were reduced to the untimely death of a character they came to identify with in a war movie they had seen. The Vietnam War had been understood, prior to their visit to Vietnam, as a distinctly American tragedy, "traumatic for American society" (Schwenkel 2009: 2). But travel to Vietnam had done for them what popular culture could not: catalyze Americans to reflect on the Vietnamese experience from a point of view other than their own. And, judging from their incorporation of Vietnam War popular culture, tourists' previous experiences consuming Vietnam *illuminate* the plight of the Vietnamese during their tourist ventures.

The existing literature on this subject, of which there is little (though see Dittmar and Michaud 1990; Donald 2001), suggests that representations of war depicted in Western movies reinforce the dichotomy between the hegemonic, masculine Self and the savage, feminine Other (see Said 1978). The tour experiences of the students that day offer an alternative to such stereotypical dichotomies: as Americans come to grips with the similarities between the movies they reference and the war tourism sites experienced *in situ*, they come to question the scope and impact of the Vietnam War in the United States beyond the stories some of their favorite war movies tell. Perhaps more consequentially, the seeds of understanding and sympathizing with alternative perspectives on war are sown out of the collision between popular media representations of war and trips as tourists. My analysis shows that popular movies of the Vietnam War, which often depict the Vietnamese as a hostile and surreptitious group of fighters, are recalled and challenged by American tourists visiting Vietnam's war sites. Memories of the Vietnam War drawn from movie representations combine with tourism encounters in Vietnam to open the war's impact to American tourists.

What role, if any, do Vietnam tour guides play in the perpetuation of aiding and clarifying understandings of the Vietnam War, which are themselves drawn largely from the intersection between film and holiday? For a possible answer we return to the weather-stricken Cu Chi Tunnels visit. The group reached the bus, which was awaiting our arrival in the parking lot, and everyone filed in with relief (Figure 11.1).

Thanh took the bus's microphone, as he always did, to share the rest of the day's plans. Speaking slowly, Thanh began not by mentioning our dinner plans

Figure 11.1 Virginia Tech group about to board the bus after their impromptu hike (photo: Jamie Gillen).

but by comparing Vietnam's current economic growth with his family's role in the American War. *"Xin chào các bạn* [hello my friends]," he said. "Right now Vietnam is developing very quickly. You can see the progress in the streets of Ho Chi Minh City. We are building our economy, our infrastructure, and our higher education. Vietnamese people today have more opportunity now than before." Then he recounted his family's plight during the war. His father was an officer in Saigon for the Army of the Republic of Vietnam, the primary South Vietnamese military unit that fought alongside the Americans for South Vietnamese sovereignty. Growing up in Saigon at the time, Thanh said, was a very exciting time for his family. There, his family could practice their Catholicism freely and were pleased that the United States had decided to join them in their fight against Communism. He continued speaking lovingly about his parents, siblings, and American support when he was a boy.

What seemed to be happening at that moment between Thanh and his tourist group was the laying out of what Jay Winter calls "fictive kinship," whereby war and its aftermath, while destroying intimate community relations, also provides the context for cross-cultural reconciliation on the basis of "the power of human creativity to confront its mechanism of destruction and embrace its ruins" (Winter 1995, cited in Kwon 2008: 84). Much like the students, Thanh was weaving together a story of his experience of the American war that was regenerative in its undertaking and therapeutic in its intent. The American war in official party language is confrontational and divisive (see below), making Thanh's story of his family coexisting peacefully and happily among the American troops both startling and unique. If Vietnamese–American history for the Americans on this trip was bound up in American actor portrayals of valorous heroes, here was a Vietnamese person's history bound up in positive, hopeful interactions with American troops that also spoke to American heroism and optimism. Here was a story that both the tourists and the tour guide could not only relate to, but stand behind. Here both the Americans and the Vietnamese were heroes, co-stars in a story unencumbered by traditional narratives of the Vietnamese–American relationship that circle around the complications or failures of the US government in Vietnam, and lacking the questions of human rights that doggedly stand in the way of a more complete diplomatic relationship between the two countries today (Hayton 2010).

"And before we knew it, the Americans left us behind," Thanh continued, adding a darker bookend to his recollections.

> My dad was in trouble because he worked side by side the Americans. He decided that we should leave Vietnam and travel to Thailand as refugees. The year was 1974 and I was seven years old. We stayed there for over six years. My mom, brothers, and sisters returned to Saigon but my father stayed behind until 1984.

Thanh paused as the students silently weighed the consequences of supporting the American cause in South Vietnam at the time.

> However, when my father returned from the refugee camp he became an English-language tour guide. He is retired now, but he began learning English working for the Americans, and he was very grateful to the Americans for teaching him English, including some naughty words and slang.

At this the group collectively laughed, and Thanh smiled. With that, his brief explanation of his past was over, and he moved on to discuss plans for the rest of the afternoon and evening.

Michael Bibby has stated that "the (Vietnam) war's dismembered ghosts continue to haunt American culture" (2000: 149, cited in Kwon 2008: 13), pointing to the detrimental memory of the war on the spirit of the American psyche. What I have highlighted in this section of the chapter is that the hopefulness and possibility for reconciliation apparent in memories of the war are a part of the "haunting" of American culture that is missing from Bibby's account. Abetted by tours to Vietnam and the tour guides who support them, the lure of the war in Vietnam endures, even thirty years after its reunification and the fall of Saigon. Popular representations of the Vietnam War engage and mix with new understandings of the tragedy of the experience on the Vietnamese and Americans.

Not comfortable letting American tourists rest on these new revelations, Vietnamese tour guides, illustrated by Thanh's narrative, feature discourses of shared American–Vietnamese feelings of longing, separation, pain, and, in contemporary times, a shared sense of optimism. Presenting a shared sense of confidence is not typically a key feature of post-war investigations of the uneasy process of relationship building between Vietnam and the United States. Instead, commentators focus on the "gift" of neoliberalism shared with (and/or forced upon) Vietnam by the United States (Schwenkel 2009), the cautiousness by which Vietnam proceeds into the global economy (Drummond and Thomas 2003), or the ways in which American tourism guidebooks reinforce stereotypes of the native, violent, and exotic Other (Laderman 2009). We could reasonably ask whether statements from tour guides, such as Thanh's narrative, are intended to invoke sympathy and solidarity in order to garner a bigger tip from the group. In the vignette in the next section we see that guides indeed use the violence of the American war to generate revenue for themselves and their kin. But in this section it is useful to evaluate the emotional imprint developed by relationship building among American tourists and Vietnamese tour guides on its own terms, as one facet of the tourist–tour guide relationship, because it is often these encounters that tourists find most important and transcendent in their travels. The memories of shared loss and a collective voice of friendship between two former enemies are the serendipitous, extraordinary components of the tourist experience that "place the human body and all its sensory capacities in unfamiliar, sometimes unsettling circumstances" (Gibson, C. 2008: 419). Even if the piercing rain, bomb crater, and Thanh's narrative were deliberately assembled to dig deeper into tourist pockets, for American tourists, the day's events and discourses lead to a type of unfettered reconciliation that only leisure travel can provide.

This section shows that the Vietnamese–American War is also used as a catalyst to clarify the shared experiences of pain, violence, and national unease that continue to exist among both Americans and Vietnamese. The next section discusses what Americans do with their newfound clarity, and how Vietnamese tour guides encourage and instruct them as both groups confront the violence and pain of the war that continues to simmer in striking ways today.

Exploring the art of the "spontaneous" sale in Vietnamese tour excursions

Using a university group as an example of a leisure encounter in contemporary Vietnam between tourists and tour guides, the line dividing "us" from "them" is not as hard and fast as it is often portrayed in popular depictions (such as movies) and tourist understandings of the Vietnam War. Various scholars have highlighted the divisive nature of Vietnam War sites, especially among Western overseas tourists (Laderman 2009; Schwenkel 2009), without incorporating the power of tourism to transform rather than reinforce stereotypes of the former enemy. The section above has sought to rectify this gap by bridging tourist needs for mutual understanding and openness with the ideological baggage many tourists from the United States and other Western countries bring with them to Vietnam; movies have taught them that the Vietnam War was a very difficult war to win, polarized the American public, brought about gruesome and numerous deaths of Americans and Vietnamese, and resulted in a totally razed Vietnamese landscape. Continuing today, the Western news media frequently refer to the Vietnam War as an example of the permanent differences between the "needs" of Western and non-Western civil society. By pacifying the US' role in Vietnam during war time, by attempting to bridge the plight of both groups and harmonize the time period when the American military sent over 500,000 troops to protect South Vietnam from the threat of Communism, Vietnamese tour guides such as Thanh seek to establish a new baseline for the relationship between Americans and Vietnamese. This is an important mechanism in the new American "involvement" in Vietnam: a shared sense of the nobility of the joint partnership between Americans and South Vietnamese military (at least in south Vietnam today) eases the stereotype that the American military was confounded during its presence in Vietnam by a homogeneous and mysterious citizen base that, if not overtly antagonistic toward the American invasion and occupation, certainly did not share in the responsibilities for "freeing" Vietnam of Communism. These cues are invaluable tools in efforts to appease a very attractive consumer base, and for American tourists this kind of dialogue provides some clarity and opportunity for resolution in what is often understood as a faraway land inhabited by an inscrutable, resilient, and hostile people.

Perhaps more tangibly, however, the American tourist–Vietnamese tour guide relationship rests on everyday, small-scale financial investments. These transactions facilitate and support moments of reconciliation between Vietnamese and Americans in the tourist experience. They also equip Americans with a familiar and welcome type of monetary currency for which they are coveted: Vietnamese tour guides categorize Americans according to their seemingly infinite amount of expendable income, and their generosity and naivety in spending it (Gillen 2008). For these reasons, it is fair to say that Americans are the most attractive tourist–consumers in Vietnam, whose activities, needs, and interests when visiting Vietnam are most predictable (Gillen 2008).

From the guides' perspective, there are generally three levels of economic exchange in the typical American tourist–Vietnamese tour guide relationship. The first and most conventional is the cost incurred to take a trip in Vietnam. Paid in most cases to a tourism company for which a Vietnamese tour guide is employed, tourists usually only see the handful of company employees who serve as the faces of the company, and the tourists therefore forget, do not understand, or do not seem to care that their official tour fees are not going solely into the pockets of the guides, which leads to misunderstandings about extra costs incurred by tourists, such as tipping. To rectify the situation, Vietnamese tour guides go through a tour group leader intermediary in requesting tips to be paid out at the end of a trip. This is the second form of tour guide repayment, and the most coveted, valuable, and unpredictable: "voluntary" gratuity.

Tipping Vietnamese tour guides operates in much the same manner as the tipping culture in the United States. Longer trips are compensated more handsomely than day-long jaunts, of course, as are higher-end tours. Americans typically pay out 15–20 percent of the cost of the tour in tips at the conclusion of a multi-day trip. American tour groups in Vietnam are popular because they are understood to appreciate the importance of gratuities in the service industry and because they tip handsomely. This form of payment is also desired because it comes in cash (often, and preferably, in US currency), which, in contrast to payment from the tour company, can be used immediately.

The third form of guide compensation, and the subject of this section of the chapter, is compensation from third parties involved in a tour group itinerary. Stopping along a route toward or returning from the official destination of the day (for example, in between the central Ho Chi Minh City hotel and the Cu Chi Tunnels), guides will often show tour groups to an interesting site, a small market, or another venue that sells "local" wares. These stops, although they are pitched as spontaneous, are in fact designed, arranged, and negotiated with precision ahead of time among family members, friends, acquaintances, and/or business associates. Guides unleash tourists to shop, spend, and gawk at goods, eat the local fare, or a combination of these. Guides usually receive a flat price from the venue operator for the privilege of unloading their commodities to Western tourists, with wildly inflated price tags. These are "Western" (*người tây*) prices, and if sales are strong, or the guide stops at a given spot regularly, he or she can also receive a percentage of the total revenue drawn from the visit. This aspect of profit seeking – as standard to the Vietnamese tourism economy as formal payment – is generally either not understood or weakly acknowledged by American tourists as they press the flesh with local vendors, primarily because there is no equivalent in American forms of formal economic exchange. It is axiomatic in the Vietnamese tourism industry that these "impromptu" stops along a tourist visit are considered "tricking" (*lừa đất ai*) tourists, but in fact it may be that tourists welcome these serendipitous experiences, as Judd and Fainstein explain: "Travel seems to remove the constraints that normally prompt people to restrict their consumption" (1999: 16).

On one overnight visit to Cần Thơ from Ho Chi Minh City, a fishing and port city on the Mekong River, I experienced firsthand how monetary forms of (re)payment to third-party vendors and tour guides were given meaning through the mutual desire for rapprochement between American and Vietnamese people. The group participating in the tour that weekend was a hodge-podge group of American tourists ranging from businesspeople interested in exploring the economic climate in Vietnam to couples on vacation. Each participant or smaller group had booked independently with a high-end travel company and were organized according to their nationality. I tagged along because I was friendly with the president of the company and she had promised me a free trip in exchange for my feedback on the tour guide, who was one of their newer recruits.

Roughly two hours into the journey, the tour guide, named Hiệp, announced that we would be stopping at a rest area to use the bathroom and because he needed to find a venue with a strong cellphone signal so he could call ahead to the Cần Thơ hotel to make sure they were ready for us. We stopped at a large marketplace with a number of individual vendors, two restaurants, and a gas station. On leaving the bus, the group was swarmed with young children pushing trinkets on us. The adults braced themselves behind their kiosks and began barking out "You, you!" in order to get everyone's/anyone's attention.

A few people scurried off to the bathroom while others fanned out to check out the available commodities. Hiệp spoke quickly on the phone and hung up within a minute. "The hotel is ready for us in one hour, but now you can have a snack and enjoy some shopping at your leisure!", he said. A few purchased conical hats, while others loaded up on lacquerware and T-shirts. Approaching the central market area, a young man around thirty years old came walking up to the group. He had no arms, only small, handless nubs that were squeezing together a package of photographs and postcards in the middle of his chest. Some of the tourists saw the man, and they began moving closer together, forming a tight semicircle. Hiệp excitedly walked over to the group, which was by now paying attention to the salespeople and the disabled man. "Hello!" exclaimed the disabled man. "My name is John, and I live here in this village. Do you want to hear about my village and my family?" he added. Hiệp chimed in and said, "Everyone, this is a very good friend of mine. He has a very interesting story to tell." In perfect English, John began to describe in candid detail how it came to be that his arms are deformed. He began by saying through his smile, "I think you can tell that I do not have arms and hands like you do." The region in which he grew up, close to Cần Thơ, had been victimized by the long-term spraying of Agent Orange, the defoliant used by the Americans to clear canopy, expose villages, and kill valuable crops during the Vietnam War. His mother had not known of the effects of the herbicide on her reproductive abilities, and he was born with a severe birth defect that caused his arms to look this way. "Today," he continued, "we know about the problems caused by the chemical on our bodies, but it is too late for me." By this time other tour group members strayed over. "My arms cannot do what your arms can do," he announced, "but I still must work and provide for my family. My family owns a few kiosks here at this marketplace." John pointed to a cluster of stalls next to one of the restaurants, and the vendors waved enthusiastically back. The crowd glanced over to the stalls and waved. At this moment, John summoned Hiệp over to him and they exchanged a brief, whispering comment between them. Hiệp then took the stage from John and said:

> Please enjoy this time to meet John and his family, and if you are hungry you are welcome to enjoy a bite to eat at the restaurant. If you wish to ask John and his family about their life today or during the American war, they will answer your questions and share some stories from their past with you.

The crowd began moving in a pack over to the cluster of stalls identified as John's, and I overheard the other vendors, who had previously been negotiating with the American tour group, utter frustrated profanities over their lost business. Our group ended up staying at that particular marketplace for over an hour, eating and drinking with John and his family, purchasing goods from their stalls, and having various photographs taken with John and his family.

In his book on war ghosts haunting the everyday lives of Vietnamese villagers, Kwon explores the concept of "*giải ngục*" (translated literally as "liberating the prison"), which is the set of practices performed by Vietnamese families who seek to stabilize the disruptive spirits of their ancestors who have died violently and tragically, most often in war (Kwon 2008: 152). Traditional practices of ancestor worship extend beyond the household to include regular payments to other, more venerated and stable village spirits, who many believe have a say in the condition and temperament of their relatives' haunted ghosts (and, by extension, on the fortunes of the living). Money is also paid to soothsayers and village elders who, after being remitted, can intervene in the afterworld to calm and appease disruptive ghosts in ways commoners cannot. Vietnamese people – as offspring and relatives of those who perished under unnatural circumstances – are *accountable* to these spirits in financial terms that transcend the spiritual and material worlds. The dead are embedded in the living's lives in such a way that the living, by virtue of the dead's violence acting in chaotic and destructive ways on their everyday lives, are not permitted to forget or disavow the tragic demise and haunting of themselves or their relatives.

Although the spiritual and material consequences of violent death on everyday Vietnamese livelihoods may not on the surface compare with the mundane practices of American tourists being drawn to stories of lingering disabilities that play on emotions of culpability, I would like to suggest that there are both spiritual and material dimensions to American tourists' responses to the war, and that these practices relate to the desire for American tourists to liberate themselves and their countrymen from their responsibility and guilt toward the Vietnam tragedy. As I rejoined the tour group there was little in the way of negotiation between the vendors and tourists over the cost of wares. The impetus to give back – the dominant attribute of voluntourism and philanthrotourism – had taken on a very personal and intimate tone during the encounter between this group and their merchants that day. Later, on the bus to Cần Thơ, the group was energized by their experiences with John's family and largely felt that they had finally been able to validate their vacation to Vietnam by atoning for the sins of their forefathers through their purchases. The group mentioned their satisfaction, which included a hint of relief at being able to help and give back to the Vietnamese, and they were especially pleased that they had been able to financially provide for a family victimized by the American war effort. This tour group, like the university group, tacitly and explicitly expressed remorse over the destruction the war caused to Vietnam. Most prominently, the conversation among the tourists centered on John's and his family's optimism and sunny disposition toward them, the former enemy. Many wondered aloud if Americans would be as sympathetic to Vietnamese tourists on visits to the United States. No matter that this group of tourists may not have openly acknowledged that their spending that day was connected to their desire to compensate Vietnamese for the war; it was clear that they all shared in delight and incredulity at the peacefulness of the Vietnamese spirit, as well as the low prices they offered to their new American friends.

After seeing Hiệp give John a wad of cash before he boarded the bus with the group, I sat next to him for the rest of our journey and we discussed his relationship with the market's vendors. Hiệp was an old high school friend of John's, and since they had grown up together and were friends for many years, Hiệp threw business John's way in exchange for John and his family looking after Hiệp's family, who remained close by in a village, away from Hiệp in Ho Chi Minh City.

What I hope to have shown through this event is that travels to Vietnam provide an opportunity for American tourists to address, in monetary terms, the violence incurred by Vietnamese at the hands of their fellow Americans. From the Vietnamese side of things, this section has evaluated how monetary compensation is generated through alternative, processual and reciprocal imaginations of the war that are not solely based on the divisions between misunderstood and regretful Americans and a resilient and distant Vietnamese. American–Vietnamese War tourist sites and experiences, I argue, are locus points for Americans and Vietnamese to assuage and transform their feelings of guilt, sadness, and, for some, animosity toward the war. My findings in the south Vietnam tourist landscape establish a tourism sector based on atonement, shared practices (such as *giải ngực*), and the mutual desire for connection. More broadly, they also suggest that the Global South is not just the passive recipient of Westerners' tourist payments, but can actively, confidently, and cannily manage local narratives to maximize profit in a competitive market-place – a marketplace whose complex contours many Westerners do not under-stand. Most leisure theory problematizes the impact of tourism on unnamed and vaguely defined Third World communities and livelihoods, which in turn asserts Western hegemony and the corresponding neediness of the Global South concerning Western payments (Hughes 2008; Gibson, C. 2009;

Winter *et al.* 2009). My research shows that the Vietnamese tour guide is the savvy marketer and the American tourist is a susceptible yet willing participant in leisure transactions that are marked by their capacity for reconciliation as well as profit. In sum, then, and following from this volume's goals, these tourism experiences unsettle notions of the predictability of leisure encounters and complicate understandings of the practices and spaces of tourism, which themselves are often built on the backs of economic inequalities between the Global North and South (Mowforth and Munt 2009).

Despite the efforts on the part of both Vietnamese tour guides and American tourists to forge a new path in their post-war relationship, the content and campaign of the official war sites in south Vietnam assure that resolution is never fully attainable. The next section addresses the official position of the Vietnamese government toward the American war in prominent war sites, which illustrates that the divisions between Americans and Vietnamese remain raw and fresh to even the most casual tourist observer and tourism producer.

Reconciliation or division? The Vietnamese–American war from the party's perspective

Not surprisingly, the Vietnamese tourist landscape's most popular sites for foreign tourists are those dedicated to the American war. These sites include the "Hanoi Hilton," the prison where US Arizona senator John McCain spent five and a half years as a prisoner of war; the Cu Chi Tunnels; and the War Remnants Museum in Ho Chi Minh City, which houses graphic images and exhibits of American ruthlessness "in country." The point conveyed in these sites is twofold: the brutality of the Americans during the invasion of Vietnam, and the underestimation of the strength and cohesiveness of the Vietnamese in the face of extraordinary loss and destruction.

At the War Remnants Museum there are canisters filled with the deformed fetuses of Vietnamese stillborn to women affected by Agent Orange, photographs of American soldiers smiling widely as they hold the decapitated heads of Vietnamese, images of Vietnamese being thrown out of airborne helicopters in order to petrify insurgents on the ground and persuade Vietnamese prisoners to talk, and photographs of graphic physical and emotional abuse mounted alongside soldiers setting fire to villages, livestock, crops, and Vietnamese citizens (see also Chapter 2 in this volume). There is a reproduction of a Tiger Cage, a makeshift cell often used by Americans to hold Vietnamese combatants. At the Cu Chi Tunnels, as in the War Remnants Museum, there are American tanks, helicopters, and other arms captured during the war on display (Figures 11.2 and 11.3). At the "Hanoi Hilton" (Figure 11.4), in contrast, there are photographs of McCain in good health after being "rescued" by ordinary Vietnamese when his plane was shot down in Hanoi in 1967.

The overarching sense one has when visiting these tourist spots is that the United States, despite the depraved, brutal, and enduring manner in which they

Figure 11.2 The entrance way to the War Remnants Museum, Ho Chi Minh City. Note the captured US Air Force plane on display at right (photo: Jamie Gillen).

Figure 11.3 Captured American military tank, Cu Chi Tunnels. Note that the tour guide is dressed as a Viet Cong guerrilla fighter from the Vietnamese–American War (photo: Jamie Gillen).

Figure 11.4 Outside Hoa Lo Prison, the "Hanoi Hilton" (photo: Jamie Gillen).

carried out the war against Vietnam, was unsuccessful in its mission. This position is intentional and serves two primary goals. The first is that the rhetoric espoused by the Vietnamese government through the American war sites is part of a broader program aimed at promoting "rich people, a strong nation, and an equitable and civilized society" domestically and internationally. Much of Vietnamese propaganda is laced with messages such as this one, which proclaims Vietnam's socialist ideals and support for the Communist Party of Vietnam. Showing the United States as the aggressor facilitates its opposite, the presentation of harmonious Vietnam society.

The second goal, and one that corresponds to the first, is to upset common Western notions of imperialism's reach and successes in the non-Western world. The Vietnamese revolutionary spirit is a commonplace assertion in each of these sites, and it is used as a tool to foment nationalism and, by extension, discredit Western and foreign forms of hegemony. The stalwartness of the Vietnamese people is contrasted with brutal and unsuccessful attempts to expand into Vietnam, most often articulated through France and the United States, but also on occasion through China. In this part of the message the actions of the US, and more generally "outside" countries and peoples in Vietnam, are emphasized over the Vietnamese response. Foreign leaders are tyrants or dictators, foreign countries are invaders, and foreign military are imperialists.

For guides, American protests and frustrations at these sites present a host of problems in their work harmonizing the American–Vietnamese contemporary relationship. It is not uncommon for payments or tips to be withheld after a visit to the War Remnants Museum or the Cu Chi Tunnels. Some visitors refuse to participate in further trips outside of their immediate hotel area in protest, while others openly wonder why, the truthfulness of official party claims notwithstanding, a country dependent on foreign investment would submit American tourists to these kinds of images and discourse. The more mundane and regular frustrations resulting from the perception of distortion, irregularities, and propaganda are managed by a number of equally mundane responses from Vietnamese tour guides that do little to reconcile, and indeed can exacerbate, the divisions posed by the narrative of the official war site.

When evaluating dark tourism or thanatourism more generally, the party's discourses at official war tourism sites challenge assumptions about formerly war-torn countries favoring a narrative of a bland and palatable contemporary "peace" easily understood and digested by tourists at their war sites (regarding Japan, see Yoneyama 1999; regarding Germany, see Till 2005).

A primary strategy invoked by tour guides to respond to Americans who harbor resentment toward Vietnam is to ignore tourist complaints or questions completely, preferring to save the "face" of both themselves and their country (Jamieson 1995). Other times tour guides, using comments popular in Western imaginations of war, state that "the winners get to tell the story" or "to the winner goes the spoils" in shaping the history of the Vietnamese–American War. Some, in an attempt to ease tourists, prefer to restate the one-sidedness of the party's stance and laud the Americans for their support of the South Vietnamese quest for freedom. Just as there is no common sentiment among American tourists about the truthfulness of the Vietnamese war experience, there is no regularity or common response by tour guides to the narratives that accompany foreign tourists in Vietnam. But, as I suggest in this section, the sustained cadence of anti-American/anti-Western sentiment invoked in Vietnam's American war sites is echoed by a related message of the strength and sacrifice of the Vietnamese. Despite the intentions of Vietnamese tour guides and American tourists to highlight and build on contemporary understandings of regret and nostalgia for the Vietnamese–American conflict, popular war sites in the Vietnamese landscape prevent reconciliation from being a realistic goal for tourists and tour guides. In effect, attempts to resolve the past through tourism encounters work in tandem with efforts by the Communist Party to assert difference and assign success and failure in unequivocal terms. These discourses tend to unfold in parallel to one another, fluctuating in importance and impact in the daily American tourist itinerary, yet framing the experiences of both tourists and tour guides. It is when they intersect, in popular sites such as the War Remnants Museum, Hanoi Hilton, or the Cu Chi Tunnels, that both tourist and tour guide are paralyzed by the divisions that remain between them, despite their substantial collective intention to find harmony in the ruins of Vietnam. In other words, it is not that the everyday interactions between tour groups and their guides supersede official party rhetoric in importance, it is that attempts at resolution are always shadowed by sustained reminders of hostility and division. Looking at things differently, the work of finding common ground among American tourists and Vietnamese tour guides continues in spite of the official party campaign haunting and disrupting their relationship.

Conclusions

In this chapter I have shown that Vietnam's adversarial role in the everyday imagination of the US does not account for the geniality, compromise, and harmonization that occur as a result of the encounters between Vietnamese tour guides and American tourists in south Vietnam. Instead of showing how Vietnam War movies continue to scar the American psyche and frame the collective imagination of the country, I have preferred to highlight how popular representations about the Vietnam War are used as building blocks in alternative conceptions of the war and its aftermath. Vietnamese tour guides use war sites to abridge the official party discourse and emphasize the qualities in Vietnam that have resulted from American interests in the country. Tour guides and tourists also share and learn from each other in financial terms.

Vietnamese and American values on the tourist path include the desire to remit in symbolic and monetary ways to the dead for their pain, to understand their own and their former opponent's relationship to the war more clearly, and to forge a new level of reciprocal understanding that uses the benefits that come from tourism and leisure as a new baseline for relationship building. Although these values are often realized, they are cautioned by official documentation of the American war, which centers on the fallibility and destruction of the American cause in Vietnam, and the persistence and recoil of the Vietnamese population. Despite efforts by tourists and tour guides in Vietnam to ignore or bypass the party's position, the official line continues to draw attention to contemporary leisure experiences for Americans and the Vietnamese tour guides that serve them. Thus, the official tourism narratives authored by the party stand in contrast to the contemporary "peacefulness" that surrounds dark tourism sites such as Hiroshima and Berlin, yet are countered by everyday interactions between American tourists and Vietnamese tour guides.

This tension, between alternative meanings of moving past and memorializing the Vietnamese–American War, sits at the heart of the chapter. To resolve the issue by giving credence to one of the positions is, I think, to cheapen the richness of the American tourism experience in Vietnam, while instead this experience also serves to illuminate broader questions of diplomatic accountability and post-war relations. In conventional terms, tourism is seen as a departure from the norm, a means to escape from the mundane and everyday in order to experience the profound and the surreal, and often as a way to appreciate and understand the mundane and everyday in new and exciting ways

(Kingsbury 2005; Malam 2008; Gibson, C. 2010; Chapters 2 and 6 in this volume). But what are the consequences for Western tourism and leisure when the profound and surreal in the non-Western world are destructive, painful, violent, and linger, and are of the West's own making? Indeed, although Vietnam and the United States have gained a "normal," if not strong diplomatic relationship since the bilateral relations were resumed in 1995, the typical Vietnamese–American negotiating platform is often upset by the Vietnamese desire for Agent Orange reparations from the United States, a position the US has until now (August 2011) refused to agree to. Perhaps the post-war imagery of Agent Orange disability in Vietnam's museums is a means to highlight the injustices of the past and of the present to a group of tourists and tour guides who are intent on transforming the complexion of the US–Vietnam relationship. It may be a way to caution domestic and overseas visitors against overstating the significance of contemporary post-war relationships between former foes. It is most certainly a means for Vietnam to assert its freedom, character, and fight to a tourist audience that continues to harbor stereotypes against and feel vulnerable toward Vietnam.

In a *New York Times* article from 2009 about the long American occupation of Afghanistan, US Army Lt Colonel Jonathan Neumann insisted, "We had to fight our way to the people. It took some time for [Afghan] folks to realize that we weren't leaving" (Schmitt 2009: A18). Colonel Neumann may not have known in 2009 how right he was. If compared with Vietnam – a government and a people who keep the United States invasion and occupation alive and well, and at the core of its tourism representations and encounters – then it is assured that the United States will never truly exit Iraq and Afghanistan. Tourism in formerly war-plagued areas can thus be used as a lens into assessing the historical arbitrariness of the timelines that Western powers create and espouse for invasion and occupation of, and withdrawal from, non-Western countries, as well as a way to show how countries such as Vietnam, Afghanistan, and Iraq can transform dark periods of war into invaluable and widely consumed chapters in the promotion of nationhood.

References

Abbott, W.F. and Monsen, R.J. (1979) "On the measurement of corporate social responsibility: self-reported disclosures as a method of measuring corporate social involvement." *Academy of Management Journal*, 22: 501–515.

Abramson, D. (2009) "The dialectics of urban planning in China." In F.L. Wu (ed.) *China's Emerging Cities: The Making of New Urbanism*. London and New York: Routledge.

Adam, B. (1995) *Timewatch: The Social Analysis of Time*. Cambridge: Polity.

Adam, B. (1998) *Timescapes of Modernity*. London: Routledge.

ADB (2007a) "Building a dynamic future: the Indonesia-Malaysia-Thailand (IMT-GT) roadmap to development, 2007–2011." Asian Development Bank. Available online at: www.adb.org/Documents/Books/IMT-Roadmap-Development/roadmap-development.pdf (accessed 19 March 2009).

ADB (2007b) "The IMT-GT Roadmap 2007–2011 Action plan: status and updates." 14 September. Asian Development Bank. Available online at: www.adb.org/Documents/IMT-GT/action-plan.pdf (accessed 28 October 2008).

Adkins, L. (2001) "Cultural feminization: 'money, sex and power for women'." *Signs: Journal of Women in Culture and Society*. 26(3): 669–695.

Adkins, L. (2003) "Reflexivity: freedom or habit of gender?" *Theory, Culture and Society*, 22(1): 21–42.

Adkins, L. and Jokinen, E. (2008) "Introduction: gender, living and labour in the fourth shift." *NORA-Nordic Journal of Feminist and Gender Research*, 16(3): 138–149.

Agamben, G. (1993) *The Coming Community*. Trans. M. Hardt. Minneapolis, MN: University of Minnesota Press.

Agamben, G. (1998) *Homo Sacer*. Stanford, CA: Stanford University Press.

Agamben, G. (2004) *The Open: Man and Animal*. Trans. K. Attell. Stanford, CA: Stanford University Press.

Aitchison, C., Macleod, N.E. and Shaw, S.J. (2000) *Leisure and Tourism Landscapes: Social and Cultural Geographies*. London: Routledge.

Allcock, A. (2004) *National Tourism Development Strategy for Lao PDR 2005 to 2015*. Lao National Tourism Administration (LNTA), Lao PDR.

Alneng, V. (2002a) "What the fuck is a Vietnam? Touristic phantasms and the popcolonialization of (the) Vietnam (war)." *Critique of Anthropology*, 22: 461–489.

Alneng, V. (2002b) "The modern does not cater for natives: travel ethnography and the conventions of form." *Tourist Studies*, 2: 119–142.

Ansorge, R. (2006) "More Americans seeking surgery abroad." *Healthwatch,* CBS News, 18 October. Available online at: www.cbsnews.com/stories/2006/10/18/health/webmd/main2104425.shtml (accessed 2 December 2006).

Arlt, W. G. (2006) *China's Outbound Tourism.* London and New York: Routledge.

Association of Private Hospitals of Malaysia (2008) "Medical tourism statistics for 2002–2007." Email (9 April).

Asuke Tourism Association (2005) *History of Creating Local Culture: Asuke's Tourism for 50 Years.* Asuke: Asuke Tourism Association.

Ateljevic, I., Pritchard, A. and Morgan, N. (eds) (2007) *The Critical Turn in Tourism Studies: Innovative Research Methodologies.* Advances in Tourism Research Series. Amsterdam: Elsevier Science.

Augé, M. (1995) *Non-Places: Introduction to an Anthropology of Supermodernity.* London and New York: Verso.

Bærenholdt, J.O., Haldrup, M., Larsen, J. and Urry, J. (2004) *Performing Tourist Places.* Aldershot: Ashgate.

Baird, I.G. and Shoemaker, B. (2007) "Unsettling experiences: internal resettlement and international aid agencies in Laos." *Development and Changes,* 38(5): 856–888.

Bakken, B. (2000) *The Exemplary Society: Human Improvement, Social Control, and the Dangers of Modernity in China.* Oxford: Oxford University Press.

Balooni, K. (1997) "Green consumerism – the new challenge." *Indian Management,* October.

Bangkok Post (2009) "Growth Triangle tourism cooperation." *The Bangkok Post,* 28 February. Available online at: www.bangkokpost.com/breakingnews/136968/growth-triangle-tourism-energy-cooperation (accessed 19 March 2009).

Baran, M. (2008) *Poorism: The Economics of Exploitation.* Secaucus, NJ: Travel Weekly.

Baranowski, S. (2004) *Strength through Joy: Consumerism and Mass Tourism in the Third Reich.* Cambridge: Cambridge University Press.

Barnett, C. (2001) "Culture, geography, and the arts of government." *Environment and Planning D: Society and Space,* 19: 7–24.

Barnett, C. (2005a) "The consolations of 'neoliberalism'." *Geoforum,* 36: 7–12.

Barnett, C. (2005b) "Ways of relating: hospitality and the acknowledgement of otherness." *Progress in Human Geography,* 29(1): 5–21.

Barrientos, S. and Dolan, C. (2006) *Ethical Sourcing in the Global Food System: Challenges and Opportunities to Fair Trade and the Environment.* London: Earthscan.

Bassin, M. (1987) "Race contra space: the conflict between German Geopolitik and National Socialism." *Political Geography Quarterly,* 6: 115–134.

Bataille, G. (1985) *Visions of Excess: Selected Writings 1927–1939.* Trans. A. Stoekl, with C. Lovitt and D. Leslie (eds). Minneapolis, MN: University of Minnesota Press.

Bataille, G. (2001) *Eroticism.* London: Penguin.

Baum, T. (2007) "Human resources in tourism: still waiting for change." *Progress in Tourism Management,* 28(6): 1383–1399.

Bauman, Z. (1991) *Modernity and Ambivalence.* Ithaca: Cornell University Press.

Bauman, Z. (1998) *Globalization.* Cambridge: Polity.

Bebbington, A. (2003) "Global networks and local developments: agendas for development geography." *Tijdschrift voor Economische en Sociale Geografie,* 94: 297–309.

Becchetti, L. and Huybrechts, B. (2008) "The dynamics of Fair Trade as a mixed-form market." *Journal of Business Ethics*, 81: 733–750.

Belhassen, Y., Caton, K. and Stewart, W.P. (2008) "The search for authenticity in the pilgrim experience." *Annals of Tourism Research*, 35(3): 668–689.

Bell, D. (2007) "Moments of hospitality." In J. Germann Molz and S. Gibson (eds) *Mobilizing Hospitality: The Ethics of Social Relations in a Mobile World*. Aldershot: Ashgate.

Bendell, J. and Lake, R. (2000) "New frontiers: emerging NGO activities to strengthen transparency and accountability in business." In J. Bendell (ed.) *Terms for Endearment*. Sheffield: Greenleaf Publishing.

Benhabib, S. (2004) *The Rights of Others: Aliens, Residents and Citizens*. Cambridge: Cambridge University Press.

Bennett, O., Roe, D. and Ashley, C. (1999) *Sustainable Tourism and Poverty Elimination Study*. London: Deloitte & Touche.

Bennett, T. (1998) *Culture: A Reformer's Science*. London: Sage.

Bergmark, R., Barr, D. and Garcia, R. (2008) "Mexican immigrants in the US living far from the border may return to Mexico for health services." *Journal of Immigrant and Minority Health*, 12(4): 610–614.

Berking, H. (1999) *Sociology of Giving*. New Delhi: Sage.

Berman, M. (1982) *All that Is Solid Melts into Air: The Experience of Modernity*. New York: Simon & Schuster.

Bettio. F. and J. Plantenga (2004) "Comparing care regimes in Europe." *Feminist Economics*, 10(1): 85–113.

Bhabha, H.K. (2004) *The Location of Culture*. London: Routledge.

Bianchi, R. (2000) "Migrant tourist-workers: exploring the 'contact zones' of post-industrial tourism." *Current Issues in Tourism*, 3(2): 107–137.

Bibby, M. (2000) *The Vietnam War and Postmodernity*. Amherst, MA: University of Massachusetts Press.

Biles, A., Lloyd, K. and Logan, W. (1999) "A tiger on a bicycle: the growth and character of international tourism in Vietnam." *Pacific Tourism Review*, 3: 11–24.

Binkley, S. (2009) "The work of neoliberal governmentality: temporality and ethical substance in the tale of two dads." *Foucault Studies*, 6: 60–78.

Birtchnell, T. and Büscher, M. (2011) "Stranded: an eruption of disruption." *Mobilities*, 6(1): 1–9.

Blowfield, M. (2005) "Corporate social responsibility: reinventing the meaning of development?" *International Affairs*, 81: 515–524.

Blowfield, M. and Frynas, J.G. (2005) "Setting new agendas: critical perspectives on Corporate Social Responsibility in the developing world." *International Affairs*, 81: 499–513.

Blyth, E. and Farrand, A. (2005) "Reproductive tourism – a price worth paying for reproductive autonomy?" *Critical Social Policy*, 25(1): 91–114.

Bonini, S.M.J., Mendonca, J.T. and Oppenheim, J.M. (2006) "When social issues become strategic." *The McKinsey Quarterly*, 2: 20–31.

Bookman, M.Z. and Bookman, K.R. (2007) *Medical Tourism in Developing Countries*. New York: Palgrave Macmillan.

Boupha, K. (2007) "Village consolidation and village development cluster in relation to permanent occupations and resident for local people." Paper presented at Village Consolidation and Village Development Cluster Conference, Vientiane, Lao PDR, 9–10 May 2007.

Bourdieu, P. (1984) *Distinction: A Social Critique of the Judgement of Taste*. London: Routledge.

Bourdieu, P. (1990) *The Logic of Practice*. Palo Alto, CA: Stanford University Press.

Bowden, J. (2005) "Pro-poor tourism and the Chinese experience." *Asia Pacific Journal of Tourism Research*, 10(4): 379–398.

Boyatzis, R.E. (1998) *Transforming Qualitative information: Thematic Analysis and Code Development*. Thousand Oaks, CA: Sage.

Braun, V. and Clarke, V. (2006) "Using thematic analysis in psychology." *Qualitative Research in Psychology*, 3(2): 77–101.

Bremer, J.A. (2008) "How global is the Global Compact?" *Business Ethics: A European Review*, 17: 227–244.

Briassoulis, H. (2002) "Sustainable tourism and the question of the commons." *Annals of Tourism Research*, 29: 1065–1085.

Briedenhann, J. and Wickens, E. (2003) "Tourism routes as a tool for the economic development of rural area: vibrant hope or impossible dream?" *Tourism Management*, 25: 71–79.

Briggs, J. and Sharp, J. (2004) "Indigeneous knowledges and development: a post-colonial caution." *Third World Quarterly*, 25: 661–676.

Britton, S. (1982) "The political economy of tourism in the Third World." *Annals of Tourism Research*, 9: 331–358.

Brohman, J. (1995) "Economism and critical silences in development studies: a theoretical critique of neoliberalism." *Third World Quarterly*, 16(2): 297–318.

Brohman, J. (1996) "New directions in tourism for Third World development." *Annals of Tourism Research*, 23(1): 48–70.

Brooker, E. and Go, F.M. (2006) "Health care tourism: a classic example of disruptive innovation." Paper presented at Travel and Tourism Research Association Canada Chapter Conference, Montebello, Quebec, Canada, 15–17 October. Available online at: www.linkbc.ca/torc/downs1/BrookerGoHealthCareTourism.pdf?PHPSESSID=1af5d3726db65f254c03bd209277786a (accessed 16 February 2009).

Buie, S. (1996) "Market as mandala: the erotic space of commerce." *Organisation*, 3: 225–232.

Bumrungrad (2010) "Overview." Available online at: www.bumrungrad.com/overseas-medical-care/about-us/overview.aspx (accessed 21 July 2010).

Burke, L. and Logsdon, J.M. (1996) "How corporate social responsibility pays off." *Long Range Planning*, 29: 495–502.

Butcher, J. (2003) *The Moralisation of Tourism: Sun, Sand . . . and Saving the World?* London and New York: Routledge.

Butler, J. (1999) *Gender Trouble: Feminism and the Subversion of Identity*. New York and London: Routledge.

Butler, J. (2009) *Frames of War: When Is Life Grievable?* London and New York: Verso.

Butler, J. (2010) "On the relationship between precariety and state power." *Transform!*, 6. Available online at: www.transform-network.net/en/home/journal-transform europe/english/issue-062010/display-anzeige-not-in-menu/article//On-the-Relationship-Between-Precariety-and-State-Power.html (accessed 26 April 2011).

Butler, R.W. (1990) "Alternative tourism: pious hope or Trojan horse?" *Journal of Travel Research*, 3: 40–45.

Butler, R.W. (1993) "Tourism: an evolutionary perspective." In J.G. Nelson, Butler, R.W. and Wall, G. (eds) *Tourism and Sustainable Development: Piloting, Planning,*

Managing. Waterloo, Ontario: Department of Geography Publication Series, No. 37, University of Waterloo.

Buzzanco, R. (1999) *Vietnam and the Transformation of American Life*. London: Blackwell.

Carrera, P.M. and Bridges, J.F.P. (2006) "Globalization and healthcare: understanding health and medical tourism." *Expert Review of Pharmacoeconomics Outcomes Research*, 6(4): 447–454.

Carroll, A.B. (1999) "Corporate social responsibility: evolution of a definitional construct." *Business and Society*, 38: 268–295.

Carroll, C. (2009) "'My mother's best friend's sister-in-law is coming with us': exploring domestic and international travel with a group of Lao tourists." In T. Winter, P. Teo and T. Chang (eds) *Asia on Tour: Exploring the Rise of Asian Tourism*. London: Routledge.

Cartier, C. (2005) "Introduction: touristed landscapes/seductions of place." In C. Cartier and A.A. Lew (eds) *Seductions of Place: Geographical Perspectives on Globalization and Touristed Landscapes*. London: Routledge.

Cartier, C. and Lew, A.A. (eds) (2005) *Seductions of Place: Geographical Perspectives on Globalization and Touristed Landscapes*. London: Routledge.

Cavalletti, A. (2005) *La Citta' Biopolitica*, Milan: Mondadori.

Chakrabarty, D. (2000) *Provincializing Europe*. Princeton, NJ: Princeton University Press.

Chamber, R. (1995) "Poverty and livelihoods: whose reality counts? ," *Environment and Urbanization*, 7(1): 173–204.

Chatterton, P. and Maxey, L. (2009) "Introduction: whatever happened to ethics and responsibility in geography?" *ACME: An International E-Journal for Critical Geographies*, 8: 429–439.

Chazée, L. (1999) *The People of Laos: Rural and Ethnic Diversities*. Bangkok: White Lotus Press.

Chee H.L. (2007) "Medical tourism in Malaysia: international movement of healthcare consumers and the commodification of healthcare." *Asia Research Institute Working Paper Series*, 83, January.

Chio, J. (2009) "The internal expansion of China: tourism and the production of distance." In T. Winter, P. Teo and T. Chang (eds) *Asia on Tour: Exploring the Rise of Asian Tourism*. London: Routledge.

Chio, J. (2010) "China's campaign for civilized tourism: what to do when tourists behave badly." *Anthropology News*, 51(8):14–15 (November).

Chok, S., Macbeth, J. and Warren, C. (2007) "Tourism as a tool for poverty alleviation: a critical analysis of 'pro-poor tourism' and implications for sustainability." *Current Issues in Tourism*, 10(2–3): 144–164.

Chomsky, N. and Foucault, M. (1994) *De la Nature Humaine, Justice contre Pouvoir*. Paris: Gallimard.

Clancy, M.J. (1999) "Tourism and development evidence from Mexico." *Annals of Tourism Research*, 26(1): 1–20.

Clarke, A. (2009) "Introduction: gender and reproductive technologies in East Asia." *East Asian Science, Technology and Society: An International Journal*, 2(3): 303–326.

Cleverdon, R. and Kalisch, A. (2000) "Fair trade in tourism." *International Journal of Tourism Research*, 2: 171–187.

Clifford, J. (1997) *Routes: Travel and Translation in the Late Twentieth Century*. Cambridge, MA: Harvard University Press.

Cloke, P. and Perkins, P. (1998) " 'Cracking the canyon with the awesome foursome': representations of adventure tourism in New Zealand." in *Environment and Planning D: Society and Space*, 16: 185–218.

Cohen, E. (1987) "Alternative tourism: a critique." *Tourism Recreation Research*, 12: 13–18.

Cohen, P.T. (2009) "The post-opium scenario and rubber in northern Laos: alternative Western and Chinese models of development," *International Journal of Drug Polity*, 20(5): 424–430.

Conlon, D. (2010) "Fascinatin' rhythm(s): polyrhythmia and the syncopated echoes of the everyday." In T. Edensor (ed.) *Geographies of Rhythm: Nature, Place, Mobilities and Bodies*. Aldershot: Ashgate.

Connell, J. (2006) "Medical tourism: sea, sun, sand and surgery." *Tourism Management*, 27, 1093–1100.

Connell, J. (2011) *Medical Tourism*. Wallingford: CABI.

Connell, R. (2007) *Southern Theory*. Cambridge: Polity.

Cooper, M. (2008) *Life as Surplus: Biotechnology and Capitalism in the Neoliberal Era*. Seattle, WA: University of Washington Press.

Cortez, N. (2008) "Patients without borders: the emerging global market for patients and the evolution of modern health care." *Indiana Law Journal*, 83, SMU Dedman School of Law and Legal Studies Research Paper no. 00–24.

Cosgrove, D. (2003) "Landscape and the European sense of sight – eyeing nature." In K. Anderson, M. Domosh, S. Pile and N. Thrift (eds) *Handbook of Cultural Geography*. London: Sage.

Crang, M. (1997) "Picturing practices: research through the tourist gaze." *Progress in Human Geography*, 21: 359–373.

Crang, M. (1999) "Knowing, tourism and practices of vision." In D. Crouch (ed.) *Leisure/Tourism Geographies*. London: Routledge.

Crang, M. (2004) "Cultural geographies of tourism." In A.A. Lew, C.M. Hall and A.M. Williams (eds) *A Companion to Tourism*. Oxford: Blackwell.

Crang, M. (2005) "Travel and tourism." In D. Atkinson, P. Jackson, D. Sibley and N. Washbourne (eds) *Cultural Geography: A Critical Dictionary of Key Concepts*. London: IB Tauris & Co.

Crang, M. (2006) "Circulation and emplacement: the hollowed out performance of tourism." In C. Minca and T. Oakes (eds) *Travels in Paradox: Remapping Tourism*. Boulder, CO: Rowman & Littlefield.

Crang, P. (1997) "Performing the tourist product." In C. Rojek and J. Urry (eds) *Touring Cultures: Transformations of Travel and Theory*. London: Routledge.

Cranston, E.A. (1993) *A Waka Anthology: Volume 1, The Gem-Glistening Cup*. Translated, with a commentary and notes by Edwin A. Cranston. Stanford, CA: Stanford University Press.

Crawshaw, C. and Urry, J. (1997) "Tourism and the photographic eye." In C. Rojek and J. Urry (eds) *Touring Cultures: Transformations of Travel and Theory*. London: Routledge, 176–195.

Cresswell, T. (2001) "The production of mobilities." *New Formations*, 43: 11–25.

Cresswell, T. (2006) *On the Move: Mobility in the Modern Western World*. London: Routledge.

Cresswell, T. (2011) "The vagrant/vagabond: the curious career of a mobile subject." In T. Cresswell and P. Merriman (eds) *Geographies of Mobilities: Practices, Spaces, Subjects*. London: Ashgate.

Crick, M. (1989) "Representations of international tourism in the social science: sun, sex, sights, savings, and servility." *Annual Review of Anthropology*, 18: 307–344.

Crouch, D. (2003) "Spacing, performing and becoming: tangles in the mundane." In *Environment and Planning A*, 35: 1945–1960.

Crouch, D. (2004) "Tourist practices and performances." In A.A. Lew, C.M. Hall and A.M. Williams (eds) *A Companion to Tourism*. Oxford: Blackwell.

Crouch, D. (2005) "Flirting with space: tourism geographies as sensuous/expressive practice." In C. Cartier and A.A. Lew (eds) *Seductions of Place: Geographical Perspectives on Globalization and Touristed Landscapes*. London: Routledge.

Crouch, D. and Lubbren, N. (2003) "Introduction." In D. Crouch and N. Lubbren (eds) *Visual Culture and Tourism*. Oxford: Berg.

Crouch, D., Aronsson, L. and Wahlström, L. (2001) "Tourist encounters." *Tourist Studies*, 1: 253–270.

D-8 Secretariat (2008) "Malaysian Air Asia facilitates health tourism with low-cost carrier business." Developing Eight Countries, 19 August. Available online at: www. developing8.org/2008/08/20/malaysian-air-asia-facilitates-health-tourism-with-lowcost-carrier-business/ (accessed 19 March 2009).

Dahl, H.M. (2010) "An old map of state feminism and an insufficient recognition of care." *NORA – Nordic Journal of Feminist and Gender Research*, 18(3): 152–166.

Dahlman, C. (2008) "Diaspora." In J.S. Duncan, N.C. Johnson and R.H. Schein (eds) *A Companion to Cultural Geography*. London: Blackwell.

Daniels, I. M. (2001) *The Fame of Miyajima: Spirituality, Commodification and the Tourist Trade of Souvenirs in Japan*. PhD thesis. London: University of London.

Dann, G. (2003) "Noticing notices: tourism to order." *Annals of Tourism Research*, 30(2): 465–484.

Darling, J. (2010) "A city of sanctuary: the relational re-imagining of Sheffield's asylum politics." *Transactions of the Institute of British Geographers*, 35: 125–140.

Davis, G.F., Whitman, M.v.N. and Zald, M.N. (2006) "The responsibility paradox: multinational firms and global corporate social responsibility." Ross School of Business Working Paper Series, Working Paper No. 1031.

Davydova, O. (no date) "Venäjän lännestä suomen itään: sukupuolittunut maahan-muutto ja haurastuneet työmarkkinat." In S. Keskinen, J. Vuori and A. Hirsiaho (eds) *Monikulttuurisuuden sukupuoli: kansalaisuus ja erot hyvinvointiyhteiskunnassa*. Unpublished manuscript.

Davydova, O. and Pöllänen, P. (2010) "Gender on the Finnish–Russian border." In J. Virkkunen, P. Uimonen and O. Davydova (eds) *Ethnosexual Processes: Realities, Stereotypes and Narratives*, Helsinki: Kikimora Publications, Aleksanteri Series 6.

Degen, M. (2010) "Consuming urban rhythms: let's Ravalejar." In T. Edensor (ed.) *Geographies of Rhythm: Nature, Place, Mobilities and Bodies*. Aldershot: Ashgate.

de Kadt, E. (1979) *Tourism: Passport to Development*. Oxford: Oxford University Press.

Deloitte (2008) "Disruptive innovation in health services." Deloitte Center for Health Solutions, November. Available online at: www.deloitte.com/dtt/article/0,1002, sid%253D80772%2526cid%253D219071,00.html (accessed 16 February 2009).

Dentchev, N.A. (2004) "Corporate social performance as a business strategy." *Journal of Business Ethics*, 55: 397–412.

De Petra, F. (2010) *Comunità, Comunicazione, Commune: Da Georges Bataille a Jean-Luc Nancy*. Rome: Derive Aprrodi.

Derrida, J. (2000) *Of Hospitality: Anne Dufourmantelle Invites Jacques Derrida to Respond*. Trans. R. Bowlby. Stanford, CA: Stanford University Press.

Derrida, J. (2002) *Negotiations: Interventions and Interviews, 1971–2001*. Trans. E. Rottenberg. Stanford, CA: Stanford University Press.

DFID (2004) "Socially responsible business team strategy: April 2001–March 2004." London: Department for International Development.

Dicks, B. (2003) *Culture on Display: The Production of Contemporary Visitability*. Maidenhead: Open University Press.

Dieke, P.U.C. (2000) "The nature and scope of the political economy of tourism development in Africa." In P.U.C. Dieke (ed.) *The Political Economy of Tourism Development in Africa*. New York: Cognizant Communication.

Dikeç, M. (2002) "Pera peras poros: longings for spaces of hospitality." *Theory, Culture and Society*, 19(1–2): 227–247.

Dikeç, M., Clark, N. and Barnett, C. (2009) "Extending hospitality: giving space, taking time." *Paragraph*, 32(1): 1–14.

Diken, B. and Laustsen, C. B. (2004) "Sea, sun, sex and the discontents of pleasure." *Tourist Studies*, 4(2): 99–114.

Dittmar, L. and Michaud, G. (eds) (1990) *From Hanoi to Hollywood: The Vietnam War in American Film*. New Brunswick, NJ: Rutgers University Press.

Donald, R.R. (2001) "Masculinity and machismo in Hollywood's war films." In S.R. Whitehead and F.J. Barrett (eds) *The Masculinities Reader*. Oxford: Blackwell.

Drummond, L.B.W. and Thomas, M. (eds) (2003) *Consuming Urban Culture in Contemporary Vietnam*. London: RoutledgeCurzon.

Duara, P. (2000) "Local worlds: the poetics and politics of the native place in modern China." *South Atlantic Quarterly*, 99(1): 13–45.

Duncan, J.S. and Duncan, N.G. (2004) "Culture unbound." *Environment and Planning A*, 36: 391–403.

Dunlop, F. (2004) "California dreaming through Chinese eyes." BBC News (11 December). Available online at: http://news.bbc.co.uk/2/hi/programmes/from_our_own_correspondent/4085607.stm (accessed 26 April 2011).

Economic Planning Unit (EPU) (2010) "Tenth Malaysia Plan (2011–2015)." Putrajaya: Prime Minister's Department.

Edensor, T. (1998) *Tourists at the Taj: Performance and Meaning at a Symbolic Site*. London: Routledge.

Edensor, T. (2001) "Performing tourism, staging tourism: (re)producing tourist space and practice." *Tourist Studies*, 1: 59–82.

Edensor, T. (2006a) "Sensing tourism spaces." In C. Minca and T. Oakes (eds) *Travels in Paradox: Remapping Tourism*, Oxford: Rowman & Littlefield.

Edensor, T. (2006b) "Reconsidering national temporalities: institutional times, everyday routines, serial spaces and synchronicities." *European Journal of Social Theory*, 9(4): 525–545.

Edensor, T. (2007) "Mundane mobilities, performances and spaces of tourism." *Social and Cultural Geography*, 8: 199–215.

Edensor, T. (2010) "Introduction: thinking about rhythm and space." In T. Edensor (ed.) *Geographies of Rhythm: Nature, Place, Mobilities and Bodies*. Aldershot: Ashgate.

Edensor, T. and Holloway, J. (2008) "Rhythmanalysing the coach tour: the ring of Kerry, Ireland." *Transactions of the Institute of British Geographers*, 33: 483–501.

Edensor, T. and Kothari, U. (2004) "Sweetening colonialism: a Mauritian themed research." In D.M. Lasansky and B. McLaren (eds) *Architecture and Tourism: Perceptions, Performance and Place*, New York: Berg.

Ehrbeck, T., Guevara, C. and Mango, P.D. (2008) "Mapping the market for medical travel." *The McKinsey Quarterly*, May. Available online at: www.medretreat.com/templates/UserFiles/Documents/McKinsey%20Report%20Medical%20Travel.pdf (accessed 16 February 2009).

Ehrenreich, B. and Hochschild, A.R. (eds) (2003) *Global Woman: Nannies, Maids and Sex Workers in the New Economy*. London: Granta Books.

Ek, R. and Hultman, J. (2008) "Sticky landscapes and smooth experiences: the biopower of tourism mobilities in the Öresund region." *Mobilities*, 3(2): 223–242.

El Taguri, A. (2007) "Medical tourism and the Libyan National Health System." *Libyan Journal of Medicine*, 2(3):109–110.

Emmanuel, M. (2008a) "Farrali wellness resort a shot in the arm for Penang." *The Business Times*, 29 September. Available online at: www.btimes.com.my/Current_News/BTIMES/Monday/Nation/FRALI.xml/Article/index_html (accessed 19 March 2009).

Emmanuel, M. (2008b) "Firefly plans code-share talks with regional carriers." *The Business Times*, 5 July. Available online at: www.btimes.com.my/Current_News/BTIMES/Saturday/Nation/ffly-2.xml/Article/index_html: (accessed 19 March 2009).

Emmanuel, M. (2008c) "Penang casts net wider for foreign investment." *The Business Times*, 14 June. Available online at: www.btimes.com.my/Monday/OurPick/fmari 13–2.xml/Article (accessed 19 March 2009).

Emmanuel, M. (2008d) "Sriwijaya to make Penang aviation hub." *The Business Times*, 9 September. Available online at: www.btimes.com.my/Current_News/BTIMES/Tuesday/Nation/wijay.xml/Article/ (accessed 19 March 2009).

England, K. (2007) "Caregivers, the local-global, and the geographies of responsibility." In P. Moss and K.F. Al-Hindi (eds) *Feminisms in Geography: Rethinking Space, Place, and Knowledges*. New York: Rowman & Littlefield.

Enloe, C. (1989) *Bananas, Beaches and Bases: Making Feminist Sense of International Politics*. Berkeley, CA: University of California Press.

Epprecht, M., Minot, N., Dewina, R., Messerli, P. and Heinimann, A. (2008) *The Geography of Poverty and Inequality in the Lao PDR*, Swiss National Centre of Competence in Research North–South. Available online at: www.laoatlas.net/links/PDF/The%20Geography%20of%20Poverty%20and%20Inequality%20in%20the%20Lao%20PDR.pdf (accessed 10 March 2009).

Escobar, A. (1995) "Imagining a post-development era." In J. Crush (ed.) *Power of Development*. London: Routledge.

Escobar, A. (2001) "Culture sits in places: reflections on globalism and subaltern strategies of localization." *Political Geography*, 20: 139–174.

Escobar, A., Rochelau, D. and Kothari, S. (2002) "Environmental social movements and the politics of place." *Development*, 45: 28–36.

Eshoo, P. (2008) "Implementation of natural eco-tourism project in Xe Pian NPA. Champasak, Lao PDR." Paper reported for World Wildlife Fund (WWF), Lao PDR.

Esposito, R. (1998) *Communitas: Origine e Destino della Comunità*. Turin: Einaudi.

Esposito, R. (2002) *Immunitas: Protezione e Negazione della Vita*. Turin: Einaudi.

Esposito, R. (2004) *Bíos: Biopolitica e Filosofia*, Turin: Einaudi.

Esposito, R. (2008) *Bios: Biopolitics and Philosophy*. Trans. T. Campbell. Minneapolis, MN: University of Minnesota Press.

Esposito, R. (2009) *Communitas: The Origin and Destiny of Community*. Trans. T. Campbell. Stanford, CA: Stanford University Press.

European Commission (2004) "Corporate social responsibility: European multi-stakeholder forum on CSR." Luxembourg: Office for Official Publications of the European Communities.

Evrad, O. and Goudineau, Y. (2004) "Planned resettlement, unexpected migrations and cultural trauma in Laos." *Development and Changes*, 35(5): 937–962.

Ewen, E. and Ewen, S. (2006) *Typecasting: On the Arts and Sciences of Human Equality*. New York: Seven Stories.

Exotissimo Travel (2009–2010) "Responsible travel." Available online at: www.exotissimo.com/travel/responsible%20travel/ (accessed 22 September 2010).

Fabian, J. (1983) *Time and the Other: How Anthropology Makes its Object*. New York: Columbia University Press.

Falconer, E. (2009) "Stories of the body: the sensual experiences of female backpackers." Paper presented at the Annual Conference of the Institute of British Geographers, Manchester.

Featherstone, M. (1995) *Undoing Culture: Globalization, Postmodernism, and Identity*. London: Sage.

Focken, K. (2007) "Marketing strategy for Lung Namtha and marketing action plan and initial promotional plan." Paper prepared for The Nam Ha Ecotourism Project, Lung Namtha, Lao PDR.

Foster, R. (2008) *Coca-Globalization: Following Soft Drinks from New York to New Guinea*. New York: Palgrave Macmillan.

Foti, A. (2004) "Precarity and n/European identity: an interview with Alex Foti (ChainWorkers)." Available online at: www.sindominio.net/metabolik/alephandria/txt/Foti_Precarity.pdf (accessed 26 April 2011).

Foucault, M. (1978) *The History of Sexuality, Vol. 1: An Introduction*. London: Penguin.

Foucault, M. (1990) [1984] *The History of Sexuality, Vol. 3: The Care of the Self*. London: Penguin.

Foucault, M. (1994) *The Birth of the Clinic*. New York: Vintage Books.

Foucault, M. (2003) *Society Must Be Defended: Lectures at the Collège de France, 1975–1976*. New York: Picador.

Foucault, M. (2004a) *Society Must Be Defended: Lectures at the College de France, 1975–1976*. Basingstoke: Palgrave Macmillan.

Foucault, M. (2004b) *Naissance de la Biopolitique: Cours au Collège de France, 1978–1979*. Paris: Seuil/Gallimard.

Foucault, M. (2005) *The Hermeneutics of the Subject: Lectures at the Collège de France 1981–1982*. New York: Picador.

Foucault, M. (2008) *The Birth of Biopolitics: Lectures at the Collège de France 1978–1979*. New York: Palgrave Macmillan.

Frankental, P. (2001) "Corporate social responsibility: a PR invention?" *Corporate Communications*, 6: 18–23.

Franklin, A. (2003) *Tourism: An Introduction*. London: Sage.

Franklin, A. (2004) *Tourism*. London: Sage.

Franklin, A. (2008) "The tourism ordering: taking tourism more seriously as a globalising ordering." *Civilisations*, 57(1–2): 25–39.

Franklin, A. and Crang, M. (2001) "The trouble with tourism and travel theory?" *Tourist Studies*, 1(1): 5–22.

Fraser, N. (1994) "After the family wage: gender equity and the welfare state." *Political Theory*, 22(4): 591–618.

Frykman, J. and Löfgren, O. (eds) (1996) "Introduction." In *Forces of Habit: Exploring Everyday Culture*. Lund: Lund University Press.

Gainsborough, M. (2007) "Globalisation and the state revisited: a view from provincial Vietnam." *Journal of Contemporary Asia*, 37: 1–18.

Gardiner, M. (2000) *Critiques of Everyday Life*. London: Routledge.

Garland, A. (1996) *The Beach*. London: Viking.

Garriga, E. and Mele, D. (2004) "Corporate social responsibility theories: mapping the territory." *Journal of Business Ethics*, 53: 51–71.

Germann Molz, J. (2009) "Representing pace in tourism mobilities: staycations, slow travel and the amazing race." *Journal of Tourism and Cultural Change*, 7(4): 270–286.

Germann Molz, J. (2010) "Performing global geographies: time, space, place and pace in narratives of round-the-world travel." *Tourism Geographies*, 12(3): 329–348.

Germann Molz, J. and Gibson, S. (2007) "Introduction: mobilizing and mooring hospitality." In J. Germann Molz and S. Gibson (eds) *Mobilizing Hospitality: The Ethics of Social Relations in a Mobile World*, Aldershot: Ashgate, pp. 1–26.

Gesler, W.M. and Kearns, R. (2002) *Culture, Place and Health*. London: Routledge.

Giaccaria, P. and Minca, C. (2011) "Nazi geopolitics and the dark geographies of the Selva." *Journal of Genocide Research*, 13(1–2): 67–84.

Gibson, C. (2008) "Locating geographies of tourism." *Progress in Human Geography*, 32: 407–422.

Gibson, C. (2009) "Geographies of tourism: critical research on capitalism and local livelihoods." *Progress in Human Geography*, 33: 527–534.

Gibson, C. (2010) "Geographies of tourism: (un)ethical encounters." *Progress in Human Geography*, 34: 521–527.

Gibson, J.J. (1986) *The Ecological Approach to Visual Approach*. London: Erlbaum.

Gibson, S. (2003) "Accommodating strangers: British hospitality and the asylum hotel debate." *Journal for Cultural Research*, 7(4): 367–386.

Gibson, S. (2006) " 'The hotel business is about strangers': border politics and hospitable spaces in Stephen Frear's *Dirty Pretty Things*." *Third Text*, 20(6): 693–701.

Gill, R. and Pratt, A. (2008) "In the social factory? Immaterial labour, precariousness and cultural work." *Theory, Culture and Society*, 25(7–8): 1–30.

Gillen, J. (2008) "Disruptions of a dialectic and a stereotypical response: the case of the Ho Chi Minh City, Vietnam, tourism industry." In T. Winter, P. Teo, and T.C. Chang (eds) *Asia On Tour: Exploring the Rise of Asian Tourism*. London: Routledge.

Glinavos, I. (2008) "Neoliberal law: unintended consequences of market-friendly law reforms." *Third World Quarterly*, 29(6): 1087–1099.

Goffman, E. (1977) "The arrangement between the sexes." *Theory and Society*, 4: 301–331.

Goodwin, H. (2010) "Reflections on 10 years of pro-poor tourism." *Journal of Policy Research in Tourism, Leisure and Events*, 1(1): 90–94.

Graburn, N. (2009) "Openings and limits: domestic tourism in Japan." In T. Winter, P. Teo and T. Chang (eds) *Asia on Tour: Exploring the Rise of Asian Tourism*. London: Routledge.

Gregory, S. (2007) *The Devil Behind the Mirror: Globalization and Politics in the Dominican Republic*. Berkeley, CA: University of California Press.

Gren, M. (2001) "Time-geography matters." In J. May and N. Thrift (eds) *Timespace: Geographies of Temporality*. London: Routledge.

Guiver, J. and Jain, J. (2011) "Grounded: impacts of and insights from the volcanic ash cloud disruption." *Mobilities*, 6(1): 41–55.

Gunawan, A. (2007) "Residents go overseas for check-up." *The Jakarta Post*, 1 November. Available online at: www.thejakartapost.com/print/161284 (accessed 25 March 2009).

Gutiérrez-Rodríguez, E. (2010) *Migration, Domestic Work and Affect: A Decolonial Approach on Value and the Feminization of Labour*. New York and London: Routledge.

Haanpää, M., Hakkarainen, M., Kylänen, M., Laakkonen, S., Tuulentie, S., Valkonen, J., Valtonen, A. and Veijola, S. (2005) "Tourism as work." Unpublished research plan, University of Lapland, The Academy of Finland.

Hadi, A. (2009) "Globalization, medical tourism and health equity." Paper presented in Symposium on the Implications of Medical Tourism for Canadian Health Policy, Ottawa, Canada, 13 November. Available online at: www.globalhealthequity.ca/electronic%20library/Hadi%20Globalization%20Medical%20Tourism.pdf (accessed 5 December 2009).

Hage, G. (2009) "Waiting out the crisis: on stuckedness and governmentality." In G. Hage (ed.) *Waiting*. Melbourne: Melbourne University Press.

Hägerstrand T. (1985) *Time-geography: Focus on the Corporeality of Man, Society, and Environment: The Science and Praxis of Complexity*. Tokyo: The United Nations University.

Hall, C.M. and Jenkins, J. (2004) "Tourism and public policy." In A.A. Lew, C.M. Hall and A.M. Williams (eds) *A Companion to Tourism*. Malden, MA: Blackwell.

Hall, C.M. and Page, S. (eds) (2000) *Tourism in South and Southeast Asia: Issues and Cases*. Oxford: Butterworth-Heinemann.

Hall, C.M. (ed.) (2007) *Pro-poor Tourism: Who Benefits? Perspectives on Tourism and Poverty Reduction*. Clevedon: Channel View Publications.

Hall, C.M. (2008) *Tourism Planning: Policies, Processes and Relationships*. Essex: Pearson.

Hall, T. (2010) "Urban outreach and the polyrhythmic city." In T. Edensor (ed.) *Geographies of Rhythm: Nature, Place, Mobilities and Bodies*. Aldershot: Ashgate.

Haraway, D. (1999) "A Cyborg manifesto: science, technology, and socialist-feminism in the late twentieth century." In D.J. Haraway (ed.) *Simians, Cyborgs and Women: The Reinvention of Nature*. New York: Routledge.

Harrell, S. (1995) "Jeeping against Maoism." *Positions*, 3(3): 728–758.

Harrison, D. (1994) "Learning from the Old South by the New South? The case of tourism." *Third World Quarterly*, 15(4): 707–721.

Harrison, D. (2008) "Pro-poor tourism: a critique." *Third World Quarterly*, 29(5): 851–868.

Harrison, D. and Schipani, S. (2007) "Lao tourism and poverty alleviation: community-based tourism and the private sector." *Current Issues in Tourism*, 10(2–3): 194–231.

Harrison, P. (2000) "Making sense: embodiment and the sensibilities of the everyday." *Environment and Planning D: Society and Space*, 18: 497–517.

Hart, G. (2004) "Geography and development: critical ethnographies." *Progress in Human Geography*, 28: 91–100.

Hart, S.L. (1997) "Beyond greening: strategies for a sustainable world." *Harvard Business Review*, 75: 66–76.

Harvey, D. (2005) *A Brief History of Neoliberalism*. Oxford: Oxford University Press.

Harwood, R. (2009) "Negotiating modernity at China's periphery: development and policy interventions in Nujiang Prefecture." In E. Jeffreys (ed.) *China's Governmentalities: Governing Change, Changing Government*. London and New York: Routledge.

Hawkins, D.E. (2006) *Corporate Social Responsibility: Balancing Tomorrow's Sustainability and Today's Profitability*. London: Palgrave.

Hayton, B. (2010) *Vietnam: Rising Dragon*. New Haven, CT: Yale University Press.

Heap, S. (1998) "NGOs and the private sector: potential for partnerships?" Occasional Papers Series Number 27. Oxford: INTRAC.

Heller, A. (1999) *A Theory of Modernity*. Oxford: Blackwell.

Herr, M. (1991) *Dispatches*. New York: Vintage.

Hobson, K. (2006) "Environmental responsibility and the possibilities of pragmatist-orientated research." *Social and Cultural Geography*, 7: 283–298.

Hopkins, L., Labonte, R., Runnels, V. and Packer, C. (2009) "Medical tourism today: a narrative review of existing knowledge." Paper presented in Symposium on the Implications of Medical Tourism for Canadian Health Policy, Ottawa, Canada, 13 November 2009. Available online at: www.globalhealthequity.ca/electronic%20library/Medical%20Tourism%20Final%20Draft%20November%202009.pdf (accessed 5 December 2009).

Hopkins, M. (2003) *The Planetary Bargain: Corporate Social Responsibility Matters*. London: Earthscan.

Horne, D. (1992) *The Intelligent Tourist*. McMahons Point, NSW: Margaret Gee.

Horowitz, M.D., Rosenweig, J.A. and Jones, C.A. (2007) "Medical tourism: globalization of the healthcare marketplace." *Medscape General Medicine*, 9(4). Available online at: http://medgenmed.medscape.com/viewarticle/564406 (accessed 04/11/2009).

Hughes, A., Wrigley, N. and Buttle, M. (2008) "Global production networks, ethical campaigning, and the embeddedness of responsible governance." *Journal of Economic Geography*, 8: 345–367.

Hughes, R. (2008) "Dutiful tourism: encountering the Cambodian genocide." *Asia Pacific Viewpoint*, 49: 318–330.

Hulupi, M.E. (2006) "Foreign hospitals still gaining ground." *The Jakarta Post*, 16 April. Available online at: www.thejakartapost.com/print/134199 (accessed 25 March 2009).

Husted, B.W. and Allen, D.B. (2007) "Strategic corporate social responsibility and value creation among large firms: lessons from the Spanish experience." *Long Range Planning*, 40: 594–610.

IMTJ (2008) "Revised 2009 growth forecast for medical travel industry." *International Medical Travel Journal*, 27 November. Available online at: www.imtjonline.com/news/malaysia-revised-2009-growth-forecast-for-medic (accessed 11 January 2009).

IMTJ (2010a) "Indonesia: new hospital may reduce medical tourism among Indonesians?" *International Medical Travel Journal*, 3 February. Available online at: www.imtjonline.com/news/?entryid82=181831 (accessed 3 February 2010).

IMTJ (2010b) "Singapore: Singapore medical tourism business grows despite competition." 25 November. Available online at: www.imtj.com/news/?entryid82=259944 (accessed 25 November 2010).

Inhorn, M.C. and Pasquale, P. (2009) "Rethinking reproductive 'tourism' as reproductive 'exile'." *Fertility and Sterility*, 92(3): 904–906.

IRIN (2009) "Indonesia: healthcare system failing millions." *IRIN*, 6 August. Available online at: www.irinnews.org/Report.aspx?ReportId=85600 (accessed 13 July 2010).

Iyer, P. (1988) *Video Night in Kathmandu*. New York: Vintage.

Jagyasi, P. (2008) "Marketing and serving GCC and Islamic patients in global healthcare." Paper presented in First Medical Travel World Congress, Kuala Lumpur, Malaysia, 25–28 February.

Jakarta Post (2008) "Govt increases airport exit tax fee to Rp 2.5m." *The Jakarta Post*, 24 December. Available online at: www.thejakartapost.com/news/2008/12/24/govt-increases-airport-exit-tax-fee-rp-25m.html (accessed 25 March 2009).

Jamieson, N. J. (1995) *Understanding Vietnam*, Berkeley, CA: University of California Press.

Jamieson, W. and Nadkarni, S. (2009) "A reality check of tourism's potential as a development tool." *Asia Pacific Journal of Tourism Research*, 14(2): 111–123.

Jenkins, J. (1997) "The role of the Common Wealth Government in rural tourism and regional development in Australia." In C.M. Hall and J. Jenkins, (eds) *Tourism Planning and Policy in Australia and New Zealand: Cases, Issues and Practice*. Sydney: Irwin Publishers.

Jenkins, R. (2005) "Globalization, corporate social responsibility and poverty." *International Affairs*, 81: 525–540.

Jenner, E.A. (2008) "Unsettled borders of care: medical tourism as a new dimension in America's health care crisis." *Research in the Sociology of Health Care*, 26: 235–249.

Johnston, L. (2001) "(Other) bodies and tourism studies." *Annals of Tourism Research*, 28(1): 180–201.

Jokinen, E. (2005) *Aikuisten arki*. Helsinki: Gaudeamus.

Jokinen, E. (2009) "Home, work and affect in the fourth shift." In H. Johansson and K. Saarikangas (eds) *Homes in Transformation: Dwelling, Moving, Belonging*. Helsinki: Suomalaisen Kirjallisuuden Seura.

Jokinen, E. and Jakonen, M. (2011) "Rajaton hoiva." In E. Jokinen, J. Könönen, J. Venäläinen and J. Vähämäki (eds) *Yrittäkää edes! Prekarisaatio Pohjois-Karjalassa*. Helsinki: Tutkijaliitto.

Jokinen, E. and Veijola, S. (1990) *Oman Elämänsä Turistit*. Helsinki: VAPK.

Jokinen, E. and Veijola, S. (1997) "The disoriented tourist: the figuration of the tourist in contemporary cultural critique." In C. Rojek and J. Urry (eds) *Touring Cultures: Transformations of Travel and Theory*. London and New York: Routledge.

Jokinen, E. and Veijola, S. (2003) "Mountains and landscapes: towards embodied visualities." In D. Crouch and N. Lubbren (eds) *Visual Culture and Tourism*. Oxford: Berg.

Jokinen, E., Könönen, J., Venäläinen, J. and Vähämäki, J. (eds) (2011) *Yrittäkää edes! Prekarisaatio Pohjois-Karjalassa*. Helsinki: Tutkijaliitto.

Jones, O. (2010) "'The breath of the moon': the rhythmic and affective time-spaces of UK tides." In T. Edensor (ed.) *Geographies of Rhythm: Nature, Place, Mobilities and Bodies*. Aldershot: Ashgate.

Jordan, G. (1995) "Flight from modernity: time, the other and the discourse of primitivism." *Time and Society*, 4(3): 281–303.

Judd, D. and Fainstein, S.S. (1999) *The Tourist City*. New Haven, CT: Yale University Press.

Julkunen, R. (1990) "Women in the welfare state." In P. Setälä (ed.) *The Lady with a Bow: The Story of Finnish Women*. Keuruu: Otava.

Julkunen, R. (2010) *Sukupuolen Järjestykset Ja Tasa-Arvon Paradoksit*. Tampere: Vastapaino.

Kabeer, N. (1994) *Reversed Realities: Gender Hierarchies in Development Thought*. London and New York: Verso.

Kaisone Phomvihane (1986) "Political Review of Central Committee of Lao People's Revolutionary Party." Paper presented to the 4th Party Congress, Vientiane, Lao PDR.

Kakwani, N., Datt, G. and Sisouphanthong, B. (2002) "Poverty in Lao PDR During the 1990s." Paper prepared for National Statistic Center. Available online at: www.nsc.gov.la/index.php?option=com_content&view=article&id=26&Itemid=27& lang=en (accessed 12 June 2009).

Kalisch, A. (2000) "Corporate social responsibility in the tourism industry." *Tourism Concern: Fair Trade in Tourism*. Bulletin 2. Available online at: www.tourism concern.org.uk/downloads/pdfs/corp-soc-responsibility.pdf (accessed 25 July 2010).

Kangas, B. (2010) "Traveling for medical care in a global world." *Medical Anthropology*, 29(4): 344–362.

Kaplan, C. (1996) *Questions of Travel: Postmodern Discourses of Displacement*. Durham, NC: Duke University Press.

Kapoor, I. (2004) "Hyper-self-reflexive development? Spivak on representing the Third World 'Other'." *Third World Quarterly*, 25: 627–647.

Kapoor, I. (2005) "Participatory development, complicity and desire." *Third World Quarterly*, 26: 1203–1220.

Kärrholm, M. (2009) "To the rhythm of shopping: on synchronisation in urban landscapes of consumption." In *Social and Cultural Geography*, 10(4): 421–440.

Katz, S.J., Cardiff, K., Pascali, M., Barer, M.L. and Evans, R.G. (2002) "Phantoms in the snow: Canadians' use of healthcare services in the United States." *Health Affairs*, 21(3): 19–31.

Kerr, D. and Kuehn, J. (2007) "Introduction." In D. Kerr and J. Kuehn (eds) *A Century of Travels in China: Critical Essays on Travel Writing from the 1840s to the 1940s*. Hong Kong: Hong Kong University Press.

Keskinen, S., Tuori, S, Irni, S. and Mulinari, J. (eds) (2009) *Complying With Colonialism: Gender, Race and Ethnicity in the Nordic Region*. Burlington, VT: Ashgate.

Kiatpongsan, S. and Sipp, D. (2008) "Offshore stem cell treatments." *Nature Reports Stem Cells*, 3 December. Available online at: www.nature.com/stemcells/2008/0812/ 081203/full/stemcells.2008.151.html (accessed 11 November 2009).

Kiely, R. (1998) "Neo liberalism revised? A critical account of World Bank concepts of good governance and market friendly intervention." *International Health Services*, 28(4): 683–702.

Kim, A.M. (2008) *Learning to Be Capitalists: Entrepreneurs in Vietnam's Transition Economy*. Oxford: Oxford University Press.

King, C.A. (1995) "What is hospitality?" *International Journal of Hospitality Management*, 14(3/4): 219–234.

Kingsbury, P. (2005) "Jamaican tourism and the politics of enjoyment." *Geoforum*, 36: 113–132.

Kirshenblatt-Gimblett, B. (1998) *Destination Culture: Tourism, Museums, and Heritage*, Berkeley, CA: University of California Press.

Knudsen, D.C., Metro-Roland, M.M., Anne K.S. and Greer, C.E. (eds) (2008) *Landscape, Tourism, and Meaning,* Aldershot: Ashgate.

Kojève, A. (1980) [1947] *Introduction to the Reading of Hegel: Lectures on the "Phenomenology of Spirit."* Trans. J.H. Nichols, Jr., R. Queneau and A. Bloom (eds). New York: Cornell University Press.

Könönen, J. (2011) "Naisena suomeen." In E. Jokinen, J. Könönen, J. Venäläinen and J. Vähämäki (eds) *Yrittäkää edes! Prekarisaatio Pohjois-Karjalassa.* Helsinki: Tutkijaliitto.

Korf, B. (2007) "Antinomies of generosity moral geographies and post-tsunami aid in Southeast Asia." *Geoforum,* 38: 366–378.

Kraus, N. and McLaughlin, E. (2002) *The Nanny Diaries.* London: Penguin Books.

Kwon, H. (2008) *Ghosts of War in Vietnam.* Cambridge: Cambridge University Press.

Labelle, B. (2008) "Pump up the bass: rhythm, cars and auditory scaffolding." *Senses and Society,* 3(2): 187–204.

Laderman, S. (2002) "Shaping memory of the past: discourse in travel guidebooks in Vietnam." *Mass Communication and Society,* 5: 87–110.

Laderman, S. (2009) *Tours of Vietnam: War, Travel Guides, and Memory.* Minneapolis, MN: University of Minnesota Press.

Larsen, J. (2004) *Performing Tourist Photography.* PhD thesis. Roskilde: Roskilde University.

Larsen, J. (2008) "De-exoticising tourist travel: everyday life and sociality in the move." *Leisure Studies,* 27(1): 21–34.

Lash, S. (1999) *Another Modernity: A Different Rationality.* Oxford: Blackwell.

Lashley, C. and Morrison, A. (2000) *In Search of Hospitality: Theoretical Perspectives and Debates.* Oxford: Butterworth-Heinemann.

Lautier, M. (2008) "Export of health services from developing countries: the case of Tunisia." *Social Science and Medicine,* 67: 101–110.

Law, J. (1994) *Organizing Modernity.* Oxford: Blackwell.

Lawson, V. (2007) "Geographies of care and responsibility." *Annals of the Association of American Geographers,* 97(1): 1–11.

LCPC (2006) *National Socio-Economic Development Plan 2006–2010.* Lao PDR: Lao Committee for Planning and Cooperation.

Lee, J.Y.N., Kearns, R. and Friesen, W. (2010) "Seeking affective health care: Korean immigrants' use of homeland medical services." *Health and Place,* 16(1): 108–115.

Lefebvre, H. (1996) *Writings on Cities.* E. Koffman and E. Lebas (eds). Oxford: Blackwell.

Lefebvre, H. (2004) *Rhythmanalysis: Space, Time and Everyday Life.* Trans. S. Elden and G. Moore. London: Continuum.

Lemke, T. (2000) "Foucault, governmentality, and critique." Rethinking Marxism Conference, University of Amherst, MA.

Leung, W.T. (1989) "Culture and the state: manufacturing traditions for tourism." *Critical Studies in Mass Communication,* 6: 355–375.

Lewis, M.E. (2006) *The Construction of Space in Early China.* Albany: SUNY Press.

Li, T. (2007) *The Will to Improve: Governmentality, Development, and the Practice of Politics.* Durham, NC: Duke University Press.

Liljeström, M. (1995) *Emanciperade till underordning: Det sovjetiska könssystemets uppkomst och diskursiva reproduction.* Turku: Åbo Akademis förlag.

Lim, F.K.G. (2009) "'Donkey friends' in China: the internet, civil society and the emergence of the Chinese backpacking community." In T. Winter, P. Teo and

T.C. Chang (eds) *Asia on Tour: Exploring the Rise of Asian Tourism*. London and New York: Routledge.

Linhart, S. (1998) "The Japanese at play: a little-known dimension of Japan." In S. Linhart and S. Frühstück (eds) *The Culture of Japan as Seen through Its Leisure*. Albany: State University of New York Press.

Lister, R. (2009) "A Nordic nirvana? Gender, citizenship, and social justice in the Nordic welfare states." *Social Politics: International Studies in Gender, State and Society*, 16(2): 242–278.

Littlewood, I. (2001) *Sultry Climates: Travel and Sex Since the Grand Tour*. London: John Murray.

LNTA (2005) *Tourism Law*. Lao PDR: Lao National Tourism Administration.

LNTA (2008a) *Lao PDR Tourism Strategy 2006–2020*. Lao PDR: Lao National Tourism Administration.

LNTA (2008b) *Statistical Report on Tourism in Laos*. Lao PDR: Lao National Tourism Administration.

Löfgren, O. (1999) *On Holiday: A History of Vacationing*. Berkeley, CA: University of California Press.

LPMO (2001) *Instruction of Prime Minister on Poverty Reduction, No. 010/PM*. Lao PDR: Lao Prime Minister's Office.

LPMO (2004) *National Growth and Poverty Eradication Strategy*. Lao PDR: Lao Prime Minister's Office.

LPMO (2008) *Instruction of Prime Minister on Village Consolidation and Development Cluster, No. 13/PM*. Lao PDR: Lao Prime Minister's Office.

LPMO (2009) *Prime Minister's Notification, No. 285/PM*. Lao PDR: Lao Prime Minister's Office.

LPRP (1994) *Decree of Rural Development*. Lao PDR: Lao People's Revolutionary Party.

LPRP (2004) *Instruction of Prime Minister on Village Consolidation and Development Cluster, No. 09/LPRP*. Lao PDR: Lao People's Revolutionary Party.

Lukas, S. (2008) *Theme Park*. London: Reaktion.

Lynch, P., Germann Molz, J., McIntosh, A., Lugosi, P. and Lashley, C. (2011) "Theorising Hospitality." *Hospitality and Society*, 1(1): 3–24.

MacCannell, D. (1999) [1976] *The Tourist: A New Theory of the Leisure Class*. New York: Schocken Books.

McDonald, D.A., Mashike, L. and Golden, C. (2000) "The lives and times of African migrants and immigrants in post-apartheid South Africa." In D.A. McDonald (ed.) *On Borders: Perspectives on International Migration in Southern Africa*. Kingston, Canada: Southern African Migration Project.

McDowell, L. (1991) "Life without father and Ford: the new gender order of post-Fordism." *Transactions*, 16(4): 400–419.

McDowell, L. (2008) "The new economy, class condescension and caring labour: changing formations of class and gender." *NORA–Nordic Journal of Feminist and Gender Research*, 16(3): 150–165.

McFarlane, C. (2006) "Transnational development networks: bringing development and postcolonial approaches into dialogue." *The Geographical Journal*, 172: 35–49.

Macnaghten, P. and Urry, J. (2001) "Bodies of nature: Introduction." In P. Macnaghten and J. Urry (eds) *Bodies of Nature*. London: Sage, pp. 1–11.

McNay, L. (1999) "Gender, habitus and the field: Pierre Bourdieu and the limits of reflexivity." *Theory, Culture and Society*, 16(1): 95–117.

MacReady, N. (2007) "Developing countries court medical tourists." *The Lancet*, 369: 1849–1850.

Malam, L. (2008) "Geographic imaginations: exploring divergent notions of identity, power, and place meaning on Pha-ngan Island, Southern Thailand." *Asia Pacific Viewpoint*, 49: 331–343.

Manyara, G. and Jones, E. (2007) "Community-based tourism enterprises development in Kenya: an exploration of their potential as avenues of poverty reduction." *Journal of Sustainable Tourism*, 15(6): 628–644.

Marks, L. (2002) "Maldives: time stands still." *The Daily Telegraph*, 30 April.

Marling, K.A. (ed) (1997) *Designing Disney's Theme Parks: The Architecture of Reassurance*. Paris: Flammarion.

Massey, D. (2004) "Geographies of responsibility." *Geografiska Annaler*, 86B: 5–18.

Massey, D. (2005) *For Space*. London: SAGE Publications.

Mathaba (2008) "Penang welcomes Firefly's inaugural flight from Sumatra." *Mathaba*, 26 October. Available online at: http://mathaba.net/news/?x=609893 (accessed 19 March 2009).

Matten, D. and Crane, A. (2003) "Corporate citizenship: towards an extended theoretical conceptualization." Research Paper Series No. 4–2003. Nottingham: International Center for Corporate Social Responsibility, Nottingham University Business School.

May, J. and Thrift, N. (eds) (2001) "Introduction." In J. May and N. Thrift (eds) *Timespace: Geographies of Temporality*. London: Routledge.

Mayo Clinic (2009) "Patient and visitor guide." Mayo Clinic. Available online at: www.mayoclinic.org/ (accessed 3 December 2009).

Mbaiwa, J.E. (2005) "The socio-cultural impacts of tourism development in the Okavango Delta, Botswana." *Journal of Tourism and Cultural Change*, 2(3): 163–184.

Meazza, C. (2010) *La comunità s-velata: Questioni per Jean-Luc Nancy*. Naples: Guida Editore.

Meethan, K. (2001) *Tourism in Global Society: Place, Culture, and Consumption*. Basingstoke: Palgrave.

Mels, T. (2004) "Lineages of a geography of rhythm." In T. Mels (ed.) *Reanimating Places: A Geography of Rhythms*. Aldershot: Ashgate.

Merriman, P. (2004) "Driving places: Marc Augé, non-places and the geographies of England's M1 motorway." In *Theory, Culture and Society*, 21(4–5): 145–167.

Meštrović, S.G. (1997) *Postemotional Society*. London: Sage.

Micheletti, M. (2003) *Political Virtue and Shopping: Individuals, Consumerism, and Collective Action*. New York: Palgrave Macmillan.

Milstein, A. and Smith, M. (2006) "America's new refugees – seeking affordable surgery offshore." *New England Journal of Medicine*, 355(16): 1637–1640.

Minca, C. (2007) "The tourist landscape paradox." *Social and Cultural Geography*, 8(3): 433–453.

Minca, C. (2009) "The island: work, tourism and the biopolitical." *Tourist Studies*, 9(2): 88–108.

Minca, C. and Oakes, T. (2006) *Travels in Paradox: Remapping Tourism*. Lanham, MD: Rowman & Littlefield.

Mitchell, T. (1988) *Colonizing Egypt*. Cambridge: Cambridge University Press.

Mitchell, T. (2002) *Rule of Experts: Egypt, Techno-Politics, Modernity*. Berkeley, CA: University of California Press.

Mitra, M. (2007) *It's Only Business! India's Corporate Social Responsiveness in a Globalized World*. Oxford: Oxford University Press.

MOH (2002) *Malaysia's Health 2002: Technical Report of the Director-General of Health*, Malaysia: Ministry of Health.

Mol, A. (2008) *The Logic of Care: Health and the Problem of Patient Choice*. London and New York: Routledge.

Morgan, D. (2003) "Medical tourism: ethical baggage and legal currencies." Paper presented in Medical Ethics Tomorrow, United Kingdom, 3 December. Available online at: www.bma.org.uk/ap.nsf/Content/MedicalEthicsTomorrowConfPapers/$file/MedTourism.pdf (accessed 14 July 2005).

Morgan, N. and Pritchard, A. (1998) *Tourism, Promotion and Power*. New York: Wiley.

Morini, C. (2007) "The feminization of labour in cognitive capitalism." *Feminist Review*, 87(1): 40–59.

Mowforth, M. and Munt, I. (2003) *Tourism and Sustainability: Development and New Tourism in the Third World*, 2nd edn. London: Routledge.

Mowforth, M. and Munt, I. (2009) *Tourism and Sustainability: Development, Globalisation and New Tourism in the Third World*, 3rd edn. New York: Routledge.

Mowforth, M., Charlton, C. and Munt, I. (2007) *Tourism and Responsibility: Perspectives from Latin America and the Caribbean*. London and New York: Routledge.

Munshi, D. and Kurian, P. (2005) "Imperializing spin cycles: a postcolonial look at public relations, greenwashing, and the separation of publics." *Public Relations Review*, 31: 513–520.

Nadkarni, S. (2008) "Knowledge creation, retention, exchange, devolution, interpretation and treatment (K-CREDIT) as an economic growth driver in pro-poor tourism." *Current Issues in Tourism*, 11(5): 456–472.

Nancy, J. (1991) *The Inoperative Community*. Trans. P. Conor *et al*. Minneapolis, MN: University of Minnesota Press.

Nash, D. (1996) *The Anthropology of Tourism*. Tarrytown, New York: Elsevier Science.

NCER (2009) "Tourism." *Northern Corridor Economic Region*. Available online at: www.ncer.com.my/ (accessed 19 March 2009).

Nepal, S. K. (2007) "Tourism and rural settlements in Nepal's Annapurna Region." *Annals of Tourism Research*, 34(4): 855–857.

Neumann, M. (1992) "The trail through experience: finding self in the recollection of travel." In C. Ellis and M. Flaherty (eds) *Investigating Subjectivity: Research on Lived Experience*. London: Sage.

NST (2008) "Air Asia to fly to Jakarta from Penang." *The New Straits Times*, 6 March. Available online at: www.cuti.com.my/news.php?op=show_article&aid=3342 (accessed 19 March 2009).

Nye, R.A. (2003) "The evolution of the concept of medicalization in the late twentieth century." *Journal of History of the Behavioral Sciences*, 39(2): 115–129.

Nyiri, P. (2005) "Scenic spot Europe: Chinese travellers on the western periphery." *EspacesTemps*. Available online at: http://espacestemps.net/document1224.html (accessed 26 April 2011).

Nyiri, P. (2006) *Scenic Spots: Chinese Tourism, the State, and Cultural Authority*. Seattle, WA: University of Washington Press.

Nyiri, P. (2009) "Between encouragement and control: tourism, modernity and discipline in China." In T. Winter, P. Teo and T. Chang (eds) *Asia on Tour: Exploring the Rise of Asian Tourism.* London: Routledge.

Oakes, T. (1998) *Tourism and Modernity in China.* London and New York: Routledge.

Oakes, T. (2009) "Asia." In R. Kitchen and N. Thrift (eds) *The International Encyclopedia of Human Geography, Volume 1.* Oxford: Elsevier.

Obrador, P. (2007) "A haptic geography of the beach: naked bodies, vision and touch." *Social and Cultural Geography,* 8(1):123–141 .

Obrador, P., Crang, M. and Travlou, P. (2009) "Introduction: taking Mediterranean tourists seriously." In P.O. Pons, M. Crang and P. Travlou (eds) *Cultures of Mass Tourism: Doing the Mediterranean in the Age of Banal Mobilities.* Aldershot: Ashgate.

O'Dell, T. (2007) "Hospitality, kinesthesis and health: Swedish spas and the market for well-being." In J. Germann Molz and S. Gibson (eds) *Mobilizing Hospitality: The Ethics of Social Relations in a Mobile World.* Aldershot: Ashgate.

Ong, A. (1999) *Flexible Citizenship: The Cultural Logics of Transnationality.* Durham, NC: Duke University Press.

O'Reilly, K. (2000) *The British on the Costa del Sol: Transnational Identities and Local Communities.* London: Routledge.

Ormond, M. (2011) "International medical travel and the politics of therapeutic place-making in Malaysia." PhD thesis. School of Geography and Geosciences, University of St Andrews. Available online at: http://hdl.handle.net/10023/1681 (accessed 1 March 2011).

Pearce, D.G. (1987) *Tourism Today: A Geographical Analysis.* New York: Wiley.

Pennings, G. (2002) "Letters to the editor: reply: reproductive exile versus reproductive tourism." *Human Reproduction,* 20(12): 3571–3572.

Pennings, G. (2004) "Legal harmonization and reproductive tourism in Europe." *Human Reproduction,* 19(12).

Pennings, G. (2005) "The last commodity: post-human ethics and the global traffic in 'fresh' organs." In A. Ong and S.J. Collier (eds) *Global Assemblages: Technology, Politics, and Ethics as Anthropological Problems.* Malden, MA: Blackwell.

Pennings, G. (2007) "Ethics without boundaries: medical tourism." In R.E. Ashcroft, A. Dawson, H. Draper and J.R. McMillan (eds) *Principles of Healthcare Ethics.* London: Wiley & Sons, pp. 505–510.

Peters, H. and Achilles, A. (2007) "Mid-term assessment." Paper prepared for *Nam Ha Ecotourism Project Phase 2,* Lung Namtha, Lao PDR.

Pieprzak, K. (2010) *Imagined Museums: Art and Modernity in Postcolonial Morocco.* Minneapolis, MN: University of Minnesota Press.

Pink, S. (1997) *Women and Bullfighting: Gender, Sex and the Consumption of Tradition.* Oxford and New York: Berg.

Polanyi, K. (1957) [1944] *The Great Transformation: The Political and Economic Origins of Our Times.* Boston, MA: Beacon.

Poon, S. (2008) "Religion, modernity, and urban space: the City God Temple in Republican Guangzhou." *Modern China,* 34(2): 247–275.

Popke, J.E. (2007) "Geography and ethics: spaces of cosmopolitan responsibility." *Progress in Human Geography,* 31: 509–518.

Potts, T. (2010) "Life hacking and everyday rhythm." In T. Edensor (ed.) *Geographies of Rhythm: Nature, Place, Mobilities and Bodies.* Aldershot: Ashgate.

Power, M., Mohan, G. and Mercer, C. (2006) "Postcolonial geographies of development: introduction." *Singapore Journal of Tropical Geography*, 27: 231–234.

Pradhan, M., Saadah, F. and Sparrow, R. (2007) "Did the health card program ensure access to medical care for the poor during Indonesia's economic crisis?" *The World Bank Economic Review*, 21(1): 125–150.

Praptini, M.N. (2007) "Health tourism, good service divide Indonesia from neighbours," *The Jakarta Post*, 31 October. Available online at: www.thejakartapost.com/print/153821 (accessed 25 March 2009).

Pratt, M. (1992) *Imperial Eyes: Travel Writing and Transculturation*. London: Routledge.

Precarias a la Deriva (2003) "First stutterings of 'Precarias a la Deriva'." Available online at: www.sindominio.net/karakola/antigua_casa/precarias/balbuceos-english.htm (accessed 26 April 2011).

Precarias a la Deriva (2004) "Adrift through the circuits of feminized precarious work." *Feminist Review*, 77: 157–161.

Precarias a la Deriva (2009) *Hoivaajien kapina. Tutkimusmatkoja prekaarisuuteen.* Helsinki: Like and Tutkijaliitto.

Precarias a la Deriva (no date) "A very careful strike: four hypothesis," Available online at: http://zinelibrary.info/files/A%20Very%20Careful%20Strike.pdf (accessed 26 April 2011).

Price, M. (1994) *The Photograph: A Strange, Confined Space.* Stanford, CA: Stanford University Press.

Pritchard, A., Morgan, N., Atelejevic, I. and Harris, C. (2007) "Tourism, gender, embodiment and experience." In A. Pritchard, N. Morgan, I. Atelejevic and C. Harris (eds) *Tourism and Gender: Embodiment, Sensuality and Experience*. Wallingford: CABI Publishing.

Raghuram, P., Madge, C. and Noxolo, P. (2009) "Rethinking responsibility and care for a postcolonial world." *Geoforum*, 40, 5–13.

Rajeev, A. and Latif, S. (2009) "Study of the knowledge, attitude and experience of medical tourism among target groups with special emphasis on South India." *Online Journal of Health and Allied Sciences*, 8(2). Available online at: www.ojhas.org/issue30/2009–2-6.HTM (accessed 15 December 2009).

Rakodi, C. (2002) "A livelihoods approach-conceptual issues and definitions." In C. Rakodi and T. Lloyd-Jones (eds) *Urban Livelihoods: A People-centered Approach to Reducing Poverty*. London: Earthscan.

Rama, M. (2008) *Making Difficult Choices: Vietnam in Transition*. Washington, DC: World Bank.

Reid, J. (2011) "The vulnerable subject of liberal war." *South Atlantic Quarterly*, 110(3): 770–779.

Responsibletravel.com. (2010) "Rebellious tourist – notes from the edge of tourism …" Available online at: www.responsibletravel.com/copy/introducing-the-rebellious-tourist (accessed 7 May 2010).

Responsibletravel.com. (2011) "Care for children in Goa, India." Available online at: www.responsibletravel.com/holiday/2354/care-for-children-in-goa-india (accessed 26 April 2011)

Richter, L.K. (1989) *The Politics of Tourism in Asia*. Honolulu, HI: University of Hawaii Press.

Robertson, R. (1992) *Globalization: Social Theory and Global Culture*. London: Sage.

Robinson, F. (1999) *Globalizing Care: Ethics, Feminist Theory and International Relations*. Boulder, CO: Westview Press.

Rojek, C. (1995) *Decentering Leisure: Rethinking Leisure Theory*. London: Sage.

Roome, N. (2005) "Some implications of national agendas for CSR." In A. Habisch, Jonker, J., Wegner, M. and Schmidpeter, R. (eds) *Corporate Social Responsibility Across Europe*. Berlin: Springer.

Rose, N. (2001) "The politics of life itself." *Theory, Culture and Society*, 18(6): 1–30.

Rotkirch, A., Temkina, A. and Zdravomyslova, E. (2007) "Who helps the degraded housewife? Comments on Vladimir Putin's demographic speech." *European Journal of Women's Studies*, 14(4): 349–357.

Sadler, D. and Lloyd, S. (2009) "Neo-liberalising corporate social responsibility: a political economy of corporate citizenship." *Geoforum*, 40: 613–622.

Said, E. (1978) *Orientalism*. London: Routledge.

Saldanha, A. (2002) "Music tourism and factions of bodies in Goa." In *Tourist Studies*, 2(1): 43–62.

Sanberg, E. (2008) "When hotels practice what we preach." *Go Green Travel Green: Travel Tips for the Eco-Conscious Traveller*. Available online at: http://gogreen travelgreen.com/green-hotels-green-accommodation/when-hotels-practice-what-we-preach/ (accessed 3 May 2010).

Schech, S. and Haggis, J. (2000) *Culture and Development: A Critical Introduction*. Oxford: Blackwell.

Scheper-Hughes, N. (2000) "The global traffic in human organs." *Current Anthropology*, 41(2): 191–224.

Scheyvens, R. (2002) *Tourism for Development: Empowering Communities*. Harlow: Pearson Education.

Schilcher, D. (2007) "Growth versus equity: the continuum of pro-poor tourism and neoliberal governance." *Current Issues in Tourism*. 10(2–3): 166–192.

Schipani, S. (2007) "Ecotourism as an alternative to upland rubber cultivation in the Nam Ha National Protected Area, Luang Namtha." *Juth Pakai*, 8. Vientiane, Lao PDR: UNDP. Available online at: www.undplao.org/newsroom/juthpakai.php (accessed 25 October 2010).

Schipani, S. (2008) *Impact: The Effects of Tourism on Culture and the Environment in Asia and the Pacific: Alleviating Poverty and Protecting Cultural and Natural Heritage through Community-Based Ecotourism in Luang Namtha, Lao PDR*. Bangkok: UNESCO.

Schmitt, E. (2009) "Unit's experience offers glimpse of next phase of the Afghan war." *New York Times*, New York, A18.

Schuurman, F. (1996) "Introduction: development theory in the 1990s." In F. Schuurman (ed.) *Beyond the Impasse: New Direction in Development Theory*. London: Zed Books.

Schwenkel, C. (2009) *The American War in Contemporary Vietnam: Transnational Remembrance and Representation*. Bloomington, IN: Indiana University Press.

Seamon, D. (1980) "Body-subject, time-space routines, and place-ballets." In A. Buttimer and D. Seamon (eds) *The Human Experience of Space and Place*. London: Croom Helm.

Semmens, K. (2005) *Seeing Hitler's Germany: Tourism in the Third Reich*. New York: Palgrave.

Seth, V. (1987) *From Heaven Lake: Travels Through Sinkiang and Tibet*. New York: Vintage.

Sevenhuijsen, S. (1998) *Citizenship and the Ethics of Care: Feminist Considerations on Justice, Morality and Politics*. London and New York: Routledge.

Sharp, J. (2008) *Geographies of Postcolonialism: Spaces of Power and Representation*. London: Sage.

Sharp, J. and Briggs, J. (2006) "Postcolonialism and development: new dialogues?" *The Geographical Journal*, 172: 6–9.

Sheller, M. and Urry, J. (2006) "The new mobilities paradigm." *Evironment and Planning A: Environment and Planning*, 38: 207–226.

Shi, W. (2008) "Rubber boom in Lung Namtha: a transnational perspective." Paper prepared for *GTZ RDMA*, Lao PDR. Available online at: www.greengrants.org. cn/file/pub/rubberboom.pdf (accessed 12 November 2010).

Shields, R. (1991) *Places on the Margin: Alternative Geographies of Modernity*. London: Routledge.

Simon, D. (2006) "Separated by common ground? Bring (post) development and (post) colonialism together." *The Geographical Journal*, 172: 10–21.

Sin, H.L. (2006) "'Involve me and I will learn': a study of volunteer tourism originating from Singapore." Singapore: National University of Singapore.

Sin, H.L. (2010) "Who are we responsible to? Locals' tales of volunteer tourism." *Geoforum*. Article in press.

Sinclair, T. M. (1997) *Gender, Work and Tourism*. London and New York: Routledge.

Singkeo, P. (2009) *Comparative Study of the Yield of Para Rubber in Different Scale of Planting*. Paper prepared for undergraduate study. National University of Laos, Lao PDR.

Skeggs (2010) "The value of relationships: affective scenes and emotional performances." *Feminist Legal Studies*, 18(1): 29–51.

Slow Travel (no date). *About Slow Travel*. Available online at: www.slowtrav. com/vr/index.htm (accessed 26 August 2010).

Smith, D.M. (1998) "How far should we care? On the spatial scope of beneficence." *Progress in Human Geography*, 22: 15–38.

Smith, K. (2008) "Medical tourism: for richer or poorer." Paper presented in Ownership and Appropriation Conference, University of Auckland, New Zealand, 8–12 December.

Smith, M. and Duffy, R. (2003) *The Ethics of Tourism Development*. London: Routledge.

Smith, M. and Puczkó, L. (2009) *Health and Wellness Tourism*. Burlington, MA: Butterworth-Heinemann.

Smith, R.D., Chanda, R. and Tangcharoensathien, V. (2009) "Trade in health-related services," *The Lancet*, 373(9663): 593–601.

Smith, S.J. (2005) "States, markets and an ethic of care." *Political Geography*, 24: 1–20.

Smith, V.L. (1989) *Hosts and Guests: The Anthropology of Tourism*. Philadelphia, PA: University of Pennsylvania Press.

Smith-Cavros, E. (2010) "Fertility and inequality across borders: assisted reproductive technology and globalization." *Sociology Compass*, 4(7): 466–475.

Smyth, F. (2005) "Medical geography: therapeutic places, spaces and networks." *Progress in Human Geography*, 29(4): 488–495.

Socio-Economic and Environmental Research Institute (2004) "Economic briefing to the Penang State Government: health tourism in Penang," *Socio-Economic and Environmental Research Institute*, 6(11): 1–8.

Sparke, M. (2009) "On denationalization as neoliberalization: biopolitics, class interest and the incompleteness of citizenship." *Political Power and Social Theory*, 20: 287–300.

Spivak, G. (1988) "Can the subaltern speak?" In C. Nelson and L. Grossberg (eds) *Marxism and Interpretation of Culture*. Chicago, IL: University of Illinois Press.

Squire, S. J. (1994) "Accounting for cultural meanings: the interface between geography and tourism studies re-examined." *Progress in Human Geography*, 18: 1–16.

Staeheli, L. and Brown, M. (2003) "Where has welfare gone? Introductory remarks on the geographies of care and welfare." *Environment and Planning A*, 35: 771–777.

Steiner, C. (2006) "Tourism, poverty reduction and the political economy: Egyptian perspectives on tourism's economic benefits in a semi-rentier state." *Tourism and Hospitality*, 3(3): 161–177.

Stiglitz, J. (2007) *Making Globalization Work*. London: Penguin.

Suhaimi, I. (2009) "Penang has lost much of its lustre in the economic down-turn." *The Star*, 7 April. Available online at: http://biz.thestar.com.my/news/story.asp?file=/2009/4/7/business/3641975&sec=business (accessed 25 April 2009).

Suntikul, W. (2007) "The effects of tourism development on indigenous populations in Lung Namtha Province, Laos." In R. Butler and T. Hinch (eds) *Tourism and Indigenous Peoples: Issues and Implications*. Amsterdam: Butterworth-Heinemann.

Suntikul, W., Butler, R. and Airey, D. (2008) "A periodization of the development of Vietnam's tourism accommodation since the open door policy." *Asia Pacific Journal of Tourism Research*, 13(1): 67–80.

Suvantola, J. (2002) *Tourist's Experience of Place*. Aldershot: Ashgate.

Svensson, M. (2010) "Tourist itineraries, spatial management, and hidden temples: the revival of religious sites in a water town." In T. Oakes and D. Sutton (eds) *Faiths on Display: Religion, Tourism, and the State in China*. Lanham, MD: Rowman & Littlefield.

Swain, M. B. (1995) "Gender in tourism." *Annals of Tourism Research*, 22: 247–266.

Sylvester, C. (2000) *Producing Women and Progress in Zimbabwe: Narratives of Identity and Work from the 1980s*. Portsmouth: Heinemann.

Takai-Tokunaga, N. (2007) *Beyond the Western Myth of the Japanese Tourist: Career Development in Holidaymaking*. PhD thesis. Reading: The University of Reading.

Tao, T.C.H. and Wall, G. (2009) "A livelihood approach to sustainability." *Asia Pacific Journal of Tourism Research*, 14(2): 137–152.

Tedre, S. (1999) *Hoivan sanattomat sopimukset: Tutkimus vanhusten kotipalvelun työntekijöiden työstä*. PhD thesis. Joensuun yliopiston yhteiskuntatieteellisiä julkaisuja nr. 40: University of Joensuu.

Telfer, D. J. and Sharpley, R. (2008) *Tourism and Development in the Developing World*. London: Routledge.

Tellmann, U. (2009) "Foucault and the invisible economy." *Foucault Studies*, 6: 5–24.

Teo, P. and Chang, T. (2009) "Singapore's postcolonial landscape: boutique hotels as agents." In T. Winter, P. Teo and T. Chang (eds) *Asia on Tour: Exploring the Rise of Asian Tourism*. London: Routledge.

Thompson, C. (2008) "Medical tourism, stem cells, genomics: EASTS, transnational STS and the contemporary life sciences." *East Asian Science, Technology and Society: An International Journal*, 2: 433–438.

Till, K. (2005) *The New Berlin: Memory, Politics, Place*. Minneapolis, MN: University of Minnesota Press.

Touraine, A. (1995) *Critique of Modernity*. Oxford: Blackwell.

Tourism and Convention Division, Department of Industry and Labour, Aichi (2007) *Tourism and Recreation Statistics in Aichi Prefecture*. Japan.

Tourism for Tomorrow (2009) "La Ruta Moskita, Honduras community benefit award winner 2008." Available online at: www.tourismfortomorrow.com/bin/pdf/original_pdf_file/la_ruta_moskitia_honduras.pdf (accessed 26 April 2011).

Tourist Studies (2009) "Special issue: Tourism as work." *Tourist Studies*, 9(2).

Tronto, J.C. (1999) "Care ethics: moving forward." *Hypatia*, 14(1): 112–119.

Tucker, H. (2009) "Recognizing emotion and its postcolonial potentialities: discomfort and shame in a tourism encounter in Turkey." *Tourism Geographies*, 11: 444–461.

Turegano, M.A.S. (2006) "Dependency and development patterns in tourism: a case study in the Canary Islands." *Tourism and Hospitality Planning and Development*, 3(2): 117–130; 3(3): 161–177.

Turner, L. (2007a) "'First world health care at third world prices': globalization, bioethics and medical tourism." *BioSocieties*, 2: 303–325.

Turner, L. (2007b) "Medical tourism: family medicine and international health-related travel." *Canadian Family Physician*, 53: 1639–1641.

Turner, L. (2009) "Commercial organ transplantation in the Philippines." *Cambridge Quarterly of Healthcare Ethics*, 18: 192–196.

Turner, L. and Ash, J. (1976) *The Golden Hordes: International Tourism and the Pleasure Periphery*. New York: St Martin's.

Turner, V. and Turner, E. (1973) *Image and Pilgrimage in Christian Culture*. New York: Columbia University Press.

UNDP (2004) "Pro-poor growth: concepts and measurement with country case studies". United Nations Development Programme. Available online at: www.ipcundp.org/pub/IPCWorkingPaper1.pdf (accessed 26 April 2011).

UNESCO (1998) *Nam Ha Ecotourism: Integrated Planning for Cultural and Ecologically Sustainable Tourism Development through District and Local Community Management*. Bangkok, Thailand.

Urry, J. (2000) *Sociology Beyond Societies: Mobilities for the Twenty-First Century*. London and New York: Routledge.

Urry, J. (2002) *The Tourist Gaze*. 2nd edn. London: Sage.

Vähämäki, J. (2011) "Takaisin tehdasasetuksiin." In E. Jokinen, J. Könönen, J. Venäläinen and J. Vähämäki (eds) *Yrittäkää edes! Prekarisaatio Pohjois-Karjalassa*. Helsinki: Tutkijaliitto.

Valkonen, J. and Veijola, S. (2008) *Töissä tunturissa: ajatuksia ja kirjoituksia matkailutyöstä*. Rovaniemi: Lapland University Press.

Valtonen, A. (2009) "Small tourism firms as agents of critical knowledge." *Tourist Studies*, 9(2): 127–143.

Valtonen, A. and Veijola, S. (2011) "Sleep in tourism." *Annals of Tourism Research*, 38(1): 175–192.

Vasantkumar, C. (2009) "'Domestic' tourism and its discontents: Han tourism in China's 'Little Tibet'." In S. Singh, (ed.) *Domestic Tourism in Asia*. London: Earthscan.

Veijola, S. (2006) "Heimat tourism in the countryside: paradoxical sojourns in self and place." In T. Oakes and C. Minca (eds) *Travels in Paradox: Remapping Tourism*. Lanham, MD: Rowman & Littlefield Publishers.

Veijola, S. (2009a) "Gender as work in the tourism industry." *Tourist Studies*, 9(2): 127–143.

Veijola, S. (2009b) "Introduction: tourism as work," *Tourist Studies*, 9(2): 83–87.

Veijola, S. and Jokinen, E. (1994) "The body in tourism." *Theory, Culture and Society*, 11: 125–151.

Veijola, S. and Jokinen, E. (2008) "Towards a hostessing society? Mobile arrangements of gender and labour." *NORA–Nordic Journal of Feminist and Gender Research*, 16(3): 166–181.

Veijola, S. and Valtonen, A. (2007) "The body in tourism industry." In A. Pritchard, N. Morgan, I. Atelejevic and C. Harris (eds) *Tourism and Gender: Embodiment, Sensuality and Experience.* Wallingford: CABI Publishing.

Virno, P. (2002) *A Grammar of the Multitude: For an Analysis of Contemporary Forms of Life.* Los Angeles, CA: Semiotext(e).

Vives, A. (2004) "The role of multilateral development institutions in fostering corporate social responsibility." *Development*, 47: 45–52.

Vogel, D. (2006) *The Market for Virtue: The Potential and Limits of Corporate Social Responsibility.* Washington, DC: Brookings Institution Press.

Vosko, L.F., MacDonald, M. and Campbell, I. (2009) "Introduction: gender and the concept of precarious employment." In L.F. Vosko, M. MacDonald and I. Campbell (eds) *Gender and the Contours of Precarious Employment.* London and New York: Routledge.

Wachter, R.M. (2006) "The 'dis-location' of US medicine: the implications of medical outsourcing." *The New England Journal of Medicine*, 16 February.

Wahab, S. (1974) *Elements of State Policy in Tourism.* Turin: Italgraphica.

Waldby, C. and Mitchell, R. (2006) *Tissue Economies: Blood, Organs, and Cell Lines in Late Capitalism.* Durham, NC: Duke University Press.

Walraven, G., Manaseki-Holland, S., Hussain, A. and Tomaro, J.B. (2009) "Improving maternal and child health in difficult environments: the case for "cross-border" healthcare." *PLoS Medicine*, 6(1).

Wang, D. (2003) *Street Culture in Chengdu: Public Space, Urban Commoners, and Local Politics, 1870–1930.* Stanford, CA: Stanford University Press.

Wang, M. (2006) "'Great tradition' and its enemy: the issue of 'Chinese culture' on the southeastern coast." In C.B. Tan (ed.) *Southern Fujian: Reproduction of Traditions in Post-Mao China.* Hong Kong: Chinese University Press.

Wang, N. (2000) *Tourism and Modernity: A Sociological Analysis.* Oxford: Pergamon.

Wang, Y. and Wall, G. (2005) "Resorts and residents: stress and conservatism in a displaced community." *Tourism Analysis*, 10(1): 37–53.

Warren, H. (2005) *NGO Funding Trends: A Comparison of NGO Income.* Oxford: INTRAC.

Waters, H., Saadah, F. and Pradhan, M. (2003) "The impact of the 1997–98 East Asian economic crisis on health and health care in Indonesia." *Health Policy and Planning*, 18(2): 172–181.

WCED (1987) *Our Common Future* (Brundtland Report). Oxford: Oxford University Press.

Weaver, D.B. (1991) "Alternatives to mass tourism in Dominica." *Annals of Tourism Research*, 18: 414–432.

Weaver, D.B. (1995) "Alternative tourism in Montserrat." *Tourism Management*, 16: 593–604.

Wheaton, B. (ed.) (2004) *Understanding Lifestyle Sports: Consumption, Identity and Difference*. London: Routledge.

Whittaker, A. (2008) "Pleasure and pain: medical travel in Asia." *Global Public Health*, 3(3): 271–290.

Whittaker, A. (2009) "Global technologies and transnational reproduction in Thailand." *Asian Studies Review*, 33(3): 319–332.

Wilkinson, R. and Pickett, K. (2010) *The Spirit Level: Why Equality is Better for Everyone?* London: Penguin Books.

Williams, A. (2004) "Toward a political economy of tourism." In A.A. Lew, C.M. Hall and A.M. Williams (eds) *A Companion to Tourism*. Malden, MA: Blackwell.

Williams, R. (1961) *The Long Revolution*. London: Chatto & Windus.

Williams, R. (1983) *Keywords: A Vocabulary of Culture and Society*. New York: Oxford University Press.

Wilson, A. (2010) "Medical tourism in Thailand." In A. Ong and N. Chan (eds) *Asian Biotech: Ethics and Communities of Fate*. Durham, NC: Duke University Press.

Winter, J. (1995) *Sites of Memory, Sites of Mourning: The Great War in European Cultural History*. Cambridge: Cambridge University Press.

Winter, T., Teo, P. and Chang, T.C. (eds) (2009) *Asia on Tour: Exploring the Rise of Asian Tourism*, New York: Routledge.

Wolvaart, G. (1998) "Opportunities and challenges for developing countries in the health sector." *International Trade in Health Services: A Development Perspective, UNCTAD-WHO Joint Publication*, Geneva, 63–70.

Wood, R.E. (1993) "Tourism, culture and the sociology of development." In M. Hitchcock, V.T. King and M.J.G. Parnwell (eds) *Tourism in Southeast Asia*. London: Routledge.

Woodman, J. (2008) *Patients Beyond Borders*, 2nd edn. Chapel Hill, NC: Healthy Travel Media.

World Economic Forum (2002) "Global corporate citizenship: the leadership challenge for CEOs and boards." The Prince of Wales International Business Leaders Forum and World Economic Forum CEOs, Geneva. Available online at: www.weforum.org/pdf/GCCI/GCC_CEOstatement.pdf (accessed 24 September 2010).

Wylie, J. (2005) "Single day's walking: narrating self and landscape on the South West Coast Path." *Transactions of the Institute of British Geographers*, 30: 234–247.

Wylie, J. (2007) *Landscape*. London: Routledge.

Yap, J.C.H. (2006) "Medical tourism and Singapore." *International Hospital Federation Reference Book 2006/2007*. Ferney Voltaire: International Hospital Federation.

Yeh, J.H.-Y. (2009) "Still vision and mobile youth: tourist photos, travel narratives and Taiwanese modernity." In T. Winter, P. Teo, and T.C. Chang (eds) *Asia on Tour: Exploring the Rise of Asian Tourism*. London: Routledge.

Ying, T. and Zhou, Y. (2007) "Community, governments and external capitals in China's rural cultural tourism: a comparative study of two adjacent villages." *Tourism Management*, 28: 96–107.

Yoneyama, L. (1999) *Hiroshima Traces: Time, Space, and the Dialectics of Memory*. Berkeley, CA: University of California Press.

York, D. (2008) "Medical tourism: the trend towards outsourcing medical procedures to foreign countries." *Journal of Continuing Education in the Health Professions*, 28(2): 99–102.

Young, R.J.C. (2001) *Postcolonialism: An Historical Introduction*. Oxford and Malden, MA: Blackwell Publishers.

Young, R.J.C. (2003) *Postcolonialism: A Very Short Introduction*. Oxford: Oxford University Press.

Yúdice, G. (2003) *The Expediency of Culture: Uses of Culture in the Global Era*. Durham, NC and London: Duke University Press.

Zadek, S. (2004) "The path to corporate responsibility," *Harvard Business Review*, 82: 125–132.

Zampoukos, K. and Ioannides, D. (2011) "The tourism labour conundrum: agenda for new research in the geography of hospitality workers," *Hospitality and Society*, 1(1): 25–45.

Zhai, M. (2002) "Hongcun's pain," *Nanfang Zhoumou*, 21 March.

Zhao, W. and Ritchie, J.R.B. (2007) "Tourism and poverty alleviation: an integrative research framework." *Current Issues in Tourism*, 10(2–3): 119–143.

Interviews

Anonymous Deputy-Director of Department, LNTA (2008) Personal interview with Saithong Phommavong, 18 June.

Anonymous group of villagers (2010) Personal interview with Saithong Phommavong, Namtalan village, Namtha District, Luangnamtha Province, Lao PDR, 21 July.

Anonymous Head of Champasak Provincial Agricultural and Forestry Department (2008) Personal interview with Saithong Phommavong, Champasak Province, Lao PDR, 27 June.

Anonymous Malaysian medical travel agent (2008) Personal interview with Meghann Ormond, Kuala Lumpur, Malaysia, 12 February.

Anonymous Malaysian private hospital marketing representative (2008) Personal interview with Meghann Ormond, Malacca, Malaysia, 21 March.

Anonymous Malaysian private hospital public relations officer (2008) Personal interview with Meghann Ormond, Georgetown, Penang, Malaysia, 4 March.

Anonymous Namtalan village tourism manager (2010) Personal interview with Saithong Phommavong, Namtalan village, Namtha District, Luangnamtha Province, Lao PDR, 21 July.

Anonymous private lodge owner (2008) Personal interview with Saithong Phommavong, Kietngong village, Pathoumphone District, Champasak Province, Lao PDR, 15 February.

Anonymous tourism service unit (TSU) officer (2010) Personal interview with Saithong Phommavong, Champasak Province, Lao PDR, 10 August.

Anonymous tourism service unit (TSU) officer (2010) Personal interview with Saithong Phommavong, Luangnamtha Province, Lao PDR, 22 July.

Anonymous village headman (2008) Personal interview with Saithong Phommavong, Done Deng village, Pathoumphone District, Champasak Province, Lao PDR, 16 February.

Anonymous village headman (2010) Personal interview with Saithong Phommavong, Samyord village, Namtha District, Luangnamtha Province, Lao PDR, 20 January.

Anonymous villagers (2008) Personal interview with Saithong Phommavong, Nalan Tai village, Namtha District, Luangnamtha Province, Lao PDR, 31 May.

Anonymous Xepian eco-tourism project adviser (2008) Personal interview with Saithong Phommavong, Champasak Province, Lao PDR, 30 June.

Boua (head of gardening section, La Folie Lodge) (2009) Personal interview with Saithong Phommavong, Don Deng village, Pathoumphone District, Champasak Province, Lao PDR, 3 August.

Clarke, S. (2009) Personal interview with Harng Luh Sin, Sattahip, Thailand, 16 November.

Colomès, O. (2009) Personal interview with Harng Luh Sin, Bangkok, Thailand, 14 December.

Dee (villager) (2009) Personal interview with Saithong Phommavong, villager, Nam Koy village, Namtha District, Luangnamtha Province, Lao PDR, 9 February.

Eng, K. (2010) Personal interview with Harng Luh Sin, Bangkok, Thailand, 19 January.

Hilton, N. (2010) Personal interview with Harng Luh Sin, Bangkok, Thailand, 14 January.

Ka (former headman) (2010) Personal interview with Saithong Phommavong, Namtalan village, Namtha District, Luangnamtha Province, Lao PDR, 21 July.

Kwanjai, N. (2009) Personal interview with Harng Luh Sin, Sattahip, Thailand, 18 November.

Lee (2009) Personal interview with Harng Luh Sin, Sattahip, Thailand, 2 December.

Lim, F. (2008) Personal interview with Meghann Ormond, Malacca, Malaysia, 22 March.

Matzig, L. (2009) Personal interview with Harng Luh Sin, Bangkok, Thailand, 22 December.

Phim (villager) (2009) Personal interview with Saithong Phommavong, Done Deng village, Pathoumphone District, Champasak Province, Lao PDR, 3 August.

Phoumy (villager) (2008) Personal interview with Saithong Phommavong, Nalan Tai village, Namtha District, Luangnamtha Province, Lao PDR, 31 May.

Pieper, M. (2010) Personal interview with Harng Luh Sin, Bangkok, Thailand, 8 February.

Sichanh (village headman) (2010) Personal interview with Saithong Phommavong, Namtavanh village, Namtha District, Luangnamtha Province, Lao PDR, 20 January.

Sichanh (village headman) (2010) Personal interview with Saithong Phommavong, Namtavanh village, Namtha District, Luangnamtha Province, Lao PDR, 20 July.

Sisavanh, S. (head of Luangnamtha Department of Tourism) (2008) Personal interview with Saithong Phommavong, Luangnamtha Province, Lao PDR, 27 June.

Sivone (villager) (2008) Personal interview with Saithong Phommavong, Nam Koy village, Namtha District, Luangnamtha Province, Lao PDR, 1 June.

Tongyang (village tourism manager) (2010) Personal interview with Saithong Phommavong, Samyord village, Namtha District, Luangnamtha Province, Lao PDR, 20 January.

Vanh (villager) (2010) Personal interview with Saithong Phommavong, Samyord village, Namtha District, Luangnamtha Province, Lao PDR, 20 July.

Vieng (village vice-headman) (2009) Personal interview with Saithong Phommavong, Don Deng village, Pathoumphone District, Champasak Province, Lao PDR, 4 August.

Weingand, P. (2010) Personal interview with Harng Luh Sin, Bangkok, Thailand, 12 January.

Yan (2009) Personal interview with Harng Luh Sin, Sattahip, Thailand, 25 November.

Index